Divided Power in Ancient Greece

Divided Power in Ancient Greece

Decision-Making and Institutions in the Classical and Hellenistic Polis

ALBERTO ESU

OXFORD
UNIVERSITY PRESS

Great Clarendon Street, Oxford, OX2 6DP,
United Kingdom

Oxford University Press is a department of the University of Oxford.
It furthers the University's objective of excellence in research, scholarship,
and education by publishing worldwide. Oxford is a registered trade mark of
Oxford University Press in the UK and in certain other countries

© Alberto Esu 2024

The moral rights of the author have been asserted

All rights reserved. No part of this publication may be reproduced, stored in
a retrieval system, or transmitted, in any form or by any means, without the
prior permission in writing of Oxford University Press, or as expressly permitted
by law, by licence or under terms agreed with the appropriate reprographics
rights organization. Enquiries concerning reproduction outside the scope of the
above should be sent to the Rights Department, Oxford University Press, at the
address above

You must not circulate this work in any other form
and you must impose this same condition on any acquirer

Published in the United States of America by Oxford University Press
198 Madison Avenue, New York, NY 10016, United States of America

British Library Cataloguing in Publication Data
Data available

Library of Congress Control Number: 2023945795

ISBN 978–0–19–888395–1

DOI: 10.1093/oso/9780198883951.001.0001

Printed and bound in the UK by
Clays Ltd, Elcograf S.p.A.

Links to third party websites are provided by Oxford in good faith and
for information only. Oxford disclaims any responsibility for the materials
contained in any third party website referenced in this work.

Preface

This book examines the notion of divided power and its institutionalization in the political decision-making of the Greek city-states of the Classical and Hellenistic periods. It aims to illuminate how institutional design shaped the behaviour of citizens when making decisions in councils, assemblies, boards of magistrates, and lawcourts. Traditional analyses have either focused on a formalist understanding of political power, or adopted an extra-institutional perspective emphasizing rhetorical, sociological, and ideological factors.

My aim, in undertaking the research that has led to this book, was to provide a study showing that the power of creating binding norms was systematically divided and dispersed among different decision-making institutions. The mechanism of divided power fostered distinctive behaviours in citizens acting in various, layered institutional environments, and was supported by different discourses, formal and informal practices, and ideas relevant to the different institutional settings. The methodological premise of the book is that a careful study of the relevant institutions and of the mechanisms that governed their interaction is the most effective way to approach deliberative practices—as well as their underlying power dynamics and discourses—across different political regimes and city-states of the Classical and Hellenistic Greek world. The book tests this thesis through a series of case studies discussed in Chapters 2–6 and shows that the notion of divided power was institutionalized around the mechanisms of delegation of deliberative power, and of legal control over the enactments of councils and assemblies.

This book, therefore, hopes to be of interest not only to students of the history of ancient Greek political and legal institutions, but also to those tackling the history of ancient ideas and political thought.

This book is a revised and expanded version of my doctoral thesis written at the University of Edinburgh under the supervision of Mirko Canevaro and Benjamin Gray. My interest for ancient Greek politics and institutions started during my studies at the Università di Cagliari when writing my Master's dissertation. I am grateful to Tristano Gargiulo, Patrizia Mureddu, Gianfranco Nieddu, and Elisabetta Poddighe for those formative years.

In pursuing a PhD, the School of History, Classics & Archaeology of the University of Edinburgh proved the ideal environment for undertaking this project and I have been very fortunate to benefit from the kind guidance of a thriving community of world-class scholars. My warmest thanks goes to Mirko Canevaro, my doctoral supervisor, to whom I owe an immense debt of gratitude.

vi PREFACE

With his typical generosity, Mirko supported me at every step of my doctorate, often going beyond his duty as supervisor. He shared ideas, engaged critically with my views, and dedicated time to correct and improve my work. Through endless conversations at the National Museum of Scotland or in front of an espresso, Mirko encouraged me to submit my first articles, co-author an article together, and revise my dissertation for publication. I have greatly benefitted from Mirko's inspirational teaching and collaborative approach to research over many years during which I learnt more than ever. I am also very grateful to Benjamin Gray, my secondary supervisor, who has read and generously commented a first draft of this book and offered many insightful comments on Greek epigraphy, Hellenistic history, and ancient political thought, which helped me to nuance and improve my argument and restrain my Athenocentric tendencies.

In working on this book, I have incurred several debts of gratitude with a number of outstanding scholars and academic institutions. First, I owe an enormous debt of gratitude to Edward M. Harris, who has never failed to act through the years as an incredibly generous and insightful advisor. As one of my Viva examiners, Edward read and thoroughly commented the first version of this book and again the revised manuscript offering invaluable suggestions and constructive criticisms by sharing his expertise and unpublished work, which strengthened my argument in many important ways.

A heartfelt thanks goes to Peter Liddel for his unfailing and kind support over the past few years. Peter examined the original thesis as external examiner and provided invaluable advice, rigorous comments, and stimulating questions during my Viva which have substantially improved the final product. I am also greatly indebted to Douglas Cairns and David Lewis who offered me feedback on Chapters 4 and 5 of this book and whose meticulous, thoughtful, and expert comments have helped to sharpen them and avoid some mistakes. Naturally, all remaining errors are my own.

Most of the revision work for this book was generously supported by a Study Abroad Studentship awarded by the Leverhulme Trust which funded a postdoc at the University of Mannheim from 2019 to 2022. I am deeply grateful for the generosity and encouragement of Christian Mann, who acted as my mentor, and Melanie Meaker, Alexander Meeus, and Mareile Rassiller, who made me feel most welcome during my time at the *Lehrstühl für Alte Geschichte*, a fruitful period of research and friendship, even in the difficult years of the Covid-19 pandemic.

The final stage of the preparation of the manuscript was carried out at the University of Nottingham. I want to express my most sincere gratitude to all my colleagues of the Department of Classics and Archaeology, and in particular to Chrysanthi Gallou, Helen Lovatt, Simon Malloch, Davide Massimo, Matt Myers, Oliver Thomas, Matt Thompson, Edmund Stewart, and George Woudhuysen for their support. I am grateful to Gabriel Bernardo and Philip Davies for sharing with me their published and forthcoming work on Sparta. I am particularly indebted to

PREFACE vii

Stephen Hodkinson for our great conversations about Greek history at Nottingham and for kindly agreeing to read and comment on parts of the manuscript. His generous feedback improved Chapters 1 and 4.

I owe a great deal to Pasquale Pasquino, whose seminal work on the very notion of divided power has inspired the topic of this book, and whose stimulating comments, at a workshop on the mixed constitution in Edinburgh in 2017, further oriented my work. A big thanks goes to Matteo Barbato, who has commented on several parts of this book and has been a supportive friend over the years. I am grateful to many scholars and friends including Christian Ammitzbøll Thomsen, Stefanos Apostolou, Sebastiano Bertolini, Sarah Cassidy, Luca Deiana, Laura Donati, Roseanna Doughty, Sam Ellis, Sabina Espis, Giacinto Falco, Stefano Ferrucci, Jakub Filonik, Zilong Guo, Alison John, Juan Lewis, Laura Loddo, Lucia Michielin, Giovanni Pontis, Linda Rocchi, Giulia Sagliardi, Emil Skaarup, Bas Willems, Matteo Zaccarini, and Sara Zanovello who have provided moral support and academic advice along the way.

At OUP, I extend my gratitude to Charlotte Loveridge for supporting the publication of this monograph. I am also thankful to Alexander Hardie-Forsyth, Kripadevi Prabhakar, and Tim Beck for their expert guidance throughout the book's production. Matthew Simonton and the other OUP anonymous reader provided meticulous evaluations and invaluable constructive criticism in their reader reports, strengthening this book's depth of analysis and scholarly relevance.

I am also grateful to all my colleagues at the *Historisches Seminar* of the University of Zurich and in particular to Victor Walser and Benjamin Straumann for support and advice.

I am in debt to the various institutions that funded the work necessary for completing this book: the Scottish Graduate School for Arts and Humanities (SGSAH/AHRC), the University of Edinburgh, the Gerda-Henkel and Jacobi Fellowship at the *Kommission für Alte Geschichte und Epigraphik* in Munich, the Leverhulme Trust, and the University of Nottingham.

Some parts of this book are based on articles that I have published elsewhere. Section 1.2 touches upon and expands on some points about the Aristotelian methodology for constitutional analysis presented in Canevaro and Esu (2018), 'Mixed Constitution and Extreme Democracy in Theory and Practice: *Nomophylakia* and Fourth-Century *Nomothesia* in the Aristotelian *Athenaion Politeia*', in C. Bearzot, M. Canevaro, T. Gargiulo, and E. Poddighe (eds), *Athenaion Politeiai tra storia, sociologia e politica: Aristotele e Pseudo-Senofonte*, Milan, 105–45. Chapter 4 is a revised and expanded version of Esu (2017), 'Divided Power and *EYNOMIA*: Deliberative Procedures in Ancient Sparta', *Classical Quarterly* 67.3, 353–73. Chapter 5 is a slightly revised and reframed version of Esu (2021a), '*Adeia* in Fifth-Century Athens', *Journal of Hellenic Studies* 141, 153–78. Section 6.2 is a heavily expanded version of some arguments presented in Esu (2020: 75–85), 'After the Empire: Judicial Review and Interstate

viii PREFACE

Relations in the Age of Demosthenes, 354–22 BCE', in E. Cavanagh (ed.), *Empire and Legal Thought: Ideas and Institutions from Antiquity to Modernity*. Leiden, Brill–Nijhof, 69–104.

Finally, my deepest gratitude goes to my parents, Roberta and Fernando, to my sister Laura, and to my partner Eva. This book is dedicated to them. None of this would have been possible without their love, support, and patience.

Alberto Esu

Zurich,
October 2023

Contents

List of Abbreviations	xi
1. Introduction	1
1.1 Sovereignty or Divided Power? Power and Institutions in the Greek City-States	3
1.2 Ancient Greek Political Thought on Political Decision-Making and Institutional Design: An Overview	14
1.3 Political Decision-Making and Legislation	24
1.4 Methodology: Taking Institutions Seriously	26
1.4.1 From *Staatsaltertümer* to the Sociological Approach	26
1.4.2 A 'New Institutionalist' Approach to Political Decision-Making in Ancient Greece	30
1.5 Decision-Making Institutions as Manifestation of Divided Power	37

I. DIVIDED POWER AND DELEGATION

2. Divided Power in Athenian Decree-Making	43
2.1 The Athenian Council and Institutional Design	43
2.2 The Institutional Values of the Council: The Bouleutic Oath and Bouleutic Discursive Practice	45
2.3 The 'Deliberative' Expertise of the Athenian Council	54
2.4 *Autokratōr*-Clauses: Delegation of Power to the Council in Fifth-Century Decree-Making	61
2.5 *Kurios*-Clauses: Delegation of Power in Fourth-Century Athenian Decrees	70
2.6 Athenian Delegation: A Standard Institution of the Decree-Making	92
3. Divided Power in Mytilene and Megalopolis: Delegation Practice beyond Athens	94
3.1 Delegation in Two Non-Athenian Case Studies	94
3.2 Mytilene from the Archaic Period to the Macedonian Conquest	96
3.3 The Decree on Concord and the Decree on Reconciliation	98
3.4 Megalopolis: The Institution of *Sunedrion*	111
3.5 Path Dependence and Conversion in Greek Divided Power	119

X CONTENTS

II. DIVIDED POWER AND CONTROL OF LEGALITY

4. Divided Power and *Eunomia*: Deliberative Procedures in
   Ancient Sparta   125
   4.1 Spartan Political Institutions and the *Mirage Spartiate*   125
   4.2 Spartan Decision-Making Institutions: Kings, *Gerousia*,
       and Ephors   130
   4.3 Interaction between Ephors and *Gerousia*: 'Divided'
       Probouleusis and *Nomophulakia*   136
   4.4 Non-Democratic Divided Power   150

5. Divided Power in the Athenian Assembly: *Adeia* and
   Fifth-Century Deliberative Ideology   152
   5.1 Institutional Complexity in the Athenian Assembly   152
   5.2 'Absence of Fear': The Expressive Terminology of Immunity   156
   5.3 Procedure: Legal Change and Divided Power in Fifth-Century
       Decision-Making   163
   5.4 *Adeia*: An Incomplete Rule of Legal Change   172
   5.5 Dividing Deliberation in the Athenian Assembly   175

6. Divided Power and Judicial Review: *Graphē Paranomōn* in
   the Decision-Making of the Greek *Poleis*   177
   6.1 Divided Power and Legal Hierarchy in Ancient Athens   177
   6.2 *Graphē Paranomōn* in Classical Athens: The Role of
       Judicial Review in Democratic Decision-Making   182
   6.3 Judicial Review outside Athens   199
   6.4 Courts as Part of Divided Power in Ancient Greece   212

7. Epilogue   214

Bibliography   227
Index Locorum   265
General Index   276

List of Abbreviations

Ancient authors and works are abbreviated according to the fourth edition of the *Oxford Classical Dictionary*. Journal abbreviations follow the *Année philologique*. All other abbreviations are listed below.

Agora XV	B. D. Meritt and J. Traill, *The Athenian Councillors* (Princeton, 1974).
Agora XVI	A. G. Woodhead, *Agora Inscriptions: The Decrees* (Princeton, 1997).
BCH	*Bulletin de correspondance hellénique* (Paris, 1877–).
BE	*Bulletin épigraphique* (Paris, 1938–).
CIG	*Corpus Inscriptionum Graecarum* (Berlin, 1828–77).
DK	H. Diels and W. Kranz, *Die Fragmente der Vorsokratiker* (Berlin, 1951–2).
FD III	*Fouilles de Delphes, III. Épigraphie* (Paris, 1929–).
FGrH	F. Jacoby, *Die Fragmente der griechischen Historiker* (Berlin, 1923–).
HGK	R. Herzog, *Heilige Gesetze von Kos* (Berlin, 1928).
I.Eleusis	K. Clinton, *Eleusis. The Inscriptions on Stone. Documents of the Sanctuary of the Two Goddesses and Public Documents of the Deme* (Athens, 2005–8).
I.Erythrai und Klazomenai	H. Egelmann and R. Merkelbach, *Die Inschriften von Erytrhai und Klazomenai*, 2 vols (Bonn, 1972).
I.Kyme	H. Engelmann, *Die Inschriften von Kyme* (Bonn, 1972).
Labraunda	D. F. McCabe, *Labraunda Inscriptions. Texts and List* (Princeton, 1991).
IG	*Inscriptiones Graecae* (Berlin, 1873–).
IGBulg.	G. Mihailov, *Inscriptiones graecae in Bulgaria repertae* (Sofia, 1958–70, 1997).
I.Magnesia	O. Kern, *Die Inschriften von Magnesia am Meander* (Berlin, 1900).
IvO	W. Dittemberger and K. Purgold, *Die Inschriften von Olympia* (Berlin, 1896).
IPArk	G. Thür and H. Taeuber, *Prozessrechtliche Inschriften der griechischen Poleis: Arkadien* (Vienna, 1994).
IvP	M. Fränkel, *Inschriften von Pergamon I* (Berlin, 1890–5).
I.Priene²	W. Blümel and R. Merkelbach, *Inschriften von Priene (Inschriften griechischer Städte aus Kleinasien 69)* (Bonn, 2014).
IscM	D. M. Pippidi, *Inscriptiones Daciae et Scythiae Minoris antiquae. Series altera: Inscriptiones Scythiae Minoris graecae et latinae*, Vol. 1: *Inscriptiones Histriae et vicinia* (Bucharest, 1983).
KA	R. Kassel and C. Austin, *Poetae Comici Graeci* (Berlin, 1983–).
ML	R. Meiggs and D. M. Lewis, *A Selection of Greek Historical Inscriptions to the End of the Fifth Century* (Oxford, 1969).
I.Milet	G. Kawerau and A. Rehm, *Das Delphinion in Milet* 1.3 (Berlin, 1914).
Miletos	D. F. McCabe, *Miletos Inscriptions. Texts and List* (Princeton, 1984).

xii LIST OF ABBREVIATIONS

Nomima	H. Van Effenterre and F. Ruzé, *Nomima: recueil d'inscriptions politiques et juridiques de l'archaisme grecque I* (Rome, 1994).
RC	C. B. Welles, *Royal Corrispondence in the Hellenistic Period: A Study in Greek Epigraphy* (New Haven, 1934).
RO	P. J. Rhodes and R. Osborne, *Greek Historical Inscriptions, 404–323* BCE (Oxford, 2003).
OR	R. Osborne and P. J. Rhodes, *Greek Historical Inscriptions, 478–404* BCE (Oxford, 2017).
SEG	*Supplementum Epigraphicum Graecum* (Leiden, 1923–).
IdCos	M. Segre, *Iscrizioni di Cos* (Rome, 1993).
Schmitt SdA	H. A. Schmitt, *Staatsverträge des Altertums*, Vol. 3: *Veträge der griechisch-römischen Welt von 338–200 v. Chr.* (Munich, 1969).
SGDI	*Sammlung der griechischen Dialekt-Inschriften II* (Göttingen, 1885–99).
Syll.	*Sylloge Inscriptionum Graecarum* (Leipzig, 1883).
Voigt	E. A. Voigt, *Sappho et Alcaeus. Fragmenta* (Amsterdam, 1972).
West	M. West, *Iambi et elegi graeci ante Alexandrum cantati* (Oxford, 1989–92).

1
Introduction

Most decisions made by the political institutions of the Classical and Hellenistic Greek *poleis* took the form of decrees. The Greeks referred to this form of political enactment with different terms such as *psēphisma* ('voted thing'), *rhētra* (with a focus on the orality), *dogma*, *graphos*, or *diagramma*.[1] Despite the terminological variety, a decree was usually enacted in the name of the people or another decision-making institution, and provided the relevant regulations binding the entire community about the key aspects of civic life ranging from international treaties to religious regulations, taxation, military, naval administration, and grants of civic honours.

The aim of this book is to offer an institutional history of ancient Greek decree-making as a system of divided power. This study concentrates on the institutional design and the attached ideologies regulating decree-making and political decision-making in the Classical and Hellenistic *poleis*. As a result, this book aims to be a contribution to the history of Greek political and legal institutions as well as to the history of ideas of political power and 'sovereignty' expressed by these institutions.[2] The main contention of this book is that Greek decree-making is to be conceived as the result of a complex system of interaction and delegation of deliberative power among different institutions: councils, probouleutic officials, assemblies, and lawcourts. This multi-layered system of constitutional interaction provided for a decision-making process in which power was divided and dispersed between several institutions. I argue, therefore, that decree-making procedures were gradually designed during the process of institutionalization of Greek *poleis* in order to implement a form of divided power, a constitutional framework that informed ideologically both democracies and non-democratic regimes. As the following chapters of this book will discuss, the institutionalization of divided power took different forms because it legitimized the social groups in power in different political regimes by shaping the collective behaviour of citizens when acting as decision-makers within the institutions.

The first traces of the concept of divided power can already be found in the political culture of the Archaic Greek *poleis* as opposed to the arbitrary power of

---

[1] Quass (1971) 11; Rhodes with Lewis (1997) 557–8; Hölkeskamp (1999); Hansen (2000) 612; Liddel (2020b) 1–4 with references to councils and assemblies in other ancient, medieval, and modern city-states.
[2] On the use of the term 'sovereignty' see pp. 9–11 below.

Divided Power in Ancient Greece: Decision-Making and Institutions in the Classical and Hellenistic Polis. Alberto Esu, Oxford University Press. © Alberto Esu 2024. DOI: 10.1093/oso/9780198883951.003.0001

2 DIVIDED POWER IN ANCIENT GREECE

one-man rule. This meant curtailing the power and tenure of magistrates through accountability procedures and collegiality in order to avoid concentration of power.[3] These very values informed the deliberative procedures which influenced the political behaviour of citizens sitting in the councils to draft a *probouleuma*, in the assembly to debate and vote on the final draft of a decree, or in a court of law as judges reviewing the legality of a decree. As a result, when a decree was discussed in the council, debated in the assembly and reviewed by a lawcourt, each of these institutions added to the decree-making process its own expertise, as well as ideologies, practices, and discourses embedded in the different institutions.[4]

By adopting models from the political sciences, and in particular from historical institutionalism, this book provides a theoretically informed study of political decision-making and a more sophisticated and nuanced view of the relationship between institutional design and political action. Through the analysis of these processes, this book provides a fresh approach to institutional and political history and the ways political actors related to power and law in the ancient Greek *polis*. I suggest that Greek political decision-making of both democracies and oligarchies should be understood as a multi-layered system that institutionalized the idea of divided power. While traditional work on ancient Greek institutions has tried to identify the locus of sovereignty in a specific institution or in social and cultural forces, I argue that the authority to enact binding norms was shared among multiple institutional actors, that is councils, boards of officials, assemblies, and courts, which interacted according to a system of delegation of deliberative authority and horizontal accountability. The institutionalization of divided power had a twofold effect. First, it prevented the concentration of power in a single institution and allowed the dominant social group in a *polis* to control itself through the formal legal procedures, the discursive practice, and normativity embedded in the decision-making institutions. Second, Greek divided power favoured the creation of expertise in administration through participation in the different state institutions in which political power was distributed.

This study proposes a renewed attention to institutions as social and political organizations consisting of formal rules, procedures, ideas, and discourses which produce recurrent patterns of behaviour. This approach to Greek institutions attempts to bridge the gap between traditional institutional approaches to political decision-making, which were mainly concerned with descriptive accounts of the constitutional machinery of the Greek *poleis*, and more recent approaches that

---

[3] The law of Dreros, the earliest written Greek law dated at the seventh century BCE, concerns the limits for the office of *kosmos*. For the law of Dreros see Gagarin and Perlman (2016); for Archaic Crete see Seelentag (2015). The same concern for curbing one-man rule is envisaged in the legislation of Solon, and Solon himself in his poetry refuses the title of tyrant for himself (cf. fr. 32 West). For a discussion of this see Harris (2006) 3–39; Canevaro (2017b), (2022). For a study showing the substantive nature of Archaic legislation see Harris and Lewis (2022).

[4] For the definition of 'ideology' adopted in this book, see pp. 35–6.

INTRODUCTION 3

have stressed the role of ideological and discursive values as key factors to understand ancient Greek politics and the nature of political regimes.

This introduction establishes the methodological and theoretical foundations that inform my interpretation of the ancient literary and epigraphical evidence for the procedures of decree-making in the ancient Greek city-states. First, I discuss the state of the art of the major studies on decree-making and political decision-making in modern scholarship. Contextually, I introduce the key concept of divided power, which constitutes the focus of the book, and distinguish it from the traditional concept of 'separation of powers'. I then explore the concept of divided power and institutional mixing in the deliberative realm in ancient political thought, in particular in the works of Plato and Aristotle. Building on this discussion of ancient political thought, the following section defines and distinguishes between decree-making and law-making in Greek ideology and practice within the broader category of political decision-making. The next section lays out my methodological framework and is structured into two parts. In the first, I present an overview of the scholarship on Greek institutional history and set out the new theoretical perspective adopted in this book. The second part presents my methodology, which is informed by historical institutionalism. I situate this approach within the wider scholarly trend in political science labelled 'new institutionalism', and I explain the benefits of adopting this typology of neo-institutionalism. The final section then provides an outline of the book's chapters.

1.1 Sovereignty or Divided Power? Power and Institutions in the Greek City-States

Every Greek state had an assembly which ideally gathered all citizens.[5] Membership of the assembly could, in fact, vary from *polis* to *polis* according to the particular constitutional arrangement. Yet everywhere in Classical and Hellenistic Greece the civic assembly ratified the decisions of the people. Unlike in the Roman Republic, where there was no unified assembly of the Roman people but different types of assemblies with limited powers vis-à-vis the magistrates, Greek assemblies always played a central role in the affairs of the Greek city-states. This was the case both in democracies, where all the free male citizens attended the assembly, and in oligarchic regimes, where membership could be restricted by census requirements or open to all citizens, yet with a much larger degree of authority invested in the magistracies.[6] The substantive aspects of Greek

---

[5] Hansen (1998); Brock (2015).

[6] Cf. the Spartan example in Chapter 4. Simonton (2017) 36 shows that oligarchy was a 'byword for rule of the wealthy'. For the sociological composition of the assemblies in oligarchies and the balance between popular assembly and the magistrates in these regimes, see Simonton (2017) 35–40. Cf. e.g. the census-based oligarchy imposed by Antipater on the Athenians in 322 with Poddighe (2002). For

4 DIVIDED POWER IN ANCIENT GREECE

constitutional law, such as boards of officials enforcing laws and decrees, final audits for magistrates, lawcourts manned by citizens, probouleutic councils, and assemblies were shared by the large majority of the Greek city-states. This unity in the substance of Greek constitutionalism allows us to study the political institutions of different *poleis* on the basis of these shared features that are found across the Greek world from the Archaic period onwards.[7] Building on this fundamental baseline, this section will explore the role of institutions in Greek political practice. It will revise modern interpretations of the nature and role of Greek political institutions and how such reconstructions have shaped scholarly understanding of Greek power. Finally, this section will discuss the use of the concept of sovereignty applied to ancient Greek political systems and will introduce the alternative notion of divided power.

As early as in the Homeric poems both the Achaeans and the Trojans made decisions in assemblies (*agorai*), and even the gods gathered and discussed matters of concern in assemblies (e.g. *Il.* 4.1–72; *Od.* 1.22–95).[8] Although these are not formally regulated institutions, Homeric councils and assemblies already work as a forum for expressing public opinion vis-à-vis that of prominent leaders.[9] By the Classical period, assemblies were fully institutionalized as decision-making bodies, and attendance at the assembly by the citizens, regulated by laws, became a cornerstone of Greek deliberative practice. It is within the assembly that all the major political affairs of the *polis* had to be discussed or at least conclusively ratified by the people in the form of decrees and laws.

Along with the constitutional centrality of the popular assemblies, a second key aspect of Greek deliberative practice was the principle of *probouleusis* (preliminary deliberation). Most Greek *poleis* started their decision-making process in councils or boards of officials which set the agenda and drafted motions to be submitted for ratification in the assembly. The aims of *probouleusis* were to make decision-making smoother as well as to favour wide deliberation before ratification. In the *Politics*, Aristotle highlights the necessity of *probouleusis* in order to secure effective deliberation (Arist. *Pol.* 1299b30–1300a). Yet again, while this institutional function is found in all Greek communities, the rules for

---

Roman Republican assemblies with a sensible discussion on their limited 'democratic credentials' see Mouritsen (2015) 152–4, (2017) 15–21; Cornell (2022). For a Roman perspective on Greek assemblies see Ferrary (1987–9); cf. Cic. *Rep.* 1.26. 42, 1.27.43, 1.31.47, 3.33.45 in which Cicero criticized the excessive powers of Greek assemblies compared to the Roman *comitia*. For Cicero's negative view on Greek decrees see also Liddel (2020b) 237–8. On the role of the Roman *populus* as both an institution and as a social group see Russell (2020).

[7] Harris (2006) 3–28.

[8] Raaflaub and Wallace (2007) 25; Elmer (2020) 293–5; for the assemblies of Homeric gods as based on consensus see Flaig (1994), (2013) 41–51.

[9] On Homeric councils and assemblies see Ruzé (1997) 19–105; Hammer (2002); Raaflaub and Wallace (2007); Barker (2009) 17–20 and 34–56; Schulz (2011) 5–88. For a compelling view of the strong, yet often disruptive role of the Homeric and Archaic *dēmos* vis-à-vis the elites see van Wees (2008) 38.

INTRODUCTION 5

implementing *probouleusis* differed in each constitution. Aristotle distinguished between two basic applications of preliminary deliberation: in oligarchic governments preliminary deliberation is the task of a restricted board of magistrates, such as the *probouloi* (ἡ τῶν προβούλων αὕτη γὰρ οὐ δημοκρατική), while in democracies it is exercised by a council (βουλὴ δὲ δημοτικόν).

Actual institutional practice seems to be consistent with Aristotle's statement. The principle of *probouleusis* implied an active interaction in decision-making between the council or officials in charge of drafting proposals and the citizens' assembly. This relationship was structured according to different constitutional arrangements, reflecting the very nature of deliberation—democratic or oligarchic—in each *polis*. In democratic Athens all citizens met regularly in the assembly at least four times in each prytany ([Arist.] *Ath. Pol.* 43.2).[10] In the assembly all the main decisions were taken by the whole civic body through several speeches and amendments from the floor, and a final vote to ratify the decree.[11] In addition, the tribe-based council of Five Hundred played a crucial role by preparing motions for discussions in the assembly ([Arist.] *Ath. Pol.* 21.3).[12] This constitutional principle is often remarked upon in the Athenian sources. In the Aristotelian *Athenaion Politeia* it is clearly stated that no decree can be enacted by the assembly, unless it is advanced through a *probouleuma* of the council ([Arist.] *Ath. Pol.* 45.4). In *Against Androtion*, Demosthenes states that Androtion's decree was illegal, because it had been enacted by the assembly without prior approval by the council (Dem. 22.5–6; *Andr. hyp.* 1.2, 1.9).[13]

Peloponnesian states adopted a similar mechanism in their decision-making. The Megarian decrees (*dogmata*) preserved on stone show that the decisions of the city were always made by the council (*boula*) and the assembly (*damos*).[14] During the Classical period, we know that Argos had a council, because inscriptions mention the name of a chairman and secretary of the council (e.g. *SEG* 33.275).[15] Sparta also had a probouleutic council. According to the Great Rhetra, the Spartan *gerousia*—a council composed of twenty-eight elders and the two kings—had the task of advancing proposals that were then ratified by the Spartan

---

[10] On Classical Athenian citizenship see Blok (2017), who shows the active role of Athenian women in the democracy and their status as citizens (*politis, astē*). But on the important role of political institutions and offices in the conceptualization of citizenship see Fröhlich (2016) and Faraguna (forthcoming).

[11] Harris (2006) 81–120 shows that more than four meetings could be called in a prytany; cf. [Dem.] 25.20. For the number of meetings of the assembly see Harris (1986), (2006); *contra* Hansen (1977), (1983), (1987a), (1991). Cf. Gauthier (1987) 314; MacDowell (2000) 266–7; Rhodes and Osborne (2003) 323.

[12] Rhodes (1972) 52; Hansen (1991) 246; Rhodes with Lewis (1997) 475; Wallace (2013) 192–3.

[13] See Chapter 2 for the decision-making role of the Athenian council.

[14] On Megarian decree culture see Liddel (2009). For the local history of Megara see now the essays in Beck and Smith (2018).

[15] Rhodes with Lewis (1997) 476.

6 DIVIDED POWER IN ANCIENT GREECE

assembly without any possibility of amending the text.[16] Unlike the Athenian council, the *gerousia* shared its probouleutic power with the ephors, and did not represent the tribal divisions of the Spartan *damos*. Aristotle considered it to be an oligarchic feature of the Spartan constitution.[17]

More generally, *probouleusis* appears to have been very widespread and is found in *poleis* of different sizes and with different kinds of constitutions from the Archaic period onwards.[18] A probouleutic council is attested in sixth-century Chios, where the council, described as δημοσίη (popular), had probouleutic functions as well as judicial powers.[19] In a sixth-century decree from an unknown city in Ozolian Locris, we find a mention of the *preiga*, a probouleutic body of elders (e.g. *IG* IX 1² 609: ἒ ψᾶφον διαφέροι ἐν πρείγαι). In Phocis, Elatea had a probouleutic *sunedrion* (e.g. *IG* IX 1 109.10: ἔδοξε τοῖς συνέδροις), which made proposals to the assembly.[20] In addition, councils were common across the city-states of the Aegean islands, as the decrees of Cos demonstrate (e.g. *SGDI* 3621). After independence from Athens, the decrees of Delos followed the Athenian probouleumatic formula, attesting the presence of a local council and an assembly (e.g. *IG* XI, 4 541).[21] In the cities of Lesbos, the probouleutic functions were carried out by the council (*bolla*) which prepared *probouleumata* for the assembly (*damos*).[22] In Asia Minor, the Carian *polis* of Iasos had a council since the fifth century (e.g. *SEG* 36.982 B1: ἔδοξεν τῆι βουλῆι καὶ τῶι δήμωι), which had at least 111 members during the Hellenistic period.[23]

Councils did not always perform the task of submitting proposals to the assembly. Probouleutic officials are found in many Greek states. Thucydides says that *probouloi* were chosen in Athens after the Sicilian expedition before the establishment of the oligarchic government of the Four Hundred (Thuc. 8.1.3; [Arist.] *Ath. Pol.* 29.2–31.3);[24] again, in the late fourth century, it seems that Demetrius of Phalerum introduced *nomophulakes* (guardians of the laws) in

---

[16] For a full discussion of deliberative procedures in Sparta see Chapter 4. The Spartan assembly was called ἐκκλησία. Cf. Thuc. 1.87.1, 5.77.1, 6.88.10; Xen. *Hell.* 3.2.23, 4.6.3. de Ste. Croix (1972) 346–8; Nafissi (2010) 94–5; Rhodes (2015).

[17] Arist. *Pol.* 1265b37–8. For Aristotle's view on Sparta see Schütrumpf (1994); Bertelli (2004) 13–31.

[18] Cf. Rhodes with Lewis (1997) 475–8 for a broad overview of Greek councils. Rhodes with Lewis (1997) 476 for the absence of councils in very small *poleis*.

[19] ML 8, 10–2: πρησσέτο τὰ δῆμο καὶ δίκα[ς ὁρό]σαι. Forrest (1960); Ampolo (1983) 401–16; Robinson (1997) 99–102.

[20] Rhodes with Lewis (1997) 145. Cf. *SEG* 3.416.

[21] Vial (1984); Constantakopoulou (2017) 2–29.

[22] See Chapter 3 for a discussion on delegation to the council in late fourth-century Mytilene.

[23] Hansen and Nielsen (2004) 81–3; Fabiani (2012) 119–25; Wallace (2013) 93; for some institutional exceptions see Rhodes (2015) 19–21.

[24] For different interpretations of this constitutional document see Rhodes (1981) 362–415; Ostwald (1986) 339; Harris (1990).

INTRODUCTION 7

Athens in order to set out proposals and control the activity of the assembly.[25] Similar officials are also attested in Corcyra at the end of the fourth century (e.g. *IG* IX 1 682, 686), and fifth-century Corinth had eight *probouloi*.[26]

Both the epigraphic evidence and Aristotle show that probouleutic bodies played an important part in the institutional machinery of the Greek *poleis*. This role has been long recognized in scholarship, especially with reference to Classical Athens, whose abundant evidence has made it possible to reconstruct the details of the probouleutic procedure.[27] In his seminal monograph on the Athenian *boulē*, Rhodes offered a more comprehensive account of the powers of the council. He provided a detailed reconstruction of the probouleutic procedure via careful scrutiny of the enactment and motion clauses in the Classical and Hellenistic Athenian decrees preserved on stone.[28] Rhodes expanded his analysis to Greek decision-making beyond Athens by engaging in an epigraphical survey of the decree-making practices in the entire Greek world. In the volume *The Decrees of Greek States*, the last systematic work on decrees and decision-making procedures in the Greek *poleis*, Rhodes and Lewis collect and comment on an impressive amount of epigraphical material from all over the Greek world in order to reconstruct documentary practices as preserved by inscriptions. An entire section of the book is dedicated to a survey of *probouleusis* in the Greek city-states as well as to other special procedures. In this landmark study, Rhodes and Lewis conceive of decree-making as a fundamentally one-way process that begins with *probouleusis* and finishes with assembly ratification. Little attention is paid to the interaction between different institutions and to the connection between institutional design in shaping ideological attitudes in decree-making and collective choices.

Other scholars have engaged with the abundant epigraphical and literary evidence for Athenian decision-making. In a series of publications, Hansen reconstructed the overall decision-making system of fourth-century Athenian

---

[25] Bearzot (2007), (2012); Banfi (2010) 142–5; Canevaro (2013c) 66–9. Cf. Arist. *Pol.* 1323a. In this passage, Aristotle describes the *nomophulakes* as an aristocratic magistracy. The *nomophulakes* are attested in Hellenistic city-states (e.g. oligarchic Cyrene: *SEG* 9.1, 32–4). For a comparison between the constitution of Cyrene and the Athenian constitution of Demetrius of Phalerum see Saldutti (2022) 159–90. In Iasos, after the third-century constitutional reform, the *prutaneis* had wide powers of limiting the assembly's autonomy by a preliminary scrutiny of bills, quite like the *nomophulakes*: see Fabiani (2012) 156–7.

[26] *IG* IX 1 682, 686; Tréheux (1989); Pietragnoli (2010); Canevaro (2014) 315–16.

[27] Andrewes (1956); Rhodes (1972) 52–87; De Laix (1973); Rhodes with Lewis (1997) 475–501; Fröhlich (2013) 255.

[28] Rhodes (1972) 52–87 with 246–58 (table of probouleumatic decrees) and 259–66 (table of non-probouleumatic decrees). See also De Laix (1973); Oliver (2003) 46; and, in particular, Lambert (2017) 227–74 who analyses the decrees for the period 352–323 BCE, and shows a majority of non-probouleumatic decrees in the epigraphical evidence of the second half of the fourth century. On Hellenistic *probouleusis* and decree proposers at Athens see Byrne (2004).

8   DIVIDED POWER IN ANCIENT GREECE

democracy, with emphasis on the separation of powers between institutions.[29] Hansen made an influential case for a change in the nature of Athenian democracy from the fifth to the fourth century. As a result, in Hansen's view, Athenian democracy after 403 BCE was substantially different from, and more moderate than, the fifth-century 'radical' democracy.[30] Building on the hierarchical distinction between *nomoi* and *psēphismata* introduced in 403 BCE, he argued for a hierarchical separation of powers in the restored democracy of the fourth century. While in fifth-century Athens sovereignty rested in the assembly, it shifted to law in the fourth-century democracy. This meant that the locus of sovereignty was to be found in the law-making and adjudicating bodies: the *nomothetai* and the lawcourts.

According to Hansen, Athens developed a rigid two-tiered system of decision-making which mirrored the juridical superiority of laws over decrees. On the one hand, the initiative-taking institutions, that is, the council, the magistrates, and the individual citizens (*hoi boulomenoi*), had the limited role of setting in motion the democratic decision-making and the implementation of the decrees and laws. Hansen singled out, on the other hand, the 'sovereign' institutions, that is the assembly and especially the lawcourts and the *nomothetai*, which made all the most important decisions and were hierarchically superior.[31] These institutions were the only ones possessing decision-making authority, in contrast to institutions in charge of enforcing political decisions, such as the council and the officials.[32]

Other studies tried to identify the 'sovereignty' of a single institution or institutional arrangement, for example the law, in Greek decision-making.[33] Ostwald argued that only fifth-century Athens was a popular democracy with a sovereign assembly, while the Athenian system shifted to the sovereignty of law in the fourth century.[34] Wallace claims that in the years between 350 BCE and 323 BCE, the council of the Areopagus increased its powers and became the dominant Athenian institution until the end of the Classical democracy.[35] In her recent work about late fourth-century Athens, Rohde also makes a similar argument

---

[29] Hansen (1974), (1975), (1987b). Several specific studies on the Athenian assembly published between 1976 and 1989 are collected in Hansen (1983) and (1989a). On the *apagōgē, endeixis,* and *ephēgēsis* see Hansen (1976), but see now also Rocchi (2023a).

[30] Hansen (1976), (1978), (1991), (2010).

[31] Hansen (1976), (1983), (1991) 215–43, (2010) 300. Against this particular formulation of 'sovereignty', cf. Rhodes (1981) 318; Ostwald (1986) 34–5; J. K. Davies (1994); Ober (1996) 108; Blanshard (2004).

[32] Pasquino (2010) 48. In his reply to Pasquino, Hansen distinguishes between 'immediate sovereignty' and 'ultimate sovereignty' according to the theory of Baker. The latter type is that of the final and unappealable institution. On the definition of sovereignty, see below pp. 9–11.

[33] For a sophisticated definition of institution from a legal perspective see MacCormick's definitions of 'institution-agency' (e.g. a court), 'institution-arrangement' (e.g. a contract), and 'institution-thing' (an abstract legal category): MacCormick (2007) 21–37.

[34] Ostwald (1969), (1986); and also Sealey (1987).

[35] Wallace (1989) followed by Todd (1993) 170 n. 201.

INTRODUCTION 9

about the increasing power of the Areopagus, and in general of a political and economic elite of experts which transformed Athens in a *Zustimmungsdemokratie* (democracy of consent).[36] Beyond Athenian scholarship, Schulz has dedicated a study to the Spartan *gerousia* arguing that the council of elders held sovereignty (*Machtfülle*) in the Spartan constitution.[37]

The problems with these views of Greek decision-making institutions are twofold. These approaches raise issues concerning both the reconstruction of institutional arrangements and procedures of Greek decision-making, as well as the conceptual understanding of its nature. It is worth examining these two intertwined problems. First, the idea that Athenian, and Greek political decision-making in general, was a rigid process, dominated by a single institution and shaped by a one-way interaction is problematic. When interaction is envisaged, such as in Hansen's model of decision-making, this reconstruction is always underpinned by a strong functionalist view that does not take into account the different expertise, discursive practices, and behavioural patterns embedded in each institution and constitutional arrangement. For example, the role of the Athenian council in the decree-making process is understood as limited to the drafting of *probouleumata* and to the strict implementation of the assembly's decisions, without considering how the relevant administrative expertise of this body was able to influence and shape actual decree-making practices. Decisions could in fact be delegated to the council, which shows that sovereignty did not ultimately reside within a single institution, but could be divided, transferred, and delegated in order to inject into the decree-making process the expertise and the values embedded in a specific institution.[38] I will return to this subject at length in the next chapter.

The second problem concerns the use of the concept of sovereignty and the relevant terminology, which opens a series of methodological issues when applied to ancient Greek decision-making and politics. The terms 'sovereignty' and 'sovereign' are often used to translate the Greek τὸ κύριον and other related terms. The term and the notion of sovereignty are in fact dependent on the historical context in which this concept assumed theorical relevance. Even if the word sovereignty already existed in medieval terminology, the modern concept only emerged as a result of religious and civil conflicts in Western Europe during the sixteenth and seventeenth centuries.[39] This notion of sovereignty was conceptualized as a remedy to the disruption of the medieval political order after the Reformation.[40] This concept was first systematized in the sixteenth century in Jean

---

[36] Rohde (2019).

[37] Schulz (2011) for a detailed analysis of this argument see Chapter 4.

[38] For an analysis of the Athenian council as decision-making institution see Chapter 2.

[39] On the origin of the English term from medieval Latin *superanus* via old French *souveraineté* see David (1954); Wilks (1963); Dennert (1964).

[40] Grimm (2015).

10   DIVIDED POWER IN ANCIENT GREECE

Bodin's work *Six Livres de la République*, and then further developed by Thomas Hobbes in his *Leviathan*.[41] Both Bodin and Hobbes thought of a unified sovereignty as made of two intertwined aspects: the monopoly of authority and unbound power to legislate in a given territorial domain. In the historical circumstances of early modern Europe, the monarch came to be the sole holder of sovereignty as described by the political theorists of the time.[42]

Yet, with the decline of the *ancien régime* societies, and the gradual establishment of constitutional representative governments during the nineteenth and twentieth centuries, the people became a 'constituted power' (*pouvoir constitué*), that is, a legal entity created by the constitution and that exercises its power through elective representatives.[43] This political development made the classic monistic conception of popular sovereignty unfit even to describe the modern democracies, which are characterized by institutional pluralism and the distribution of power among several decision-making levels. Thus, avoiding the use of the word sovereignty is not only a matter of anachronistic or pedantic nominalism. It actually prevents substantial theoretical misunderstandings and the misleading application to ancient Greek history of concepts that are embedded in the history of the idea of sovereignty in modern European political and legal thought.[44]

In an institutional framework centred around the interaction of many institutions, like that of the Greek *poleis* during the Classical and Hellenistic periods, there could be no single sovereign political institution. Accordingly, when discussing the ancient material about decree-making procedures, I will avoid the terms 'sovereignty' and 'sovereign' and will consistently adopt the concept of *divided power* to refer to the constitutional systems of the Classical and

---

[41] Bodin (1606); Hobbes (1651).

[42] See the sensible comments on the 'non-usability' of sovereignty in ancient Greece in J. K. Davies (1994).

[43] For the expression coined by Seyes of *pouvoir constitué* see Pasquino (1998) and the important discussion of popular sovereignty in Pasquino (2019). Cf. the collection of essays in Leijssenaar and Walker (2019).

[44] For the intellectual history of sovereignty see Bourke (2016) and the essays in Bourke and Skinner (2016). Among them, the account by Hoekstra (2016) of fifth-century popular sovereignty at Athens conceptualized as 'popular tyranny' is problematic. This view is open to several objections. First, his claim is substantiated by sources that cannot represent the Athenian popular understanding of democratic power and sovereignty. Ancient thinkers such as Plato and the 'Old Oligarch' are openly anti-democratic (see Marr and Rhodes [2008] 26–39; Ferrucci [2013]; and Mosconi [2021] 33–54). Other pieces of evidence, such as Thucydides' Mytilenean debate and Aristophanes' *Knights*, pinpoint the shortcomings of Athenian imperial policies during the Peloponnesian War and their supporters in the assembly, such as Cleon. Second, accepting the idea of the unaccountability of the *dēmos* as a whole risks falling into the conceptual trap of ancient anti-democratic theories. Not only were the Athenians legally accountable when serving as officials through the procedures of *euthunai, eisangelia* to the council, *apocheirotonia*, and several *graphai*, but every speaker of the assembly could be indicted for proposing an illegal decree through the *graphē paranomōn* (see Chapter 6) or simply being indicted through the *dokimasia rhētorōn* for not behaving according to the shared value system of the community enshrined in the laws (cf. Aeschin. 1). In this latter case, the penalty was *atimia*, which meant the loss of all the civic rights attached to the status as member of the *dēmos*.

INTRODUCTION 11

Hellenistic Greek city-states.[45] Pasquino introduced the notion of divided power in ancient Greek decision-making in a series of important publications.[46] The expression divided power should not be taken as a synonym for the concept of 'separation of powers' in the classic tripartition of executive, legislative, and judiciary which is typical of modern representative democracies. It is thus important to specify the distinctiveness of such a notion and the differences from other definitions of limited or divided government.

The tripartite separation of powers (or rather state functions) is based on the idea that the legislation and political decision-making—even in the presence of bicameralism and veto power—was the exclusive prerogative of a legislative institution, that is, a legislative assembly whose legitimacy is derived from a system of election.[47] In the classic separation of powers, the legislative power is accountable to the electors who authorize the elected representatives to exert the law-making power on their behalf.[48]

Divided power is a constitutional order that distributes the power of making laws and binding norms among different institutions, such as magistrates, assemblies, and courts. In Pasquino's words, only an institutional 'polyarchy' can in fact implement the principle of the rule of law, through political and legislative decision-making distributed among different bodies.[49] Pasquino's definition describes a political regime based on institutional pluralism where 'there is no monocratic *sovereign* governmental agency' and accountability between institutions is organized horizontally, without constitutional hierarchies between institutions.[50] Such a concept underpins a constitutional system in which political decision-making is regulated by a set of sophisticated institutional layers establishing a mechanism of interaction and control between distinct legislative institutions.

If the label of divided power is eminently etic, this does not mean that the Greeks did not have their own emic understanding of such concept. In the case of ancient Greece, the intellectual foundation of divided power can be traced back to the Archaic period and to the activity of the early lawgivers (cf. §1.3 below) whose concern was to limit the concentration of power and to divide it among several institutions. For example, in Solon's poetry, we read: 'To the people I gave as much privilege as was sufficient / Neither removing nor granting more honour. / As for those who have power and excel in wealth / I saw to it they suffered no harm' (fr. 5 West). Here, the Athenian lawgiver gives an account of how he has distributed

---

[45] Pasquino (2010) 49 problematizing the use of Barker's idea of sovereignty.

[46] Pasquino (2010). See also Pasquino (2005).

[47] Pasquino (2015) 159–61. This is the classic separation of powers that was exemplified in the US constitution before the US Supreme Court obtained judicial review power.

[48] Legal and political theorists refer to this process as vertical accountability as opposed to the concept of horizontal accountability, see the essays in Bovens, Goodin, and Schillemans (2014).

[49] Pasquino (2012) 132.   [50] Pasquino (2003), (2005), (2010) 27–8.

12 DIVIDED POWER IN ANCIENT GREECE

prerogatives (*timē*) to each group in Athenian society in order to avoid excessive concentration of economic and political power. In the realm of institutions, the same concern can be seen in Solon's legislation about the creation of the council of Four Hundred which balanced the fact that the assembly and the lawcourts were open to every citizen without property qualification as well as in the division of power among the archons ([Arist.] *Ath. Pol.* 8.4).

The widespread cultural acceptance among the Greeks of the idea that power should be divided and limited according to the laws and by means of institutional devices is found in numerous sources.[51] When introducing his charge against the decree of Ctesiphon, Aeschines provides a constitutional reflection. He outlines the features of three kinds of existing constitutions: tyranny, oligarchy, and democracy. While tyrannies and oligarchies are governed by the personal temperament of the rulers (διοικοῦνται δ' αἱ μὲν τυραννίδες καὶ ὀλιγαρχίαι τοῖς τρόποις τῶν ἐφεστηκότων), whose power is unlimited (or undivided), democracy is the only political system ruled by the laws (αἱ δὲ πόλεις αἱ δημοκρατούμεναι τοῖς νόμοις τοῖς κειμένοις).[52] Aeschines first highlights that when an Athenian enters the court to judge a *graphē paranomōn* and respects his oath to cast his vote according to the laws, he is protecting his own right of free speech and the democracy based on the laws (Aeschin. 3.6). Later in the speech, while recalling the oligarchic regime of the Thirty, who abolished the *graphē paranomōn*, Aeschines emphatically declares: 'when the *graphē paranomōn* is abolished, the democracy is overthrown' (Aeschin. 3.191). The general tone of Aeschines' statement is not surprising. We can find many passages in speeches of the Attic orators showing that the Athenians believed that the democracy was the only legitimate system of government implementing the principles of the rule of law. What is particularly interesting here is that Aeschines not only appeals to the reverence for the supremacy of the law and to abstract democratic values;[53] the orator locates Athenian divided power in a specific institution, that is, the *graphē paranomōn*. He sees this institution as the best way to safeguard the Athenian democratic *politeia* and its laws.[54]

Understanding the institutional manifestations of divided power in Greek politics also has important implications for our historical interpretation of the discourse, norms, and ideas of power in the Greek *poleis*. The normative aspects of Greek divided power were entrenched in the institutional design of the political

---

[51] Cf. Archaic and Classical laws where authority is distributed among different boards of magistrates with the power to fine each other in case of illegal conduct: e.g. *Nomima* I 62 (early sixth-century Chios); Körner (1993) n. 7 (fifth-century Olympia); *I.Erythrai* 1 (fifth-century Erythrai).

[52] Aeschines employs widespread stereotypes about tyranny which are also applied to oligarchies. For the prototypical character of the sole ruler in Greek culture and political thought, see Luraghi (2013), (2015), (2018).

[53] For the reverence of the laws, often expressed in terms of fear for the laws in Greek culture, see Esu (2021a) 155–9 and Chapter 5.

[54] Cf. Chapter 6 for divided power and the Athenian *graphē paranomōn*.

INTRODUCTION 13

institutions and can be better identified through careful study of the procedures and laws. This is not only relevant for our knowledge of legal mechanisms of decision-making, but also for understanding the nature of political power and how social actors abided by the normative system and the informal practice of their political community and accessed political decision-making and legislative power in practice. If Greek deliberative power was in the hands of the people as a social entity, this was institutionally divided and distributed among different institutions, which cooperated and interacted horizontally to run the decision-making and enact decrees and laws.

The capacity of the *dēmos* to control itself and respect individual obligations and rights—usually expressed with the terminology of *timē*—in the decree-making function was entrusted to laws and to different institutional devices and procedures designed to allocate power in a flexible fashion, yet without undermining the respect of the higher-order rules.[55] This means that the procedure to implement the concept of divided power could vary from *polis* to *polis*, but the substance of dividing the power among different institutions in order to protect the rule of law and the individual prerogatives attached to individual statuses remained fundamentally the same across the Greek world. Such mechanisms included various forms of legislative review performed by lawcourts or by boards of officials according to different procedures but with the same aim of securing legal consistency between laws and decrees. Similarly, power could be divided between the deliberative bodies through a delegation procedure from one body to another in the decree-making or by establishing special voting procedures within the assembly. Studying the procedures and institutions of Greek divided power is therefore not only a contribution to Greek institutional and legal history, but also a way to unearth the nature of Greek political deliberation and a contribution to the intellectual and political history of popular power in antiquity.

The concept of divided power is therefore incompatible with the idea of the superiority of a given institution in the decision-making system. Instead, it envisages a form of decision-making that is the outcome of multi-institutional

---

[55] The complex system of mutual obligations and rights between individuals in Greek communities was expressed through the concept of *timē* (honour) and the relevant terminology and connected concepts. *Timē* is a bidirectional notion that encompasses both one's own claims to honour and the respect coming from others (cf. Hdt. 9.28.1–3; Cairns [1993], [1996], [2011], [2019c]; Scodel [2008]; Canevaro [2018e]; Keim [2018]). The concept of *timē* underpins any given values system and involves both self-assertiveness and limitations to one's own claims vis-à-vis the community. As such, *timē* is a central mechanism in the institutions that connect the individuals to the community. The *timē* of citizens (cf. e.g. Dem. 23.1) entailed their status and their subjective rights and obligations towards the community. The extent of such rights and obligations, enforced by the relevant institutions, could vary in different political communities. For *timē* as right see Canevaro (2020) and especially Canevaro and Rocchi (forthcoming) with Arist. *Pol.* 1278a35–6; Hdt. 4.145.4. On *atimia* as loss of legal prerogatives attached to citizenship, see e.g. [Arist.] *Ath. Pol.* 22.8, 53.5–6, 63.3, 67.5; Andoc. 1.74; Xen. *Lac.* 9.6; Dem. 9.44; *IG* I³ 40.6–7, 33–4.

14   DIVIDED POWER IN ANCIENT GREECE

interaction between different bodies, each one playing a distinctive and relevant role in the shaping of decrees. Recent studies on specific institutions of fourth-century Athenian democracy have pushed this understanding against previous accounts of the working of Athenian decision-making institutions. Canevaro's new reconstruction of the *nomothesia* procedure sheds light on the pivotal role played by the assembly in law-making after 403 BCE, which did not envisage any reduction or shift of power from the assembly to the *nomothetai*, but rather a more sophisticated procedure to enact laws combining legal stability and popular decision-making, which was based on the interaction between different bodies and unfolded in distinct procedural set-ups.

These recent studies demonstrate the limits of the old institutionalist approach to Greek political decision-making, and the necessity of redefining the deliberative practices of the Greek *poleis* according to the notion of 'divided power', which underscores the importance of the interaction between different institutional settings in processing political deliberation. Institutional division of power and constitutional mixing in political decision-making was not unknown to ancient political thought. The concept of the mixed constitution played a significant role in the theories of ancient philosophers and historiographers, especially Plato, Aristotle, and Polybius. Their ideas of mixed government have been extremely influential in shaping early modern and later constitutionalism, but ancient views on political deliberation and institutional mixing also help distinguishing between the theory and practice of ancient Greek constitutionalism.

1.2 Ancient Greek Political Thought on Political Decision-Making and Institutional Design: An Overview

The previous section has introduced the concept of divided power as a multi-layered decision-making system. This section explores how Greek political thought conceptualized political decision-making as a function of the constitution (*politeia*), and how ancient political thinkers and historiographers elaborated the concept of mixed constitution, and the interaction between different political bodies. Such theorizations do not usually match the concept of divided power as is clearly found in the constitutional procedures of the Greek *poleis*, and show a tension between theoretical models and institutional practice. The divergence between philosophical accounts, especially Platonic and Aristotelian models, and Greek constitutional practice is not surprising considering the generally negative assessment of popular participation given by the two major Classical Greek philosophers and their schools. Yet, the unfavourable view of the popular participation expressed by Plato and, in a more nuanced fashion, by Aristotle can only partially explain the minor analytical role of institutions in their

INTRODUCTION 15

theoretical frameworks.[56] It is the basic methodology used to assess the nature of constitutions, especially in the Aristotelian school, that reveals a certain lack of interest in institutions as a meaningful heuristic category.

Greek political thought was in fact not particularly interested in defining constitutional mixture before the complex theories of Plato and Aristotle. From Solon to Herodotus, political thought mostly focused on how to govern a *polis*, concentrating on the polarity between lawfulness and unlawfulness (e.g. Hes. *Op.* 225–60; Sol. fr. 5 West). Herodotus' constitutional debate is the first attempt in the Greek literary tradition to engage in a more sophisticated reflection on different constitutional models: democracy, oligarchy, and monarchy (Hdt. 3.80-2).[57] Herodotus' assessment of the three constitutional categories is based on moral categories that are typical of Greek ethics.[58] However, traces of the necessity of dividing power, in line with the concerns of Archaic Greek legislation, are found in Otanes' proposal of a democratic constitution for the Persians. Otanes' take on democracy is built in opposition to monarchy, which assumes the contours of tyranny. Monarchy is characterized by the absence of accountability (τῇ ἔξεστι ἀνευθύνῳ ποιέειν τὰ βούλεται) which leads even the best men to commit *hybris* moved by resentment (*phthonos*) (3.80.1-4). The rule of the people is different, first because it is called *isonomia* (equality before the law), and second because power and offices are allocated by lot (πάλῳ μὲν ἀρχὰς ἄρχει), are subject to accountability (ὑπεύθυνον δὲ ἀρχὴν ἔχει), and all issues are referred to the public (3.80.6).[59] Otanes' speech reveals traces of a concern for divided power. His definition of democracy illustrates a decision-making power that is shared and open. Political offices are open to everyone through the use of the lot and the people are in charge of the accountability of the officials.

Thucydides' assessment of the constitution of the Five Thousand provides the first example in Greek literature of the concept of institutional 'mixture in control of the few and the many' (Thuc. 8.97.2: μέτρια γὰρ ἥ τε ἐς τοὺς ὀλίγους καὶ τοὺς πολλοὺς ξύγκρασις).[60] According to Thucydides, this constitutional compromise between the wealthiest and the many allowed the Athenians to be better governed than under their previous democratic regime. Thucydides subscribes to a socio-logical view of political power that is typical of Greek political thought. What

---

[56] For the problematic relationship between Plato and the restored Athenian democracy, see Trampedach (1994) 278-9; Haake (2009) 118-19, and (2020) 67-74 showing the elitist social milieu of the members of the Academy. They belonged to 'the upper classes of the Greek cities around the Mediterranean and the Black Sea'; see Haake (2020) 74.

[57] For early Greek political thought see Raaflaub (2000); for Greek political theory before Plato see esp. Bertelli (2017) 11-66. On Herodotus' political thought, see Raaflaub (2002), (2013); Forsdyke (2006). On Archaic Greek thought see especially Fisher (1992); Cairns (2013b); and Canevaro (2022).

[58] For moral historiography in Herodotus see Hau (2016) 172-93.

[59] Lanza (1977) 225-32; Pelling (2002).

[60] Hahm (2009) 178-9. A similar fifth-century philosophical approach is that of the Anonymus Iamblichi who advocated the mixing of citizens as a way to promote civic harmony, see Anonymus Iamblichi 7.2 DK. For Thucydides' political thought see Ober (2006); *contra* Balot (2017).

16 DIVIDED POWER IN ANCIENT GREECE

made the constitution of the Five Thousand a good *politeia* was not the institutional design of the new arrangement, but the sociological mixing of the civic body. Thucydides had already adopted a similar perspective in Athenagoras' staunch defence of the democracy (Thuc. 6.39), where the Syracusan leader praises democracy for representing all the people (δῆμον ξύμπαν ὠνομάσθαι), while oligarchy only speaks on behalf of a part (ὀλιγαρχίαν δὲ μέρος). Athenagoras also distinguishes the relevant functions of advising (βουλεῦσαι) and making decisions (κρῖναι) which are better performed on an equal share in a democracy (ταῦτα ὁμοίως καὶ κατὰ μέρη καὶ ξύμπαντα ἐν δημοκρατίᾳ ἰσομοιρεῖν). Here, Thucydides sketches a constitutional reflection based on both a sociological understanding of the *politeia* and on the relevant institutional functions, which will be developed in a highly sophisticated way in Aristotle's *Politics* and his theory of the 'parts of the city'.[61] I will return to this view more extensively when discussing Aristotle's constitutional taxonomy.

Plato was one of the first political thinkers to engage more systematically with institutional design, and in particular with the notion of a 'mixed constitution'.[62] In his major political dialogue, the *Republic*, Plato theorizes a utopian and ideal city ruled by wise philosophers and designed for 'gods and children of gods';[63] however, it is in the *Laws* that the Athenian philosopher actually deals with institutional mixing and the division of powers for the potentially real *polis* of Magnesia.[64] The mixed constitution proposed in the *Laws* is for Plato the second best, after the ideal-type of the *Republic*.[65] Yet, in Book 3 of the *Laws*, Plato identifies in Sparta a distinctive type of *politeia*.[66] By referring back to an old tradition that saw Sparta as a model of good government and well-established laws,[67] Plato observes that the Spartan constitution consists of a double kingship which is mixed (*mignusi*) with an aristocratic council of elders, who were constrained in their power by the ephors who in turn were elected by the people in the assembly. As a result, the Spartan kingship did not become a tyranny and was mixed (*summiktos*) with other powers.[68]

As Piérart has shown, the model Plato used in the *Laws* for the city of Magnesia was not Spartan institutions; his is mainly a critical account of the contemporary

---

[61] The terminology is revealing of the predominance of a sociological and ethical approach. Athenagoras divides up the society into *aristoi* (the best or the wealthy), *xunetoi* (the wise people), and *polloi* (the many).

[62] A unique example of the discussion of the Spartan mixed constitution which emphasizes the democratic aspect is found in fr. 4 of *On Law and Justice* attributed to the Pythagorean philosopher Archytas of Tarentum. See the translation and analysis in Horky and Johnson (2020).

[63] For the methodology of Plato's *Republic* and *Statesman*, see Lane (1998); Schofield (2000a); Rowe (2007); and the essays in Dimas, Lane, and Sauvé Meyer (2021).

[64] Pl. *Leg.* 739d–e. Plato's *Epistles* show a connection between Plato's plan for Syracuse and the *Laws*; see *Ep.* 337a, *Ep.* 337d. See Schofield (2000b).

[65] For the relationship between the *Laws* and Plato's other political dialogues see Laks (2000).

[66] Hodkinson (2005) 227–31.   [67] On the Spartan 'mirage' see Chapter 4 with bibliography.

[68] Pl. *Leg.* 691d–692a.

INTRODUCTION   17

constitutional and legal arrangements of fourth-century Athens.[69] The *Laws* are especially important as this dialogue shows the tension between Plato's theoretical analysis and the Athenian manifestation of divided power, which constituted for him the critical baseline for his philosophical model. This becomes immediately clear in Book 6 of the *Laws*, where he discusses political offices, most of which clearly resemble those of contemporary Athens. Plato lists military officials (*stratēgoi, hipparchoi, phularchoi,* and *taxiarchoi*), a council with *prutaneis, nomophulakes,* religious officials (priests and priestesses, *tamiai* and *exēgētai*), *astunomoi, agronomoi,* and *agoranomoi,* officials in charge of education, elected judges, and *euthunoi.*[70] Citizenship was divided into four census classes, like the Solonian classes, and Plato designed membership of deliberative bodies, the council and the assembly, in such a way as to secure the participation of every class. The complex selection procedures envisaged for appointing the councillors were combined with a system of fines for the rich who failed to attend the assembly. This had the purpose of mitigating the political influence of the wealthiest on the one hand, and of keeping under control the poorest classes on the other.

Plato's advice about the appointment of officials displays the philosophical and ideological principles that underpinned his view of mixed constitutions. Military officials and treasurers were selected by a mix of sortition, as in Athens, and election. Meanwhile, the officials in charge of applying and protecting the laws, such as the *nomophulakes,* the *euthunoi,* and the judges, were selected only from and among the most educated and most virtuous citizens, who were not necessarily the richest. Plato's theory of mixed government was not predicated directly on socio-economic criteria and was instead built on his psychological theory.[71] In order to prevent rulers as well as citizens from being led by irrationality, education and institutions should play a key role.[72] For Plato, institutional mixing and complex constitutional devices are meant to influence and constrain the behaviour of rulers towards virtue and rationality.[73] Plato's idea of the mixed constitution is based on the assumption that the rationality embedded in the laws would help prevent a constitution from degenerating into an autocracy or an excess of freedom for the people—as had happened to Athenian democracy.[74] As a result, Plato generally increases the powers of magistrates in decision-making, especially the power of *nomophulakes* and *euthunoi* vis-à-vis larger

---

[69] Piérart (2016); Bartels (2017).   [70] Pl. *Leg.* 6.751a–768c.

[71] Nippel (1980); Hahm (2009) 184.

[72] Plato links the good morality of a political community to the good morality of its citizens (*Resp.* 435d–436a). For a detailed analysis of Plato's tripartite soul metaphor in Book 4 of the *Republic* see Cairns (2021).

[73] Hahm (2009) 181.

[74] See Filonik (2019) 4–10, 12–15, and 17–18 showing the bias of Athenian thinkers about the alleged excess of freedom enjoyed by individuals under the Athenian democracy. Cf. also the transformation of the democratic concept of *parrhēsia* by Isocrates and Plato in Filonik (forthcoming).

18   DIVIDED POWER IN ANCIENT GREECE

participative institutions, such as the council and the assembly. Institutional mixing and division of power, in Plato's view, did not entail a socio-economic mix of different segments of society; he rather sees institutions as a way to curb and put a check on the psychology of both rulers and citizens. This is important because Plato introduces a concept akin to the notion of institutional checks and balances, which was then adopted and revised by Polybius and later by Montesquieu.[75]

In the *Politics*, Aristotle does not seem particularly interested in the constitutional mechanisms and the normativity of institutions per se. Aristotle's method for constitutional analysis is, for instance, apparent in his treatment of the Spartan *politeia*. Similarly to his teacher Plato, Aristotle considered Sparta an example of *mixis* between democracy and oligarchy, yet with particular emphasis on the ephorate as an institution that sociologically represented the people.[76] Aristotle engages in a systematic critique of the Spartan *politeia* in Book 2 of the *Politics*, in which he condemns the Spartan slave system, the unequal distribution of land, the excessive freedom enjoyed by women, the social status of the ephors, and the life-long tenure of the elders (Arist. *Pol.* 1269a29–1271b19). These sharp judgements on Sparta's socio-economic institutions reveal a different Aristotelian approach to constitutional analysis compared with Plato's. Unlike for Plato, the methodological baseline for Aristotle's discussion of political regimes in the *Politics* is primarily sociological.

Aristotle makes his sociological perspective clear in Book 3, where he provides a systematic discussion of the different constitutions and their deviant and correct forms. In chapter 6 of Book 3, Aristotle solves the riddle of the multiplicity of constitutional forms by introducing the notion of *politeuma*, that is, the body of the citizens enjoying full political rights.[77] Aristotle defines the constitution (*politeia*) as the arrangement of civic offices and especially of the *politeuma* (body politic), which everywhere has supreme authority (κύριον μὲν γὰρ πανταχοῦ τὸ πολίτευμα τῆς πόλεως) (1278b6–11).[78] Aristotle then gives examples of *politeumata* in democracies and oligarchies. When the *dēmos* (as *politeuma*) has the supreme authority, then the constitution is a democracy, while when the few are the *politeuma* the constitution is an oligarchy. The same concept is reaffirmed later at 1279a22–8 when Aristotle states that the *politeuma* has supreme authority in the city, and by necessity the *politeuma* is composed either by the few or by the many which can rule either in the interest of their social group or in the common

---

[75] Nippel (1980).

[76] See Hodkinson (2005) 234–7. For the Spartan mixed constitution as part of the Spartan mirage see Chapter 4 pp. 125–8.

[77] Levy (1993); Hansen (1994); Accattino and Curnis (2013) on *politeuma* as 'body politic' in Aristotle's *Politics*.

[78] Similar formulations of the *politeia* and the problem of the variety of constitutions occurs also at Arist. *Pol.* 1274b38, 1275a38, 1276b1 and 31–5, 1278a15.

INTRODUCTION 19

interest of the *polis*.[79] In Aristotle's theory, sovereignty is attributed to the *politeuma* and this is an eminently sociological category.[80]

Similarly, in chapter 3 of Book 4 of the *Politics*, Aristotle provides again the conceptual background for his method of constitutional analysis, and sets out what he believes are the reasons for the variety of existing constitutions. The reason is identified in the theory of the parts of the city or what Accattino has defined as *l'anatomia della città* (the anatomy of the city).[81] According to Aristotle every city is composed by 'multiple parts' (*merē* or *moirai* of the *polis*). These parts are conceived in socio-economic terms: the poor, the *mesoi*, and the rich. The very nature of a constitution is determined by the numerically dominant part of the city within a given constitution. Democracy exists when all partake in political power, while oligarchy emerges when only few are in charge. The *mesē politeia* is Aristotle's best option, in which the *mesoi* hold power. For Aristotle, the differences between the most extreme democracy and the most extreme oligarchy depend on sophisticated and nuanced divisions in the parts of the *polis*, whereas institutions, legal procedures, and mechanisms seem to play no part in his theoretical model.[82] The nature of political power is therefore characterized foremost by the social composition of the citizenry.

Aristotle, however, is aware that in most cases the Greek *poleis* are either democracies or oligarchies, as the *mesoi* constitute a very small social class. This is the reason why he introduces another option, the mixed constitution (*memigmenē politeia*), which is a mix of democracy and oligarchy. Yet, in order to have a mixed constitution, the constitutional functions (political deliberation, judiciary, and magistracies) need to be shared and allocated to different parts of the city. It is at this point that the sociological approach becomes unfit to describe the *memigmenē politeia*, and Aristotle changes his methodology. In chapters 14–16 of Book 4, Aristotle introduces institutional analysis as a means to mix democracy and oligarchy. As Accattino has noted, this represents a new methodology, a second 'anatomy of the city', in opposition to the socio-economic

---

[79] The discussion on *politeuma* offers a way to identify 'deviant' and 'correct' constitutions. In deviant constitutions, the social agents who constitute the *politeuma* rule exclusively for their self-interest. In correct constitution the social group in charge rule for the common interest. See Accattino and Curnis (2013) 173–4.

[80] Hansen (1994) 74–5 argues that since *kurios* does not indicate an abstract concept of sovereignty and could be applied to an agent, this means that ancient political thought could conceptualize an institution as the sovereign of the city. The Aristotelian use of the term *kurios* does not warrant this conclusion, especially because his constitutional analysis is focused on the social groups who hold the supreme power in a given constitution. For a discussion of the terms *autokratōr* and *kurios* in Athenian institutional practice see §§2.4 and 2.5.

[81] Accattino (1986); Canevaro (2014) 279–80.

[82] For Aristotle's methodology for constitutional analysis see Canevaro and Esu (2018) with bibliography.

20 DIVIDED POWER IN ANCIENT GREECE

anatomy of the city, one in which Aristotle adopts a functionalist approach based on institutions.[83]

At the beginning of chapter 14 (*Pol.* 1297b35–40), Aristotle no longer discusses the 'parts of the city' in socio-economic terms, but talks about 'parts of all *politeiai*' and singles out three state functions: the deliberative power (τὸ βουλευόμενον περὶ τῶν κοινῶν), the magistracies (τὸ περὶ τὰς ἀρχάς), and the judicial function (τὸ δικάζον). Aristotle's classification was not a novelty. He uses a tripartition that was common in previous Greek political and constitutional thought.[84] This categorization, however, does not match exactly the modern liberal-democratic conception of the division of powers into legislative, executive, and judiciary. The Greeks postulated a division between the political and the judicial functions.[85] They did not isolate, however, executive power proper. Instead, the magistrates carried out administrative tasks which frequently overlapped with the deliberative sphere and the judicial realm. The very expression τὸ περὶ τὰς ἀρχάς reveals Aristotle's difficulty in treating officials as an abstract notion in parallel with the deliberative and judicial functions.[86] In Book 4 of the *Politics*, Aristotle gives an account of the institutional functions and the relevant subjects on which each function has authority (*kurios*). When he comes to describing political decision-making, at *Politics* 1298a3–7, he states that the deliberative function has authority over four matters: foreign policy (περὶ πολέμου καὶ εἰρήνης καὶ συμμαχίας καὶ διαλύσεως), laws (καὶ περὶ νόμων), sentences of death and exiles and confiscation (καὶ περὶ θανάτου καὶ φυγῆς καὶ δημεύσεως), and appointment and audits of magistrates (καὶ περὶ ἀρχῶν αἱρέσεως καὶ τῶν εὐθυνῶν).[87]

Moving away from this general account of the areas governed by the deliberative function; in the rest of chapter 14 of Book 4 the Aristotelian analysis turns into a minute and detailed description of different institutional ways of organizing the deliberative institutions of democracies, oligarchies, and aristocratic regimes. Aristotle lists four different kinds of democratic arrangements, three oligarchic ones, and one aristocratic type. For example, Aristotle describes a model of moderate democracy in which the franchise for taking offices and attending the assembly is very low (Arist. *Pol.* 1298a12–19). The number of rich, *mesoi*, and

---

[83] Accattino (1986) 77–8.

[84] The division of the *politeia* into three parts was older than the Aristotelian theorization; cf. Bertelli (1994) 27–84; Miller (1997) 165–6; Harris (2006) 31–2; Canevaro (2014) 282. Cf. Hdt. 3.81; Eur. *Suppl.* 403–8, 426–55. In [Dem.] 25.20 laws are described as the foundation for the meetings of council and assembly (τὴν βουλὴν συλλέγεσθαι, τὸν δῆμον εἰς τὴν ἐκκλησίαν ἀναβαίνειν), the filling of the lawcourts (τὰ δικαστήρια πληροῦσθαι), and the turnover of magistrates (τὰς ἕνας ἀρχὰς ταῖς νέαις ἑκούσας ὑπεξιέναι). For a slightly different tripartition between lawgiver, assembly, and judges see also Arist. *Rhet.* 1.1.1354b4–8.

[85] Harris (2006) 30–1.   [86] For *archē* in Aristotle's *Politics* see Carlier (2004).

[87] Arist. *Pol.* 1297b35–1298a7, 300b19–20. Cf. Canevaro (2014) 279–90, 356–7. Institutional systems that made officials accountable were common in all Greek states from the Archaic until the Imperial period; see Fröhlich (2004). In Sparta, the ephors held audits of officials and even kings; see Chapter 4. Cf. [Arist.] *Ath. Pol.* 43.4, 48.3; Piérart (1971); Fröhlich (2004) 333–62.

poor is balanced. Political decision-making is in the hands of the whole civic body, which deliberates in the council and in the boards of magistrates. The assembly is gathered only rarely, to appoint magistrates and to pass laws.[88] What determines the political nature of a regime, however, even in the context of Aristotle's institutional analysis, is not its institutional design and how power is institutionally divided, but which socio-economic part of the *polis* has access to political decision-making. Aristotle also applies the same methodology in chapters 15 and 16, where he discusses respectively the organization of the magistracies and the lawcourts. The importance of institutions and constitutional arrangements is clearly not unknown to Aristotle, who identifies the complexity of institutional arrangements in the reality of the Greek *poleis*, and sees that the three functions of the *politeia*, that is, the deliberative, the judiciary, and the offices were in fact divided across different institutions, and that such divisions had an impact in the nature of the constitution. Yet, divided power and constitutional design are always methodologically understood as subordinated to the socio-economic anatomy of the city—what determines the nature of a constitution is what socio-economic part of the city has control of particular state functions. Institutional mixing is only relevant inasmuch as it succeeds in assigning different roles and functions to different socio-economic parts of the city.

Within this framework, it is clear why for Aristotle historical examples of divided power such as the one he could see in fourth-century Athens, with its complex system of deliberative and judicial institutions controlling each other, could not be models of a good constitution. In those cases there was no socio-economic mixing of the parts of the city and no recognition of a plurality of grounds for worth and therefore for claiming honour and political prerogatives. It was the same sociological part of the city, namely the *dēmos*, that was in control of all the three parts of the *politeia* (the deliberative, the judiciary, and the magistracies).[89] In Aristotle's framework, regardless of the institutional complexity of Athenian divided power, it was the *dēmos*, with its claims and notions of fair distribution of honour and resources, that ultimately dominated the constitution.

The interaction of Aristotle's sociological and ethical methodologies with his institutional analysis of constitutions is also relevant to his theory of constitutional change (*metabolē*) and *stasis*. In this case, it serves to explain how institutionalized forms of divided power break down and change. In *Politics* 5, Aristotle discusses *stasis* within his study of the preservation and failure of constitutions anticipated in Book 4 (*Pol.* 1289b23–6). Aristotle explains that social agents usually trigger *stasis*, and consequentially *metabolē*,[90] when their own notion of distributive

---

[88] Canevaro (2014) 295–7; B. D. Gray (2015) 101–3.
[89] This argument is developed in Canevaro and Esu (2018) with emphasis on the interaction between Aristotle's political theory and its use in the *Athenaion Politeia*.
[90] For *metabolē* in Aristotle see Bertelli (2018) 71–86.

22   DIVIDED POWER IN ANCIENT GREECE

justice clashes with the institutionalized system of power and recognition. This means that the allocation of power and offices (*timai*) is not arranged in accordance with the social agents' internalized notions of proportional equality, that is, equality by worth (*κατ' ἀξίαν*).[91] The grounds for worth that are considered relevant are more inclusive for democrats, and more exclusive for oligarchs and aristocrats, as demonstrated by the different ways democracies and oligarchies establish access to honours, offices, and institutions.[92]

This is consistent with the Aristotelian definition of proportional equality in the *Nicomachean Ethics*, where the philosopher states that proportional equality regards honour, resources, and everything else that is divisible (*τῶν ἄλλων ὅσα μεριστά*) among those who participate in the *politeia* (Arist. *Eth. Nic.* 5.2.1130b31–3).[93]

Aristotle's analysis of *stasis* provides the tools for clarifying two interrelated points about divided power, institutional design, and social conflict in Greek political thought. First, as the most important ancient theorist of *stasis*, Aristotle makes clear that *stasis* was not in fact an intrinsic feature of functioning constitutional arrangements (which entailed versions of divided power). In other words, *stasis* is not equated to normal political conflict within a well-functioning constitutional order in which the power of making political decisions is distributed across different institutions. *Stasis* represented the breakdown of social ties, political practices, and institutional rules. Second, Aristotle's account shows that *stasis* could happen for several causes, but the fundamental cause rested on a social group rejecting the notions of distributive justice which underpinned the existing constitution. This triggered and paved the way for constitutional change.[94] *Stasis*, therefore, occurred when the legitimacy of the current divided-power arrangements in a given *polis* were altogether challenged and a social group attempted to produce a new constituent moment. The purpose was that of restructuring the constitutional order according to a new system which could

[91] A strong case for the way Aristotle analyses *stasis* as a matter of distribution of resources as well as recognition and status is made and developed in great detail by Cairns, Canevaro, and Mantzouranis (2022).

[92] At 5.2–3, Aristotle identifies three causes which interact with the disposition of the agents (*diathesis*) in provoking *stasis*: (1) a different notion of distributive justice; (2) *timē, kerdos, atimia*, and *zēmia*; and (3) several various factors that include behaviour (*hybris*), emotions (fear), contempt, and demography, which are all underpinned by the fundamental cause of a different notion of distributive justice: see Cairns, Canevaro, and Mantzouranis (2020) 551–70.

[93] Aristotle's analysis of power as 'struggle for recognition' shows the limits of some analysis of power in Greek thought as detached from notions of justice. Cf. Gotter's important article (2008) 179–99. For example, Gotter takes Eteocles' speech in Eur. *Phoen.* 503–24 as paradigmatic of the way 'the Greeks spoke about power'. Eteocles wants to defend his *turannis* and reputation in any possible way, yet his point of view is totally antisocial. While he worships *Philotimia*, his mother Jocasta reproached him (536, 542) by opposing to his view that of the goddess Equality (*Isotēs*). See Cairns (1993) 266 for a detailed analysis. For 'struggle for recognition', see the seminal book by Honneth (1995).

[94] For a discussion of examples of breakdown of the system of divided power see Chapter 7.

INTRODUCTION   23

involve a new divided-power arrangement recognizing a different allocation of honours and resources.[95]

The analyses of institutional design and constitutional change in both Plato and Aristotle sheds light on two different ways in which the mixed constitution could curb power: while Plato's constitutional mix is based on his psychological theory of rulers, Aristotle adopts a sociological methodology which privileges a constitution mixing the sociological parts of a city through institutions. Yet, for both philosophers, the mixed constitution was only a second-best option. Plato's idea of the mixed constitution inspired Polybius in his analysis of the Spartan and the Roman constitutions, both understood as mixed governments. For Polybius, however, the mixed government was the best type of constitution. Polybius adopted Plato's view of checks and balances as a way to preserve the stability of the constitution, but in a different way. According to Polybius, a mixed constitution is not comprised of a combination of different bodies, with each one keeping the others in check, but involves the mixing of three governments (*politeumata*): kingship, aristocracy, and democracy.[96] In Polybius' view, power becomes stable if it is divided between three key institutions, each one representing a *politeuma*. In Sparta the *basileis* represented kingship, the *gerousia* aristocracy, and the ephors democracy (Polyb. 6.10).[97] Such a constitution was only surpassed by the Roman one, which not only prevented degeneration through a careful division of powers, but also promoted institutional unity in the implementation of policies.[98]

The fourth-century theories of Plato and Aristotle identified the existence of institutional complexity and the necessity to divide power in different bodies of governments working together to run a *polis*. Yet for both Plato and Aristotle, divided power was not per se the solution to the conundrum of creating well-ordered regimes in the Greek *poleis*. Both the constitutional ideal-types of Plato's *Republic* and of Aristotle's *Politics* 8, as well as their notions of the mixed constitution, are not based on a theory of institutions, but on other philosophical premises. With the very partial exception of the model of Sparta, the other Greek constitutions, and especially the Athenian democracy—implicitly criticized by Plato in the *Laws* and by Aristotle in the *Politics*—did not show any trace of an effective division of power. The contemporary versions of institutional mixing, as we can reconstruct them from literary and epigraphical evidence, never satisfied Plato's and Aristotle's requirements. In their perspective, it was always the *dēmos*

---

[95] For constituent power and its relationship with popular power, see Arato (2017); Rubinelli (2020), providing a history of the concept from Seyes to post-World War II. For the relationship between constituent power and the law, see the important book by Colón-Ríos (2020). A useful review of the different discussions on this concept in constitutional theory is Arvidsson, Brännström, and Minkkinen (2020) 1–7.

[96] Cf. Polyb. 6.3.5–4.5 for his identification of the three simple constitutions: kingship, democracy, and aristocracy.

[97] See also the discussion in Chapter 4.

[98] For Polybius' political theory see F. W. Walbank (1972); Hahm (1995) 7–47 and (2009) 190–6.

24 DIVIDED POWER IN ANCIENT GREECE

that was in charge of controlling the political decision-making, passing decrees and laws in the council and the assembly, appointing officials, and manning the lawcourts. And the *dēmos* could not in fact control itself, however much its power was divided up between different institutional roles and agencies. This is an important gap between ancient political theory and institutional practice. It is in the analysis of the latter realm that we find the popular understanding of divided power.

1.3 Political Decision-Making and Legislation

Another important distinction must be introduced in order to provide a comprehensive definition of divided power in the realm of ancient Greek deliberation: the peculiar place of law-making within Greek political decision-making.

The previous section has shown that Aristotle considered the enactment of laws as a constitutive part of political decision-making. This is coherent with other accounts in the Aristotelian corpus and in the works of other Greek philosophers. In his account of the deliberative function in the *Rhetoric*, Aristotle lists revenues, war and peace, imports and exports, defence of the land, and law-making, while other important subjects such as taxation and grants of citizenship are missing (Arist. *Rhet.* 1359b19). Similarly, the Old Oligarch remarks that the Athenian deliberative bodies are in charge of the officials' audits, legislation, war and peace, allies and their tributes, administration of temples, and the armoury ([Xen.] *Ath. Pol.* 3.2).

The fact that all the Athenian accounts of deliberation single out a separate category for *nomoi* is important since it carries vast implications for our understanding of political decision-making and divided power. In terms of legal sources, the Greeks, and especially the Athenians, distinguished between *nomoi* (laws), permanent and general rules, and *psēphismata* (decrees), ad hoc and temporary enactments (Andoc. 1.87; Dem. 20.92, 22.43, 23.87, 24.30).[99] Most of the topics listed in the philosophical and theoretical definition of political decision-making were enacted in the form of decrees that made up most of the business of councils and assemblies. By contrast, especially in Athens after 403 BCE, laws were made hierarchically superior to decrees, which in turn had to conform to the *nomoi*. Such a distinction originates in the Archaic period when the Greek communities distinguished between the day-by-day administration carried out by the political bodies of the *polis* and law-making performed by authoritative *nomothetai* during extraordinary times.[100] This conceptualization of law-making is exemplified in

---

[99] Hansen (1978); Canevaro and Harris (2012) 117–19; Canevaro (2013a) 75–6.

[100] On the first lawgivers and especially Solon see Szegedy-Maszak (1978) 199–209; Thomas (1994); Harris (2006) 6–14; Canevaro (2015); Loddo (2018).

INTRODUCTION 25

widespread traditions of legendary or idealized lawgivers, such as Draco and Solon in Athens, Lycurgus in Sparta, Zaleucus in Locris, and Charondas in Catania. Archaic legislation received its authority because of the higher status of the lawgivers and was understood as unchangeable.[101]

In deliberative practice, however, the Greeks did legislate in their assemblies, in contrast with this legal ideology. Canevaro has shown that in fifth-century Athens laws were passed in the assembly without acknowledging their nature as *nomoi* through a process of 'tacit legal change' that did not officially change the statutes enacted by Solon.[102] During the last decade of the fifth century, the Athenians introduced a set of broad legal reforms, as well as reviewed and republished all their statutes, which aimed to solve contradictions and preserve coherence within their legal system. These new measures included the introduction of the *graphē paranomōn*—the public action against illegal decrees. As a result of the formalization of the hierarchy between *nomoi* and *psēphismata* in 403 BCE, the assembly passed only *psēphismata*, while a separate and complex procedure for legislation (*nomothesia*) was introduced in order to institutionalize legal change with a comprehensive procedure that gave to the *dēmos*, and not to special lawgivers, the power of legislation.[103]

The *nomothesia* was enforced by the *graphē nomon mē epitēdeion theinai*, a new public action, which aimed to prosecute the enactment of unsuitable laws.[104] The very term *epitēdeion* (suitable) shows that the purpose of this judicial procedure was to protect the coherence of the legal system as a whole, acting as a bulwark against statutes that did not fit within the system of Athenian laws. During the fourth century some very relevant areas of Athenian public life were regulated by laws passed or modified through *nomothesia*. For instance, Athenian finances were organized into a series of separate funds allocated to different spending authorities through the *merismos*, which was a law passed by the *nomothetai* that regulated the entire Athenian budget.[105]

Nomothesia was a key aspect of Athenian political decision-making, and a fundamental feature of divided power in the Athenian democracy. While I will often make reference to it as a point of comparison with the procedures of decree-making, in this study I shall not discuss the features of Athenian legislation in the fourth century. The reason for this choice is twofold. First, this would require

---

[101] For the tradition of lawgivers in the ancient sources see Diod. 12.7; Dem. 24.139–41 for Zaleucus; [Arist.] *Ath. Pol.* 7.2 and Plut. *Sol.* 25 for Solon.

[102] See also Esu (2021a).

[103] Canevaro and Harris (2012); Canevaro (2013a), (2016c). The *nomothesia* is a paradigmatic instance of institutional complexity of Athenian decision-making. For a detailed reconstruction see Canevaro (2013a); *pace* MacDowell (1975); Hansen (1978), (1979a); Rhodes (1987). For the identity of the *nomothetai* see Canevaro and Esu (2018) 130–6.

[104] Canevaro (2016a), (2016b).

[105] The earliest attestation of the *merismos* in the epigraphical evidence is in 386/5 BCE, see RO 19, 18–22. On Athenian finances see Rhodes (2013) 203–31; Migeotte (2014).

26 DIVIDED POWER IN ANCIENT GREECE

another comprehensive and complementary study on law-making practices and ideologies in ancient Greece. Second, the Athenian law-making procedures were understood and conceptualized as separated from those of decree-making and day-by-day administration of the *polis*. While identical law-making procedures are unparalleled outside Athens, there is evidence that suggest that separate procedures, which included interaction between assemblies and judicial bodies in enacting laws, could have been set up in other *poleis* during the Hellenistic period.[106] By focusing on divided power and decree-making, this study aims to examine only those procedures related to the preparation, discussion, and judicial revision of decrees, without addressing the issue of the creation, change, and preservation of *nomoi*.

1.4 Methodology: Taking Institutions Seriously

This last section sets out the methodology adopted in this study and defines some important theoretical notions and recurrent terms used throughout. It is organized into two parts. The first provides a concise account of different approaches to Greek institutional history, from the old institutionalism to the more recent behaviouralist and sociological perspectives, and discusses the limits of such approaches. Building on these premises, the second part introduces my methodology, which is informed by historical institutionalism. I explain the principles of historical institutionalism and highlight how this approach provides a new way to study ancient Greek political decision-making through a renewed attention to institutions.

1.4.1 From *Staatsaltertümer* to the Sociological Approach

The study of ancient Greek legal and political institutions has long been at the centre of Greek history.[107] Until the second half of the nineteenth century, the study of Greek institutions was conceived of as *Staatsaltertümer*, a collection of antiquarian curiosities ranging from inscriptions to various names of civic and religious officials and legal texts.[108] This conception started to change with Boeckh's *Staatshaushaltung der Athener*, a book on the public economy of Athens, published in 1817. Boeckh's work was one of the first attempts to use

---

[106] See Canevaro (2016a). §6.3 provides a study of these sources.

[107] See the concise surveys by Ehrenberg (1969) 256–9; Rhodes (2003a) 34–44; and Beck (2013) 1–2.

[108] Some works of this period, for example Schoemann (1819), contributed to introducing a more systematic approach to the history of Athenian institutions. On the antiquarian use of Greek inscriptions see Guarducci (1967) 27–42; on early modern and modern antiquarianism of ancient Greece, see Stoneman (1987).

INTRODUCTION 27

inscriptions as historical sources, and founded the modern study of Greek political institutions.[109] Interest in political institutions and separation of powers is also found in Grote's *History of Greece*, in which the British historian envisaged a division of powers in Classical Athens by distinguishing the relevant roles of the assembly and the lawcourts with reference to the *graphē paranomōn* and the *nomothetai*.[110] This institution-based approach became dominant with the rise of German *Altertumswissenschaft* in the second half of the nineteenth century. In particular, the studies by Mommsen on Roman *Staatsrecht* (constitutional law) promoted a normative and positivistic perspective on ancient institutions and law with an emphasis on the juridical classification of constitutional procedures and political bodies. This influenced the work of contemporary and later Greek historians. The most comprehensive of these later studies is Busolt's two-volume *Griechische Staatskunde* (vol. 1, 1920; vol. 2, 1926), which was partially completed by Swoboda. This study collates a large amount of material on several aspects of the Greek states, from political institutions to financial and military organization.[111]

Works inspired by the German tradition of *Staatskunde* flourished in other European countries during the first half of the twentieth century. A Francophone tradition started with Glotz's *La Cité Grecque*, and continued with Robert and Gauthier. This important school established a scholarly tradition that focused on the careful scrutiny of inscriptions as a way of studying Greek institutions, especially in the Hellenistic World. Recent works stemming from this tradition have examined many different institutions, for example, the *euthunai*, *dokimasia*, Hellenistic councils, and Eretrian decrees of *proxenia* and citizenship.[112] These studies emphasize the diachronic development of a number of institutional arrangements in each *polis* across the Hellenistic world. Adopting a similar approach, but with a different focus, an English-speaking scholarly strand has focused on the study of the political institutions of the Classical Athenian democracy (cf. also §1.1). This view of the Athenian decision-making institutions is especially exemplified by the seminal works of Rhodes and Hansen, respectively, on the Athenian council and the Athenian assembly

---

[109] For the use of inscriptions as historical sources before Boeckh see de Biagi (1785). For the reception of ancient inscriptions see Cooley (2000); Liddel and Low (2013) esp. 1–32.

[110] Grote (1906) 18–26 (vol. 6, Dent edition). Grote's analysis had important implication for modern liberal democratic thought; see Urbinati (2002) 62–4. For another early attempt to single out divided power in ancient Greece see Van Dyke Robinson (1904).

[111] See also the studies on law-making and political offices by Kahrstedt (1922), (1934), (1938a), (1938b).

[112] Knoepfler (2001); Fröhlich (2004); Hamon (2005); Feyel (2009). Other French-speaking scholars have studied Archaic and Classical institutions, or institutions in their longer temporal development: see e.g. Brun (1983) on the Athenian war taxes; Carlier (1984) on Greek kingship; Ruzé (1997) on deliberation in the Archaic and Classical periods; van Effenterre and Ruzé (1994) on Greek laws of the Archaic period; Richer (1998) on the Spartan ephors (and see Chapter 4); Piérart (2000) on the Athenian *nomothetai*.

28 DIVIDED POWER IN ANCIENT GREECE

in the fourth century, which have shed light on several aspects of the constitutional workings of the institutions of Athens.[113]

Such an approach, interested in the formal mechanisms and the institutional procedures of the Greek city-states, started to be criticized in the English-speaking world at the end of the 1980s.[114] In a famous review article of Hansen's book on the Athenian assembly, J. Ober criticized Hansen's work for 'narrowly framing' his research questions, and concentrating on 'abstruse' constitutional matters.[115] His critique is reminiscent of Finley's assessment of scholarship focused on institutional analysis of political life as 'the constitutional-law trap', which he considered unable to explain political and social dynamics.[116] The central point of Ober's argument, extensively explored in his classic book *Mass and Elite in Democratic Athens: Rhetoric, Ideology and the Power of the People*,[117] is the concept of democratic ideology. It was ideology, rather than complex constitutional mechanisms and institutional separation of powers, that allowed the *dēmos* to control the public realm and keep in check the power of the wealthy elites. Ober's contention was that legal and institutional analysis can be used to give an account of formal political machinery, but it does not say much about social and political behaviour in practice. The work of Ober and other scholars paved the way for the sociological and behavioural study of Greek politics and political systems,[118] and opened a division between institutional and extra-institutional approaches.[119] Following Ober's work that identified the Athenian lawcourts as an arena for intra-elite political conflict, many other studies dealt with Athenian litigation and Athenian law by stressing the role of social and extra-legal norms, and the self-helping behaviour allegedly at work in the lawcourts or in Athenian society. The Greek *polis* has even been described as a stateless society.[120] In stark opposition with the old institutional tradition, this new trend of studies heavily downplayed

---

[113] Cf. above §1.1 for a review of the works of Rhodes and Hansen. To name a few among many works on institutions within this Athens-focused tradition in English: Cohen (1973) on Athenian maritime courts; MacDowell (1975) on fourth-century law-making, and (1978) on Athenian law; Traill (1975) on the political organization of Attica; Osborne (1981–3) on naturalization in Athens; Whitehead (1986) on the Athenian demes; Wallace (1989) on the Areopagus; Lambert (1993) on the phratries; Boegehold (1995) on the Athenian lawcourts; Stroud (1998) on the Grain-Tax Law of 374/3 BCE; Gabrielsen (1994) on the Athenian trierarchy; Hamel (1998) on the Athenian generals; Rubinstein (2000) on supporting speakers in Athenian trials.

[114] A similar debate is also found in France in the different approaches of the institutional tradition of Robert and Gauthier, and the anthropological school of Vernant, Mossé, and Vidal-Naquet, whose approach focused on religion and ritual as key tools for understanding Greek civic life. Cf. Murray's opposition between the German account of the *polis* as 'handbook of constitutional law' and the French *polis* as a form of 'Holy Communion'; Murray (1990) 3.

[115] Ober (1989b) 322–34. For a reply to Ober see Hansen (1989a).

[116] Finley (1983) 56. Cf. Ober (1989a) 42.   [117] Ober (1989a).

[118] Cf. also Osborne (1985b).

[119] For a review of these approaches see Azoulay and Ismard (2007).

[120] e.g. Hunter (1994); Cohen (1995); Christ (1998), (2006), (2012); Lanni (2006), (2016). For Athens as a stateless society see Berent (2000). But see Hansen (2002) 17–47; Herman (2006); Anderson (2009); and Harris (2013c) 21–59.

INTRODUCTION 29

the role of formal rules, institutions, and constitutional arrangements in shaping social and political behaviour in the ancient Greek *polis*.[121]

Recently, scholarship has moved further away from institutional analysis of Greek political and social history. A new perspective stresses the importance of social networks and informal associations beyond the formal institution of the *polis*, as extra-institutional settings in which citizens could interact with other groups: metics, slaves, and women.[122] Informed by actor network theory, this approach has refreshed the studies on Greek social history and pushed scholars to think harder about the definition of institutional spaces, even if the clear-cut line between the political and social life of Greek societies, and the formal institutions (i.e. the political assemblies, councils, lawcourts, and boards of officials), should not be overestimated.[123] Private associations, in fact, tended to reproduce the basic institutions of the Greek polis, such as boards of magistrates, assembly of members enacting decrees, or procedures for accountability of officials.[124]

However, interest in Greek political institutions has never disappeared. Along with recent works on well-defined Hellenistic institutions, recent scholarship has also produced wide-ranging studies, for example, on the council of elders in Sparta and in other Greek *poleis*, on civic government in Hellenistic and Roman Asia Minor, as well as Beck's *Companion on Greek Government*, Mack's comprehensive study on the institution of *proxenia*, and Simonton's *Classical Greek Oligarchy*.[125] Other recent works on Greek history have provided fruitful engagement with ancient and modern political theories for the interpretation of both literary and epigraphical evidence in order to study Greek political thinking and practice; for instance, Liddel's volume on civic obligation in Classical Athens, and Gray's work on *stasis* and exile in Classical and Hellenistic Greece.[126]

After much emphasis on the role of law and law-making, recent scholarship has drawn our attention to the significance of decree culture in the Greek world. Liddel's new monumental study on Athenian decrees in the literary sources breaks new ground in this direction. Not only does this work complement the rich epigraphical record of fourth-century Athens with a careful analysis of literary-preserved decrees, but it also offers a sophisticated understanding of the decree as an institution made of practices, ideas, and norms which defined Greek political

---

[121] For more recent work by Ober which adopts a rational-choice methodology and acknowledges the importance of institutions, see Ober (2008), (2015).

[122] Vlassopoulos (2007).

[123] Gottesman (2014); C. Taylor and Vlassopoulos (2015) 2–31. A similar debate is also emerging concerning the study of the political history of the Hellenistic *polis*: see Roubineau (2015); Fröhlich (2016); Sebillotte Cuchet (2017); Ando (2018); Moatti and Müller (2018).

[124] Gabrielsen (2009) 179–205; Gabrielsen and Thomsen (2015); cf. the remarks in Gabrielsen and Paganini (2021) 16 about private associations creating parallel as well as complementary values to that of the *polis*.

[125] Dmitriev (2005); Giannakopoulos (2008); Schulz (2011); Beck (2013); Mack (2015); Simonton (2017).

[126] Liddel (2007); B. D. Gray (2015).

30 DIVIDED POWER IN ANCIENT GREECE

culture and provided an authoritative source of social capital for the proposers and of norms and collective memory for the Athenian community.[127] Forster has collected the epigraphical evidence of honorary decrees for citizens across the Greek world and has emphasized the importance of decrees as both political and cultural tools of the Hellenistic *poleis* for shaping their changing civic culture in the Hellenistic period.[128]

Building on these recent approaches to Greek institutions, law, and political culture, this book attempts to promote a novel perspective for the study of political institutions, and to advance our understanding of ancient Greek political decision-making through a close analysis of its institutional and legal mechanisms, and the interaction of different institutions in decree-making. The discussion of the ancient evidence for political decision-making in different Greek *poleis* will be informed by the theoretical models of historical institutionalism. This analysis will demonstrate that formal institutions and procedures are key factors in shaping political behaviour, and in enhancing specific expertise through the relevant institutional set-ups and arrangements of deliberative institutions (probouleutic bodies and assembly) and judicial-review institution (lawcourts). The next section will define the features of historical institutionalism within the broader trend in political science labelled as new institutionalism, and will show the heuristic advantages of adopting methods and theories of historical institutionalism for understanding the institutions of ancient Greek political decision-making.

1.4.2 A 'New Institutionalist' Approach to Political Decision-Making in Ancient Greece

While the field of ancient history was shifting focus to a more sociological and behavioural approach during the 1980s and 1990s (see §1.4.1), social and political sciences were undergoing a shift in the opposite direction. As a reaction to behaviouralism and rational-choice theories that had dominated the field of political science until the 1970s,[129] March and Olsen in 1984 published a programmatic article calling for a 'new institutionalism', and encouraged political scientists to bring back institutions to the centre of their research.[130] March and Olsen argued against approaches that saw policy-making as just an aggregation of individual actors seeking self-interest, or as merely a reflection of society. Their

---

[127] Liddel (2020b) 14–58.   [128] Forster (2018).

[129] Behaviouralism was a reaction to the 'old institutionalism' in political sciences that was only concerned with the analysis of politics and formal legal institutions and constitutional issues, in a way similar to what happened in the field of ancient history. For a very similar trend in economics see North (1990). On old institutionalism in political sciences see R. A. W. Rhodes (2006).

[130] March and Olsen (1984); and the classic volume by March and Olsen (1989).

analysis instead stressed the importance of institutionalized rules, practices, norms, and standard procedures in shaping political behaviour. New institutionalism sees institutions as stable social organizations that give order to social and political relations and enhance recurrent patterns of behaviour according to a 'logic of appropriateness'. As a result, political actors act within an institution by following a set of formal and informal rules and practices, including discursive rules, symbolic gestures, and behaviours that are considered appropriate (or inappropriate) within an institution and are derived from the *ethos* of the institution itself. The logic of appropriateness is particularly important in the study of political and institutional history as it can override mere self-interest and rational calculation when specific 'values and identity are at stake'.[131] In March and Olsen's view, the study of the institutional settings and the formal procedures that regulate political life is the key tool for understanding how political behaviour is shaped in practice.

The new institutionalist revolution was so successful in political science that in 2002 the political scientists Pierson and Skocpol stated that 'we are all institutionalists now'.[132] Yet, within the large scholarship on political institutions, different approaches have been developed under the heading of new institutionalism. Despite considerable overlap, these approaches adopt different methodologies and distinct theoretical tools when studying contemporary institutional arrangements. Before concentrating on historical institutionalism, which provides the theoretical framework of my study, it is important to identify the three main strands within the new institutionalism: rational-choice institutionalism, sociological institutionalism, and historical institutionalism.[133]

Rational-choice institutionalism (RI) focuses on institutions as systems of incentives for political actors. Institutions are understood as 'arenas for conflict', which are shaped by institutional norms and procedural rules for maximizing advantages or disadvantages for individual actors. Rational-choice institutionalists privilege micro-level analysis. They look at how institutions constrain the behaviour or solve the problems of rational actors who put their self-interest and preferences as the drivers of their political activity.[134] Differently, sociological institutionalism (SI) thinks of institutions as institutionalized cultural norms of a given society. Institutions originate from the cultural and social norms of society and are viewed as exogenous and independent entities. Unlike RI, sociological institutionalism sees individuals as acting according to cultural rules, such as

---

[131] March and Olsen (1989) 38; Lowndes (2005) 294.   [132] Pierson and Skocpol (2002) 706.

[133] A fourth typology of new institutionalism, called discursive or constructivist institutionalism, has emerged recently. It focuses on the concepts of ideas and discourse in the institutional analysis. See Hay (2006); Schmidt (2008), (2010). For the relationship between discursive and historical institutionalism see Blyth, Helgadottir, and Kring (2016) 143–59. For a recent work in the field of Athenian democracy adopting this approach see Barbato (2020).

[134] For a recent analysis of rational-choice institutionalism see Shepsle (2006) 23–38.

32 DIVIDED POWER IN ANCIENT GREECE

a sense of obligation, embedded in the institution. SI provides institutional analysis on a macro-level to explain why and how cultural norms are created and shared.[135] Historical institutionalism (HI) stresses the concept of the continuity of institutional arrangements over time. Historical institutionalism sees institutions as real entities that shape the collective or individual behaviour of political actors. Political scientists adopting this approach rely on a distinctive analytical toolbox. Their approach strictly connects temporal phenomena and political institutions, which are understood as stable and 'sticky'. Historical institutionalists are especially interested in how institutions create constraints for political action and how power is institutionally organized over time.[136]

To interpret the ancient literary and epigraphical sources, I have drawn theoretical models from historical institutionalism. This strand has proved to be the most suitable for the study of ancient Greek decision-making. Among the new institutionalist strands historical institutionalism is the one most interested in exploring political power and what the institutional manifestations of power can tell us about the nature and evolution of political processes.[137] This proves fundamental for advancing our understanding of Greek divided power. With its stress on the role of temporal development of institutions and empirical evidence, historical institutionalism provides a flexible as well as theoretically sophisticated framework to discuss change and the impact of formal procedures and institutions in the Greek world over a long period of time. This approach differs from rational-choice institutionalism, which adopts an actor-based approach to institutions and concentrates on a highly theoretical and normative level of microanalysis of individual preference. As a result, rational-choice institutionalism emphasizes the 'coordinative' aspect of institutions which are seen as structures aggregating individual preferences, formed outside the institutions, and constraining behaviour through 'pay-offs' for rational actors and individual preferences.[138] In historical institutionalism, on the other hand, institutions are stable not only in time but also when there is a change of conditions, that is, the underlying structure of power that created institutions in the first place. As a result, historical institutionalism analyses not only stability but also the durability of institutions in different political situations.[139] Historical institutionalism therefore attempts to study, to use the words of Pierson and Skocpol, 'the forest as well as trees', by combining

---

[135] For a discussion of sociological institutionalism see Hall and Taylor (1996) 946–50.

[136] For a general overview of historical institutionalism see Sanders (2006) 39–55; Fioretos, Falleti, and Sheingate (2016) 4–22.

[137] Pierson (2016) 125–91 with sensible critiques to behaviouralists and experimentalists studying only micro-level phenomena in the modern political science.

[138] In a rational-choice perspective, Sheple's seminal article describes institutions as 'standing between the individual qua bundle of tastes and the alternatives comprising available social choices'; Shepsle (1986) 51. For a recent study adopting rational-choice institutionalism on Athenian democracy see Ober (2008) esp. 6–12.

[139] Levitsky and Murillo (2009) 117.

specific patterns of socio-political and institutional development with a general and broad understanding of institutions, conceptualized as a set of rules, norms, and practices that structure social relations.[140] Historical institutionalism sees institutions not only as organizations that coordinate the actions and preferences of social actors, but as structures that shape and change the collective behaviour and preferences of those acting within the institutional framework over time.[141]

Some distinctive conceptual tools of historical institutionalism are consistently used in this book. In particular, I will often refer to the notion of path dependence, a mechanism that explains the persistence of institutions and the attached ideology over time, even when the historical circumstances that created a specific institution have elapsed. Path dependence has been defined as a logic of 'increasing returns'. This expression indicates that the institutionalization of a specific policy or arrangement implies a choice inducing further choices, which are difficult to reverse.[142] Thus, institutions maintain path dependence, primarily because of their 'structured nature' which influences individual and collective agency.[143] As Pierson rightly emphasizes, the concept of path dependence does not mean that social and political change does not happen. It entails, however, that it is often a 'bounded change' which is shaped by, and happens within, existing institutional frameworks.[144] Political and social scientists have studied a number of modern institutions that have shown institutional continuity according to a logic of path dependence, such as state bureaucracies, political parties, associations, and welfare systems.[145] A classic example of institutional path dependence is provided by the analysis of welfare institutions. In his study on welfare institutions in the US and Britain, Pierson shows that welfare institutions such as housing and old-age pensions survived the attempts of dismantling by the conservative governments of the 1980s and early 1990s and remained entrenched in society, despite the decline of the political parties and social constituencies that created and supported them in the first place. This was possible because of a system of formal mechanisms and structures, social and human capital, and identification with those welfare institutions that ultimately made change more difficult.[146] Lowdnes also points out that the self-reinforcing power of institutions and the logic of path dependence can be either virtuous or vicious. By studying the reform of local authorities in England and Wales, Lowdnes shows that

---

[140] Pierson and Skocpol (2002) 711.

[141] For an in-depth analysis of the difference between rational-choice and historical institutionalism see the foundational volume of Steinmo, Thelen, and Longstreth (1992), which also coined the label 'historical institutionalism'. An effective synthesis is also provided by Fioretos, Falleti, and Sheingate (2016) 7–10.

[142] This has been especially studied by Pierson (2000a), (2000b). See Palier (2010) 19–35 for historical institutionalist perspectives on the Bismarckian welfare state.

[143] Lowdnes (2005).   [144] Pierson (2000a) 265.

[145] See a brief overview in Mahoney (2006) 129–39.

[146] Pierson (1995). Cf. a recent reconsideration of Pierson's book by Jensen, Wenzelburger, and Zolnhöfer (2019).

institutional arrangements remained locked in despite top-down reforms. She notes that the Local Government Act introduced in 2000 with the purpose of making local executive leaderships more accountable failed to radically change the institutional decision-making at the local level, which mostly kept following practices of the previous committee-based system of government.[147]

The concept of path dependence allows for a better understanding of many important aspects of institutional development. It clarifies the origin of institutions and formal procedures during particular historical moments, what historical institutionalism calls 'critical junctures', and the political and ideological features that were embedded at the creation of an institution. Institutional change can happen as a consequence of 'exogenous forces', such as war or strong ideological shifts in the political environment, and as a result of endogenous changes in the social structure.[148] The concept of path dependence, therefore, contributes to understanding institutional change from the original arrangement and the re-enactment of institutional set-ups in a different context. Scholarship in historical institutionalism has also developed other more nuanced analytical tools which cast light on the modality of gradual institutional change such as the concepts of 'drift' and 'conversion', defining respectively the change of existing rules due to shifts in the environment and the repurposing of existing rules to new ends.[149]

Through this model, micro- and macro-levels of historical analysis can be combined to re-evaluate ancient Greek political and social behaviours within their wider institutional context. This methodological approach has already informed recent innovative works in the field of Greek history.[150] For example, Harris explores the legal procedures and institutions which the Athenians created to implement the ideal of the rule of law, and demonstrates how these procedures shaped the behaviour of individuals acting within and outside the lawcourts and discouraged feuding behaviour.[151] Canevaro has similarly drawn from the theoretical model of historical institutionalism in a series of studies tracing the development of Athenian legislation from the Archaic period to the early Hellenistic period. Canevaro explains the institutional change that Athens experienced in 403 BCE, with the establishment of the formal hierarchy between *nomoi* and *psēphismata*, and the introduction of a separate procedure for law-making (see above §1.3) in terms of path dependence. Even when the Athenians abandoned the ideology that did not allow for legal change, they enshrined many of those principles in the new institution of *nomothesia*, which is underpinned by the idea

---

[147] Lowdnes (2005) 296.   [148] Lowdnes and Roberts (2013) 114–15.

[149] On 'drift' and 'conversion' see especially Chapter 3.

[150] See also recent important work on Roman political culture which adopts a perspective informed by historical institutionalism, such as the essays in Arena and Prag (2022).

[151] Harris (2013c).

INTRODUCTION   35

that legislation is not managed according to the ordinary assembly procedures.[152] Elsewhere, Mackil shows the key role of path dependence in the formation of federal institutions, for example in Classical Boeotia, which was influenced by pre-existing political and social institutional arrangements.[153] Mack has also adopted a new institutionalist theoretical framework in his recent study of the institution of *proxenia*. According to Mack, path dependence illustrates the long-term development of *proxenia*, and especially its resistance to change in the politically fragmented world of the Greek *poleis*.[154] Simonton has fruitfully studied the political institutions and social strategy of Classical oligarchies using models of historical institutionalism.[155]

Political decision-making and the relevant institutional arrangements in the Greek *poleis* are still in need of a theoretically informed study which renews the focus on the role of institutional design and legal procedures by avoiding a merely descriptive and positivistic perspective. My contention in this book is that Greek deliberative procedures and decision-making institutions shaped the behaviour of political actors performing within them. They acted in accordance with ideological values that were enshrined in each institution from its foundation.

Throughout the book I will often refer to the different ideological values enshrined in institutions and adopted by political actors in different decision-making institutional contexts. It is first important to define what I mean by the 'ideology' adopted by Greek institutions with particular reference to democratic Athens. In the case of Classical Athens, all *polis* institutions were committed to the ideological principles of the democracy, which includes political equality, the rule of law, individual freedom for free citizens, piety towards the gods, and obligations towards the *polis*.[156] In his classic study on Athenian democracy and its ideology, Ober adopted a definition of ideology as a fixed set of political principles shared by both the mass and the elites. As Barbato has recently demonstrated, Athenian democratic ideology was not a static set of shared ideas, but the result of a fluid and continuous process of ideological practice and interpretation of values within the Athenian institutions.[157] As a result, citizens acting within different decision-making institutions could emphasize different aspects of democratic ideology which were appropriate to the relevant institutional context. For example, the

---

[152] Canevaro (2013c), (2015). For an institutional perspective to Athenian popular culture see Canevaro (2017c).

[153] Mackil (2013) 10–15.   [154] Mack (2015) 23–4.   [155] Simonton (2017).

[156] These basic features can already be found in Solon's legislation, especially in his ban of enslavement of citizens due to debts (in fr. 30 G.-P.² = 36 West) and in the right for a citizen to block a magistrate's verdict and to be judged by the *dēmos* (fr. 3 G.-P.² = 4 West; [Arist.] *Ath. Pol.* 9.1): Harris (2006) 6–14; Pelloso (2016), (2017); Loddo (2018) 113–18; Canevaro (2022). Cf. Thuc. 2.37.1. See Liddel (2007) on the concepts of obligations and liberty as fundamental aspects of Athenian democratic citizenship.

[157] Ober (1989a) 38–9; Barbato (2020) 5–10 and 3–5 for a discussion of the previous bibliography on Athenian public ideology. Cf. Loraux (1981) for a classic work adopting a Marxist interpretation of Athenian ideology.

36 DIVIDED POWER IN ANCIENT GREECE

ideals of commitment to justice and respect of the laws in the context of the council and the assembly were concerned with the notion of distributive justice, such as allocation of civic honours and respect of obligations with the allies and benefactors. The Athenians qua judges in a court of law were instead concerned with applying the complementary concept of corrective justice, that is, to assess if the defendant had violated specific laws.[158] This process of ideological practice influenced by the institutions allowed Athenian decision-making to accommodate the (occasionally conflicting) values of common advantage, typical of the deliberative institutions, as well as the values of the rule of law in court.

Greek decision-making is better understood as a complex system of interaction between several decision-making bodies, such as councils, boards of officials, assemblies, and lawcourts, in which each institution possessed complementary expertise and a well-defined institutional and ideological role within the policy-making process. This study also shows that Greek decision-making procedures broadly shared a common institutional toolset as well as the framework of divided power. It was through the sophisticated combination of these institutional tools and mechanisms that deliberative practice unfolded. For example, the role of *probouleusis* and the constitutional balance between probouleutic bodies and assembly could determine the democratic or oligarchic features of the decision-making and the relevant political behaviour of individuals. Institutional design is therefore a key factor that shapes the very nature and quality of political deliberation. Each institutional arrangement in decree-making gradually developed to perform a specific function and to add the relevant expertise of a body to the final outcome of a multi-layered decision-making system. In a Greek *polis* like Classical Athens, a decree could be transferred from one body to another before gaining legal force, for example through delegation from the assembly to the council in order to complement the assembly's decision with the relevant administrative expertise of the council. Similarly, boards of officials or lawcourts could be in charge of checking the legal consistency of a decree with the laws of the city.

This book's approach differs from previous studies on Athenian democracy and Greek political systems that have concentrated on descriptive analysis of the institutional arrangements. At the same time, this study aims to rediscover the importance of institutional analysis and reconcile it with approaches that have emphasized the role of political ideology and cultural forces in politics. In other words, this book focuses on the institutional design of councils, assemblies, and lawcourts, on the relevant ideological values embedded in their formal rules, on their institutionalized procedures and routine practices. It shows how the interaction of these institutions shaped the behaviour of individuals, and enhanced the

---

[158] See Arist. *Eth. Nic.* 1130b–1a. For a discussion on the different discursive parameters of Athenian institutions see Harris (2013a), (2017a); Barbato (2020) 57–80.

INTRODUCTION 37

specific expertise (e.g. administrative expertise in the council or legal expertise in the lawcourts) within the relevant institutions and in the decision-making as a whole.

1.5 Decision-Making Institutions as Manifestation of Divided Power

In this Introduction, I have first given an account of scholarship on Greek political decision-making, and in particular on decree-making, and introduced the concept of divided power. I have then discussed the ancient philosophical views of institutional mixing and the institutional complexity in the realm of Greek deliberation. I have defined what I mean with ancient Greek political decision-making by distinguishing between decree-making and legislation. I have then moved to sketch an overview of old and more recent approaches to the study of political institutions in ancient Greek history, and have laid out my methodological framework informed by historical institutionalism.

This introduction has laid the analytical foundation and has clarified the key terms for a new study of Greek divided power. This concept and the relevant ideology and discourse are enshrined and reflected in the formal procedures and in the institutional complexity of political decision-making. The emphasis on the institutional manifestation of divided power is justified by the attempt to construct divided power in practice, as a notion embedded in Greek institutions which in turn shaped the collective behaviour of citizens while making decisions by decree.

This aim is reflected in the structure of the monograph. The book is divided into two thematic parts. Part I includes Chapters 2 and 3 and discusses the notion of delegation as a key part of Greek divided power. Part II includes Chapters 4, 5, and 6 and explores the balance between deliberation and legal control as another key aspect of divided power in Greek decree-making. While a large part of this volume is dedicated to Classical Athens, this book adopts a comparative approach by investigating Classical and Hellenistic case studies from Athens, Mytilene, Megalopolis, Sparta, Demetrias, Alexandria Troas, and the Achaean League. For each case study, I provide an analysis of the relevant institutional procedures within its historical context, which allows me to offer a broader picture of Greek decree-making. The structure of the book follows an institutional ordering rather than a chronological sequence. It starts with the analysis of councils and *sunedria*, where decrees were initially drafted, and their delegated power to complete the assembly's enactments; and it concludes with a discussion of the judicial review power of lawcourts and foreign judges, which was the last step in Greek decree-making.

Chapter 2 opens the section about delegation and divided power. This chapter analyses the role played by delegation clauses in Athenian decrees of the Classical

38 DIVIDED POWER IN ANCIENT GREECE

period with which the assembly empowered the Athenian council to decree additional measures. In this chapter, I argue that even though the Athenian council was an *archē*, its role was not only limited to *probouleusis* and ordinary administration but also played an important policy-making role as enshrined in the bouleutic oath. This chapter first offers a detailed examination of the ideology of the Athenian council, the relevant discourse practice found in the *dokimasia* speeches and the creation of expertise through participation and deliberation in the council. The chapter then moves to an analysis of the delegation clauses of inscribed decrees (i.e. *autokratōr*-clauses during the fifth century, and the fourth-century *kurios*-clauses). This chapter draws important conclusions on the workings of the deliberative bodies of Classical Athens and on democratic practice in a legal and political perspective. First, despite the usage of different formulas in different historical periods, the two clauses outlined the same legal procedure, showing continuity in democratic practice in the fifth and the fourth centuries. Second, epigraphical and literary evidence (Andoc. 1.15) agree in showing that delegation was an actual transfer of deliberative authority to the council, which had a free hand in making decisions. The careful study of the delegation clauses thus sheds light on the administrative power of the council. It demonstrates that, unlike other magistrates, the council played a proper policy-making role through the enactment of a decree, which was the product of the council's expertise in specific matters, such as religious affairs, foreign policy, and the navy.

Chapter 3 builds on the findings of the previous chapter, and shows the workings and development of delegation clauses to the council in two extra-Athenian examples over the *longue durée*. First, I explore the delegation of deliberative authority in fourth-century Mytilene. A decree from democratic Mytilene of 334–332 BCE (reconciliation decree *SEG* 36.752 = RO 85) shows evidence of the delegation of authority from the Mytilenian assembly to the council in accordance with the Athenian model. The Mytilenian example shows that delegation clauses and a multi-faceted decision-making process existed beyond Athens. Like in Athens, the power delegated to the council is not limited to the execution of provisions decided by the assembly, but envisages proper deliberative authority transferred to the Mytilenian council. I then analyse a second-century *diagramma* from Megalopolis (*IG* V² 433). This statute mentions delegation clauses (*kurios*-clauses) to the city *sunedrion*, which is authorized to fill gaps in the laws. By building on recent work on Hellenistic councils and political decision-making, the analysis of this document shows the endurance of delegation in deliberative practice in a census-based and non-democratic constitution, in which the democratic *boulē* has become an elistist *sunedrion*.

Chapter 4 continues the exploration of divided power beyond Classical Athens. It deals with the deliberative procedures of Classical and Hellenistic Sparta and introduces the important issue of the balance between the people's deliberation and the stability of the legal order, which form the focus of Part II of the book.

INTRODUCTION   39

The chapter illuminates the institutional interactions as well as the ideology of deliberation in the non-democratic context of the Spartan *eunomia*. Literary evidence shows that the Spartan decision-making process involved the assembly and two probouleutic institutions: the *gerousia* and the five ephors. The analysis and discussion of the literary evidence shows that the Spartans could not modify a bill submitted by the *gerousia* during the meetings of the assembly, but could only ratify or reject the *gerousia*'s proposal. The Spartan 'divided power' envisaged that the *gerousia* shared the probouleutic power with the ephors who could independently submit the bill to the assembly. The Spartan assembly then could approve the decree, which needed a second vote in the *gerousia* in order to get the final approval. In my reconstruction of Spartan deliberative practice, I envisage a veto power a posteriori of the *gerousia*, which performed the role of guardianship of the laws of the Spartan constitutional system. This chapter shows that divided power and the need of legal stability were addressed by Spartan institutions, but with different results owing to the wider probouleutic powers of officials.

Chapter 5 moves to special procedure for decree-making in the Athenian Assembly. This chapter discusses the role played by the legal procedure of *adeia* in fifth-century deliberative decision-making in the assembly. It provides a new comprehensive account of this legal institution which replaces two old-fashioned and incomplete works on this topic.[159] My analysis of the passages from Athenian forensic oratory (e.g. Dem. 24.45; Andoc. 1.15) and especially inscriptions (*IG* I³ 52b, 370) shows that *adeia* was an institution designed to reconcile the official nomothetic ideology and the democratic deliberative practice of the assembly. *Adeia* instituted a pre-nomothetic procedure, according to which the assembly could change an entrenched piece of legislation or decree without clashing with the nomothetic ideology. Although this procedure did not rely on a delegation of power from a body to another institution, it was the first attempt to impose different institutional set-ups and mechanisms in decree-making in order to take different decisions and promote distinctive behaviour and considerations within the same institution. This new study puts *adeia* in its broader legal and political context of the last decades of the fifth century. My analysis demonstrates that *adeia* was the product of the same legal awareness that created the judicial review procedure of *graphē paranomōn*, which is the subject of the next chapter.

Chapter 6 examines the relationship between political decision-making and judicial review in the Greek *poleis*. The first section discusses the Athenian *graphē paranomōn*, the public charge against an illegal decree. This procedure aimed to safeguard the legality of Athenian decrees through a judicial review process. Anyone could indict the proposer of an illegal decree by bringing a charge in front of the *thesmothetai* and writing up a plaint which included the relevant

---

[159] Goldstaub (1889); McElwee (1975).

40 DIVIDED POWER IN ANCIENT GREECE

statutes broken by the decree. This chapter explores the role and rationale of the *graphē paranomōn* in Athenian deliberative procedure. Hansen has argued that a decree charged of illegality before the approval of the assembly could be upheld by the court according to political considerations. If the court did not rule out the decree, this was upheld without a vote of the assembly.[160] More recently, Lanni has argued that when judging *graphē paranomōn* cases, the lawcourts played a role equivalent to that of a second chamber of a parliament in bicameral systems. This assumption is not confirmed by the evidence and is based on a political view of the Athenian trial. A thorough analysis of the legal procedure and of its institutional design shows that deliberative decisions were made within the framework of the rule of law, and the *graphē paranomōn* enforced this principle. This did not imply an institutional prominence of the lawcourts in the Athenian decision-making, because the institutional role of the lawcourts was to perform a democratic judicial review, rather than replacing the council and the assembly in making political decisions. The lawcourts should be understood as one part of the decree-making system. Courts performed an important role in the deliberative process through providing a safeguard of legal consistency, which was ensured by legal expertise of the judges and the majoritarian decision-making in court. This complemented the consensus decision-making of the council and the assembly and made the process of decree-making more balanced. The second part of the chapter is dedicated to the discussion of extra-Athenian evidence of judicial review and the multi-faceted role of the Hellenistic practice of appointing foreign judges in adjudicating public lawsuits.

The themes, approach, and findings of the book are summarized in Chapter 7. It draws some general conclusions about the Greek political decision-making as a system of divided power within modern political theory on sovereignty. The chapter also analyses cases of the breakdown of divided power, while stressing the normativity of divided-power institutions as the standard way the Greeks understood their political decision-making.

---

[160] Hansen (1974) 49.

PART I
DIVIDED POWER AND DELEGATION

2

Divided Power in Athenian Decree-Making

2.1 The Athenian Council and Institutional Design

A scholiast commenting on Aeschines' speech *Against Ctesiphon* glossed the term *boulē* with the expression μικρὰ πόλις (mini-*polis*) emphasizing the council's role as a representative institution of Athenian democracy (Schol. A. III *Ctes.* 4, Dilts 14). A closer look at the design of the Athenian council confirms the vivid picture of this scholiast. In 508/7 BCE Cleisthenes established a new tribal system from which the five hundred councillors were appointed by lot. The Athenian councillors were chosen from among those citizens who had reached the age of 30, and they stayed in office for one year and could serve again after an interval of two years.[1] The Aristotelian *Athenaion Politeia* provides a full account of the council's powers in all areas of Athenian administration ([Arist.] *Ath. Pol.* 43.2–49.5). The *boulē* played a leading role in the management of public finances, supervision of public works, religious cults, the army, and the navy.[2] The council also had some judicial powers in specific jurisdictions. For instance, *eisangeliai* against magistrates and some *dokimasiai* started in the council.[3] As a deliberative institution, the council was a cornerstone of Athenian decree-making: every matter was first discussed in the council before being submitted to the assembly in the form of fully drafted decrees (closed *probouleumata*) or open subjects of the agenda (open *probouleumata*). In addition to drafting *probouleumata* for the assembly, the council enacted its own decrees (*psēphismata boulēs*) on matters pertaining to all fields of Athenian public administration.

The constitutional powers of the council have long been recognized by scholars in a series of fundamental studies on political institutions of Classical Athens.

---

[1] Rhodes (1972) 5–6, (1980) 307–9, (1984).
[2] Cf. [Arist.] *Ath. Pol.* 47–8; Rhodes (1972) 88–143, (1981) 549–64. For Athenian finances see Linders (1975); Faraguna (1992); Samons (2000); Blamire (2001); Burke (2010); Rhodes (2013); Migeotte (2014); Pritchard (2015).
[3] For a comprehensive analysis of the evidence of *eisangelia* with a new reconstruction of the legal procedure see Harris with Esu (2021) *contra* Hansen (1975) 21–8, (1980); Rhodes (1979). For *eisangelia* to the council see Harris with Esu (2021) 79–90; cf. [Arist.] *Ath. Pol.* 45.2, 59.4; [Dem.] 47.42–3. Canevaro (2013b) 152–4 for the legal document on *eisangelia* in Dem. 24.63. On *dokimasia* in the Athenian council see Rhodes (1972) 171–8, (1981) 542–3, 564–8, 570. For *dokimasia* procedures in the Greek *poleis* see Feyel (2009).

Divided Power in Ancient Greece: Decision-Making and Institutions in the Classical and Hellenistic Polis. Alberto Esu, Oxford University Press. © Alberto Esu 2024. DOI: 10.1093/oso/9780198883951.003.0002

44   DIVIDED POWER IN ANCIENT GREECE

Rhodes's seminal work offers the fullest and most comprehensive treatment of the Athenian council's constitutional powers.[4] Hansen stressed the definition of council as an *archē* (magistracy) and conflated the council with other magistrates.[5] Hansen's classification is instrumental to his reconstruction of the division of powers in fourth-century Athenian democracy, which he identified in the distinction between initiative-taking magistrates vis-à-vis the decision-making powers of assembly, lawcourts, and *nomothetai*.[6] Other scholars have instead understood the council as a more active institution in Athenian deliberation.[7] In her classic study on Greek deliberation, Ruzé emphasized the essential role of the council as a deliberative forum of the democracy, yet she also problematizes the relationship between the council and the assembly in terms of institutional sovereignty.[8] In an important work, Ober identifies a connection between the Athenian council and civic expertise. Ober draws attention to the role of the council as an aggregator of the dispersed knowledge of Athenian society. In Ober's view, Athens was an epistemic democracy and the council bridged the gap between the state institution and the social networks that each Athenian had outside the council.[9]

This influential body of scholarship does not envisage any relevant transfer of authority from the assembly to the council in Classical Athens, but only a one-way relationship. The council had specific competences and served the assembly in an advisory role, making its workings smoother by organizing its agenda and performing a certain amount of preliminary deliberation on the matters to be decided by the *dēmos*. Moreover, an Athenian councillor would gain little expertise by active involvement in the council, but the effective functioning of this institution would rely on external networks and individual expertise which was then aggregated within the council.

This chapter aims to advance our understanding of the council in the Athenian decision-making system. I argue that the council was not only a cornerstone of Athenian deliberation but also of the Athenian conceptualization of divided power. An analysis of discursive practice in the council provides a means to unearth the endogenous values of this institution. I argue that the council was primarily understood as a deliberative forum, in which deliberative dynamics were at play not only during *probouleusis* but for all the range of bouleutic activities, including the daily administration. Examination of the formal procedure also shows that direct involvement in the council was intertwined with the creation

---

[4] Rhodes (1972); De Laix (1973); Hansen (1978), (1981), (1991); Rhodes with Lewis (1997). For a review of these studies see Introduction §1.2.

[5] Hansen (1981) 350–1.   [6] Hansen (1981) 351–7.

[7] Ober (1989a), (2008); Pecorella Longo (2004) 96–103; Harris (2016a) 73–85.

[8] Ruzé (1997) 437–70; cf. emblematically the title of the chapter, '*Conseil et Peuple. Probouleusis et Souveraineté*'.

[9] Ober (1996), (2008) 142–51.

DIVIDED POWER IN ATHENIAN DECREE-MAKING   45

of collective expertise and allows us to appreciate both the institutional dimension, and its ideological implication for Athenian divided power.

In this chapter, I first discuss the bouleutic oath and the constituent values underpinning the bouleutic discourse as attested in the Athenian oratorical sources. I then explore how the institutional constraints and the formal and informal rules of the council promoted the acquisition of expertise. Building on these conceptual premises, the chapter focuses on the working of Athenian divided power in actual deliberation. The two sections investigate Athenian epigraphical evidence for delegation of decree-making authority to the council in the Classical period (420–324/3 BCE). My investigation shows that the decree-making power was divided according to well-defined rules that allowed the council to add its own institutional expertise without limiting the decision-making power of *dēmos* in the assembly.

2.2 The Institutional Values of the Council: The Bouleutic Oath and Bouleutic Discursive Practice

Every year the five hundred councillors, who were selected by lot from the Athenian tribes, had to pass their *dokimasia* and swear an oath before taking office.[10] Civic oaths were widely used in Classical Athens; oaths were a powerful tool to induce obligation in officials and citizens alike to their public role.[11] The bouleutic oath was no exception and is our best available source to understand how the Athenians approached the office of *bouleutēs* and which normative values the councillors had to uphold. Similarly to the judicial oath, the text of the bouleutic oath included several clauses, which ancient sources have not preserved in their entirety. However, the main clauses of the oath can be reconstructed based on the mentions found in several literary sources as well as a very fragmentary inscription from the late fifth century (*IG* I³ 105). According to the reconstruction made by Rhodes, the oath included the following ten pledges.[12]

1. I will deliberate according to the laws (Xen. *Mem.* 1.1.18).
2. I will deliberate for the best of the people of the Athenians (Lys. 31.1; [Dem.] 59.4).

---

[10] Aristotle also includes the council within the category of *archai* in the *Politics* when discussing the role of magistrates in democratic constitutions (Arist. *Pol.* 1299b30–2, 1317b30–1, 1322b12–17). Cf. Dem. 39.10. In the Aristotelian *Athenaion Politeia*, the council is included in the discussion of the deliberative function according to the traditional tripartition of the *politeia* into deliberative realm (42–9), magistracies, and judiciary; cf. §1.2. For the methodology used in this treatise see Hansen (1974) 10–2; Harris (2006) 31–2; Bertelli (2017) 551–77; Canevaro and Esu (2018).

[11] On oaths and civic obligation see Liddel (2007) 133; Hansen (2015).

[12] Rhodes (1972) 194; Sommerstein and Bayliss (2013) 40–3.

46 DIVIDED POWER IN ANCIENT GREECE

3. I will not imprison any Athenian citizen who offers three sureties taxed in the same class as himself, except any person found guilty of conspiring to betray the city or to overthrow the democracy, or any tax-farmer or his sureties or collector being in default (Dem. 24.144).

4. I will neither exile, nor imprison, nor put to death anybody without trial ([Andoc.] 4.3).

5. I will denounce anyone who has been appointed by lot who I know is unsuitable to serve in the council (Lys. 31.2).

6. I will sit in the letter section to which I am allotted (Philoch. *FGrH* 328 F 140).

7. If someone coins money of silver in the *poleis* and does not use Athenian coins or weights or measures, but uses foreign coins and weights and measures, I shall charge him according to the former decree of Clearchus (*IG* I³ 1453 + *SEG* 28.2).

8. I am no less than 30 years old (Xen. *Mem.* 1.2.35).

9. I will not allow any *endeixis* or *apagōgē* arising out of past events, except in the case of those who fled (Andoc. 1.91).

10. I will not put to the vote anything contrary to the laws (Xen. *Mem.* 1.1.18, 1.7.14).

The clauses of the oath can be divided into two groups. One includes clauses three, four, six, seven, eight, and nine, and deals with the limits to the powers of the council, membership requirements, and internal procedures. Another group includes clauses one, two, five, and ten, which set the founding principles of the *ethos* of the council. Scholarly interpretations of the bouleutic oath have especially focused on the implications of the former group of clauses in order to reconstruct the constitutional limits imposed upon the council.[13] By contrast, clauses one, two, and five have been particularly disregarded. Rhodes defines these pledges as 'patriotic generalities' forming the original part of the oath and does not identify the important implications of these clauses in defining the task of the councillors.[14]

These clauses are the most frequently mentioned parts of the oath in the ancient sources. The first, the second, and the fifth pledges are closely related and bound the councillors to make the best decisions for the Athenians according to the laws. Bayliss has argued that the bouleutic oath could be used as a 'rhetorical device' in a way similar to what the Attic orators did when alluding to the judicial oath in forensic speeches.[15] Yet, allusions to the judicial oath in court speeches were not simple rhetorical devices, but clear evidence for how the Athenians conceptualized the role of the judges and the values that they had to uphold.

The bouleutic oath played the very same role in Athenian civic discourse and clearly defines the job of the councillors. To acquire a fuller understanding of the

---

[13] Rhodes (1972) 190–6; Hansen (1991) 227; Koch (1995–6).   [14] Rhodes (1972) 195.

[15] Sommerstein and Bayliss (2013) 41–2.

DIVIDED POWER IN ATHENIAN DECREE-MAKING 47

bouleutic values, it is necessary to analyse the allusions and mentions of the oath in the *dokimasia* speeches in the council. Four of the surviving *dokimasia* speeches were written by Lysias and delivered during *dokimasiai* before the council which carried out the preliminary scrutiny of prospective councillors, archons, and the disabled (*adunatoi*) ([Arist.] *Ath. Pol.* 49.2).[16] Candidates going through a *dokimasia* were not judged on their skills, but on their public conduct and the formal requirements for taking office. The orators referred to the oath to remind the councillors of the values that they should uphold while examining a councillor or a magistrate.

The first reference to the bouleutic oath occurs in Lysias' speech *Against Evander* (Lys. 26). Evander was appointed as a prospective archon, but was accused of being unfit for this office at his *dokimasia*. This procedure consisted in a preliminary examination in the council and in a second before a lawcourt. The nature of the allegation against Evander is twofold; first, he and his family were supporters of the oligarchy and were involved with the rule of the Thirty (26.2–4). Second, Evander is polluted and cannot perform the sacrifices and religious rituals attached to his office of archon (26.6–8). After presenting his allegations, the speaker reminds the councillors of their oath and asks them to bear in mind whether they have 'sworn to appoint to public office a person who has not passed his *dokimasia*, or else to conduct a *dokimasia* and then to crown the person who is worthy of office. This is what you should consider' (ὑμεῖς ὠμόσατε εἰς τὴν ἀρχὴν ἀδοκίμαστον καταστήσειν, ἢ δοκιμάσαντες τὸν ἄξιον τῆς ἀρχῆς στεφανώσειν. ταῦτα γὰρ σκοπεῖσθε). The speaker also relies on appeals to the intent of the lawgiver to remind the councillors about their duties as members of a democratic institution. At section 9, the speaker emphasizes that the man who designed the law on *dokimasia* would have found it terrible to confirm an oligarch in office. Likewise at 26.21, the prosecutor affirms that it is the task of the councillors (ὑμέτερον δὴ ἔργον ἐστίν) to choose whether their deliberation would be better (ἄμεινον βουλεύσαισθε) if they trusted him or Thrasybulus, Evander's defender. Here, the speaker closely paraphrases the second clause of the bouleutic oath (τὰ βέλτιστα βουλεύσειν) when asking the council to reach the better deliberation (ἄμεινον βουλεύσαισθε). The speaker's point is further reinforced by the use of the expression ὦ ἄνδρες βουλευταί. This is the only occurrence of the vocative ὦ ἄνδρες βουλευταί within the corpus of the Attic orators. The orators usually address the council with the most common expressions ὦ βουλή or with the generic ἄνδρες Ἀθηναῖοι.[17] The form ὦ ἄνδρες βουλευταί resembles the more attested form ὦ ἄνδρες δικασταί of forensic speeches, which is especially employed when the

---

[16] Rhodes (1972) 171–8, (1981) 542.

[17] For ὦ βουλή: Lys. 16.1, 3, 8, 9, 12, 15, 16, 19, 20; 24.1, 3, 7, 8, 10, 11, 12, 13, 15, 21, 22, 23, 26; 31.1, 8, 33; Dem. 51.1. For ἄνδρες Ἀθηναῖοι: Dem. 51.3, 8, 22. The only occurrence in historiography is in Xenophon's *Hellenica* (2.3.24) when in 404 BCE, Critias addressed the council to justify the actions taken by the Thirty to establish their rule, and accused Theramenes.

48   DIVIDED POWER IN ANCIENT GREECE

orators urge the judges to consider the importance of a law, reminding the court of their institutional role.[18] Similarly, in this passage, Lysias uses ὦ ἄνδρες βουλευταί to remind the councillors of their task (ἔργον) in deliberating for the best interest of the Athenians. If the councillors confirm Evander in office, they would break their oath and the values enshrined in it. These notions did not only include respect for the spirit of the law on *dokimasia* and the general obligation of abiding by the laws, but also the civic obligation of deliberating for the best interest of the Athenians.[19] A similar point based on the bouleutic oath is made in Xenophon's *Hellenica* (Xen. *Hell.* 1.1.18, 1.7.15). During the controversial trial of the generals of the Arginusae in 405 BCE, Socrates was the chairman (*epistatēs*) of the *prutaneis*, the presiding committee of the council and the assembly. The assembly instructed the council to draft a *proboulema* for the trial of the generals. In the assembly, Callixenus proposed an illegal motion prescribing an immediate vote to punish the generals as a single group with the death penalty. The *prutaneis* were forced to put the motion to the vote, but Socrates was the only member of the board who refused because the proposal was against the bouleutic oath.[20]

The Athenians viewed the council as the highest deliberative institution of the state, which had to apply the laws as well as make decisions for the advantage of the people according to the values embedded in the law. This last point is important for understanding the deliberative role of the council. Like the magistrates and the judges, the councillors had to follow the laws when in office. However, the Athenian magistrates could not make independent decisions on policy, as they were bound to enforce the laws and the decrees of the council and the assembly.[21] The oath of office taken by the nine archons offers a good example of the behaviour that the Athenians expected from their magistrates. After passing their *dokimasia*, the nine archons were brought before a stone in the agora where victims were cut up for sacrifice and they swore that 'they will hold the office of archon justly and according to the laws, they will not to take any gifts on account of their office, and if they should take anything they shall set up a golden statue' ([Arist.] *Ath. Pol.* 59: ὀμνύουσιν δικαίως ἄρξειν καὶ κατὰ τοὺς νόμους, καὶ δῶρα μὴ λήψεσθαι τῆς ἀρχῆς ἕνεκα, κἄν τι λάβωσι ἀνδριάντα ἀναθήσειν χρυσοῦν). The oath of the archons singles out two pledges: the obligation to act according to the laws and the prohibition against taking bribes while in office.[22] On a normative level, the oath of the archons reveals the pervasive concern for compelling magistrates to respect the laws and for preventing bribery. Unlike the bouleutic oath, this oath does not mention any obligation for the archons to give the best counsel nor to formulate political decisions on behalf of the Athenians because these functions were understood as separate from implementation and fell outside the

---

[18] Cf. Martin (2006) 79; Canevaro (2016c) 178.   [19] Liddel (2007) 134.
[20] Cf. also Pl. *Ap.* 32b.   [21] [Arist.] *Ath. Pol.* 55.5.3; cf. also the ephebic oath (RO 88).
[22] See Dein. 3.2 for the provision against taking gifts in oath of the generals.

DIVIDED POWER IN ATHENIAN DECREE-MAKING 49

prerogatives of Athenian magistrates. As Rubinstein notes, even the participation of a magistrate as a prosecutor in court was seen as a breach of his duty to remain impartial (Lys. 15.3).[23]

On the other hand, the council was in charge of the everyday administration as well as of democratic deliberation both during bouleutic debates and, in the case of *prutaneis* and *proedroi*, as chairmen of the assembly. The profile of each *bouleutēs* had to conform to the institutional constraints and the formal rules embedded in the bouleutic oath. Such formal norms were complemented by and consistent with the informal rules setting out the etiquette to be followed in the council, which was similar to what happened in the lawcourts and in the assembly. Evidence for the council's behavioural norms is unfortunately very limited, but they seem to overlap with those of the assembly in which personal attacks, display of wealth and public service, and delegitimization were not accepted. Some passages in the forensic speech *Against Androtion* (Dem. 22) give a general account of what was considered inappropriate regarding the conduct of the councillors. At 22.37–8, Demosthenes condemns the partisan behaviour of prominent politicians, such as Androtion and the clerk Antigenes, whom he accuses of attempting to control the councillors. When anticipating some of Androtion's arguments, Demosthenes alleges that his opponent will claim to speak before the court in favour of the whole council, but that Androtion is only concerned with his personal advantage and to provide an honorific decree as evidence of his good conduct at his *euthunai*.

We can appreciate Athenian expectations concerning the behaviour of the councillors in another *dokimasia* speech by Lysias; in *Against Philon* (31), the speaker, who was a *bouleutēs* himself, attacks Philon of Acharnai, who was selected to serve as a member of the council. All of Lysias' charges aim to depict Philon as an anti-democratic and corrupt citizen who does not deserve to serve on the council. Lanni argues that these arguments were legally irrelevant in *dokimasiai*.[24] Yet, as Feyel points out in his comprehensive study of *dokimasia*, arguments based on personal conduct and democratic values were not in opposition to the formal questions asked to the candidates; the *dokimasia* included questions on the candidate's respect for their family cult, the obligation of taking care of their parents, evidence that they belong to one of the three property classes, and on their successful fulfilment of military service (Din. 2.17).[25] Such arguments were consistent with the purpose of the legal procedure and aimed to establish whether the candidate was fit for the office of councillor according to the principles of Athenian laws and the standards of behaviour accepted by the community.

---

[23] Rubinstein (1998) 138.   [24] Lanni (2006) 59–64.

[25] Rhodes (2004) 140–1; Feyel (2009) 169. We mostly have evidence about the *dokimasia* questions for the nine archons, but it is likely that the basic questions at the *dokimasia* for councillors were similar.

50 DIVIDED POWER IN ANCIENT GREECE

At the beginning of his speech, when introducing the reasons for his accusation against Philon, the speaker recalls the importance of his own oath. He had sworn to deliberate for the best advantage of the city as well as to expose any unsuitable person who has been appointed for office (Lys. 31.1–2: εἰσῆλθον εἰς τὸ βουλευτήριον τὰ βέλτιστα βουλεύσειν τῇ πόλει, ἔνεστί τε ἐν τῷ ὅρκῳ ἀποφανεῖν εἴ τίς τινα οἶδε τῶν λαχόντων ἀνεπιτήδειον ὄντα βουλεύειν). The key term in this passage is *anepitēdeios*. This word can be translated as 'unfit', 'inappropriate', 'unsuitable', and has important parallels in Athenian legal terminology. The adjective *epitēdeios* also occurs in the name of the public action against unsuitable laws (*graphē nomon mē epitēdeion theinai*), a legal procedure directed at prosecuting an unconstitutional law. In order to be *epitēdeios*, a law should conform to the *ethos* of the *dēmos* enshrined in the system of written laws, understood as a coherent whole.[26] This meaning of *epitēdeios* is not unique to Athenian legal language. For example, Herodotus tells the story of Periander's son, Lycophron, who was sent away from his father's house. Lycophron could not find a shelter because his father forbade anyone to host him. After four days, Periander took pity on the miserable state of his son, and asked Lycophron whether he preferred his current state or would rather meet his father's expectations and receive all his possessions (Hdt. 3.52: ταῦτα ἐόντα τῷ πατρὶ ἐπιτήδεον παραλαμβάνειν). In another example, Thucydides gives an account of the manoeuvres of Archidamus in Attica during the early stage of the Peloponnesian War, where he says that the Spartan king found Acharnae to be an appropriate position for encamping (Thuc. 2.20: ὁ χῶρος ἐπιτήδειος ἐφαίνετο ἐνστρατοπεδεῦσαι).[27] In Demosthenes' *Against Androtion*, the speaker accuses Androtion of treating citizens like slaves. Demosthenes mentions two prostitutes seized by Androtion as payment for their masters' debt to the state. The speaker then affirms that it is appropriate to treat slaves harshly and to seize their bodies and properties, but it is not appropriate, according to Athenian laws, to break into free citizen's houses and to seize their properties (Dem. 22.56–7: καίτοι εἴ τισιν ἄρα δοκοῦσ' ἐπιτήδειαι 'κεῖναι παθεῖν, ἀλλὰ τὸ πρᾶγμά γ' οὐκ ἐπιτήδειον γίγνεσθαι, τηλικοῦτό τινας φρονεῖν διὰ καιρὸν ὥστε βαδίζειν ἐπ' οἰκίας καὶ σκεύη φέρειν μηδὲν ὀφειλόντων ἀνθρώπων).

The adjective *epitēdeios* is always construed in comparative terms and denotes appropriateness within a given context or for a specific purpose. The same dynamics were incorporated in the clauses of the bouleutic oath, as discussed by Lysias, which shaped the logic of appropriateness for the Athenian councillors. In the speech *Against Philon*, Lysias claims that Philon does not conform either to the values of the council or to the democratic constitution of Athens; he is thus

---

[26] For the term *epitēdeios* in Athenian legal procedure see Kremmydas (2012) 48–50; Canevaro (2016b) 73–6.
[27] For other Thucydidean occurrences of *epitēdeios* and *anepitēdeios* as expressing alikeness to a political regime see e.g. Thuc. 1.19, and for opposition to a given political inclination see e.g. Thuc. 4.113.3, 8.65.2.

DIVIDED POWER IN ATHENIAN DECREE-MAKING   51

anepitēdeios to be a councillor vis-à-vis his fellow citizens. The whole narrative of the speech is built on this notion. Philon is a criminal and has committed many wrongdoings towards fellow Athenians (3–4). He does not uphold the values of the *politeia* as he regarded his personal advantage as more important than that of the city (5–7). During the civil war for the restoration of the democracy, he fled with his property to Oropus, and did not take part in the battle against the oligarchs or help the *polis* (τι τῶν τῇ κοινῇ πολιτείᾳ συμφερόντων) (8–9). Similar arguments build up in the remaining sections of the speech, which Lysias ends by stressing once again that Philon's way of life (*epitēdeuma*) is alien to the democratic constitution (34: ἔστι γὰρ τὰ τούτου ἐπιτηδεύματα καινὰ παραδείγματα καὶ πάσης δημοκρατίας ἀλλότρια).[28]

These passages from the *dokimasia* speeches show that the Athenians took the bouleutic oath very seriously. The Aristotelian *Athenaion Politeia* (22.2–3) informs us that the Athenians established the bouleutic oath under the archonship of Hermocreon in 502/1 BCE, and the same oath was still in use at the end of the fourth century. If one accepts the validity of this statement in the *Athenaion Politeia*, this means that the values and principles regulating the *ethos* of the council and enshrined in the oath were those institutionalized soon after the constitutional foundation of the council following the reform of Cleisthenes.[29] Then, the continuity of this ideological arrangement was preserved throughout the entire Classical period of the Athenian democracy according to the phenomenon of path dependence. The bouleutic oath is a key piece of evidence for what historical institutionalism defines as the 'institutionalization of advantage' of a social or political group.[30] As the dominant social group, the *dēmos* institutionalized its political and social capital in the power-allocating structures of the *polis* and in the relevant formal and informal norms and public discourse. Paga's study on the public building of the late Archaic democracy at Athens also confirms that the archaeological and topographical evidence for completion of the old

---

[28] Interestingly, such arguments also provide parallels with those occurring in Aeschines' *Against Timarchus*, a speech delivered for a *dokimasia rhetorōn*, which was a procedure designed to check the behaviour of speakers in the assembly. Speakers in the assembly did not take the bouleutic oath, yet their role as advisors of the *dēmos* was akin to that of the councillors in the council. Speakers in the council and the assembly then had to follow similar 'deliberative requirements' and were subject to a similar institutional control. For the procedure see MacDowell (2005); for the context of the trial see Harris (1995) 101–6; Fisher (2001).

[29] For Cleisthenes see the classic work of Lévêque and Vidal Naquet (1964). On the problematic reception of Cleisthenes in Athenian ideology see Camassa (2011b) and Flaig (2011). For the debate about whether the Athenian democracy began with Cleisthenes or with the reforms of Ephialtes, see respectively Ober (1996) 32–52, (2007); Raaflaub (2007); Giangiulio (2015) 49. For a compelling study on the invention of the reforms of Ephialtes, see Zaccarini (2018) with discussion of the previous bibliography.

[30] Pierson (2016) 131–4. This concept is compatible with Gramsci's notion of 'hegemony' of a social class. On the *dēmos* and its hegemony expressed through institutions and honorific practice in Classical Athens, see Canevaro (2021); Esu (2021b). For a general discussion on the relevance of Gramsci's methodology for Classical studies, see Zucchetti (2021).

52 DIVIDED POWER IN ANCIENT GREECE

bouleutērion is consistent with the dating proposed by the *Athenaion Politeia* and shows the awareness of the democracy to sustain the institutions of the new regime with symbols of their centrality in the decision-making.[31] As a result, popular power and democratic ideology were entrenched in the institutions of Classical Athens.

When delivering speeches before the council, both elite and non-elite speakers adapted their arguments to the institutional framework, to the relevant discursive protocols that were suitable for a *dokimasia*, and to the original ideological framework of the council. References to the oath were not simple rhetorical devices, but allusions to the set of values embedded in the institutional setting. The speakers as well as the councillors clearly expected these values to be respected when performing their institutional roles. Moreover, the clauses of the oath help our understanding of the Athenians' own constitutional conceptualization of the council. The council was not only an *archē* preparing motions and implementing norms passed by the *dēmos* in the assembly; it played an active deliberative role within the decision-making process. The first and the second clauses of the oath make clear that the council had to follow the laws, but it especially had to act in the best interest of the Athenians.[32]

This last point is especially important. The verb βουλεύειν, inserted in both the first and second pledge of the oath, refers to the office of the *bouleutēs* in its deliberative capacity. Cammack has recently questioned the deliberative nature of the council, and more generally of the Athenian democracy. Through a stimulating analysis of the verb βουλεύειν and its cognates, Cammack makes a case for a sharp division between orators and *dēmos*. After listening to the speeches of the *rhētores* in the council and in the assembly, Athenians made up their minds with a fully internal process—this would be implied by the use of the middle voice of the verb βουλεύειν (βουλεύομαι) to mean the act of deliberating. However, this lexicographical approach does not in fact analyse the behaviour of the deliberative terminology in the relevant context.

A good example is found at the beginning of Demosthenes' *First Olynthiac* (1.1). The orator affirms that the people are eager to listen all those who wish to give advice (προσήκει προθύμως ἐθέλειν ἀκούειν τῶν βουλομένων συμβουλεύειν). Demosthenes then affirms that the *dēmos* should not only listen and accept useful proposals prepared in advance (οὐ γὰρ μόνον εἴ τι χρήσιμον ἐσκεμμένος ἥκει τις) by orators such as himself. He states that it is for the benefit of the Athenians, that many helpful proposals are put forward on the spur of the moment (παραχρῆμ'), so that from all these (proposals) it is easy for the *dēmos* to choose what is most

---

[31] Paga (2020) 97–102 and 293–6.

[32] My argument diverges significantly from Cammack (2013), (2020a), (2020b), and (2022a). In these important studies, Cammack makes the case for an Athenian democracy in which deliberation, even in the council and in the assembly, played a marginal role in favour of a majoritarian decision-making such as in the 'supreme' lawcourts.

DIVIDED POWER IN ATHENIAN DECREE-MAKING 53

advantageous. Here, Demosthenes gives an expressive picture of an assembly debate, where the two moments of the speech and the decision of the *dēmos* are not sharply divided. Demosthenes envisages a fluid process made of several proposals on a given topic; proposals which might arise from well-prepared orators as well as be formulated on the spot while the debate was unfolding.[33]

This dialogical deliberation was fostered by the specific procedures which were used both in the assembly and in the council, such as the *diacheirotonia*.[34] Canevaro shows that the procedures of the Athenian assembly favoured a decision-making process based on deliberative requirements and consensual decisions. In particular, the combination of the procedure of *diacheirotonia*, structured in multiple proposals and a final vote assessing the ayes and nays, with the power of the *prutaneis* and *proedroi* to stir the discussion and assess the outcome of the votes (cf. [Arist.] *Ath. Pol.* 44.2–3: τὰς χειροτονίας κρίνουσιν).[35] Another consensus-building mechanism was the *thorubos* operating both in the assembly and in the council. Far from being the symbol of passive participation and of the irrational malice of the Athenian mob, the *thorubos* allowed the orators on the platform, both expert and occasional speakers, to gauge the general mood of the *dēmos* concerning their proposal. The proposer could potentially adapt his original motion to the will of the people under the pressure of an opposing *thorubos*, or find confirmation of the consensus for his bill.[36] It did not necessarily follow that consensual deliberation always ended with the best decision. An example of this is found in Andocides' account of Pisander's controversial proposal in the council to repeal the decree of Scamander, which forbade the torture of an Athenian citizen during an investigation of the profanation of the Mysteries and the mutilation of the Herms (Andoc. 1.43). The *boulē* approved unanimously with shouts (ἀνέκραγεν ἡ βουλὴ ὡς εὖ λέγει).[37]

The council also followed the deliberative parameters enshrined in the bouleutic oath when making decisions in the day-to-day administration. The Demosthenic speech *Against Evergus and Mnesibulus* ([Dem.] 47), written for a dispute between two trierarchs, provides good evidence for this practice.[38] The speaker reconstructed the events preceding his trial and relates how he tried to recover his naval equipment from Theophemus, who served as trierarch

---

[33] Other normative statements about the deliberative nature of Athenian democracy are discussed in Canevaro (2019d). On the *prooimia* preserved in the Demosthenic corpus see Clavaud (1974); Yunis (1996); Worthington (2004).

[34] Rhodes (1972) 79.

[35] An illegal behaviour of the *prutaneis* and *proedroi* during their presidency of the council and of the assembly could be prosecuted through a *graphē proedrikē* (*Ath. Pol.* 59.2): see Rhodes (1981) 660; Harris (2014).

[36] On *thorubos* see Bers (1986) (in court); Villacèque (2013); Thomas (2016); Canevaro (2019d) 359–66. On popular will-formation from a constructivist perspective see Simonton (2021).

[37] For a discussion of the procedures during the investigation for the profanation of the Mysteries see Esu (2021a).

[38] For discussion on the speech see MacDowell (2009) 137–41; Scafuro (2011) 291–8.

54 DIVIDED POWER IN ANCIENT GREECE

before him. Theophemus refused to hand in his equipment and was convicted by a lawcourt. In spite of this, the speaker was still unable to recover the equipment and decided to approach the council with a formal complaint. In this forensic speech, the speaker closely paraphrases the institutional language of the decree and gives a vivid picture of the familiarity of citizens with this institution. The council authorized him to seize Theophemus' equipment in any way he could ([Dem.] 47.33: ἡ βουλὴ ψηφίσματι, ὃ ἀναγνώσεται ὑμῖν, εἰσπράττεσθαι τρόπῳ ᾧ ἂν δυνώμεθα).[39] The speaker also emphasizes that he was empowered by a decree of the council which was passed after many speeches (καὶ πολλῶν λόγων γενομένων ἀποκρίνεται ἡμῖν ἡ βουλὴ ψηφίσματι).[40] This account shows that even in case of routine administration, the council worked by wide deliberation. The decree was voted on and enacted after multiple speeches and open deliberation.[41]

The evidence from the Attic orators shows that the Athenian council was a deliberative institution designed to promote democratic values, which were embedded into this institution since its founding and formalized in the bouleutic oath. The relevant narratives unfolded according to a logic of path dependence adopted by political actors within this institution during the whole period of the Athenian democracy. The institutional constraints, which are central to the new institutionalist theory, had a double effect on the Athenian council: they helped preserve and perpetuate the constituent ideal of the respect for the laws as well as foster open deliberation and equal involvement in the democratic decision-making process.

As a result, the council shaped Athenian political discourse through the relevant constituent values embedded in the oath. Moreover, the procedures and the value of the oath helped the councillors to gain a minimum level of expertise through participation in the council. This expertise was an essential factor underlying deliberation and the working of a system of divided power. The way in which bouleutic expertise was created is the subject of the following section.

2.3 The 'Deliberative' Expertise of the Athenian Council

Expertise has been a contentious issue in the study of Athenian democracy.[42] According to a widespread view, only a select number of influential *rhētores*

---

[39] Cf. *IG* II² 1328.13–14. This is a standard formula of Athenian decrees. For epigraphical evidence of this legal clause outside Athens, see Rubinstein (2010) 209–12.

[40] For evidence for multiple copies of Athenian decrees written down for administrative usage see Sickinger (1999) 185–6. Athenian officials often carried copies of relevant decrees while performing their office (Ar. *Av.* 1024–5; Aeschin. 2.109–10). On the authority of Athenian decrees see the important analysis in Liddel (2020b) 14–48.

[41] *Contra* Cammack (2020a) 17–22 who downplays the deliberative nature of the council but does not consider the power of the council to issue its own decrees.

[42] Expertise also represents a challenge for modern theory and practice of deliberative democracy see Brown (2008).

DIVIDED POWER IN ATHENIAN DECREE-MAKING 55

possessed the relevant expertise to lead political decision-making, whereas the common Athenian is usually portrayed as an inexperienced citizen, who passively attended the meetings of the council and of the assembly and voted after listening to the speeches of prominent leaders.[43] Ismard has made a case for a clash between the Athenian civic ideology and the expertise of citizens in their political capacity.[44] According to Ismard, Athenian democracy was hostile to experts in the field of state administration and bureaucracy. Administrative expertise—a necessity for a state the size of Classical Athens—was embodied by the public slaves (*dēmosioi*), who de facto carried out the daily administration of the state. Public slaves supported different boards of magistrates, for example the *dokimastai*, the Eleven, and the *prutaneis*. *Dēmosioi* preserved continuity in state administration and balanced the annual rotation of officials.[45] This focus on public slaves is refreshing as it shows that the role of enslaved population was also relevant in Athenian political institutions.[46] Slaves were not totally excluded from recognition or social esteem, despite their highly asymmetrical social status; however, their role in the working of Athenian democratic machinery should not be overestimated.[47]

The employment of public slaves in the realm of public administration in Classical Athens is not evidence that public slaves were the major depositaries of expertise in this field. There is evidence for the existence of experts whose skilful knowledge was highly respected. The most prominent examples are the *exēgētai* and the Areopagus, which were regularly consulted as legal experts by citizens and were invited to give reports to the assembly (Pl. *Eutphr.* 4c8; Dem. 3.5.20; Dem. 47.67–8).[48]

If there were groups or institutions whose prestige and expertise in a given field was uncontested in Athens, it is also true that the institutional structure of Athenian democracy did not favour the creation of a citizen class of experts. However, this does not mean that the administrative knowledge to run the state machinery was in the hands of a restricted group of state-owned slaves. Ismard's

---

[43] Hansen (1991) 308–9; Kallet-Marx (1994). Cammack (2020a) offers a view of Athenian deliberation modelled on the judicial practice in lawcourts with no back-and-forth deliberation. For different views see Ober (2008) 161–7; Rhodes (2016b). On the involvement of a wide range of individuals in the political process, see now Lambert (2017) 171–225; Liddel (2020a) 23; *contra* Rohde (2019) who argues for a more passive role of the *dēmos* in the late fourth century. A similar picture of an important involvement of ordinary proposers seems to also emerge for the fifth-century democracy; see Barbato (2023).

[44] Ismard (2015).   [45] Ismard (2015) 131–92. Cf. also Todd (1996).

[46] [Arist.] *Ath. Pol.* 43.3. See the reviews of D. Lewis (2016); Hansen (2019).

[47] For the Athenian system of slavery see D. Lewis (2018) 167–96. Athenian democracy did not legally recognize any claim to *timē* for slaves vis-à-vis their master see Canevaro (2018e). For the potential of an honour relationship between slaves and masters see Canevaro (forthcoming b). For slave identity and agency see Forsdyke (2019); Vlassopoulos (2022) 92–112.

[48] On the Athenian view of legal expertise cf. also [Dem.] 59.15. See Chapter 6 on the expertise of Athenian courts. See Harris (1991); (2020).

56   DIVIDED POWER IN ANCIENT GREECE

conceptual framework in fact relies on a vertical view of expertise—typical of modern states—which did not apply to Athenian democracy.[49]

Expertise in Athenian public administration was organized horizontally. By horizontal expertise, I refer to a kind of expertise that was generated and fostered by the direct involvement of citizens in the democratic institutions and dispersed across society. Athenian citizens could initially learn the basic legal and administrative knowledge in their demes, where the demarch would gather the deme-assembly regularly according to each deme's needs (Dem. 57.7).[50] The scanty evidence for deme assemblies suggests that the deliberative practice was as central to deme assemblies as it was in the council and in the assembly. In *Against Euboulides* (Dem. 57), the speaker Euxitheus relates that the demarch Euboulides, who incidentally was also a *bouleutēs* that year, spent the day in the deme assembly giving speeches and introducing decrees (Dem. 57.9: κατέτριψε τὴν ἡμέραν δημηγορῶν καὶ ψηφίσματα γράφων). The deme assemblies carried out the procedure of enrolling new citizens (*diapsēphisis*), which consisted in checking the requirements of new *demotai*. Familiarity with this procedure at the deme level could have helped Athenian citizens gain expertise about similar (and connected) procedures held in the council such as the *dokimasiai*, discussed in the previous section.[51] The demarch selected by sortition was in charge of recording the new citizens in the *lēxiarchika grammateia* and archiving these registers in the deme. These records were compiled at the deme levels, and as Faraguna and Pébarthe note, were complex documents reporting important information for fiscal and military purposes.[52] Other expertise in public affairs was acquired while acting as member of one of the several boards of magistrates selected by lot and as a member of the council of the Five Hundred or while serving as a judge in court. This kind of expertise did not mostly rely on a restricted group of experts who were the main depositary of technical skills (vertical expertise) for the running the administrative and legal proceedings. A closer analysis of the prerogatives of the Athenian council can further substantiate this claim.[53]

The five hundred councillors were representative of the average demographic of the Athenian male population. As Hansen has shown, every year around 375–400

[49] This distinction mirrors the division between elected politicians (*la politique*) and unelected civil servants and bureaucrats in modern states. See Introduction pp. 24–6 for division between administration and legislation in Athens.

[50] Osborne (1985a); Whitehead (1986).

[51] The demes appointed their own officials who had to undergo to *dokimasia* before taking office and *euthunai* at the end of their term. On the demarch and other deme officials see Whitehead (1986) 121–48.

[52] Pébarthe (2013); Faraguna (2015c); cf. Boffo and Faraguna (2021) 151–75, 693–749 respectively for registers of citizens from the Archaic period to the fourth century and in the Hellenistic period.

[53] Similarly, Athenian lawcourts produced legal expertise by direct involvement of citizens in judicial panels. Athenian judges heard numerous legal cases and interpreted laws and decrees; cf. Ar. *Nub.* 1178–1200 for the Athenian familiarity with legal language and institutions.

DIVIDED POWER IN ATHENIAN DECREE-MAKING 57

new councillors were selected by lot from all the Attic demes to serve in the council. Because the average councillor was around 40, Hansen managed to calculate that two-thirds of Athenian men over 40 became councillors, and a good number of them became councillors twice.[54] One might argue that such a high turnout did not allow the councillors to develop a sufficient expertise of public affairs. Such a view does not take into account the institutional setting and the day-by-day duties of the councillors.

According to the Aristotelian *Athenaion Politeia*, the *prutaneis* summoned the council every day, except during festival days, and the councillors also gathered on the days in which the assembly was held.[55] As Hansen demonstrates, this means that the Athenian council was in session for 275 days in a year of 354 days, which means that the councillors were at work in the council for around 76 per cent of the year.[56] Moreover, the *prutaneis* stayed in office all day for the entire duration of their prytany. Some of them had already performed the role of councillors or other offices at local levels in their demes before, so there was a group of experienced citizens that were familiar with the institutional procedures and rules of the *boulē*. Unlike the citizens of a modern state, the average Athenian citizen was familiar with and acted at ease within the official institutions of the *polis*.[57]

During the daily sessions of the council, the councillors were faced with several technicalities of Athenian state administration. The councillors drafted all the *probouleumata* for discussion in the assembly, which almost half of the time were closed *probouleumata* that the *dēmos* ratified as probouleumatic decrees without changes in the assembly.[58] In addition, the council passed its own decrees, which were fully prepared within the council. In the previous section, I asserted that the council as much as the assembly made decisions through discussion and multiple debates. This deliberative decision-making in the council was especially relevant in case of decrees of the council, which were immediately operative and closed *probouleumata*. As the studies of Rhodes and Hansen have demonstrated, closed *probouleumata* were usually passed by *procheirotonia* in the assembly, a procedure envisaging a vote by raising the hands without discussion on the relevant bill. If the assembly was unanimous, the *probouleuma* was immediately ratified, otherwise a discussion was opened with amendments from the floor.[59] In this way, in many instances, the council did not just carry out a preliminary

---

[54] Hansen (1985b) 51–5; Hansen (1991) 249; Canevaro (2017c) 48. For the bouleutic quotas see Rhodes (1984).

[55] For the meetings and the bouleutic calendar see Rhodes (1972) 30–48, 224–30, (1981) 518–20.

[56] Dem. 22.36 has been interpreted as evidence for the scarce attendance of many councillors. Demosthenes' statement should not be taken out of context. He is accusing Androtion in a *graphē paranomōn* trial against an honorary decree for outgoing council. He needs to prove that Androtion is solely responsible for the council's failure and underestimates the participation of other councillors.

[57] Canevaro (2017c) 46–8.

[58] Probouleumatic decrees are fewer in the second half of the fourth century see Lambert (2017) 227–74.

[59] Hansen (1983) 123–30, (1991) 139–40.

58 DIVIDED POWER IN ANCIENT GREECE

deliberation on a decree, but the whole deliberation took place in the council, and the final proposal was then ratified in the assembly. Such a deliberative stage in the decision-making casts new light on the rationale of *probouleusis* in Athenian decision-making. In Athens, indeed, no matter could be discussed by the assembly without the preliminary deliberation of the council (*Ath. Pol.* 43.5; Dem. 22.5). The purpose of *probouleusis* has usually been interpreted as a remedy for the amateurism of Athenian democracy that was intended to prevent hasty decisions by the people in the assembly. This is only one possible reason for the existence of the probouleutic procedure, which should not be overestimated and is partially influenced by anti-democratic writers such as Thucydides, Plato, and Xenophon.[60] Hornblower notes several omissions about the role of the council in Thucydides' historical account making the *dēmos* in the assembly the only responsible party for unplanned, irrational, and rushed decisions.[61] In fact, a closer look at institutional practice shows that Athenians enshrined a principle into their law that requires a mandatory deliberative discussion in the council in order to promote consensus and democratic involvement before the enactment of any decree, especially when a large amount of decrees were actually passed in the assembly without a debate with the procedure of *procheirotonia*. Participation in this process of deliberation and decree-making enhanced the basic documentary and legislative expertise of the councillors and their knowledge of legal terminology, which was not seen as a discrete and obscure language of experts.[62] As Liddel suggests, the deliberative process could require some level of collaboration among the councillors and other expert politicians in drafting decrees.[63] For example, Demosthenes collaborated with a councillor to draft a decree which was then debated in the assembly (Aeschin. 3.125–8).

Another task associated with the council was the job of keeping the records of state documents: laws, decrees, official accounts, lists, and records. As Sickinger shows, from the fifth century until 368 BCE the *grammateus tēs boulēs* was the chief secretary of the Athenian state, with wide knowledge on all the administrative and bureaucratic documents produced by the council and the assembly ([Arist.] *Ath. Pol.* 54.3).[64] The *grammateus* was a member of the council elected for one prytany in order to represent all the tribes during the year. He was in charge of the actual drafting of the decrees during the session of the council and also supervised the record-keeping of the state decrees and laws in the public archive. Although the system of election might point to a selection of leading

---

[60] Ober (1996) 140–59.   [61] Hornblower (2009).
[62] Willi (2003); Harris (2006) 429; Liddel (2020b) 93–9.   [63] Liddel (2020b) 18.
[64] Sickinger (1999) 74. After the 60s of the fourth century, there was a reorganization of the secretaries. The main secretary became the *grammateus kata prutaneian*, who was selected by lot, stayed in office for one year, and was not a member of the council. On secretaries see Rhodes (1972); Henry (1977); Liddel (2020b) 31–2, and for the role of the secretary of the council in legal proceedings see Filias (2020) 197–9.

DIVIDED POWER IN ATHENIAN DECREE-MAKING   59

members of the elite for this position, as the Aristotelian *Athenaion Politeia* suggests, the names of the secretaries from the decrees preserved on stone does not show a prominence of important leaders.[65] This clearly suggests that within the council there was a relatively widespread knowledge of decree-making and documentary terminology, which supported administrative and bureaucratic skills.[66] This expertise was not acquired outside the institutional context and was not ideologically delegated to public slaves, who worked as support staff, but it was a specific form of expertise, shaped by daily participation to state affairs and favoured by the institutional setting.

Probouleutic activity and archival practice were not the only administrative activities of the council. The councillors received foreign envoys and diplomats, who were often hosted for a meal at the *prutaneion*, the official building of the *prutaneis*, as a civic honour (e.g. RO 2,74–5; 20, 36–8; *IG* II² 107. 25–6). In addition, the councillors regularly heard reports from Athenian ambassadors from their envoys abroad and they were in charge of supervising the ambassadors (Dem. 19.154). This means that, unlike the average assembly-goers, membership to the council allowed the councillors to be updated regularly on the development of Athenian and foreign diplomacy.

The council was also the principal institution involved in the administration of state finances, perhaps the most important sector of public administration.[67] The council supervised several boards of officials and treasurers. For example, the board of ten *pōlētai* set the amount of the leases, allocated the concession for the mines, and the collection of military taxes, before the council ([Arist.] *Ath. Pol.* 47.2: ἐναντίον τῆς βουλῆς).[68] The accounts were checked every prytany by a board of ten *logistai*, who were selected by lot within the council (*IG* I³ 52.59; Lys. 30.5; [Arist.] *Ath. Pol.* 48.3).[69] These were all highly technical decisions regulating fundamental sectors of the financial administration. The councillors had no passive roles, as the *Athenaion Politeia* makes clear that every decision was voted on by the council in order to become valid (καὶ κυροῦσιν ὅτῳ ἂν ἡ βουλὴ χειροτονήσῃ). Cuomo notes that public counting in Classical Athens was a highly valued democratic ritual involving the numeracy and mathematical expertise of citizens in different institutional contexts, and this act of counting together, often with auxiliary counting tools, was linked to the democratic principle of

---

[65] Sickinger (1999) 141; C. Taylor (2007).

[66] On relatively good level of literacy in ancient Greece see Pébarthe (2006); Missou (2011) with a focus on fifth-century Athens; Langdon (2015). This does not mean that levels of literacy were uniform and consistent across social classes and for the entire Classical period. New epigraphical discoveries for the sixth and the fifth century show that literacy was widespread in the Greek world; see e.g. Kritzas (2006), (2009) about the bronze tables from the Argos' archive.

[67] For Athenian financial expertise see J. K. Davies (2004).

[68] In the fifth century, the council was also in charge of supervising and assessing the collection of tributes from the Delian League, see Rhodes (1972) 89–90.

[69] These *logistai* were different from the annual board of *logistai* which controlled the final accounts of magistrates ([Arist.] *Ath. Pol.* 54.1) and also appear in *IG* I³ 52 and *IG* I³ 369.

60   DIVIDED POWER IN ANCIENT GREECE

transparent accountability.[70] Blok also shows the cognitive efficiency of Greek acrophonic numerals for accounts and tables, especially for people with modest level of literacy.[71] The internal procedures of the council favoured the acquisition of computational and accounting skills. While several officials were involved in the managing of public finances, the council, to put it in Rhodes's words, 'was involved at every point, and alone could see the whole picture'.[72]

These are only a few examples, but they show that membership in the council had a high impact on shaping the expertise of the councillors. The five hundred members of the council were involved in the active management of the state on a daily basis, and the relevant formal norms and procedures of the council made it possible for the councillors to be informed about all the main areas of state finances, military and foreign policy, and the legislative agenda. This direct daily contact with key Athenian policies must have created a relevant level of what I call 'deliberative expertise'. By this expression I mean a set of skills and basic knowledge that was acquired through participation in institutions geared towards a deliberative democracy, and in turn, allowed the councillors to deliberate for the advantage of the city. Moreover, it is worth stressing that because two-thirds of the Athenians had served as councillors, such expertise was also transferred to the assembly, where decisions were further discussed before being ratified. This expertise combined good knowledge of Athenian laws and legal practice, necessary for drafting decrees for the assembly, with financial expertise as well as access to updated information about all the other key policies.

Such expertise of the councillors in the deliberative realm was formalized in the legal procedures and is reported in the epigraphical evidence. A series of different decrees feature legal clauses in which the council is made *autokratōr* or *kurios* to make further decisions if there is anything lacking in the decree. This practice is documented throughout the entire Classical period from the earliest decree dated at around 424–410 BCE to the latest occurrence in 325/4 BCE. These decrees deal with different matters, but even a cursory look at their contents show they were concerned with typical matters in which bouleutic expertise was key, such as public honours, foreign policy, religion, and the navy: the two fifth-century fragmentary decrees deal respectively with (1) proxeny for Potamodorus, a Boeotian citizen (*IG* I³ 73); and (2) regulations for the cult of the Thracian goddess Bendis (*IG* I³ 136). The fourth-century examples are (3) an alliance between Athens, and the kings of the Thracians, Illyrians, and Paeonians (*IG* II² 127); (4) the decree for demarcation of the sacred *orgas* (*IG* II³ 1 292); and (5) the decree for an expedition to the Adriatic (*IG* II³ 1 370).

---

[70] Cuomo (2001), (2012), (2013); Netz (2002) defining Athenian democracy a 'counter culture' where numeracy was pervasive. Cf. also Sing, van Berkel, and Osborne (2022) 11–13; similar arguments on numeracy and Athenian democratic institutions see also Kallet (2022) 32–8.

[71] Blok (2021) 36–8.   [72] Rhodes (1972) 105.

DIVIDED POWER IN ATHENIAN DECREE-MAKING   61

These decrees show that delegating power to the council was a routine activity and that one of the purposes of delegation to the council was to make the decision-making quicker. However, this does not mean that it was only done for the sake of efficiency. By delegating extra power to the council for completing the regulations of a decree, the Athenians designed a legal procedure which aimed to exploit the 'deliberative expertise' of the council in the decision-making process. When the council was *autokratōr* or *kurios* to complement a decision of the assembly with another decree, its decision was independent, and did not have to be referred to the assembly. Thus, the council carried out a proper deliberative discussion with the relevant debate and vote which resulted in the enactment of another decree. This activity differs from the normal instructions given by the assembly to the council to supervise boards of magistrates or the implementation of a law or a decree of the assembly. In those cases, the council had no decree-making authority and could not make independent decisions, but only carry out the instructions set by the assembly. On the other hand, the councillors were made *kurioi* when they contributed to the decree-making, not only by drafting the preliminary proposals, but also by adding their relevant expertise to the enactment of another decision complementing the decree of the assembly.

2.4 *Autokratōr*-Clauses: Delegation of Power to the Council in Fifth-Century Decree-Making

A close analysis of the inscribed decrees within their relevant historical contexts demonstrates that the Athenian decision-making procedures were designed according to the notion of divided power, which provided for an interactive system of political decision-making. The first instance is provided by a decree of 424/3 BCE honouring three Boeotians: Potamodorus from Orchomenos, his son Eurytion, and a third man called Pythilles (*IG* I³ 73).[73] Potamodorus was probably one of the Boeotians mentioned by Thucydides when reporting that a group of exiles from Orchomenos helped the Athenians in the attempt to seize Delion in summer 424 BCE.[74] The decree would attest to the Athenian measures to renew the rewards for their Boeotian supporters after the Delion campaign. The grant of proxeny is again attested in a later honourary decree for Eurytion, which is dated 412/11 BCE (*IG* I³ 97. 1–7). According to this later decree, the grant of proxeny in 424 BCE was not the first, since it is stated that his ancestors were already *proxenoi* of the Athenians (5–8).[75]

[73] Henry (1983) 12.
[74] Thuc. 4.76, 89–102. Cf. Hornblower (1996) 252–3; *pace* M. B. Walbank (1978) n. 40.
[75] M. B. Walbank (1978) 510–18; Mattingly (1961) 129 n. 39 with Thuc. 8.60.1. On Potamodorus and his son as supporters of the democracy within the Boeotian *koinon* see also Simonton (2017) 203.

62 DIVIDED POWER IN ANCIENT GREECE

The decree in *IG* I³ 73 shows interesting patterns regarding benefits granted to the honorands. In addition to renewing the proxeny, the decree leaves open the possibility to bestow new rewards. At lines 5–7, the *stratēgoi* and the *prutaneis* are instructed to bring Potamodorus before the council and the assembly. The benefit is granted in the following clause (12–16), by providing Potamodorus and Eurytion with access to the council and the assembly any time they are in Athens, which de facto makes this a grant of *prosodos*.[76] At line 21, a new decree starts, reporting instructions for the *kōlakretai*, according to which they shall pay 500 drachmas to Potamodorus and his son. Then, at lines 39–40, we read the 'delegation clause', stating that if any further matter needs to be decided at a later stage, the council has full authority to add what is necessary.

The clause allows the council to take a new formal vote concerning the honorand. Here the verb ψηφίζεσθαι is restored, but it seems safe as the verb also occurs in the motion formula of some decrees of the council (e.g. *IG* II² 157: ἐψηφίσθαι τῆι βουλῆι), and has the generic meaning of 'to vote', 'to enact'.[77] It presupposes the enactment of a new decree, providing the needed additions decided by the council.[78] The fragmentary evidence does not allow us to reconstruct what the council actually did to complement the decree honouring Potamodorus. The evidence of this decree offers the chance to explore the terminology of divided power within Athenian deliberative bodies. It is clear that the role of the council was not only limited to drafting the decree, which was then emended in the assembly. The council was empowered to carry out the provision of the decree and add further regulations on behalf of Potamodorus and his son without referring back to the assembly.

This power is implied by the term *autokratōr*. An analysis of the institutional meaning of the term has relevant implications for understanding how delegation and divided power were implemented in decree-making. *Autokratōr* occurs in Athenian inscriptions as a key term meaning 'with authority' or 'with full powers'.[79] This word is usually employed in legal and epigraphical formulas in public documents as well as in literary texts as a synonym for the more common term *kurios*, which refers to particular offices that had the power to make decisions without being subordinate to other constitutional bodies.[80] Despite the importance of the term in Athenian institutional practice, there are only partial studies about the different meanings of *autokratōr* and the institutional implications of such a term. These studies focus especially on the ambassadors with full powers

---

[76] Henry (1983) 311–12.   [77] See Hansen (1991) 253.
[78] Quass (1971) 2–4; Staveley (1972) 93–5; Rhodes (1981) 523, 619; Canevaro (2013a) 145–6; cf. Xen. *Hell.* 1.5.18; *Mem.* 4.4.2; [Arist.] *Ath. Pol.* 43.4, 61.2.
[79] Rhodes (1972) 171, 180 n. 4, 186–8; Rhodes (1981) 402.   [80] Magnetto (2013) 229.

DIVIDED POWER IN ATHENIAN DECREE-MAKING 63

(*presbeis autokratores*).[81] The literary sources are not always consistent in adopting the term. The earliest evidence of the term is in Thucydides, who uses the term fourteen times, mostly in an institutional context (Thuc. 1.126.8, 5.27.2, 5.45.1, 5.46.1, 6.8.2, 6.26.1, 6.67.1–3, 6.72.1). However, three of these instances seem to be general occurrences of the meaning of *autokratōr*. At 4.64.1, Hermocrates calls himself master (*autokratōr*) of his own judgment and fortune (ἡγεῖσθαι τῆς τε οἰκείας γνώμης ὁμοίως αὐτοκράτωρ εἶναι καὶ ἧς οὐκ ἄρχω τύχης). Again, in Book 4, Thucydides affirms that men reject what they do not accept with arbitrary reasoning (λογισμῷ αὐτοκράτορι).[82] In spite of the Thucydidean non-institutional instances, which also recur in some other Classical sources, literary attestations indicate that *autokratōr* especially occurs in institutional contexts during the Classical period.[83] This usage occurs with reference to military magistrates, ambassadors, or to the Athenian council.

This latter use occurs frequently both in literary and epigraphical evidence. An analysis of the behaviour of the term in different institutional contexts provides a good term of comparison for understanding the power of the council *autokratōr*. Thucydides states that the Argives appointed a few men with plenipotentiary powers (ἀποδεῖξαι δὲ ἄνδρας ὀλίγους ἀρχὴν αὐτοκράτορας) to negotiate an alliance with any Greek city, except Sparta and Athens (Thuc. 5.27).[84] A similar meaning is found again later in the same book (Thuc. 5.45), when the Spartan ambassadors address the Athenian council and announce that they have come having full powers (ἐν τῇ βουλῇ αὐτοκράτορες ἥκειν).[85] However, Alcibiades asks them not to refer to their full-power mandate before the Athenian assembly, fearing the reaction of the Athenians. Magnetto rightly points out that, in this section, the title of *autokratōr* implies that the Spartan ambassadors enjoyed a higher level of delegated power than the common *presbeis* which the Athenians could easily recognize.[86] Xenophon provides a further piece of evidence (Xen. *Hell.* 2.2.19). He states that in 404 BCE the Athenians sent Theramenes and other men as *autokratores* ambassadors to Sparta to negotiate the peace. The Athenian envoys had 'full powers to treat for peace' (αὐτοκράτορες περὶ εἰρήνης). The Spartan ephors consented to summon the assembly only after ascertaining the full-power

---

[81] Mosley (1973) 30–8; Missiou-Ladi (1987); Skoczylas Pownall (1995); Harris (2000) 487–95; Magnetto (2013) 228–40 with a complete list of literary sources for *presbeis autokratores* (225–6 n. 7).

[82] Thuc. 4.108.4, 4.126.5; cf. Hornblower (1996) 344, 400; Rhodes (1998) 292, 308.

[83] There are sixty-nine occurrences of *autokratōr* in Classical sources, always in a legal or institutional context (one of these occurrences is in Dem. 18.155.11, but see Canevaro [2013b] 296–304) and of a few etymological uses (Ar. *Pax* 359 using language of decrees; Xen. *Mem.* 2.1.21; Pl. *Crat.* 413c F; *Pol.* 274a5, 299c2; *Leg.* 713c7, 875b3; *Epist.* 309b2, 324d1; Lys. 6.13, 451; Dem. 18.235, 50.52).

[84] For the Thucydidean representation of Argives see Hornblower (2006).

[85] Hornblower (2009) 252.

[86] Magnetto (2013) 229. For the use of public documents and technical words in Thucydides see Gomme (1962) 30–9; Canfora (1990) 195–216; Bearzot (2003) 267–311; Rhodes (2007) 58–60; for Thucydides' use of inscriptions see also Smarczyk (2006).

64   DIVIDED POWER IN ANCIENT GREECE

mandate of the Athenian embassy. This indicates that Theramenes had the actual power to negotiate peace with Sparta, but in this case a later ratification of the assembly was eventually needed.[87] *Presbeis autokratores* also appears in two Aristophanic plays, where the ambassadors seem to have wide negotiating power.[88] In Aristophanes' *Lysistrata*, the Athenian *proboulos* mentions ambassadors with full powers, demanding that the Spartans and the Athenian council send them to the women (Ar. *Lys.* 1009–12). In the *Birds*, envoys of the gods are sent to Cloudcuckooland, where Poseidon states that they came with full powers (Ar. *Av.* 1595). Again, Thucydides, reporting the vote on the Sicilian expedition, affirms that the Athenians appointed Alcibiades, Nicias, and Lysimachus as generals with full powers ($στρατηγοὺς αὐτοκράτορας$).[89] Literary sources do use *autokratōr* mainly as an institutional term. Although the range of powers is uneven and not defined by the term itself, the word indicates a substantial and extraordinary exercise of power by those officials who were appointed *autokratores*.[90]

A close examination of the epigraphic evidence supports this view and shows that *autokratōr* appears especially in fifth-century Athenian inscriptions and less frequently in fourth-century decrees. Such a title is not attested in inscriptions outside Attica before the last decade of the fourth century. The term *autokratōr* becomes more widespread across the rest of the Greek world only in Hellenistic inscriptions.[91] While in literary sources *autokratōr* mostly occurs with reference to ambassadors and officials, in Athenian inscriptions the word is mostly used in delegation clauses to the council, occurring in patterns similar to the Potamodorus decree.[92]

Andocides on the other hand offers different and unquestionable evidence of the institutional meaning of *autokratōr* when it is used with reference to the council. Andocides states that during the investigation following the profanation

---

[87] Cf. Lys. 13.9. Lysias uses the same definition ($περὶ τῆς εἰρήνης πρεσβευτὴν αὐτοκράτορα$). Cf. Missiou-Ladi (1987); Todd (2000) 141 n. 6. Cf. Andoc. 3.33–4, 40–1.

[88] Cf. Harris (2000) 488–90.

[89] Thuc. 6.8; cf. 6.26, 6.72, 8.67. The author of the Aristotelian *Ath. Pol.* says that the Four Hundred elected ten generals with full powers who had to consult the council. Rhodes (1981) 402 comments that 'how far and in what respects they were to be free tends not to be specified'.

[90] Magnetto (2013) 232–40 *pace* Mosley (1973) 36; Skoczylas Pownall (1995) 145–6; Hamel (1998) 202.

[91] The epigraphic evidence of the term outside Athens is quite poor, if compared with the literary evidence (cf. n. 55). See the letter of Antigonos to Skepsis in 311 BCE (Welles *RC* 1); *IvP* I 5 (*Isopoliteia* between Pergamon and Temnos, early third century); *IG* XI 4 1063 (Delos, 300–250 BCE); *IG* XII 5 444 (*Marmor Parium*, 263 BCE); *SEG* 33.637 (Rhodes, 200 BCE); *Miletos* 61 (*sympoliteia* between Miletus and Pisada 183–164 BCE); *IscM* 1 64 (Apollonia, second century BCE); *IG* Bulg. I² 388 (Apollonia, 200–150 BCE). For the use of Athenian epigraphic habit outside Attica see D. M. Lewis (1997) 51–9; Rhodes with Lewis (1997) 551–7.

[92] *IG* I³ 46. 12–3 (Brea decree, 440–434 BCE; cf. OR 142); *IG* I³ 52.9 (financial decree of Callias, 434/3 BCE); *IG* I³ 21.85 (Milesian decree, 426 BCE; cf. Papazarkadas (2009) 71–2); *IG* I³ 136.24 (decree of Bendis, 413/12 BCE); *IG* II² 28.15–17 (decree for Klazomenai 387/6 BCE); *IG* II² 44.22–3 (Alliance between Athens and Chalcis, 378 BCE).

DIVIDED POWER IN ATHENIAN DECREE-MAKING 65

of the Herms in 415 BCE, Teucrus, a metic, asked for immunity (*adeia*), so that he could come back from Megara to Athens to be a witness in the trial (Andoc. 1.15). The council, which had already been made *autokratōr* (ψηφισαμένης δὲ τῆς βουλῆς, ἦν γὰρ αὐτοκράτωρ), granted him the immunity (ἄδειαν εὑρόμενος).[93] This passage sheds light on the legal meaning of *autokratōr* in its institutional context. The key for understanding the range of powers delegated to the council is the grant of *adeia*. *Adeia* was normally enacted through a secret ballot with a quorum of 6,000 votes in the assembly. Andocides does not detail how the Athenian council voted the *adeia*, but certainly the common procedure was completely overridden. The Greek is very clear, through the use of γάρ, in showing the grammatical and logical connection between the *autokratōr* status of the council and the grant of *adeia*, which was voted because of the plenipotentiary power of the council.[94] A previous meeting of the assembly had enacted a decree giving full authority to the council, probably following the same patterns of the clause within the decree honouring Potamodorus.[95] This passage shows that the term *autokratōr* can imply a very high level of delegation of authority, since *adeia* was a prerogative of the assembly.[96] A comparison between the use of the technical label in literary sources and in Athenian inscriptions confirms that those institutional actors who were made *autokratores* were empowered to take independent and final decisions.

A similar kind of clause is restored in another fifth-century decree regulating the new cult of the Thracian goddess Bendis (*IG* I³ 136).[97] The text of the inscription is badly preserved, but at line 37 it is possible to read the clause stating that the council is made *autokratōr*. The rest of the line is not preserved, but it seems plausible—following the restoration—that the assembly gave the council the power to fill possible gaps in the decree, much in the same way as in the decree honouring Potamodorus.[98]

To figure out the substance of the delegation clause in this decree, I shall contextualize the introduction of the cult of Bendis in late fifth-century Athens. I shall then move to the analysis of the different institutional layers that worked together in regulating this new cult. The earliest Athenian evidence for Bendis is in the comedy *The Thracian Women* by Cratinus, which was performed in the 440s

---

[93] For the granting of *adeia* in the fifth-century decree-making see Chapter 5. For *adeia* and the investigation for the profanation of the Mysteries see Esu (2021a) 168–72.

[94] See Denniston (1996) 58–67.

[95] Rhodes (1972) 186. Cf. the meeting of the assembly at Andoc. 1.12.

[96] MacDowell (1962) 74. MacDowell explains the meaning of *autokratōr* in the context of the investigation for the profanation of the Mysteries as 'having the power to act without reference to higher authority'.

[97] In *IG* I³ 108.56 (410/9) Merritt and Andrewes restored a delegation clause to the council hó τι ἂν δοκεῖ ἀγαθ[ὸν τεῖ βουλεῖ], which has no parallel in the other fifth-century decrees. I follow Rhodes's restoration hó τι ἂν δοκεῖ ἀγαθ[ὸν hô δέονται] in order to have an ἄλλο ἀγαθόν clause; cf. n. 46 above.

[98] Cf. Rhodes (1972) 82 n. 2.

66   DIVIDED POWER IN ANCIENT GREECE

(Cratin. fr. 85 [*KA*]). Xenophon says that in 404 BCE there was a shrine of Bendis (*Bendideion*), located at Piraeus (Xen. *Hell.* 2.4.10). The most famous and vivid account of the cult of Bendis in Athens is given in the introduction of Plato's *Republic*. Plato's account of *Bendidea* is supposed to be set around 411–410 BCE. It begins with the description of two distinct processions, one led by Thracians and one by Athenians, which were followed by a torch-horse race and a *pannuchis*, an all-night ceremony (Pl. *Resp.* 327a).[99]

In the dialogue, Socrates affirms that this was the inaugural celebration of Bendis. The cult of the Thracian goddess was in fact formalized in Athens by 429/8 BCE, since her treasury is mentioned in the accounts of the treasurers of the Other Gods of that year.[100] However, there is no consensus on the date of the regulations inserted in *IG* I³ 136, which is variously dated between 430/29 BCE and 413 BCE in light of Plato's account.[101] The decree is too fragmentary to figure out if it refers to the first introduction of the cult or to subsequent regulations, but some elements, such as the mention of *kōlakretai* and the *pannuchis* (l. 13), whose mention is also found in Plato, point to the later date.

Regardless the uncertainty about the date, the decree shows the political involvement of the state's institutions in the organization of a foreign cult, which would play an important role in Athenian civic religion. It is important to first identify the exact role of the *polis* institutions and regulations in the administration of the festival in the fifth century. I shall review the most recent scholarship on the role of the civic institution and private association in managing the cult of Bendis, before discussing the delegation of power to the Athenian council.

The cult is reasonably well documented for the fourth and the third centuries through a set of decrees of private associations, which also make it possible to draw some parallels with the fifth-century institutional scenario. Ismard suggests that the mention of Bendis in the records of the treasurers of the Other Gods does not imply an exclusive state administration of the cult; he conceives of an interplay between the political institutions and two distinct associations of Thracian *orgeōnes*. The two associations of *orgeōnes* were based during the late fourth century respectively in the *astu* and at the Piraeus and enjoyed rights of *enktēsis* and *hidrusis* as attested by a third-century decree (*IG* II² 1283).[102] As a result,

---

[99] For the torch-race (λαμπαδεδρομία) in Athenian religion see Simms (1988) 59–66; Parker (1997) 170–5, (2005) 74, 170, 463; Jones (1999) 256–62.

[100] *IG* I³ 383. 143 (καὶ Βε[νδῖδος]); cf. Linders (1975) 15.

[101] 430/29: Ferguson (1944) 96–107; Simms (1988) 62; Versnel (1990) 111–12; Garland (1992) 112–13; Planeaux (2000) (see full bibliography on Bendis, 165 n. 2); Sears (2013) 152. For 413 as date of the decree: Pečírka (1966) 129–30; Develin (1989) 156; Parker (1997) 172; Sakurai (2014) 203–11; Arnaoutoglou (2015).

[102] Ismard (2010) 269–70. See also *IG* II² 1255 with Kloppenborg and Ascough (2011) 125–32. For other grants to foreign communities to build a sanctuary in Attica see *IG* II³ 1 337 with commentary by Brun (2005) 260–1; cf. also Simms (1988) 68; Planeaux (2000) 183–6; Ismard (2010) 270.

DIVIDED POWER IN ATHENIAN DECREE-MAKING   67

Ismard argues that the Thracian *orgeōnes* were already in charge of the main administration of the cult in the fifth century.

Ismard's depiction of the introduction of Bendis rightly goes beyond previous evolutionary reconstruction of an ancient state cult and offers an interesting picture of an interaction between political institutions and private associations.[103] Accordingly, Ismard draws particular attention to this aspect of *IG* I³ 136 and connects the mention of the *kōlakretai* (36, 39) with the financial measures concerning the cult. Although a direct involvement of the *kōlakretai* in the funding of a religious cult was not impossible, in this case the *kōlakretai* are not dealing with the financial administration of the cult of Bendis.[104] As Arnaoutoglou points out, the financial magistrates are only instructed to pay for the publication of decrees as was standard practice in the fifth century.[105]

Arnaoutoglou has convincingly shown that *IG* I³ 136 deals with a second regulation of the cult in 413 BCE. By this date, Bendis had already been integrated into the Athenian pantheon and included in the treasury of the Other Gods.[106] Building on Lambert's work on the Athenian *genē* and the *orgeōnes*, Arnaoutoglou shows that once Bendis was integrated in the Athenian pantheon, her cult was run by the Athenian *polis* institutions, while the Thracians were involved in the performance of typical Thracian elements of the cult such as the torch horseback procession.[107] The role of the association of *orgeōnes* is therefore most likely associated with ethnic requirements of the cult which had to be performed by Thracians. The civic institutions, on the other hand, seem to oversee the actual administration of the cult. This is highlighted by the decree's amendment mentioning the celebration of public sacrifices (32), which consisted—at least during the fourth century—of a hecatomb. A fourth-century decree of the *orgeōnes* of Bendis confirms that public sacrifices were held during the *Bendidea*.[108] The massive size of the sacrifice is shown by epigraphic records which claim profits of 457 drachmas earned from the sale of animal skins sacrificed during the festival, earnings which were eventually handed over to the public treasury.[109]

---

[103] De Polignac (2012). De Polignac also proposes a similar trend for the integration of the cult of Asclepius in Athens, which had an inconsistent development.

[104] Cf. *IG* I³ 7, 7–9 the decree for the Praxiergidai; cf. Rhodes (2009) 7–9; *contra* Henry (1989) 250. On the possible date of the decree see Mattingly (1996) 398 n. 35. On the relationship between traditional religious norms and *polis* regulations see Harris (2015b).

[105] Henry (1989) 248–50; for Athenian finances during the Peloponnesian War see Rhodes (2013) 210–16.

[106] Arnaoutoglou (2015) 35–8.   [107] Arnaoutoglou (2015) 40–1; Lambert (2010) 161–3.

[108] *IG* II² 1361. The inscription does not mention Bendis. However, it is stated that the sanctuary shall give two drachmas to the *hieropoioi* before the sixteenth day of *Thargelion* during which the *Bendidea* took place. Cf. Planeaux (2000) 176.

[109] *IG* II² 1496. 86 (*dermatikon*). Cf. Rosivach (1994) 62–3. During the fourth century, the City Dionysia and the *Olympieia* earned respectively 856 and 671 drachmas from the animal skin sale; see also Lambert (2012) 69–71.

68   DIVIDED POWER IN ANCIENT GREECE

It is now possible to draw some conclusions about the possible role played by the city and, in particular, by the council *autokratōr*. Both the literary and the epigraphical evidence concerning the cult of Bendis show a complex involvement of civic institutions and private associations working together for the setting up and the managing of the cult. It seems that the cult may have had an elaborate and expensive structure since the fifth century, which was, at some point, supported financially and logistically by the Athenian state. In this inter-institutional context, the delegation clause played the role of connecting the bodies of government in enacting, implementing, and improving the decree. Rhodes has pointed out that religious and financial matters were part of the council's normal duties, noting that delegation in these matters is unclear or probably subsidiary.[110] Such a strictly functionalist approach provides a very limited view. It does not make sense that the Athenians delegated subsidiary power to the council on matters, such as the supervision of cults and temples, which were anyway normally supervised by the council in its advisory role.[111] Even though a delegation of authority to the council on religious and financial matters is not a surprise, it is nevertheless significant that the Athenians decided to give full authority to the council in this context. The cult of Bendis was recently introduced in Attica, and it is not unlikely to assume that the Athenians felt that the unmediated input of the council may be necessary. The delegation to the council maximed the *boulē*'s comprehensive outlook on the administrative process. This institutional practice did not only aim to make the decision-making process more practical but also to transfer proper decision-making authority to the relevant institution, which could shape a particular policy with its own expertise. A decree of the council should not to be considered a subsidiary enactment, but the product of an important layer of the Athenian policy-making procedure. In the case of delegation clauses, the council was empowered to enact a deliberative measure, which was not the same as the normal activity of ordinary supervision.[112] The decree of the assembly provided the legal baseline which empowered the council to enact other regulations for the reform of the cult and possibly for the involvement of private associations.[113]

We do not know what further decisions the council took concerning the cult, but we do know that when the council was made *autokratōr*, it was given independent, wide-ranging powers—like the case of the grant of *adeia*—to do whatever may be useful to improve the decree. The transfer of authority does not mean that the council necessarily exercised all the delegated powers, but it is clear that the Athenians did not conceive of their deliberative power as institutionally

---

[110]   Rhodes (1972) 84 n. 3; cf. de Ste. Croix (1963) 114–5; Hansen (1991) 256.

[111]   [Arist.] *Ath. Pol.* 49.3. Hansen endorsed this opinion by saying that, in case of delegated powers, the council 'could only decide on details'; cf. Hansen (1991) 256.

[112]   For the analysis of decree for the sacred *orgas* (*IG* II² 204) see pp. 75–83.

[113]   The *polis* did not create traditional religious norms (*ta patria*) but gave the legal procedures to implement them see Harris (2015c). For the Hellenistic and Imperial regulations see Chaniotis (2009).

DIVIDED POWER IN ATHENIAN DECREE-MAKING 69

indivisible. In their political decision-making, the Athenians used the institutional complexity of the democracy to optimize their deliberations. This happened for different reasons: first, because the council, unlike the assembly, met every day, so that it could implement as well as enact further urgent or less urgent measures.[114] Second, as discussed in §2.3, because of the technical nature of the decree of Bendis concerning financial, administrative, and religious matters, a good level of administrative expertise was necessary, which could be better provided by the councillors.[115] The Athenians were obviously aware that the council was an institution with a distinct institutional personality and distinct features and abilities, and chose to exploit these features and abilities in a particular sphere of deliberative action.

If political deliberation was a single state function controlled by the *dēmos*, this was institutionally divided between the assembly and the council. Divided power does not mean that the council limited the assembly's power, but rather that the relevant powers were shared between the two bodies. Yet, as I will show in later chapters, these institutional practices were not exclusive of the council-assembly interaction. The sophistication of Athenian constitutional law reflects the democratic concern to divide the power of creating norms and provide a legal and democratic control on the political decision-making through the lawcourts.

Athenian democracy had a decision-making process in which the decisions were the joint outcome of horizontal interaction and accountability between the major deliberative institutions. The council did not only play a role during *probouleusis*, but it could complement the decision-making with another decree in which the deliberative expertise of the council was enshrined and then implemented. Even if these two fifth-century cases are limited, the decrees for Potamodorus and for the cult of Bendis show that fifth-century democracy was organized according to the principle of divided power, a notion that combined the rule of law and a sophisticated and multi-layered system of decision-making.

The way Athenian deliberative institutions, like the council, were structured to show the commitment for enacting the normative idea of divided power, which was in turn reinforced it in the political practice. As a result, the collective behaviour and the decisions of the Athenians as political actors were also shaped by the institutionalized idea of divided power both in the fifth and the fourth centuries. Although the Thirty abused of the power of Athenian institutions and used often the council as the main venue to breech the rule of law, this institution did not loose legitimacy after the restoration of the democracy in 403/2 BCE.[116] Several fourth-century Athenian decrees show that the mechanism of delegation of decision-making authority was preserved, according to a logic of

---

[114] [Arist.] *Ath. Pol.* 43.3; cf. Rhodes (1972) 30.   [115] Kallet-Marx (1994) 229–30.
[116] Esu (2021a) 168.

70   DIVIDED POWER IN ANCIENT GREECE

path dependence, even after the abolition of the democracy and the breakdown of their political system under the Thirty.

2.5 *Kurios*-Clauses: Delegation of Power in Fourth-Century Athenian Decrees

The practice of delegating decree-making authority to the council is better documented for the fourth century. After 403/2 BCE, the enactment of decrees of the council and the assembly was framed within a reformed legal order. After the restoration of the democracy, the Athenians formalized the hierarchy between laws (*nomoi*) and decrees (*psēphismata*). According to this distinction, the laws were higher permanent rules dealing with general matters, which always superseded the decrees, temporary regulations for the daily administration of the *polis*.[117] As a result, as Hansen demonstrated in a classic article, during the fourth century, the council and the assembly normally passed only decrees.[118] A separate procedure for legislation (*nomothesia*) was introduced to institutionalize legal change with a comprehensive procedure that gave to the *dēmos*, rather than special lawgivers, the power of legislating.[119] The *nomothesia* became a paramount institution for democratic divided power in Athens. While some very relevant areas of Athenian public life, such as state finances, were regulated by laws of the *nomothetai*, other decisions continued to take the form of *psēphismata*. Even after the introduction of *nomothesia*, interstate treaties, honorific decrees, and several ad hoc regulations and were passed by the council and the assembly through the standard decree-making procedure.[120]

This section will continue exploring the historical relevance for delegation clauses in the Athenian decree-making with a focus on three major decrees of the fourth century which report delegation of deliberative authority to the council. These decrees represent valuable instances of all the major policy areas of Athenian public life that were regulated by decrees: the alliance between Athens and the Thracians, Paeonians and Illyrians; the decree for the sacred *orgas*; and the decree for an expedition to the Adriatic.

It is a decree of alliance dated at 356 BCE that provides the first piece of epigraphical evidence for fourth-century delegation clauses to the council

---

[117] Cf. Andoc. 1.87; Dem. 23.86, 218, 24.18, 59, 116, 188; On the nature of *nomos* cf. Arist. *Pol.* 1292a32–7; *Eth. Nic.* 1137b13–14; [Plat.] *Def.* 415b.

[118] Hansen (1979). Canevaro and I show that the *nomothetai* were in fact the assembly summoned in special session to pass new laws, see Canevaro and Esu (2018) 130–45.

[119] See Introduction §1.3. This distinction was safeguarded by the *graphē paranomōn*. For a full discussion of this procedure within the decree-making see Chapter 6.

[120] Hansen (1979a) 31–2; for making and breaking treaties in Classical Greece see Rhodes (2008). For the ideology and practice of Greek interstate relations see Giovannini (2007); Low (2007), (2018).

DIVIDED POWER IN ATHENIAN DECREE-MAKING 71

(RO 53 = *IG* II² 127).[121] The inscription preserves a decree of the alliance between Athens and three foreign kings: Cetriporis, king of the Thracians; Lyppeus, king of the Paeonians; and Grabus, king of the Illyrians. The decree of alliance is to be analysed within the historical context of the Social War and the rise of Philip II. In 358 BCE, Philip had defeated the Illyrians and the Paeonians in battle, after the defeat of his brother Perdiccas by the Illyrians and their continuous raids in Macedon. In 357 BCE, the Macedonian king took Amphipolis, which the Athenians were previously unable to capture. Philip managed to make an alliance with the Chalcidians, to whom he gave Potidea, after taking it from Athenian control (RO 50). The seizure of Amphipolis caused the beginning of the long conflict between Macedon and Athens, which would end with the Peace of Philocrates.[122]

Athens in fact did not participate in the campaigns because of the demanding financial commitments in the Social War. Diodorus reports that the kings of the Thracians, the Paeonians, and the Illyrians attacked Philip without any mention of Athenian participation.[123] The decree gives a full report of the diplomatic steps taken to establish the alliance and shows the important involvement of the council in Athenian foreign policy.[124] As lines 35–6 of the decree shows, the council was empowered to make further additions to the decree and to play an active role in the decree-making (35–6: [το προσδέηι τόδε τ]ὸ ψή[φ]ισμ[α], τ[ὴ]ν [β]ουλ[ὴν] κυ[ρ]ίαν εἶναι). The delegation clause is closely connected with the council's power of supervision over ambassadors and Athenian foreign policy in general. This practice matches the procedure used immediately after the peace of Philocrates in 346 BCE, as reported in Demosthenes' *On the False Embassy* (Dem. 19.154). Demosthenes states that the assembly empowered the council to send the ambassadors to Philip (τὴν βουλὴν ποιήσαντος τοῦ δήμου κυρίαν), who had to swear the oath before them in order for the treaty to be valid.[125] Harris comments that a delegation of power to the council to supervise an envoy was a routine business in Classical Athens, and similar delegation-procedures were, for instance, also seen when the Areopagus was asked to report to the assembly after an investigation without undermining the principles of the democracy.[126]

---

[121] Two associated fragments of an inscription possibly dated around 365/4 BCE (*IG* II² 216/17) preserve a decree concerning the melting of sacred dedications on the Acropolis according to the decree of Androtion (cf. Dem. 22). The decree shows part of a delegation clause to the council (3–5 B). The enacting body of the decree is uncertain, since the inscription only preserves the last two letters of the enacting formula (line 5 [.................]ῆι τοὺς ταμίας [τὸς νέ]-). D. M. Lewis (1954) 39–49 suggested the restorations ἀγαθῆι τύχηι or δέδοχθαι τῆι βολῆι. Lewis opted for the former restoration, which would make it a non-probouleumatic decree of the assembly. See D. M. Lewis (1954) 39–41; Rhodes (1972) 260. The content of the decree, dealing with religious matters, is also consistent with the typical tasks of the council.

[122] For a full discussion of these events see Harris (1995) 63–100.   [123] Diod. 16.22.3.

[124] On Callisthenes, the proposer of the decree: Fantasia (1987); Rhodes and Osborne (2003) 258–9; and Canevaro (2016c) 255–7.

[125] For oaths in alliances see Sommerstein and Bayliss (2013) 162, 186–92.

[126] Harris (2006) 85–9, (2016a) 78–80.

72 DIVIDED POWER IN ANCIENT GREECE

In his important study of fourth-century Athenian decrees, Lambert has also pointed out that fourth-century delegation clauses in inscribed decrees have a close connection with the respect of the rule of law in the implementations of complex regulations enacted by the assembly.[127] Delegation clauses were one of the several manifestations of divided power of the Athenian democracy. As discussed in the previous section, delegation to the council was already used in the fifth century, showing continuity in Athenian institutional practice and in respect of the rule of law. Abiding by the law constituted the baseline for the Athenian decree-making, but delegation was not only limited to implementing this foundational principle. Delegation clauses introduced a flexible interaction in the decree-making allowing the councillors to improve the decisions of the assembly as well as to strengthen the deliberative nature of Athenian democracy by adding another decision-making layer.

The clause at *IG* II² 127.35–6 is related to the council's task of supervision of foreign policy involving also honours for the Thracian kings Cetriporis, Monounius, and Pinax, who are granted hospitality and dinner in the *prutaneion* (27–34).[128] The *xenia* in the *prutaneion* were one of the common honours bestowed by Athenian diplomacy upon foreigners and civic benefactors who showed *philotimia* towards Athens.[129] The relationship between these kinds of honours and Athenian foreign policy is underscored by the literary sources.[130] Andocides complains that Alcibiades was honoured with *sitēsis* in the *prutaneion*, although he did not bring any advantage to the city [Andoc.] 4.31.[131] In another passage, Demosthenes argues that Leucon, king of Bosphorus, was honoured with Athenian citizenship and *ateleia* because of his efforts in supplying grain to Athens. However, Leucon would have lost this privilege under the provisions of Leptines' statute, which repealed all the *ateleiai*, damaging Athenian reputation as well as its geopolitical interests.[132] Lambert has shown the same close connection between honours and Athenian foreign relations, especially anti-Macedonian policy, from the mid-fourth century to the battle of Chaeronea, providing relevant epigraphical evidence of decrees honouring foreign individuals as well as foreign

---

[127] Lambert (2017) 159–61.

[128] A similar role might be assumed for the fifth-century decree honouring Potamodorus cf. pp. 61–2.

[129] The Athenian, and Greek, euergetical system was underpinned by the notion of *timē* (honour). For the concept of *timē* in Greek culture see Cairns (2011). For some examples in Athenian decrees see *IG* I³ 85, 127; *IG* II² 1, 19, 40, 124, 226. For the language of honour in Classical Athens see Whitehead (1993) 37–55; Veligianni-Terzi (1997); Canevaro (2016c) 77–98. *Sitēsis* at the *prutaneion* could also be permanent. This was one of the *megistai timai*. On this see Gauthier (1985); Kralli (1999) 133–61; Forster (2018) 91–5 contests Gauthier's reconstruction of a comprehensive law of granting *megistai timai*.

[130] Lambert (2011a) 197; for the economy of public honours see Canevaro (2016c) 77–97 and (forthcoming a); Domingo Gygax (2016). For the forensic discourse on honours in *graphai paranomōn* and Athenian diplomacy see Esu (2020).

[131] See also Isae. 5.47.

[132] Dem. 20.29–40. Cf. Canevaro (2016c) 240–64; Canevaro (2018d). Other foreign kings, especially Thracian, were honoured with citizenship; see Mitchell (1997) 134–47.

DIVIDED POWER IN ATHENIAN DECREE-MAKING 73

communities as a whole for diplomatic purposes.[133] Liddel has singled out six different non-Athenian categories of honorands in fourth-century decrees: partisans of the restored democracy, financial benefactors, military supporters (such as Cetriporis), grain-suppliers, Macedonians, and exiles friendly to Athens.[134] This latter category is attested in a fragmentary decree is dated by Lambert between 345 BCE and 320 BCE, honouring Neapolitan exiles in Athens; Loddo has recently studied the decree and has made a convincing case to date the decree to the time of Philip's Thracian campaign against Neapolis in Thrace. This decree also includes a fragmentary delegation formula to the council about the management of the hospitality of the refugees in Athens.[135] In the decree, one can read that the exiles are to be looked after and protected by the *stratēgoi* and the council (5–6), which is also empowered to vote whatever seems the best (7–9: ἐὰν δέ του προσδέηι τόδ]ε τὸ ψήφισμα, τὴν β[ουλὴν κυρίαν εἶναι ψηφίζ]εσθαι ὅτι ἂν α]ὑτῆι δοκῆι ἄριστ[ον εἶναι·).[136] The decree also specifies that the provisions made by the council shall be applied to the exiles until they return to their fatherland (9–10: ταῦτα δὲ εἶναι α| ὑτοῖς ἕως ἂν τὴ]ν πατρίδα κομίσω[νται).[137] This is important because it shows that the relevance of the decrees of the Council. The delegated power allowed the Council to enact additional and substantial norms that were immediately applicable on the Neapolitan community of refugees living in Athens. The additional decisions by the council were valid as long as the refugees remained in Athens, making the council the main decision-making institution for the Neapolitan community during their time in Attica.[138]

The inscription shows a clear connection between the delegation clause and the foreign policy. The delegation to the council would aim for better management of the institutionalized duties of hospitality that were key tool of Athenian diplomacy and underpinned the Greek interstate relations. This confirms that along with the ordinary supervision of diplomacy, the council was also a deliberative forum, where the implementation of the assembly's orders was intertwined with another level of deliberation in the council, which crucially contributed to shaping Athenian policies by passing its own decrees.

The decree of alliance between Athens and the three kings and the decree for the Neapolitans are also important pieces of evidence for the epigraphical pattern

---

[133] Lambert (2012) 378–85. Cf. e.g. *IG* II³ 1 303, 1 304, 1 309, 1 313. The number of honorary decrees for individuals significantly increased after the 340s. See Henry (1996); Lambert (2011a) 177–8.

[134] Liddel (2016).

[135] *IG* II³ 1 404. For an epigraphical analysis of the inscription, see Lambert (2012) 211–12. The inscription does not preserve the name of the exiles. Wilhelm restores τ[ῶν Νεο]πολιτῶν. Loddo (2020b) confirms Wilhem's suggestion with additional arguments. For decrees honouring foreigners in Classical Athens see Lambert (2011a) 178–9, (2011b), (2012) 383–5; Liddel (2016) and (2020b).

[136] For this formula cf. the decree for the sacred *orgas* pp. 75–83.

[137] We should also keep in mind that most fourth-century decrees of the council dealt with honours; cf. *IG* II² 17 which shows the *sitēsis* granted by the council to a Thasian citizen. See Rhodes (1972) table G.

[138] Loddo (2020b) 219–20.

74 DIVIDED POWER IN ANCIENT GREECE

of delegation formulas (*kurios*-clauses) in fourth-century Athenian decrees.[139] The formula is easily comparable with the clauses found in three further inscriptions of the second half of the fourth century, in which the term *kurios* assumes the same meaning that *autokratōr* had in fifth-century evidence. It indicates full authority exercised by individuals or institutions in a specific domain.[140]

The two terms also occur together in a clause of the Athenian amnesty agreement of 403 BCE described in the Aristotelian *Athenaion Politeia*. The text of the amnesty states that those Athenians who want to move to Eleusis shall have full rights (*epitimoi*), full legal status (*kurioi*), and full power (*autokratores*) over themselves and their property ([Arist.] *Ath. Pol.* 39.1).[141] As this juxtaposition of the two terms shows, one should not overestimate the terminological differences between the two words, which were perceived as broadly synonymic by both the literary and epigraphical sources.[142] In [Arist.] *Ath. Pol.* 39.1 the two words reinforce the meaning of *epitimoi* (those who enjoy full rights) and refer to the former supporters of the Thirty. *Epitimos* is normally used to indicate the absence of *atimia* (as legal penalty) and indicates a restoration and preservation of rights. In this context, the author of the Aristotelian *Athenaion Politieia* use *kurios* and *autokratōr* synonymically to underline and reinforce the concept implied by the word *epitimoi*. The former supporters of the Thirty were to preserve the typical rights attached to their status of Athenian citizens that is that of right to hold land and all the legal rights protected under Athenian law.

Kurios and its denominal verb κύρόω were also used to affirm the concept of legal validity and autonomous power in a broad typology of juridical texts.[143] It is, for instance, part of the typical formulas in decrees and laws, in which the legal validity of certain clauses is explicitly stated. In the decree honouring the Samians (405/4 BCE) it is reported that the assembly had to vote on the validity of the previous enactments (κύρια|[ἐ ναι τὰ ἐψηφισ]μένα) about the Samians (*IG* II² 1.52–3).[144] A law cited in Demosthenes' *Against Aristocrates* (23.87) states that no decree should override a law (ψήφισμα δὲ μηδὲν μήτε βουλῆς μήτε δήμου νόμου κυριώτερον εἶναι).[145] In *Against Ctesiphon*, Aeschines says that it is not possible to

---

[139] For the bureaucratic standardization of Athenian public documents, cf. Henry (1977); Rhodes (1980) 308–9; Rhodes with Lewis (1997) 18; Rhodes and Osborne (2003) 19–20.

[140] Cf. *IG* II³ 1 292; *IG* II³ 1 404; *IG* II³ 1 370 cf. Miller (1997) 149–50; (2007) 106–7. For a fourth-century non-Athenian example, see B. D. Gray (2013) 370–401.

[141] On this amnesty see n. 345 in Chapter 3 with the relevant bibliography.

[142] Cammack (2022b) 477 sees a difference in conceptual meaning between *autokratōr* and *kurios* with the former applied only to delegated powers, but both terms were used in a number of institutional and non-institutional contexts to refer to 'full authority'. On this clause of the amnesty see Joyce (2022). On *epitimia* in Athenian law and legal discourse see Rocchi (2023a) 316; Canevaro and Rocchi (forthcoming).

[143] For ἄκυρος, which expresses invalidity in private and public documents, see Dimopoulou (2014) 249–76.

[144] Cf. *IG* I³ 68.43–4.

[145] Canevaro (2013b) 75. Cf. also Dem. 24.30 and Andoc. 1.87 with Canevaro and Harris (2012) 116–17.

DIVIDED POWER IN ATHENIAN DECREE-MAKING 75

call *politeia* a constitution in which invalid laws stand written among the valid statutes (ἀκύρους νόμους ἐν τοῖς κυρίοις ἀναγεγράφθαι) (Aeschin. 3.37). The same language is to be found in decrees of the demes and private associations, which resembled those of assembly.[146] The term *kurios* is also applied to private legal acts, such as contracts, leases, sales, transactions, wills, and private arbitrations (Dem. 36.34; [Dem.] 45.7).[147]

The *kurios* clauses show continuity in the delegation of decision-making authority, as a feature of divided power, throughout the Classical period. By using the term *kurios*, the clause in the decree gave legal authority to acts of the institution receiving the delegated power. This enabled the council to contribute independently to the decisions, instead of simply carrying out the assembly's decisions. It also singles out the council as a deliberative institution vis-à-vis other boards of magistrates and the council of Areopagus.

The complex decree about the sacred *orgas* (*IG* II³ 1 292 = *I.Eleusis* 144) offers one of the most valuable insights in the working of the delegation mechanism in fourth-century decree-making. In 352/1 BCE the Athenians passed a decree concerning the boundary-markers of the land sacred to Demeter and Persephone (sacred *orgas*) on the border between Attica and Megara.[148]

The decree was passed only a few years later than the alliance with the three kings against Philip II, and immediately after the Athenian defeat in the Social War. Because of the dramatic state of their finances after the war, the Athenians introduced a series of relevant financial measures to manage their revenues and expenditures in a more efficient fashion. In *Ways and Means* (3.1–7), for example, Xenophon encourages the leasing of sacred lands and temples, which interestingly matches the content of the decree in *IG* II² 204, enacted only two years later. This is also consistent with the several instances of sacred and public land leases in the second half of the fourth century.[149] A contemporary decree of the *trittys* of Epakreis shows that public real estate was leased out, possibly for religious purposes (*IG* II² 2490). The deme of Teithras enacted two decrees for leasing out the public land of the deme to private citizens, specifying that the tenants had to pay the *eisphora* on the rented land (*SEG* 24.51, 52).

The decree for the boundaries of the sacred *orgas*, thus, seems to be part of this general trend, in which sacred and public land was rented out to fund public

---

[146] Cf. *IG* II² 1275 (obligation for the members of a *thiasos*, 325–327 BCE).

[147] For a comprehensive analysis of Demosthenic speeches for and against Apollodorus see MacDowell (2009) 100–25.

[148] *IG* II³ 1 292 = *I.Eleusis* 144. For the meaning of ὀργάς as uncultivated woodland cf. Phot. s.v. ὀργάς; Harpocrat. s.v. ὀργάς; *Lex. Sud.* s.v. ὀργάς; *Etym. Magn.* s.v. ὀργάδα γῆν. See also Daverio Rocchi (1987) 97–109; Bowden (2005) 88–108. For fifth-century mentions of the *orgas* see Thuc. 1.139. On the fourth-century Attic border see Ober (1985).

[149] Xen. 4.19, 6.1–2; see Papazarkadas (2011) 248. Cf. also Faraguna (1992) 289–396; Whitehead (2019). For fourth-century leases of sacred lands cf. [Arist.] *Ath. Pol.* 47.4–5; see Papazarkadas (2011) 51–75.

76 DIVIDED POWER IN ANCIENT GREECE

expenditure. Papazarkadas suggests that the reassessment of the boundaries had the purpose of earning resources, which would have been used for the building programme in Eleusis planned by the board of *epistatai* of the Eleusinian cult of 356/2 BCE.[150]

This decree is a key source for Athenian political and economic history in the aftermath of the Social War and records the working of the different institutions of the divided power. Among several boards of magistrates cited in the decree, the council plays a central and different role through the delegation clause. As I have discussed in §2.3, Classical Athens did not have professional bureaucrats and ad hoc implementative structures, yet public officials performed the fundamental task of carrying out the decisions. Magistrates (*archai* or *timai*) were usually selected by lot and organized in boards. This activity of magistrates was separated from the realm of political decision-making.[151] The Athenian *archai* were not normally empowered to make meaningful political decisions and instead were in charge of carrying out the regulations of the relevant laws and decrees.

Similarly to the other *archai*, the Athenian council was often instructed to implement the provisions of laws and decrees. However, the powers of the council were not limited to simple implementation of the decree's instruction. The role of the Athenian council vis-à-vis the other boards of magistrates in the implementation of the decree of the sacred *orgas* introduced a new nuance in the practice of divided power. It shows how the implementation of a decree of the assembly could also include the extra-level of deliberation in the council involving speeches, consensus-building, and the vote on another decree. This was an activity related to the implementation carried out by the other magistrates mentioned in the decree, yet different and more substantial. Since the decree mentions several officials and legal procedures, a detailed discussion of the decree's content sheds new light on the role played by the delegation clauses in institutional practice. I reproduce below the text of the decree and an English translation.

$$\text{— —} \underline{I}$$

$$\text{— } \Pi E\Pi\text{-}$$

$$\text{— } \text{—οντες } \pi\text{—}$$

$$\text{— — — — — — — . — — — — — — — — — — — — — — — — — — — . } \epsilon\omega\nu \ \tau\hat{\omega}\nu \ \kappa\alpha\text{—}$$

5 [............23..........ἑλέσθαι τὸν δῆμ]ον δέκα ἄνδρα-

[ς ἐξ Ἀθηναίων ἁπάντων αὐτίκα μάλα, πέντε δὲ] ἐκ τῆς βουλῆς· ⌄

[τοὺς δὲ αἱρεθέντας........ ἐν τῶι Ἐλευσ]ινίωι τῶι ἐν ἄστ-

---

[150] Papazarkadas (2011) 256–7. Cf. also *IG* II² 1666.
[151] See Introduction §1.2 for the traditional distinction of the *politeia* in deliberative power, magistrates, and judicial power.

DIVIDED POWER IN ATHENIAN DECREE-MAKING 77

[εɩ .... 29 ....] τῆς ἱερᾶς ὀργάδος ὀ-

[............ 27 ....] μήτε χάριτος ἔνεκα μήτ' ἔ-

10 [χθρας ... 14 ....ὡς δɩ]καιότατα καὶ εὐσεβέστατα· τὰ-

[............ 19 ......ἀ]πὸ τῆς ἕκτης ἐπὶ δέκα τοῦ Ποσιδεῶ-

[νος ....16 ......] ἐπὶ Ἀριστοδήμου ἄρχοντος· παρεῖν-

[αι δὲ καὶ τὸν βασιλέ]α καὶ τὸν ἱεροφάντην καὶ τὸν δαιδοῦχο-

[ν καὶ Κήρυκας καὶ] Εὐμολπίδας καὶ τῶν ἄλλων Ἀθηναίων τὸν β-

15 [ουλόμενον, ὅπως] ἂν [ὡ]ς εὐσεβέστατα καὶ δικαιότατα τοὺς ὅρ-

[ους θῶσιν. ἐπɩ]μελεῖσθαι [δ]ὲ τῆς ἱερᾶς ὀργάδος καὶ τῶν ἄλλω-

[ν ἱερῶν τεμε]ῶν τῶν Ἀθήνησιν ἀπὸ τῆσδε τῆς ἡμέρας εἰς τὸν

[ἀεὶ χρόνον οὕ]ς τε ὁ νόμος κελεύει περὶ ἑκάστου αὐτῶν καὶ τ-

[ὴν βουλὴν τὴν] ἐ[ξ] Ἀρείου πάγου καὶ τὸν στρατηγὸν τὸν ἐπὶ τὴ-

20 [ν φυλ]ακὴ[ν τῆς χ]ώρας κεχειροτονημένον καὶ τοὺς περιπολά-

[ρχ]ους καὶ τοὺς [δη]μάρχους καὶ τὴν βουλὴν τὴν ἀεὶ βουλεύου-

[σαν] καὶ τῶν ἄλλ[ων Ἀθ]ηναίων τὸμ βουλόμενον τρόπωι ὅτωι ἂν

[ἐπ]ίστω[ν]ται. γρά[ψαι δὲ τὸ]ν γραμματέα τῆς βουλῆς εἰς δύο κα-

[ττ]ιτέρω ἴσω καὶ [ὁμοίω, εἰς μὲν] τὸν ἕτερον· εἰ λῶιον καὶ ἄμει-

25 [νό]ν ἐστι τῶι δήμ[ωι τῶι Ἀθηναίων μισ]θοῦν τὸμ βασιλέα τὰ νῦ-

[ν ἐ]νειργασμ[έ]να [τῆς ἱερᾶς ὀργάδος τὰ ἐκ]τὸς τῶν ὅρων εἰς οἰ-

[κ]οδμίαν τοῦ προ[στώιου καὶ ἐπισκευὴν το]ῦ ἱεροῦ τοῖν θεο-

ῖν· εἰς δὲ τὸν ἕτερον κ[α]ττίτ[ερον· εἰ λῶιον καὶ ἄμει]όν ἐστι

τῶι δήμωι τῶι Ἀθηναίων τὰ ν[ῦν ἐκτὸς τῶ]ν ὅ[ρων ἐ]νειργ[α]σμέν-

30 α τῆς ἱερᾶς ὀργάδος ἐᾶν ἄνετα [τοῖν θ]εοῖν· ἐπειδὰν δὲ ὁ γραμ-

ματεὺς γράψηι, λαβὼν ὁ ἐ[π]ιστάτης ὁ ἐκ τῶν προέδρων συνειλ-

ιξάτω [τ]ὸν καττί[τε]ρον· ἑ[κάτ]ερον καὶ κατειλίξας ἐρίοις εἰ-

ς ὑδρ[ί]αν [ἐμ]β[α]λ[έ]τω [χαλ]κῆν ἐναντίον τοῦ δήμου· παρασκευασ-

άντων [δ]ὲ τ[α]ῦ[τ]α οἱ π[ρ]υτάνεις, οἱ δὲ ταμίαι τῆς θεοῦ κατενεν-

35 [κόν]των ὑ[δ]ρία[ς] χ[ρ]υ[σ]ῆν καὶ ἀργυρᾶν αὐτ[ί]κα μάλ[α] εἰς τὸν δήμ-

ον, ὁ δ' ἐπ[ɩ]σ[τ]ά[τη]ς [διασ]είσας τ[ὴ]ν ὑδρίαν τὴν χαλκῆν ἑλκέτω τ-

ὸν καττ[ί]τ[ε]ρον ἑκάτερον ἐμ μέρει· καὶ τὸμ μὲμ πρότερον εἰς

τὴν [ὑδ]ρ[ίαν τὴν] χρυσῆν ἐμβαλέτω, τὸν δὲ ὕστερον εἰς τὴν ἀργ-

υρᾶν καὶ [κα]τα[δ]ησά[τ]ω, ὁ δὲ ἐπιστάτης τ[ῶ]μ πρυτάνεων κατασῃ-

40 μη[νά]σθω τ[ῆ]ι [δημ]οσίαι σφραγῖδι, παρασημηνάσθω δὲ καὶ τῶν

[ἄ]λλ[ω]ν [Ἀ]θ[ηναί]ω[ν] ὁ βουλ]όμενος· ἐπει[δ]ὰν δὲ κατασημανθῶσιν,

78 DIVIDED POWER IN ANCIENT GREECE

ἀνεν[εγ]κ[ό]ντω[ν] οἱ [ταμ]ίαι τὰς ὑδ[ρ]ίας εἰς ἀκρόπολιν· ἑλέσθω

δὲ ὁ δ[ῆμ]ος [τρ]εῖς ἄνδρας ἕν[α] μ[ὲ]ν ἐκ τῆς βουλῆς, δύο δὲ ἐξ Ἀθην-

αίω[ν ἁ]πάντων, οἵτ[ιν]ες εἰ[ς Δ]ελφοὺς ἀφικόμενοι τὸν θεὸν ἐπ-

45 ερ[ήσ]ο[ν]τ[α]ι [κα]θ' ὁ[π]ότερα τὰ γρ[άμ]ματα ποιῶ[σ]ιν Ἀθηναῖοι περ-

ὶ τῆ[ς ἱ]ερ[ᾶ]ς ὀρ[γάδ]ος ε[ἴ]τ[ε] τ[ὰ] ἐκ τῆς [χ]ρυσῆς ὑδρίας εἴτε τὰ ἐκ

τῆ[ς ἀ]ρ[γ]υρ[ᾶς· ἐπειδ]ὰν [δ]ὲ [ἤκ]ωσιν παρὰ τοῦ θεοῦ, καθελόντωσα-

ν τὰ[ς] ὑδ[ρί]α[ς καὶ] ἀνα[γ]νωσθ[ήτ]ω τῶι δήμωι ἥ τε μαντεία καὶ τὰ

[ἐ]κ τῶ[ν κα]ττ[ι]τέρω[ν] γρ[ά]μματα· καθ' ὁπότερα δ' ἂν τὰ γράμματα ὁ

50 θεὸ[ς] ἀ[ν]έ[ληι] λῶιον [καὶ ἄμειν]ον εἶναι τῶι δήμωι τῶι Ἀθηναί-

ω[ν] κα[τὰ ταῦτα π]οι[εῖν, ὅπ]ω[ς] ἂ[ν] ὡς εὐσεβέστατα ἔχει τὰ πρὸς τ-

ὼ θεὼ [καὶ μηδέποτ' εἰς τὸν λοιπ]ὸ[ν] χρόνον μηδὲν ἀσεβὲς γίγν-

ητ[αι περὶ τῆς ἱερᾶς] ὀ[ργάδος καὶ] περὶ τῶν ἄλλων ἱερῶν τῶν Ἀ-

θ[ήνησιν· νῦν δὲ ἀν]αγράψα[ι] τόδε τὸ ψήφισμα καὶ τὸ πρότερον τὸ

55 Φι[λ]ο[κ]ράτο[υς τὸ περὶ τῶν] ἱ[ερῶν] τὸν γραμματέα τῆς βουλῆς ἐ-

ν στ[ήλαιν λιθίναιν καὶ στῆσαι τὴν] μὲν Ἐλευσῖνι πρὸς τῶι π-

ρο[πύλωι τοῦ ἱεροῦ, τὴν δὲ ἐν τῶι Ἐλε]υσινίωι τῶι ἐν ἄστει· θυ-

[σαι δὲ καὶ ἀρεστήριον] το[ῖν θεοῖν] τὸν ἱ[ε]ροφάντην καὶ τὴν ἱέ-

[ρειαν τῆς Δήμητρος ... 10 ......] Ο [...] τὸν ταμίαν τοῦ δήμου τὸ

60 [........17....... δραχμάς]· δοῦ[ν]αι [δ]ὲ καὶ εἰς τὴν ἀναγρα-

φ[ὴν......15.........δραχμὰς εἰς] ἐκ[α]τέραν ἐκ τῶν κατὰ ψη-

φ[ίσματα ἀναλισκομένων τῶι δή]μωι· [δ]οῦναι δὲ καὶ τῶν αἱρεθ-

έ[ντων εἰς Δελφοὺς ἑκάστωι...] δρ[α]χμὰς εἰς ἐφόδια· δõναι δὲ κα[ὶ]

το[ῖς αἱρεθεῖσιν ἐπὶ τὴν ἱερ]ὰν ὀργάδα : Γ : δραχμὰς : ἑκάστ-

65 [ωι ἐκ τῶν εἰς τὰ κατὰ ψηφίσμα]τα ἀναλισκομένων τῶι δήμωι· π-

[αρασχεῖν δὲ ὅρους λιθίνους], ὁπόσων ἂν προσδέηι, τοὺς πωλη-

[τὰς......17..........] βουλῆ[ς μ]ίσθωμα, τούς τε προέδρος

[............22.........] συγγράψαι καθότι ἐξεργασθήσ-

[ονται......17.......... ἐπι]σταθήσονται τῆς ἱερᾶς ὀργ-

70 [άδος......16..........]σιν οἱ αἱρεθέντες· τὸ δὲ ἀργύριον

[.........20..........]ΣΟ[..]λίθ[ο]ις τοὺς ὅρους δοῦναι τὸ-

[ν ταμίαν τοῦ δήμου ἐκ] τῶν κατὰ ψηφί[σ]ματα ἀναλισκομένων [τ]-

[ῶι δήμωι]. vacat

[οἵδε ἡιρέθησαν ἐπὶ τὴν ἱερὰν] ὀργά[δ]α ἀντὶ τῶν ἐκπεπτωκό[τ]-

75 [ων νέους ὅρους θεῖναι : ἐκ τῆς β]ο[υλῆ]ς : Ἀρκεφῶν : Ἁλαιεύς.

DIVIDED POWER IN ATHENIAN DECREE-MAKING 79

[. . . . . 29 . . . .]ης : Θριάσιος, *vacat*

[. . . . . .25 . . . . :]Ἀγνούσιος· *vacat*

[ἐξ ἰδιωτῶν· : . . . . 16 . . . .]ιος [:] Ἱπποκράτης : ἐκ Κερ[α]-

[μέων, ...9 . . . .]ος : [Χαιρ]ε[φ]ῶ[ν :] ἐκ [Κ]ηδῶν : Ἐμμενίδης : ἐ[κ]-

80 [. . . . . .14 . . . . : Σ]ουν[ιεὺς : Ἀ]ριστείδης : Οἶηθεν *vacat*

[. . . . . .17 . . . .] ιος : Γλαύκων : Περιθοίδης : Φαῖδρος

[. . . .7 . . . : ἐπὶ τὸ μαν]τεῖον εἰς Δελφοὺς : ἐξ ἰδιωτῶν· *vacat*

[. . . . . .16 . . . .] εύς : Εὐδίδακτος : Λαμπτρεύς· *vacat*

[ἐκ τῆς βουλῆς· . . . 6 . . .]ος : Λαμπτρεύς : [τ]ά[δ]ε ἐπαν[ο]ρθοῦται·

85 [ἐὰν δέ το προσδέηι τόδ]ε τὸ ψήφισμα, τὴν βουλὴν κυρίαν εἶνα-

[ι ψηφίζεσθαι ὅτι ἂν αὐτῆι δ]οκῆι ἄριστον εἶναι. *Vacat*

[...] of the [...] the people shall elect straightaway ten men from all the Athenians and five from the council; and those elected shall—in the Eleusinion in the city [...] of the sacred *orgas*. [...] From neither favour nor enmity [...] but as justly and piously as possible [...] from the sixteenth of Posideon [...] in the archonship of Aristodemos; and there shall be present the [king] and the hierophant and the torchbearer and the Kerykes and the Eumolpidai and any other Athenian who wishes, so that they may place the markers as piously and justly as possible; and there shall have oversight of the sacred *orgas* and the other [sacred precincts] at Athens from this day for all time those whom the law requires for each of them and the council of the Areopagos and the general elected for the [protection] of the country and the *peripolarchoi* and the demarchs and the council in office at any time and any other Athenian who wishes, in whatever way they know how; and the secretary of the council shall write on two pieces of tin, equal and alike, on the one, if it is preferable and better for the Athenian people that the king lets out the area [of the sacred *orgas*] which is now being worked [out or in]side the markers for building the portico [and repair] of the sanctuary of the two goddesses; and on the other piece of tin, if it is preferable and better for the Athenian people to leave the area of the sacred *orgas* which is now being worked [out or in]side the markers fallow for the two goddesses; and when the secretary has written, the chairman of the *proedroi* shall take each of the two pieces of tin and roll them up and tie them with wool and put them into a bronze water jug in the presence of the people; and the prytany shall prepare these things; and the treasurers of the goddess shall bring down a gold and a silver water-jug straightaway to the people; and the chairman shall shake the bronze water-jug and take out each piece of tin in turn, and shall put the first piece of tin into the gold water-jug and the second into the silver one and bind them fast; and the prytany chairman shall seal them with the public seal and any other Athenian who wishes shall counterseal them; and when they have

80 DIVIDED POWER IN ANCIENT GREECE

been sealed, the treasurers shall take the water-jugs up to the Acropolis; and the people shall elect three men, one from the council, two from all the other Athenians, to go to Delphi and enquire of the god, according to which of the writings the Athenians are to act concerning the sacred *orgas*, whether those from the gold water-jug or those from the silver one; and when they have come back from the god, they shall break open the water jugs, and the oracle and the writings on the pieces of tin shall be read to the people; and according to whichever of the writings the god ordains it to be preferable and best for the Athenian people, according to those they are to act, so that matters relating to the two goddesses shall be handled as piously as possible and never in future shall anything impious happen concerning the [sacred *orgas*] or the other sacred places at Athens; and the secretary of the council shall [now] inscribe this decree and the previous one of Philokrates [about the sacred places] on two stone stelai and stand one at Eleusis by the [gateway of the sanctuary], the other in the Eleusinion in the city; and the hierophant and the priestess of Demeter shall also sacrifice [a propitiatory sacrifice] to the two goddesses [...] the treasurer of the people [...] drachmas; and give for inscribing [...] drachmas for each of the two from the people's fund for expenditure on decrees; and give for each of those elected to go to Delphi—drachmas for travelling expenses; and give to those elected on the sacred *orgas* five drachmas each from the people's fund for expenditure on decrees; and the *poletai* shall [supply] as many stone [markers] as may be needed [...] the contract [...] the council [...] the *proedroi* [...] draw up specifications for their manufacture [...] [and] placement on the sacred *orgas* [...] those who have been elected; and the treasurer of the people shall give the money [...] stone [...] the markers from the people's fund for expenditure on decrees. [The following were elected on the] sacred *orgas* [to put new markers] in place of the dilapidated or missing or obsolete ones. [From the council]: Arkephon of Halai, [...] of Thria, [...] of Hagnous. [From private individuals]: [...] Hippokrates of Kerameis, [...] of Kedoi, Emmenides of Koile or Hekale [...] of Sounion, Aristeides of Oe, [...] Glaukon of Perithoidai, Phaidros [...] for the oracle at Delphi. From private individuals: [...] Eudidaktos of Lamptrai. [From the council]: [...] of Lamptrai. The following correction is made: if this decree lacks anything, the council shall be empowered to vote whatever seems to it to be best.   (adapted trans. Lambert)

The decree deals with two different but interrelated issues. The first issue has international relevance and concerns the demarcation of the boundaries of the sacred *orgas* at Eleusis.[152] The second issue concerns the religious aspect. The Athenians put in place an elaborate procedure which involve sending three men to

---

[152] See Liddel (2003) 83.

DIVIDED POWER IN ATHENIAN DECREE-MAKING 81

Delphi with the task of consulting the oracle about the cultivation of the *eschatiai* around the *orgas* (23–45). Despite the previous disputes about the use of land at the border, Megara is never mentioned in the decree, which seems at first sight to imply that the matter was treated as an internal Athenian affair.[153] The decree prescribes that the boundaries are to be set by a board of fifteen men elected immediately by the assembly: five councillors and ten from all the Athenians (5–8). The committee took an oath, only partially readable on the stone, which bound them to set the boundaries neither with favour nor hostility and vote as rightly and piously as they could (9–10).[154] Scafuro suggests that the decree's procedure, described in lines 5–12, does not outline a *diadikasia* between two parts, as Foucart's first restoration implied, but a unilateral act of the Athenians against their Megarian neighbours.[155] However, the clause of the oath at lines 9–10 states that the chosen men have to vote neither according to favour nor enmity, which was typical of arbitration and was also one of the clauses of the heliastic oath. The pledges of Athenian judicial oath are often alluded to or quoted in forensic speeches, and the clause which prescribes impartiality of judgement is one of the most cited by fourth-century orators. For instance, at the beginning of the speech *On the Embassy*, Aeschines addresses the judges by stating that they are under an oath, which gives equal hearings to the parties (ἄνδρας ὀμωμοκότας τῶν ἀντιδίκων ὁμοίως ἀμφοτέρων ἀκούσεσθαι).[156] The clause therefore seems to imply the presence of a 'hidden' second party, most likely the Megarians, in the decision that the Athenian elected commissioners had to take. Papazarkadas has convincingly connected the clause with a possible interstate conflict with Megara, which may also be one reason, along with the obvious religious aspect, for consulting the Delphic oracle, giving to the demarcation of the *orgas* an interstate dimension.[157]

The elected board of fifteen Athenians had to sit from the sixteenth day of the month of Poseidon under the supervision of the *basileus*, the hierophant, the *dadouchos*, the two Eleusinian *genē* of *Kerukes* and *Eumolpidai* and anyone of the Athenians who wished to be present (13–15).[158] At line 18, the decree mentions a law, which might be a comprehensive statute about *temenē*

---

[153] RO 58. For Attic frontiers in the Archaic period see Daverio Rocchi (1987) 53–4; Rousset (1994); Freitag (2007); Canevaro (2017a) 56–7. For epigraphical evidence of *horoi* in Attica see also Lalonde (1991).

[154] For customary oaths see Low (2007) 94; Sommerstein and Bayliss (2013) 163.

[155] Foucart (1889); *contra* Scafuro (2003) 127–42. Cf. Foucart (1889) line12 [νος ἕως ἂν διαδικασθῆι]. The *diadikasia* was not a private action, but rather a judgement for bestowing a right between two or more litigants. The case was introduced by the verb ἐπιδικάζεσθαι. See Paoli (1960) 576–8, 'Diadicasia'; Harrison (1968) 214–17; MacDowell (1978) 103–8, Biscardi (1982) 200–2. Cf. Isae. 11; Dem. 43.

[156] Aeschin. 2.1; see also Dem. 18.6–7. For a complete list of the allusions to the judicial oath in Athenian orators see Harris (2013c) 353–6.

[157] Papazarkadas (2011) 252–3; *pace* Daverio Rocchi (1987) 99. See also RO 58. Cf. OR 131.64–7; OR 73.5; Thuc. 5.32; cf. also *IG* I³ 136.

[158] For the Eleusinian officials and the two *genē* see Clinton (1974) 10–68; Parker (1997) 293–7, 300–2; Papazarkadas (2011) 253.

82 DIVIDED POWER IN ANCIENT GREECE

entrusting a series of officials to look after the *orgas* as well as all the Athenian *temenē*.[159] Building on the fifth-century decree on the administration of the property of Codros, Neleus, and Basile (418/7 BCE), Papazarkadas partially reconstructs its content as the legal framework for the leasing of *temenē* in Classical Athens.[160] It is within the framework of this law that one can explain the involvement of the *basileus* in this particular task, since this magistracy was in charge of renting out sacred estates. The rentals had to be paid to the *apodektai*, who then allocated them according to the *merismos*.[161] However, the direct involvement of the Eleusinian officials and the two *genē* shows the Athenians attempted to single out impartial institutional actors due to the religious nature of the dispute. Similarly, the consultation of the oracle of Delphi complies with the Athenian respect towards the *orgas'* area as well as with the tradition of consulting the oracle for religious affairs of international relevance.[162]

The *basileus* enforced the law along with other officials and boards: the demarchs, the Areopagus, and the council as well as two military officers, the general ἐπὶ τὴν φυλακὴν τῆς χώρας and the *peripolarchoi* (18–23).[163] This provision of the decree displays the features of divided power and the implementation of a legal statute in action. The Athenian officials are to enforce a statute passed by a deliberative body following the law. Similarly, the detailed and complex procedure for consulting the oracle described at lines 30–53 required the involvement of many officials, such as the *proedroi* and the *prutaneis*, who play an eminently executive role by carrying out the legal provisions.

This is consistent with the Athenian division between legislation and administration, in which the latter is the domain of magistrates.[164] Public officials were not making political decisions since the procedure was established by the written regulations of the decree. For example, in Athenian trials magistrates had to accept a charge by following the relevant written law, without introducing any

---

[159] I follow Lambert 2012 61 who restores [ν ἱερῶν τεμε]ων at line 17; *contra* RO 58 [ν ἱερῶν ἀπάντ]ων.

[160] *IG* I³ 84.23–5; [Arist.] *Ath. Pol.* 47.4–5; Papazarkadas (2011) 59 n. 175. For *archontes* in Classical Athens cf. Rhodes (1981) 99–102, 556, 637–41.

[161] Papazarkadas (2011) 74. Cf. [Arist.] *Ath. Pol.* 48.1–2. Papazarkadas argues (84–5) that the *merismos* may have already worked in the fifth century by identifying the law mentioned in *IG* I³ 84 with a proto-allocation system. Even it is very likely that the Athenian started to organize their public budget in separate funds already in the fifth century, the system must be different in legal terms, as the *merismos* entrenched the budget and made very difficult to change it through the *nomothesia*, see Canevaro (2019c). The language of the decree clearly shows that the *apodektai* were instructed to transmit (παραδιδόντον) the money to the treasurers of the Other Gods, rather than allocating the resources. The allocation procedure is usually expressed by the forms of the verb μερίζειν or ἀναλίσκειν (e.g. *IG* II³ 1 452.43–6). The verb παραδιδόναι never occurs in Athenian inscriptions with the meaning 'to allocate' (cf. *IG* I³ 58; *IG* I³ 78; *IG* I³ 138; *IG* II² 1631).

[162] RO 58; Papazarkadas (2011) 253.

[163] For the office of general ἐπὶ τὴν φυλακὴν τῆς χώρας in Classical Athens see [Arist.] *Ath. Pol.* 61.1. See Rhodes (1981) 678–9; Hamel (1998) 15–16; RO 58, 278; Papazarkadas (2011) 258.

[164] Harris (2006) 30–1, (2013c) 29–44; see also appendix 2.

DIVIDED POWER IN ATHENIAN DECREE-MAKING 83

innovations, for which they would be otherwise prosecuted.[165] In public charges, the *thesmothetai* had to receive the charge, presented through a written document (*enklēma* or *graphē*), and check the procedural and substantive accuracy according to the written laws, under which the offence was prosecuted.[166] Magistrates could not follow unwritten laws and had no power to issue their own decree changing or interpreting the provisions of the assembly's decrees and laws.[167]

This decree provides evidence for a more nuanced picture of the process of implementation. This emphasizes a leading role of the council bringing together deliberative dimension and implementation. The decree shows at least two different levels of involvement of the council in the decision-making process. The enforcement of the statute mentioned at line 18 is the first level, at which the council carries out the implementation of the law along with the other officials. Nevertheless, as seen in the case of the decree for the goddess Bendis and the decree of the Athenian alliance with the three kings (and more cursorily in the decree for the Neapolitans), the administrative power of the council was not limited to carrying out normative prescriptions. It also consisted of active policy-making through the relevant delegated powers (85–6).[168] The administration of an important issue, such as the delimitation of sacred land with its interstate, religious, and financial implications, belonged to the political realm.

As the most important deliberative board in Athens, the council played a major role in shaping the decisions through its expertise in these matters. This did not only happen during *probouleusis*, when the council deliberated and drafted a *probouleuma* for the assembly, but Athenian divided power provided a further level of decree-making. Unlike the other *archai*, the Athenian council was a deliberative body able to enact its own decrees, which were actual political measures and a product of political deliberation, no less than the assembly's decrees.[169] The power of the council of passing new regulations by decree which were added to those already passed by the assembly is important from both an institutional and ideological perspective. The Athenians closely associated the enactment of decrees with democratic deliberation itself. Demosthenes distinguishes between the democratic decree-making and that of oligarchies and tyrannies where there is no preliminary discussion in the council (Dem. 19.185). Aeschines in *Against Ctesiphon* said that the city of Oreos should be considered

---

[165] Isae. 4.28; cf. Harris (2014) 117.

[166] Canevaro (2016c) 71–6; for the plaint in Athenian trials see Harris (2013b) 143–62.

[167] Andoc. 1.86. Their prerogatives were therefore very different from those of a Roman *praetor*.

[168] For the council's involvement in the Eleusinian Mysteries see Clinton (2008).

[169] Cf. n. 104 above. On the decrees of the council see Rhodes (1972) 82–7. The clear-cut division between political realm and bureaucratic implementation is no longer effective for the analysis of modern administrations. This makes it even less appropriate for Classical Athens which did not have professional bureaucrats. Cf. Pressman and Wildawsky (1973); Svara (2001). For implementation as a policy-making activity and the concept of 'interactive governance' see Torfing, Peters, Pierre, and Sørensen (2012); Peters (2014) 139.

84 DIVIDED POWER IN ANCIENT GREECE

a democracy, because they decide everything by decree (Aeschin. 3.103). The author of the Aristotelian *Athenaion Politeia* says that in Athens the *dēmos* was in charge of everything because decisions were taken by decrees and in the lawcourts ([Arist.] *Ath. Pol.* 41.2).[170]

A closer analysis of the delegation clause of the decree on the sacred *orgas* confirms this idea. The inscribed clause follows the pattern of the decree for the alliance with the kings of Paeonians, Illyrians, and Thracians, with the only addition of the expression ὅτι ἂν αὐτῆι δοκῆι ἄριστον εἶναι.[171] This probably represents a more detailed variant of the other delegation clauses and is consistent with the elaborate style of this decree. More remarkably, the same delegation formula is also attested in a contemporary inscription reporting an amendment of the *nomothetai* to the law of Chairemonides about the *aparchē* (*I.Eleusis* 142 = *IG* II² 140). By modifying the existing law, the *nomothetai* gave authority to the assembly to vote on whatever seemed best about the *aparchē* (lines 10–13).

> Ἐλευσίνιος εἶπ[εν· δεδόχθαι τοῖ]-
> ς νομοθέταις· τὰ [μὲν ἄλλα κατὰ τὸ]-
> ν Χαιρημονίδο νό[μον τὸν περὶ τῆ]-
> 10 ς ἀπαρχῆς, κύριο[ν δ’ εἶναι τὸν δῆμ]-
> ον ψηφίζεσθαι κ[αθ’ ὅτι ἂν αὐτῶι δ]-
> οκῆι ἄριστα ἐκλ[εγήσεσθαι ἡ ἀπα]-
> ρχὴ τοῦ καρποῦ τ[οῖν θεοῖν· τὴν δὲ]

Eleusinius proposed. The *nomothetai* decided. In other respects according to the Law of Chairemonides about the *aparchē*, but the people shall have authority to decree what it seems the best to collect the *aparchē* of the first-fruits to the two goddesses.

The inscribed law displays the division between legislation and administration.[172] This is an important documentary parallel for better understanding the language of delegation in Athens and the working of Athenian divided power. The assembly was empowered by the *nomothetai* (κύριον δ’ εἶναι τὸν δῆμον) to pass a decree about the Eleusinian first-fruits without any further restrictions, apart from the provisions of the law itself. Such a procedure shows the unfolding of divided power in Athenian law-making, which was based on the horizontal interplay between different institutions and distinct procedural set-ups.[173] The assembly is not hierarchically subordinated to the *nomothetai*, but the deliberative power of

---

[170] On the Athenian perception of decrees as democratic institution see Liddel (2020b) 32–9.
[171] Cf. also *IG* II³ 1 404 and pp. 73–4.
[172] On the division between legislation and administration see also Introduction §1.3.
[173] It was the assembly that ordered the summoning of the *nomothetai*; cf. n. 110 above.

DIVIDED POWER IN ATHENIAN DECREE-MAKING   85

legislation is shared according to distinct procedures. The *nomothetai* amended the law, and the assembly passed an ad hoc decree enforcing the amendment. The fact that the very same wording is used in the delegation from the assembly to the council is important and reflects the same concern for preserving the divided power in the decree-making. Canevaro and I have argued that the *nomothetai* are to be identified with a special session of the assembly with law-making power.[174] The identification of the *nomothetai* with the assembly, and not with a separate board, does not undermine the concept of divided power. In fact shows the importance of legal procedure in Athenian constitutionalism. Each procedural stage aimed at isolating and dividing distinct behaviours and expectations. The *dēmos* qua assembly had to perform different roles that the *dēmos* qua *nomothetai* according to the relevant institutional framework. The *dēmos* sitting as lawmaker in the assembly had to follow a distinct and institutionally complex procedure which required the interaction with the council and the lawcourts.

Like the relationship between *nomothetai* and assembly, the interaction between the Athenian assembly and the council is horizontal and not marked by institutional hierarchy. The council is there empowered to play an essential policy-making role in enacting further administrative measures; the content of which is considered complementary to the decree of the assembly rather than subsidiary. In other words, the Athenian decision-making process was much more interactive, complex, and multi-faceted than previous models argued.

The features of divided power were also evident in inscribed documents of the Lycurgan period. An important piece of evidence for delegation to the council is attested in a decree for the foundation of a colony in the Adriatic (*IG* II³ 1 370 = RO 100). The decree is preserved as part of the accounts of the supervisors of the dockyards (ἐπιμεληταί τῶν νεωρίων).[175] In this case, the text of the decree includes a delegation clause to the council as well as the relevant decision of the council ordering the *epimelētai* to add a quadrireme to the expedition (272–5: τετρήρη ἔδομεν κατὰ ψήφισμα βουλῆς). Scholars have interpreted the evidence from this inscribed decree differently. Hansen remarks on the additional decree of the council to demonstrate that the delegated power was marginal and the council's decisions pertained to small details.[176] Conversely, in his important discussion of the Adriatic decree, Ober has emphasized the role of the council as an institution aggregating the dispersed expertise of Athenian society.[177]

In line with my previous analysis of the delegation clauses in Athenian decrees, I propose to advance both these views. While Hansen's view is functional to limit the role of the council to what he has called the 'power of initiative', Ober's

---

[174] Canevaro and Esu (2018).
[175] Cf. *IG* I³ 153.19 (430–420 BCE) for the first mention of these officials. For the records of the supervisors of the dockyards see *IG* II² 1604–32. Gabrielsen (1994) 162; Rhodes (1972) 148–58. Cf. Dem. [47]; *IG* II² 1623; *IG* II² 1628; *IG* II² 1631.
[176] Hansen (1991) 255–6.   [177] Ober (2008).

86   DIVIDED POWER IN ANCIENT GREECE

argument has the merit to enhance the decision-making role of the council. Yet, Ober conceptualizes the council as an exogenous entity collecting political expertise and individual preferences. In §2.3, I suggest that the council was a producer of collective expertise by means of the bouleutic procedures and discourse fostering participation and deliberation. In fact, the Adriatic decree is not only valuable for reconstructing the formal aspect and the institutional complexity underpinning the Athenian divided power; it also provides an important epigraphic benchmark for linking formal procedures and political narratives as outlined in oratorical texts. I shall provide a concise summary of the decree's content and then move to analyse the role of the council in the decree-making.

The core of this inscription contains a non-probouleumatic decree proposed by Cephisophon of Cholargus for dispatching an expedition to the Adriatic to found an outpost (165–271).[178] This elaborated decree orders that preparation for the expedition should be done as quickly as possible (173–4: ὅπως ἂν τὴν | [ταχίσ]την πράττηται). The trierarchs should bring their ships and the relevant equipment to the jetty before the tenth day of Mounichion (183–90). In the following section, the decree prescribes different awards for the trierarchs (τὸν δὲ πρῶτον πα-| [ρακομί]σαντα στεφανωσά-|[τω ὁ δῆ]μος): a golden crown of 500 drachmas for the first trierarch, a crown of 300 drachmas for the second, and a crown of 200 drachmas for the third trierarch. The awards are to be announced by the herald of the council at the *Thargelia* and the *apodektai* are to allocate the money to reward their *philotimia* (190–204: ὅπω-|[ς ἂν ἦι] φανερὰ ἡ φιλοτι-|[μία ἡ εἰ]ς τὸν δῆμον τοῖς | [τριηρ]άρχοις). The decree outlines the procedure for pleas for exemption from service to be presented to the *thesmothetai* (204–16). At lines 233–41, the decree also postulates a fine of 10,000 drachmas for any magistrate or private citizen who does not abide by the regulations. The following section of the decree makes clear that ten dispatchers elected by the assembly are to look after the dispatch under the close supervision of the council, which is summoned continuously to the dock until the expedition leaves. The council should also punish any lack of discipline according to the laws, and a further crown is prescribed for the council and the *prutaneis* if they do a good job (251–63). The decree delegates the power of enacting a decree without repealing what the people have voted, if there is anything lacking, to the council (264–9: τὴν βουλὴν | κυρίαν εἶναι ψηφίζεσθαι | μὴ λύουσαν μηθὲν τῶν | ἐψηφισμένων τῶι

---

[178] This decree shows typical linguistic features of 'Lycurgan Athens' which connect the decree with fifth-century Athenian imperialism. Miltiades, the man in charge of the foundation, is called *oikistēs* (19, 40, 61, 160). The colony is defined as an *apoikia* (177) and the settlers are called *epoikoi* (224–5). On Lycurgan Athens see Faraguna (1992), (2011) 67–86; Azoulay and Ismard (2011); Hanink (2014). For an epigraphical perspective see Lambert (2017) 93–111. The proposer Cephisodotus was closely associated with Lycurgus see Faraguna (1992). For an analysis of decrees about grain supply see Tracy (1995) 30–5; Moreno (2007); Oliver (2007) 16–110; Engen (2010) 54–5; Lambert (2012) 384.

DIVIDED POWER IN ATHENIAN DECREE-MAKING   87

δήμωι). The text of the decree concludes at 271 with the formula 'for the defence of the country' (εἰς φυλακὴν τῆς χώρας).[179]

The delegation clause empowers the council to pass additional measures, if anything is lacking in the decree, which do not annul anything voted by the *dēmos*. This explicit restriction is unparalleled in delegation clauses to the council as analysed in this chapter.[180] This piece of evidence offers both a challenge and an opportunity to expand my analysis on Athenian divided power in the decree-making. Part of the explanation for a limited delegation might be linked to the judicial powers of the council in naval matters. As the text of the decree makes clear, the council is instructed to punish any lack of discipline in accordance with the law. In case a trierarch did not perform his duty in equipping a ship, the council had to hand him over to a court which could double his debt to the state. Yet, Rhodes notes that there also is evidence that the council could enact an 'adjusting measure', even after the lawcourt's verdict.[181] For example, in 323/2 BCE, a trierarch named Sopolis was convicted by the lawcourt to pay double his debt for not handing over his trireme; his property and some timber for oars belonging to Sopolis were confiscated. Then, the council passed a decree which ordered the *epimelētai* to reduce the penalty of three drachmas for each of the lengths of timber confiscated (*IG* II² 1631.350–403). Thus, it is conceivable that the Athenians aimed at preserving the fine of 10,000 drachmas by limiting the council's power to impose or reduce fines in naval matters, without excluding the contribution of the council to other decisions about the expedition.

Yet, balancing the judicial power of the council gives only a partial explanation to this limited delegation clause. It was commonplace in Athenian political culture to juxtapose the punishment of wrongdoers with public honours for the benefactors of the city (Dem. 19.32; Lyc. 1.9–10).[182] Such an opposition occurs frequently in fourth-century sources and this decree is no exception. The Adriatic decree prescribes severe penalties as well as distinct crowns for enhancing the *philotimia* of the trierarchs, and crowns for the council and the *prutaneis*. The grant of civic honours for officials was a routine matter in Classical Athens,

---

[179] For the clause stating εἰς φυλακὴν τῆς χώρας see Rhodes (1972) 231–5; Oliver (2007) 210–13 demonstrates that this formula was used for urgent financial measures, not necessarily related to the actual defence of the country. Cf. *IG* II³ 1 404; *IG* II² 1631.

[180] A similar clause only appears in the law about the Mysteries of Andania. In that case the delegation to the *sunedroi* is limited by the following entrenchment clause protecting the law at 191–4. Cf. also §3.3; *IG* V¹ 1390. See Gawlinski (2012) for a new edition and commentary of this law; see Hansen and Nielsen (2004) 553; for the *sunedroi* in Messene see Deshours (2004) 136–9; Hamon (2005).

[181] Rhodes (1972) 154. A similar power of 'adjustment' of a judicial verdict might be attested in a law about the Eleusinian Mysteries. A provision of the law forbids the *muesis* for those who were not member of the *Kerukes* and *Eumolpidai*. The council is requested to deliberate about the wrongdoers' (βολευέτω ἡ βολὴ ὡς ἀδικõντος) after the case was decided by the lawcourt. The involvement of this latter institution is however restored in Clinton's edition (1980) 278–80, (2008); cf. *Agora* XVI 56 A 29–30. Cf. also MacDowell (1991).

[182] On the relationship between honour and punishment see Azoulay (forthcoming).

88 DIVIDED POWER IN ANCIENT GREECE

yet a meaningful part of the political and social system of the democracy. The correct recognition of personal excellence and merits on behalf of the *dēmos* was acknowledged in the form of decrees of the assembly and often of the council. Through the delegation clause and continuous supervision over the expedition, the *boulē* was the institution in charge of assigning the crown. The council's role is thus well defined by the decree and by the delegation clause. It is the herald of the council who had to announce the awards to the trierarchs at the *Thargelia*.[183] This would have resulted in the enactment of another decree of the council, which complemented the decree of assembly without changing its text in accordance with the delegation clause.

The procedure attested in the decree for the Adriatic expedition is also consistent with the account of the Demosthenic speech *On the Trierarchic Crown* (Dem. 51). The comparison between this speech and the inscribed decree complements the epigraphical evidence and offers a valuable insight into the discursive practice of divided power and delegation to council. The speech *On the Trierarchic Crown* is the only Demosthenic oration delivered in the council and the only surviving bouleutic speech not written for a *dokimasia*.[184] This provides a rare and important glimpse into a bouleutic debate and the relevant discursive practice beyond the *dokimasia* procedure, which I discuss in §2.2.

The speech was written for a dispute about an honorific crown between Demosthenes and other two trierarchs and delivered in the council in 360/59 BCE. According to the Demosthenic account, the assembly had previously passed a decree which instructed the trierarchs to prepare quickly for launching their ships. The decree also prescribed the awarding of a crown for the first man who had his trireme ready for launch. Demosthenes claims that the crown should be awarded to him, as he was the first man to have his ship ready (51.1). Yet, two other trierarchs, holding a syntrierarchy, opposed him, and tried to claim the crown for themselves. Scholars have not clearly identified the legal procedure followed by litigants on the assumption that this was a typical judicial dispute about honours. The relevant institutional context is key to understanding the speech and the role played by the Athenian council. In his book on the Demosthenic corpus, MacDowell does not analyse the procedural issues of this case and leaves the issue open.[185] Bers suggests that this might have been a 'formal or informal *diadikasia*' for settling the dispute between two opponents claiming the same civic honour.[186] The suggestion that this speech was written for a *diadikasia* is interesting but problematic. It would be unparalleled that an official honour conferred by a decree of the assembly was the object of informal litigation between

---

[183] On the importance of publicity that produces normativity and incentives in an 'economy of esteem' see Brennan and Pettit (2004) 152–60.

[184] Libanius attributed the speech to Apollodorus, but modern scholars consider Dem. 51 an authentic Demosthenic speech. See MacDowell (2009) 133.

[185] MacDowell (2009) 133–5.   [186] Bers (2003) 39.

DIVIDED POWER IN ATHENIAN DECREE-MAKING 89

public officials and was settled by the council. A formal *diadikasia*, on the other hand, had to be presented by the relevant official to a lawcourt, which had the last word in deciding whose claim was the strongest.[187] However, Demosthenes makes it very clear that the council made the final decision and was in charge of assigning the crown.

Such a decision fell into the usual duties of the council about the navy ([Arist.] *Ath. Pol.* 46.1; Dem. 22.8). We gain a better understanding of this speech by comparing it with the decree for the Adriatic expedition. If one compares the provisions of the decree for the Adriatic expedition with the Demosthenic speech, it becomes clear that the inscribed decree and Demosthenes' account unfolded in the same institutional framework.

Demosthenes begins his speech by mentioning the decree's provision according to which the treasurer was instructed to provide money to crown the first man to get his trireme ready (νῦν δὲ τῷ πρώτῳ παρασκευάσαντι τὴν τριήρη τὸν ταμίαν προσέταξεν ὁ δῆμος δοῦναι). Like in the decree for the expedition on the Adriatic (183–90), Demosthenes reports that the decree establishing the crown had a timescale within which the ships were to be brought to the dockyards. At 51.4, Demosthenes adds that the decree prescribes that whoever fails to bring his ship by the last day of the month would be imprisoned and given over to a lawcourt. The legal foundation of Demosthenes' speech is a decree of the assembly which finds an almost exact procedural parallel in the decree for the Adriatic expedition. The epigraphical comparison shows that the council is not only performing adjudication, but it has an active policy-making role. The councillors in this context are required to make decisions about the crown, according to the provision of a previous decree of the assembly, and this implies a deliberation in the council through multiple speeches and the enactment of a decree of the council assigning the honour to one of the litigants. This bears important implications for our understanding of how institutional design, deliberation, and expertise of councillors were strictly interrelated.

First, it is important to define the nature of the litigation in the council. Unlike other disputes about civic honours, such as those witnessed in Demosthenes' speeches *On the Crown* (Dem. 18), *Against Aristocrates* (Dem. 23), and *Against Androtion* (Dem. 22), the council is not acting as a panel of judges deciding about whether the honorific decree is legal or not. This is a substantial difference. The Athenian lawcourts judged the legality of honorific decrees through the *graphē paranomōn*.[188] While Athenian judges could reject or confirm the legality of a decree, they never conferred a crown by enacting their own decrees. No Athenian lawcourt could pass a decree granting civic honour on behalf of the *dēmos*.

---

[187] For the procedure of *diadikasia* see Paoli (1960) 576–8, s.v. *Diadicasia*; Harrison (1968) 214–17; Biscardi (1982) 199–202.

[188] Cf. Chapter 6 on *graphē paranomōn* on honorific decrees.

90 DIVIDED POWER IN ANCIENT GREECE

Conversely, in *On the Trierarchic Crown* the dispute is not about the legal aspects of the decree instituting the crown and Demosthenes never tries to demonstrate the illegality or illegitimacy of the decree. This speech was part of a bouleutic dispute between Demosthenes and some opponents to decide who would be awarded the crown and the council is simply carrying out one of its normal duties rather than following a judicial procedure. The speech provides discursive protocols between judicial and deliberative arguments, but the latter arguments are predominant and are consistent with the features of this institutional setting of the council. The arguments used by Demosthenes focus on the consistency between his behaviour as trierarch and the terms of the decree establishing a crown. He aims to demonstrate that he deserves the crown from the council. Demosthenes first provides an account of how he launched his ship using his own money and recruiting the best crew, unlike the opposing claimants (5–6). His opponents do not deserve the crown, as they claim this honour without having paid for their liturgies (7–8), which is against the reciprocity underpinning the rationale of civic honours.[189] He reiterates this point at 13–14, where Demosthenes makes clear that in order to claim honours, they should have used their private wealth to restore that of the city, rather than the other way around. This leads Demosthenes to accuse his opponents of not expressing reciprocity (*charis*) and not understanding the values regulating public honours (16). Finally, Demosthenes concludes by accusing his opponents of requesting (*keleuousi*) the council to crown or not to crown whomever they want.

Thus, the council took an independent decision and played an active role in policy-making by granting an honorific crown. The appeals to reciprocity imply that the role of the council is to function as a guarantor of the right allocation of the honour according to the principle of distributive justice.[190] This institutional framework is clearly reflected in Demosthenes' arguments. This confirms that the council, unlike other magistracies, was not only a law-implementing institution, but was actively involved in putting into practice the euergetic ideology which played a central role in fourth-century democratic ideology.[191] The decrees of the council were perfectly in line with this practice. Almost all the decrees of the council preserved on stone deal with honourific decrees concerning proxenies, crowns, and other civic honours.[192] This led some scholars to underplay the political value of the decrees of the council as politically marginal.[193] However, there is no legal or political reason to support this. From a political and ideological

[189] On the concept of honour in Archaic and Classical Greece see Cairns (1993), (2011), (2015). For reciprocity and honours in Greece see Domingo Gygax (2016); Canevaro (2016c) 77–97 and (forthcoming).
[190] Cf. Arist. *Eth. Nich.* 1130b–1131b.   [191] Liddel (2016).
[192] See Rhodes (1972) 271–5 (table G: decrees of the council) and now Liddel (2020a) 966–71 for the literary evidence of decrees of the council.
[193] Rhodes (1972) 87; Hansen (1991) 255–6.

DIVIDED POWER IN ATHENIAN DECREE-MAKING 91

point of view, Liddel points out that discussion of honorific decrees was often exposed to a remarkable 'moral anxiety', demonstrating that any kind of honorific decree was not politically marginal and required broad political debate. As a result, by entrusting the council with this task, the Athenians acknowledged the council's institutional knowledge and expertise in matters such as the navy as well as its ability to assess the performance of citizens and to bestow the relevant honours.

From a legal perspective it is important to note that the law establishing the hierarchy between *nomoi* and *psēphismata* cited in Dem. 23.87 cites the decrees of the assembly and the council as on par while both were subordinated on the same ground to the *nomoi*.[194] The decrees of the council are also mentioned on an equal basis along with the decrees of the assembly as source of law on which Athenian judges took their oath of office (Dem. 19.179). Similarly, in the Demosthenic speech *Against Evergus and Mnesibulus*, the speaker provided the decree of the council as a piece of evidence during the trial ([Dem.] 47.34). After that the clerk read out the decree in the lawcourt, the speaker argued that since no one brought a *graphē paranomōn* against the decree of the council (οὐδενὸς γραφομένου παρανόμων), it was fully valid (ἀλλὰ κυρίου ὄντος). It is important that a decree of the council could be indicted for illegality, exactly like a decree of the assembly.[195]

The speech *On the Trierarchic Crown* shows that the Athenian democratic system relied on the expertise of the council at the beginning of the decision-making, during the probouleutic activity, which constituted a proper deliberative step in the decree-making, as well as after the enactment of decrees in the assembly, when the council supported the people's decisions and in the daily administration of Athens.

The fact that, in this case, the council passed another decree adding a quadrireme does not mean that the political authority of the council was marginal. It is meaningful that even when passing a detailed decree such as that for the Adriatic expedition, an additional decree of the council was required for completing the decision-making. This shows, like the previous instances of delegation clauses, that Athenian decree-making was organized according to the notion of divided power, that is a multi-layered system characterized by several deliberative steps both in the council and in the assembly. This system was not unidirectional from the council's probouleumatic activity to the assembly's ratification, but it emphasized the distinct inputs of these institutions in different moments of the decision-making.

---

[194] For discussion of the document see Canevaro (2013b) 75–6.
[195] A *probouleuma* could also be indicted of illegality as in the case of Aristocrates' decree in honour of Charidemus in Demosthenes' *Against Aristocrates* (Dem. 23) see Esu (2020).

92 DIVIDED POWER IN ANCIENT GREECE

The fourth-century epigraphical evidence for the role of council confirms that delegation was an important tool in decree-making. The Athenians did not see a reduction of the people's power with the delegation of decree-making authority to the council, which was often empowered to pass further decrees for the regulations of important sectors of the civic administration. Such a practice shows that the power of the people in Classical Athens was transferrable from one institution to another according to specific procedures and arrangements, which were meant to enhance the relevant behaviour of citizens acting in the assembly and in the council as decree-makers.

2.6 Athenian Delegation: A Standard Institution of the Decree-Making

The council of Five Hundred was a key institution for the Athenian deliberative system. Bouleutic powers mapped not only in the realm of magistracies and daily administration as well as in that of proper political decision-making. These functions were enshrined in the bouleutic oath, which preserved the constituent values of this institution and emphasized the deliberative role of the council in the Athenian political system. Understanding the values underpinning a political institution has proved essential to shed light on the Athenian conceptualization of the council beyond our normative accounts of Athenian democracy.

This chapter has shown that a close analysis of the procedures and formal rules of the council provides valuable evidence to reconstruct the implicit ideological values and the discursive protocols of political agents. The values detailed in the bouleutic oath were implemented in the institutional design and formal procedure of the council. In turn, such formal arrangements favoured open deliberation and the acquisition of expertise in the different areas of bouleutic activity. The expertise of the councillors in public administration and the deliberative requirements were necessary for the working of divided power in the decree-making and for the functioning of the Athenian deliberative system more generally. The delegation of decree-making power to the council followed these institutional and ideological premises.

Athenian inscribed decrees show consistency in institutional practice throughout the fifth and the fourth centuries in transferring authority to the council by inserting delegation clauses in decrees. The use of terms such as *autokratōr* and *kurios*, which acquired a technical meaning in epigraphical language, provided sound legal grounds for exercising an independent wide-ranging deliberative function. This evidence has helped clarify the role and the administrative powers of the Athenian council by identifying at least two levels of the council's engagement in institutional practice: the implementation of decisions under the rule of law and a policy-making role after the enactment of the assembly's decrees.

The former task was typical of public officials that carried out the implementation of the enactments of the deliberative bodies. The latter was usually performed in relation to matters in which the council could offer relevant competence and expertise, such as foreign policy, religion, public finances, and the fleet. Inscriptions such as the fifth-century decree for the cult of Bendis and the decree for the sacred *orgas* show that the council played a multi-faceted role in dealing with these issues, which were often closely related to each other, but also with different legal levels (e.g. laws of the *polis*, laws *kata ta patria*) and several institutional actors (e.g. associations and magistrates). The purpose of the delegation was therefore not limited to charging the council with the task of executing the assembly's orders, but was rather aimed at exploiting the institutional expertise of the councillors who, unlike other Athenian officials, could exercise a proper deliberative power by enacting *psēphismata*. This analysis confirms the presence of a 'divided power' in Classical Athens, without limiting the role of the council to that of a subsidiary deliberative body, by underlining its central role in shaping and making decisions as a constituent part of the deliberative power ($\tau\grave{o}$ $\beta ou\lambda\epsilon u\acute{o}\mu\epsilon\nu o\nu$ $\pi\epsilon\rho\grave{i}$ $\tau\hat{\omega}\nu$ $\kappa o\iota\nu\hat{\omega}\nu$) as described in Aristotle's *Politics*.

3

Divided Power in Mytilene and Megalopolis

Delegation Practice beyond Athens

3.1 Delegation in Two Non-Athenian Case Studies

Delegation clauses are also found in decrees from outside Classical Athens. Although attestations in Athenian literary and epigraphical sources are much more abundant than those from the other Greek *poleis*, it is still possible to identify similar practices outside Attica. A couple of interesting case studies are provided by two inscribed documents inscribed from fourth-century Mytilene and second-century Megalopolis.

The two cities differ in geographical location, size, and historical development. The Mytilenian epigraphical dossier relate to the political and institutional context of the Lesbian city at the end of the fourth century, when the city had just established a new democratic constitution under the influence of Alexander. The fragmentary inscription from Megalopolis provides insights into the late Hellenistic period, between 150 and 100 BCE, at a time when the political independence of the Greek *poleis* was coming to an end under the pressure of Rome. The institutions of Megalopolis, like those of other Greek city-states, underwent a process of institutional change due to a complex phenomenon of both endogenous and exogenous changes. The endogenous process of elite-capture institutionalized the increasing elite influence in political life according to Greek institutional traditions. As Fabiani showed in her magisterial work on Iasos, a shift towards a major role of the local elites in Iasos' decision-making already started in third century.[1] Despite preserving democratic institutions, offices such as the *prutaneis* were gradually manned by members of elites and carried out a prominent role in the agenda-setting of third-century Iasos. Hamon has also shown that the imitation and external imposition of Roman institutions significantly contributed to changing the socio-economic composition of their councils across Greece.[2]

---

[1] Fabiani (2012), (2015), and (forthcoming).
[2] Hamon (2005), (2007); cf. §3.4. Ferrary (1987–9) 206–10 also shows the relevant role played by the Roman authorities in changing the nature of many Greek councils during the second century BCE.

Divided Power in Ancient Greece: Decision-Making and Institutions in the Classical and Hellenistic Polis. Alberto Esu, Oxford University Press. © Alberto Esu 2024. DOI: 10.1093/oso/9780198883951.003.0003

Despite the difference in the historical context, the decision-making procedures of Mytilene and Megalopolis share remarkable similarities in the institutional interplay between their respective councils and assemblies through the practice of delegation of decree-making power to their councils.

This chapter explores both the relevance and the ideological purpose of this practice in the decree-making procedures of Mytilene and Megalopolis by analysing the few pieces of epigraphical evidence. This analysis provides two valuable extra-Athenian examples of delegation to the council and show the existence of procedures implementing the notion of divided power outside Athens. The study of these legal clauses in the early and late Hellenistic decrees also shows the endurance of delegation practices throughout a long period of time in two different historical contexts: a newly restored democracy and an elitist constitution. This comparison bears important implications for understanding the ideological rationale of the council-assembly relationship regulated by the delegation clauses. It shows the role of path dependence in the institutional design of the Greek *poleis* and the inseparable nature of institutional design and political ideology.

The epigraphical evidence from Mytilene provides a close parallel to the delegation practice found in Athenian inscriptions. This highlights the key role played by the council as a proper policy-making institution, which actively shaped the decisions by enacting its own decrees. The very limited epigraphical evidence from Megalopolis does not allow us to reconstruct a comprehensive picture, but it casts some light on the workings of a newly established census-based constitution, in which the civic *boulē* has become an elitist *sunedrion*. In Megalopolis, delegation to the council is still operating according to the formal rule already identified in fully democratic contexts. Such a practice demonstrates, on the one hand, the formal persistence of this legal procedure, and on the other hand, the very distinct institutional purpose of deliberative delegation in a regime where popular participation to the council was restricted.

This chapter first offers an overview of Mytilene's political and institutional history in order to frame the so-called reconciliation agreement and the relevant procedure of delegation within its historical and cultural context. The chapter will then survey the role of the *sunedrion* of Megalopolis through an analysis of the epigraphical material and discusses the persistence of delegation-procedure and divided power in the different social and cultural context of Hellenistic democracy.

Heller (2009) refers to '*hybridation institutionelle*' and emphasizes the endogenous Greek tendency to an oligarchization of political life rather than the Roman imitation, which become more evident from the early Imperial period.

96 DIVIDED POWER IN ANCIENT GREECE

3.2 Mytilene from the Archaic Period to the Macedonian Conquest

According to Herodotus, the island of Lesbos was originally divided into six *poleis*, which became five by the fifth century (Hdt. 1.151.2). Mytilene was the largest of these Aeolian *poleis*. The history of the Mytilenian political community traces back to the Archaic period, when Mytilene played a prominent role among the Lesbian cities and in the surrounding area.[3] During the seventh century, the wealthy city elites established fruitful relationships abroad in terms of prestige, economic exchange, and political power.[4]

The political history of Mytilene was characterized by several constitutional changes and episodes of *stasis* from the Archaic period to the early Hellenistic age.[5] In the *Politics* (Arist. *Pol.* 1311b19), when discussing the monarchical tyrannies (βασιλικαὶ δυναστεῖαι), Aristotle affirms that the tyrannical rule of Penthilides, who used to beat the citizens with clubs, was overthrown by the action of an opposing political group led by Megacles, possibly around 630 BCE.[6] The fall of the Penthelid dynasty was followed by a period of political instability, during which individual rulers tried to acquire supremacy by establishing tyrannies. Megacles was possibly overthrown by Myrsilus and Pittacus, who were both fiercely and famously attacked in Alcaeus' poems (Diog. Laert 1.81; Alc. fr. 70 Voigt; Arist. *Pol.* 1285a30).[7]

In the second half of the sixth century, Mytilene fell under the influence of the Persian Empire. Until 512 BCE, when the Persians established a new tyranny, the city was probably governed by an oligarchy. Mytilene remained a vassal state of Persia, since the Lesbian *polis* helped Xerxes in the invasion of Greece in 480–479 BCE (Hdt. 6.5, 14, 26–2, 31; Diod. 11.37–8). After the Persian wars, Mytilene was a founding member of the Delian League (Thuc. 3.10.2–4). Like Chios and Samos, Mytilene was initially independent and the Mytilenians supplied their own ships to the League. The Athenians did not impose any constitutional changes at this time, so that when the anti-Athenian revolt broke out, Mytilene was still ruled by an oligarchy, possibly with a citizen body restricted to one thousand oligarchs, who were subsequently executed in Athens after the revolt was suppressed (Thuc. 3.27–51, 3.50).[8] Mytilene lost its independence

---

[3] Hansen and Nielsen (2004) 1026–30. For the archaeology of ancient Lesbos see Spencer (1995).

[4] Spencer (2000) 68–81.

[5] Gehrke (1985) 117–23. For a history of Mytilene in its regional context in the Classical period see now Ellis-Evans (2019) 159–88.

[6] Carlier (1984) 451; Schütrumpf and Gehrke (1996) 561.

[7] For the role of the *aisumnētēs* see Faraguna (2005). According to Aristotle (*Pol.* 1274b18–23), Pittacus gave new laws to Mytilenes, but not a new constitution. For this tradition of tyrants administering justice which follows patterns going back to the Homeric *basileis* see J. Taylor (2022).

[8] See Gomme (1962) 326–7; Rhodes (1994) 214; Hornblower (1996) 440.

DIVIDED POWER IN MYTILENE AND MEGALOPOLIS 97

and became a cleruchy under the direct control of Athens.[9] Mytilenian inhabitants cultivated the allotments assigned to Athenian citizens by paying a rent to them. In 405 BCE, Lysander put an end to Athenian rule, and he may also have established a Spartan governor (*harmostēs*) and a board of Ten as an oligarchic government, who were eventually expelled in 390/89 BCE by the Mytilenians (Xen. *Hell.* 2.2.5; Paus. 8.52.4). The fourth-century institutional history of Mytilene is again characterized by sudden constitutional changes and political instability. In the first half of the fourth century, Mytilene became a democracy.[10] Some Mytilenian decrees show that the city had a council (*bolla*) and a people's assembly (*damos*) and democratic features can be envisaged in the fourth-century Athenian honorific decree for the Mytilenians in 369 BCE (*IG* II[2] 107 = RO 31; *IG* XII 2, 4).[11] It also seems that the city enjoyed considerable naval power as well as influence over other Lesbian *poleis* during this period.[12] Some years later, however, Demosthenes reports that the democracy was abolished in Mytilene (ὁ Μυτιληναίων δῆμος καταλέλυται) and an oligarchy was set up in Chios and Mytilene (Χίων ὀλιγαρχουμένων καὶ Μυτιληναίων), which was then followed by the short anti-Athenian tyranny of Kammys (Dem. 13.8, 15.19; [Dem.] 40.36–7).[13]

At the end of the fourth century, the Macedonians replaced the traditionally Athenian influence over Lesbos. During the years of Macedonian expansion against the Persian Empire, Mytilene experienced more *staseis* and consequent modifications in the constitutional setting. In 334 BCE, after the battle of Granicus, Alexander conquered Lesbos, but the Persians managed to recover the island once again. According to Arrian in 333–332 BCE under the leadership of Memnon, the Persian fleet conquered Chios and all the Lesbian cities (Arr. *Anab.* 2.1.1; Diod. 17.29.1). Yet, the Persians imposed the destruction of the inscribed *stelai* reporting the alliance with Alexander and established a new tyranny under Diogenes, one of those exiled by Alexander, who was supported by a Persian garrison (Arr. *Anab.* 1.18.1). The following year, the Macedonians ultimately conquered Lesbos, and Alexander favoured the establishment of a democratic government and civic reconciliation after several years of political strife.

This new and definitive institutional arrangement is attested in two epigraphical documents, which provide a vivid picture of the workings of the Mytilenian political institutions. More interestingly for our purpose, the relationship between the assembly and the council in implementing the legal clauses of the reconciliation agreement is regulated by a delegation clause (Decree B 37–8 see below),

---

[9] See Moreno (2009) 211–21. On the status of people living in the cleruchy see Zelnick-Abramovitz (2004).

[10] Robinson (2011) 178–9.

[11] Other fourth-century Athenian inscriptions mentioning Mytilene are *IG* II[2] 40; RO 22; *IG* II[2] 1437.

[12] Brun (1988) 376–7.

[13] Other tyrannical rulers are attested in Lesbos during the fourth century; see Brun (1988) 381–2.

98   DIVIDED POWER IN ANCIENT GREECE

which shows a similar pattern to the Athenian ones.[14] A close reading of the epigraphical text will shed light on the role of the Mytilenian council in this complex political and legal procedure.

3.3 The Decree on Concord and the Decree on Reconciliation

The texts of the two decrees were probably inscribed separately on two different *stelai* (*SEG* 36.750; *SEG* 36.752).[15] While the context of the decrees shows that the two documents were closely associated and enacted sometime in the 330s, the exact year is controversial. Scholars have proposed several hypotheses, between 334 and 324 BCE, but the year 332 BCE, after the second Macedonian conquest, seems to be the best option for the reconciliation decree.[16] These are the texts of the decrees:

RO 85 (A+B)

A

[ἔγ]νω βόλλα καὶ δᾶμος· περὶ τῶν οἴ [. . . . .]

[ε]ἰσάγηνται ὢς κεν οἰ πόλιται οἴκει[εν τὰμ π]-

[ό]λιν ἐν δαμοκρατίαι τὸμ πάντα χρόνον [ἔχον]-

[τ]ες πρὸς ἀλλάλοις ὢς εὐνοώτατα. τύχαι ἀγ[άθ]-

5 αι· εὔξασθαι μὲν τὰμ βόλλαν καὶ τὸν δᾶμον τ[ο]-

ῖς θέοισι τοῖς δυοκαίδεκα καὶ τῶι Διὶ τῶι Ἡ-

ραίωι καὶ Βασίληι καὶ Ὀμονοίωι καὶ τᾶι Ὀμο-

νοίαι καὶ Δίκαι καὶ Ἐπιτελείαι τῶν ἀγάθων

αἴ κε συνενίκει τῶι δάμωι τῶι Μυτιληνάων τ-

10 ὰ δόξαντα, θυσίαν καὶ πρόσοδομ ποήσασθαι τ-

ελειομένων τῶν ἀγάθωγ κατ ὄττι κε τῶι δάμω

φαίνηται· ταῦτα μὲν ηὖχθαι· ἀγάθαι δὲ τύχαι

τῶ δάμω τῶ Μυτιληνάων, ἐψάφισθαι τᾶι βόλλα

καὶ τῶι δάμωι· αἰ μέγ κέ τις δίκας γενομένας

[14] On the far-reaching nature of the Mytilenian reconciliation with the effort to reintegrate the exiled see B. D. Gray (2015) 80–6.

[15] For the standard edition of the inscriptions see Heisserer and Hodot (1986). See Bencivenni (2003) 41 with full bibliography of previous editions.

[16] 334 BCE (decree on concord) and 332 BCE (decree on reconciliation): Heisserer (1980) 131–9; Worthington (1990); Bencivenni (2003) 39–54; Rhodes and Osborne (2003); 324 BCE: Brun (1988) 255–6; Gauthier (1997) 349; Dössel (2003) 159, 170–2; Dmitriev (2005) 357–60. On these two decrees see also the recent study of Dimopoulou-Piliouni (2015) 250–67.

DIVIDED POWER IN MYTILENE AND MEGALOPOLIS 99

15 κατ τὸν νόμον φύγηι ἐκ τᾶς πόλιος ἢ ἀπυθάνη,

[χ]ρῆσθαι τῶι νόμωι· αἰ δέ κε ἄλλον τινα τρόπο-

[ν Μυτ]ιλ̣ηνάων ἢ τῶγ κατοικέντων ἐμ Μυτιλήν-

[αι ἐπὶ προ]τάνιος Δίτα Σαωνυμείω σύμβαι ἀτ-

[ιμασθέντα φυγ]αδεύθην ἐκ τᾶς πόλιος ἢ ἀπυθ-

20 [άνην . . . .]ν̣τας χρήματα τ[ού]των τινὶ

[. . . . .]. ΤΑ

The council and the people resolved. Regarding what [. . .] have introduced, so that the citizens may live in the city in a democracy for all time, having the best goodwill towards one another. For the good Fortune. The council and the people shall pray to the twelve gods and Zeus *Heraios* and the Queen and *Homonoios* and Agreement and Justice and Fulfilment of Good Things, if what is resolved benefits the people of Mytilene to make a sacrifice and a procession when the good things are being fulfilled in whatever way the people decide. Vow this. For the good Fortune of the people of Mytilene, the council and the people voted: if, after a lawsuit, someone has been exiled from the city or put to death according to the law, this shall be applied. If, in any other way, anyone of the Mytilenians or those living in Mytilene during the prytany of Ditas son of Saonymus should be declared *atimos*, and exiled from the city or put to death, [. . .] those owning money to any of these…

B

[. . . . . καὶ οἱ β]ασί̣[ληες προστί]θησ[θον τῶι κατεληλύθον]-

[τι ὡς τέχναν τεχνα]μέγ[ω] τῶ ἐ[ν τᾶι] πόλι πρόσθε [ἔοντος· αἰ δέ κέ τις]

[τῶγ κατεληλυθόν]των μὴ ἐμμένη ἐν ταῖς διαλυσί[εσ]σι ταύτ[αισι],

[μήκετι ἀπυκομι]ζέσθω πὰρ τᾶς πόλιος κτήματος μήδενος μη[δὲ στ]-

5 [ειχέτω ἐπὶ μή]δεν τῶμ παρεχώρησαν αὔτωι οἱ ἐν τᾶι πόλι πρό[σθε]

[ἔοντες, ἀλλὰ σ]τείχοντον ἐπὶ ταῦτα τὰ κτήματα οἱ παρχώρησαν[τ]-

[ες αὔτωι ἐκ τῶν] ἐν τᾶι πόλι πρόσθε ἐόντων, καὶ οἱ στρόταγοι εἰσ-

[αῦθις ἀπυφέρο]ντον ἐπὶ τὸν ἐν τᾶι πόλι πρόσθε ἔοντα τὰ κτήματα

[ὡς μὴ συναλλαγ]μένω τῶ κατεληλύθοντος, καὶ οἱ βασίληες προστί-

10 [θησθον τῶι ἐν τ]ᾶι πόλι πρόσθε ἔοντι ὡς τέχναν τεχναμένω τῶ κα-

[τεληλύθοντος]· μηδ' αἴ κέ τις δίκαν γράφηται περὶ τ[ο]ύτων, μὴ εἰσά-

[γοντον οἱ περί]δρομοι καὶ οἱ δικάσκοποι μηδὲ ἄ[λλ]α ἄρχα μηδεΐα·

[ἐπιμέλεσθαι δὲ] τοὶς στροτάγοις καὶ τοὶς β[ασίλ]ηας καὶ τοὶς πε-

[ριδρόμοις καὶ τ]οὶς δικασκόποις καὶ ταὶς [ἄλλα]ις ἄρχαις, αἴ κε

15 [μὴ γίνηται ἄπαν]τα ὡς ἐν τῶι ψ[αφίσματι γέγραπτ]αι, κατάγρεντον

[δὲ τὸν ἀθέτεντά τι τῶν ἐν τῶι ψαφίσματι γεγρα]μμένων, ὣς κε μηδ-

100   DIVIDED POWER IN ANCIENT GREECE

[εν {μηδ|εις?} . . . . *c*.30–1 . . . . π]ρὸς τοῖς ἐν τᾶι πόλι

[πρόσθε ἔοντας, ἀλλὰ ὁμόνοοι καὶ διαλε]λύμενοι πάντες πρὸς ἀλ-

[λάλοις πολιτεύοιντο ἀνεπιβολλε]ύτως καὶ ἐμμένοιεν ἐν τᾶι ἀ-

20 [ναγραφείσαι διαγράφαι καὶ ἐν τᾶ]ι διαλύσι τᾶι ἐν τούτωι τῶι ψα-

[φίσματι· διαιτάταις δὲ ἔλεσθ]αι τὸν δᾶμον ἄνδρας εἴκοσι, δέκα

[μὲν ἐκ τῶγ κατελθόντων, δέκ]ᾳ δὲ ἐκ τῶν ἐν τᾶι πόλι πρόσθε ἐόντων·

[οὗτοι δὲ σπουδαίως φυλάσσ]οντον καὶ ἐπιμέλεσθον ὡς μῆδεν ἔσ-

[ται ἐνάντιον τοῖς τε κατ]ελθόντεσσι καὶ τοῖς ἐν τᾶι πόλι πρόσ-

25 [θε ἐόντεσσι μηδετέρως]· καὶ περὶ τῶν ἀμφισβατημένων κτημάτων

[?ὑπὸ τῶγ κατελθόντων]· καὶ πρὸς τοῖς ἐν τᾶι πόλι ἔοντας καὶ πρὸς

[ἀλλάλοις ὡς πάντα μ]ὲν διαλυθήσονται, αἰ δὲ μή, ἔσσονται ὡς δικ-

[αιότατοι, καὶ ἐν τα]ῖς διαλυσίεσσι, ταῖς ὁ βασίλευς ἐπέκριννε

[ταῖς ἐν τᾶι διαγράφ]αι ἐμμενέοισι πάντες καὶ οἰκήσοισι τὰμ πό-

30 [λιν καὶ τὰγ χώραν ὁ]μονόεντες πρὸς ἀλλάλοις· καὶ περὶ χρημάτων

[ὡς ἔσται εἰς τὸ θέσ]θαι ταῖς διαλύσις ὡς πλεῖστα· καὶ περὶ ὅρκω

[τόγ κε ἀπομόσσοισι οἱ] πόλιται, περὶ τούτων πάντων ὅσσα κε ὁμο-

[λογέωισι πρὸς ἀλλάλο]ις, οἱ ἀγρέθεντες ἄνδρες φέροντον ἐπὶ τ-

[ὸν δᾶμον, ὁ δὲ δᾶμος ἀκο]ύσαις, αἴ κε ἄγηται συμφέρην, βολλεύτω·

35 [αἰ δε κε . . . . τὰ] ὁμολογήμενα πρὸς ἀλλάλοις συμφέρον-

[τα κύρια ἔσται καὶ τοῖς κα]τελθόντεσσι ἐπὶ Σμιθίνα προτάνιος

[ὅσσα κε τοῖς λοίποισι ψαφ]ίσθη· αἰ δέ κέ τι ἐνδεύη τῶ ψαφίσματος,

[περὶ τούτω ἁ κρίσις ἔστω ἐπ]ὶ τᾶι βόλλαι· Κυρωθέντος δὲ τῶ ψαφίσ-

[ματος ὑπὸ τῶ δάμω, εὔξασθαι] τὸν δᾶμον ἐν τᾶι εἰκρίσται τῶ μῆννος

40 [τῶ Μαιμάκτηρος πάντεσσι] τοῖς θέοισι ἐπὶ σωτηρίαι καὶ εὐδαι-

[μονίαι τῶμ πολίταν πάντων] γενέσθαι τὰν διάλυσιν τοῖς κατελ-

[θόντεσσι . . . . . . καὶ τοῖς] ἐν τᾶι πόλι ἐόντεσσι. τοὶ[ς δ]ὲ ἴρηας τ-

[οὶς δαμοτέλεας πάντας καὶ] ταῖς ἰρείαις ὀείγην το[ὶ]ς ναύοις καὶ

[τὸν δᾶμον πρὸς εὔχαν συνέλ]θην· τὰ δὲ ἶρα τὰ ὁ δᾶμος ηὔξατο ὅτε ἐξ-

45 [έπεμψε τοῖς ἀγγέλοις πρὸς] τὸν βασίληα ἀπυδόμεναι τοῖς βασί-

[ληας . . . .]τον· παρέμμεναι δὲ τᾶι θυσίαι καὶ

[τοῖς διαιτάταις καὶ τοῖς ἀ]γγέλοις τοῖς πρὸς τὸν βασίληα πρ[οσ]-

[πέμφθεντας τοῖς τε ἀπὺ τῶν] ἐν τᾶι πόλι ἐόντων καὶ τοῖς ἀπὺ τ[ῶγ]

[κατελθόντων. τὸ δὲ ψάφισμα τ]οῦτο ἀναγράψαντας τοῖς τ[αμίαις]

50 [εἰς στάλλαν λιθίναν θέμεναι εἰς τὸ ἶρον . . .]

DIVIDED POWER IN MYTILENE AND MEGALOPOLIS   101

The *basileis* shall favour the man who has returned if the man who was previously in the city practised a craft. If any of those who have returned does not abide by this agreement, [he will not recover] any possession from the city, nor own any of the possessions that those who were previously in the city had given to him; but let those who were previously in the city, amongst those who made over these possessions, own them; the *strotagoi* shall transfer the possessions again to the man who was previously in the city on the grounds that the man who returned has not been reconciled, and let the *basileis* favour the man who was previously in the city if the man who returned has been guilty of craft. If anyone brings a lawsuit about these matters, neither the *peridromoi* nor the *dikaskopoi* nor any other official shall introduce it. [...] the *strotagoi*, the *basileis*, the *peridromoi*, the *dikaskopoi* and the other officials [shall take care], if all the things are not done as it is written in the decree, shall condemn the man who breaks any of the written provisions in the decree, so that nothing/none [...] towards those who were previously in the city, but they may be citizens in state of concord and agreement each other without plotting, and may abide by the *diagrapha* written up and by the settlement in this decree. The people shall elect twenty men as arbitrators, respectively ten from those who returned and ten from those who were previously in the city. Those shall carefully protect and take care that there shall be nothing contrary to those who returned nor to those who were previously in the city in any way, and regarding the possession disputed by those who returned, both with those in the city and with one another, that everything shall be settled, but if not, they shall be as just as possible according to the agreements which the king settled in the *diagrapha*, and they shall live in the city and the surrounding territory in agreement with one another; and concerning the properties so that it can implement the agreement as far as possible; and regarding the oath that the citizens are to take, concerning all these things whatever they agree with each other, the elected men shall refer to the people, the people after hearing that, if it is suitable, let them deliberate. If [...] what they agree is useful to each other, it shall also be valid for those who returned during the prytany of Smithinas whatever was voted for the others [?]. If there is anything lacking in the decree, concerning this the decision is entrusted to the council. When the decree has been ratified by the people; the people shall vow all the gods on the twentieth of the month of Maimakter so that the settlement shall be for the salvation and the happiness of all the citizens for those who have returned and for those in the city. All the public priests and priestesses shall open the temples and the people shall come together for prayer. The rites which the people performed when they sent out the messengers to the king shall be offered by the *basileis* [...]. There shall be present at the sacrifice the arbitrators and the ambassadors sent out to the king both by those in city and by those who returned. This decree shall be written up by the treasurers on a stone *stele* and placed in the temple [...] (adapted trans. Rhodes and Osborne)

102   DIVIDED POWER IN ANCIENT GREECE

The delegation clause to the council is found at lines 37–8 of decree B on reconciliation. A preliminary analysis of the political context as well as the legal procedures involved in the two decrees is necessary in order to understand the role of the delegated power of the council in Mytilenian decision-making.

The first decree (A) is the foundation document of a democratic constitution which should last 'for all time' as explicitly stated at 2–3 (δαμοκρατίαι τὸμ πάντα χρόνον). Bencivenni points out that the establishment of the democracy in Mytilene may have originated from an external political input due to Alexander. This seems to be implied by references in the reconciliation decree to a king, probably Alexander (45) and to a *diagraphē* (B, 20).[17] Heisserer also argued that Alexander may have enacted a *diagramma* concerning constitutional arrangements for all the Greek *poleis* in Asia Minor, but it seems more likely that individual measures were taken for the different cities, as the *diagramma* for Chios shows.[18] This is relevant to the divided power and the decision-making process of the city, as the civic institutions had to deal with an external power, which introduced a higher level of decision above that of the *polis*.

Decree A opens with am enacting formula (ἔγ]νω βόλλα καὶ δᾶμος). The enactment bodies were the council and the assembly of the Mytilenians according to the usual democratic practice.[19] Rhodes and Lewis point out that the decree formulas in Mytilene differ from the model found in many other Greek cities (ἔδοξεν τῆι βολῆι καὶ τῶι δήμωι) and they argued that probouleumatic and non-probouleumatic formulas do not seem to envisage a difference in the decree-making procedure, like Athenian practice.[20] Most of the Mytilenian decrees followed a probouleumatic procedure. Decrees were introduced to the *damos* by a *probouleuma* or by the *strotagoi*, who were in charge of being intermediary between the council and the *damos*.[21] This seems to be the case in both the decree on concord (A) and the reconciliation decree (B). In the latter, the prescript is not preserved; however, one can reconstruct the probouleutic origin of the decree from lines. 38–9, where it is prescribed that the decree is to be valid after the approval of the assembly (Κυρωθέντος δὲ τῶ ψαφίσ[ματος ὑπὸ τῶ δάμω]), which implies that the relevant draft had been prepared by the council. This proves a first important point, it appears that in Mytilene the delegation clause to the council that we are discussing was first inserted in a *probouleuma*, and was then approved, possibly without substantial changes, in the assembly.[22]

---

[17] Bencivenni (2003) 46–7. A *diagramma* was an official letter of the Macedonian chancery, but adopted by other Hellenistic kings as a formal legal act of the king. For an analysis of the royal letters see Welles (1933); Bencivenni (2010), (2014); Ceccarelli (2014) 298–311; Mari (2018).

[18] Heisserer (1980) 137; cf. *SEG* 22.506= RO 84; Bencivenni (2003) 18–32.

[19] Rhodes with Lewis (1997) 258; see Labarre (1996) 162.   [20] Rhodes with Lewis (1997) 258.

[21] Labarre (1996) 167 with the review of Gauthier (1997) 349–61; Rhodes with Lewis (1997) 258. For the role in *probouleusis* of magistrates, especially in the Hellenistic *poleis*, see Chapter 4 on Sparta, pp. 136–50.

[22] Cf. Chapter 1 pp. 5–7.

Neither these two documents nor later decrees provide any information about the appointment and the office of the councillors in Mytilene. One may assume that, similarly to other democratic councils, every male citizen was eligible without census requirements at least in the fourth century.[23] Other Lesbian cities, such as Methymna, were divided into tribes, which might have been the basis for the appointment of the council.[24] The democratic features of such councils cannot be questioned. As Gauthier notes, in the decrees of the Lesbian cities, as in many Hellenistic *poleis*, the proposers are consistently officials or common citizens who approached the council and proposed their motion before the councillors. Then the council deliberated and drafted a formal *probouleuma* to be transmitted to the assembly.[25] Yet, even if the initiative started from outside the council, the inscribed documents make clear that the council played a key role in preparing the drafts for the assembly, which had to make decisions about restoration of the democracy and reintegration of the exiles, as a result of the royal *diagraphē*. It is important however to draw a distinction between the role of the council in the two decrees. The first decree proclaims the restoration of the democracy and the political decision to found the new constitution on ideals of civic reconciliation and reintegration of exiles, points reinforced by the invocation of deities such as *Homonoia, Dikē,* and *Zeus Homonoios*.[26] In this document, the council limits itself to initiating the deliberative procedure by submitting a draft to the assembly according to the normal probouleutic procedure.

The reconciliation decree, on the other hand, deals with the actual implementation of the reconciliation and creates the legal procedure to enforce the agreement.[27] The regulations contained in the reconciliation decree address the issue of the restoration of properties to the exiles and their integration into the civic body.[28] The decree thus shows the effort made by the citizens to involve all civic institutions in the complex legal procedure of property restoration, and at the same time, sheds light on the unfolding of divided power in Mytilene.

The decree's procedure entailed a relationship between the assembly, the officials, and the council, and singled out a distinctive role of the latter in the deliberative process. The decree first instructs the *basileis* to supervise the return of the exiles and the enforcement of their rights on their former properties in the city, whereas the *strotagoi* were in charge of transferring the restored properties to

---

[23] Labarre (1996) 165. Cf. the case of Iasos in Fabiani (2012) 119–20. In that case, however, the council's size can be more surely calculated by the councillors' votes recorded in the inscriptions.

[24] Labarre (1996) 171–3.   [25] See Gauthier (1997) 357–8 with several epigraphical examples.

[26] See B. D. Gray (2015) 80–1. Cf. also Heisserer and Hodot (1986) 122; Bencivenni (2003) 51.

[27] For a discussion on the role of amnesty in the Greek *poleis* see B. D. Gray (2013) 369–401; (2015) 89; Joyce (2008), (2014), (2015); (2022); *contra* Carawan (2013). On Hellenistic amnesty see Rubinstein (2013) and B. D. Gray (2015).

[28] On political exiles and the values and preferences underpinning their exclusion and behaviour in the Greek world see B. D. Gray (2015) 197–291; Loddo (2022) 60–3. On their political consciousness, see B. D. Gray (2015) 293–388, (2020) 231–46; Rubinstein (2018); see Loddo (2020a) 11–21 with discussion of the previous bibliography and especially Loddo (2022).

104   DIVIDED POWER IN ANCIENT GREECE

the exiled who agreed to this settlement. The exiles had to comply with the written agreement in order to have their properties returned. Lonis has pointed out that the decree prescribed only a partial reintegration of property, whereas the city guaranteed compensation for the rest of the property that was not restored according to a well-attested contemporary practice.[29] The provision makes clear that the exiles had to comply with the reconciliation settlement in order to receive part of their property and compensation from the city (2–7). In case an exile did not abide by the agreement, but brought a legal charge, the relevant judicial magistrates—the *peridromoi* and *dikaskopoi*—could not introduce it to court.

The following two sections deal with other procedural matters and also introduce a fundamental legal concept, which is especially relevant to understanding the delegation clause. At lines 13–15, the decree orders that all ordinary magistrates should enforce the agreement only according to the written text of the decree, otherwise they should condemn the man who breaks its written provisions. The decree stresses the written dimension of the enactment, which envisages the respect of the rule of law as one of the conceptual foundations of the reintegration procedure.[30] Usually, the validity of a statute was guaranteed by its clear visibility and by the fact that the citizens could read the relevant inscription or consult it in the public archives.[31] It is not surprising that in 333 BCE, when the Persians managed to briefly control Mytilene again, they ordered the destruction of the *stelai* containing the alliance with the Macedonians. In order to safeguard the aims of the reconciliation, both citizens and magistrates had to follow the written regulations of the decree and of the *diagraphē* during the implementation of the agreement.[32] In other words, the Mytilenians had established that only the written measures enacted by the king and by the *polis* should have legal force and excluded other kinds of informal agreement between the parties.

This is also consistent with the following section of the decree which describes the procedural steps to undertake to settle disputes between the two factions. The assembly had to elect as arbitrators twenty men, ten from the exiled and ten from those who were already in the city. This board served to broker a deal negotiating the interests of both groups on the basis to the royal *diagraphē*, as the king decided (ὁ βασίλευς ἐπέκρινε). The royal decree worked as the ultimate legal framework, as implied by the verb ἐπικρίνω, which identifies an unappealable decision.[33]

---

[29] Lonis (1991) 98–102. See also a similar provision in Tegea (*IPArk* 5); Arr. *Anab.* 2.1.4 (on the return of the exiles in Mytilene imposed by the Persians). For a study of the legal procedures for restoration of property rights for the entire Classical period see Mackil (2021).

[30] A principle of the rule of law is that laws are to be clear and accessible, see Harris (2013c) 7–8. For a general discussion see Gagarin (2008) 68; Bingham (2010).

[31] The nullification of a city statute was often made through the physical destruction of the *stelai*, see Culasso Gastaldi (2003) 241–3; Dimopoulou (2014) with several examples; and Dreher (2022) 7–76.

[32] See B. D. Gray (2015) 82–3.

[33] For the use of ἐπικρίνω in inscriptions see Gauthier (1972) 321 n. 96.

DIVIDED POWER IN MYTILENE AND MEGALOPOLIS 105

The arbitrators should finally refer their decisions to the *damos*, who had the right of final approval over property agreements.

It is after detailing this complex procedure that the council was empowered to make a decision, if there was anything lacking in the decree (αἰ δέ κέ τι ἐνδεύη τῶ ψαφίσματος, ‖[περὶ τούτω ἀ κρίσις ἔστω ἐπ]ὶ τᾶι βόλλαι).[34] If one accepts the restoration, it seems that the wording of the delegation clause moves away from the *autokratōr/kurios*-clauses found in Athenian decrees. Although the council was not made *kurios*, the decree empowers the council of autonomous power to make decisions about further changes regarding the decree without referring back to the people. The absence of evidence for a Mytilenian democratic discourse, like the public discourse that emerges in a number of Athenian literary sources, makes impossible to decide whether Mytilene's council already had similar powers during previous democratic periods.[35] To understand the persistence of democratic institutions in Mytilene is useful to analyse continuity, as well as moments of institutional change and restoration.

Deliberative institutions and a lively political participation are attested in Mytilene between the end of the seventh and the beginning of the sixth centuries. During his exile from political life, Alcaeus longed for hearing the speeches in the assembly (*agora*), being called by the herald, and in the meetings of the council (Alc. fr. 130b Voigt). Later, in the first half of the fourth century, a democratic council is attested in a decree (*IG* XII 2, 4.1, 4.3) which may constitute the closer model for the council of the restored democracy of the late fourth century.[36]

The restoration of a council, after the rule of a non-democratic regime, is important evidence for the institutional strength of Mytilean institutions that were created in the Archaic period. Recent scholarship on political institutions has explored the concept of 'institutional strength'—a parameter that can be assessed along two notions: 'enforcement' and 'stability'.[37] Enforcement indicates the degree by which institutions and their relevant rules are complied in practice,

---

[34] This restoration is accepted by all the editors. One might argue that a reference to the δᾶμος could be restored in the formula. However, if one accepts the standard expression περὶ τούτω, there is no space on the stone to restore τῶι δάμωι, as a definitive verbal form is needed. There is also no parallel for the *dēmos* mentioned in this kind of delegation clause. There are only two pieces of evidence for this expression in the dative τῶι δήμωι καὶ τῆι βουλῆι and τῶι δάμωι καὶ τᾶι βωλᾶι (*Agora* XV 37; *Teos* 51) which do not fit the lacuna. These two formulas are found respectively in the very fragmentary title of an Athenian *grammateus* and in the initial greetings of a letter to the Teians, which are not procedural formulas in deliberative contexts.

[35] For a general overview of the council see Dimopoulou-Piliouni (2015) 355–7.

[36] Cf. also the enactment formula in the late fourth-century decree of the council and the assembly honouring Atrometus, a citizen of Magnesia on the Meander (*SEG* 26.909).

[37] On 'institutional strength' see the important article by Levitsky and Murillo (2009) 115–33. The two scholars provide a fourfold model: (1) strong institutions that are both stable and enforced. This system is typical of modern developed countries, but also of some modern authoritarian countries. (2) Institutions that are widely enforced but are modified with relatively high frequency (see the case of Mytilene above). (3) Formal institutions are stable but not enforced, for example, this is the case of many Socialist laws on private property in modern China and Vietnam. (4) Institutions are weakly enforced and highly unstable.

106 DIVIDED POWER IN ANCIENT GREECE

while the notion of stability indicates the durability of institutions under changing social conditions and political preferences. The combination of these two factors produces a spectrum of 'institutional strength' that goes from formal institutions, characterized by strong enforcement and stability, to weak formal institutions. Between these diametrically opposite categories, one finds those cases in which institutional norms are enforced but are unstable over the time. The political history of Mytilenean institutions fits into this latter conceptual category.

As we have explored earlier in this chapter, Mytilene's political history was characterized by a complex history of *staseis* and changes of constitutional regimes. Mytilenean political decision-making was in fact organized in formal institutions from an early period. Such political institutions were in force and both the *dēmos* and the elite members, like for example the poet Alcaeus, used them as political arenas. Yet the political culture of Mytilene was highly unstable and the system often broke down. The institutionalized divided power, despite being enforced in period of social stability, did not show have enough strength to reconcile social struggle.[38] However, the restorations of formal political institutions show that Mytilene's degree of institutional strength was not minimal either and the institution of divided power persisted even after several episodes of *staseis*.[39]

The complexity of the reconciliation decree shows that the procedural steps taken by the Mytilenians to implement the reconciliation can be compared with that of the Athenian decree for the sacred *orgas* (*IG* II^2 204), already analysed in Chapter 2. Similarly to the decree for the sacred *orgas*, the Mytilenian decree for the reconciliation shows the workings of divided power in practice and draws a distinction between the boards of magistrates and the council.[40] On the one hand, the magistrates should carry out the written provisions of the decree without introducing any legal or procedural innovations. They can only apply the written regulations within the legal framework of the decree and the *diagraphē* of the king. On the other hand, the council had the power to introduce a further level of decision-making, after the enactment of the decree, by deciding about what was left unresolved by the decree. The role of the council is fundamental in the practical implementation of the decree of reconciliation,[41] and unlike other city offices, the council could make actual decisions about it. As a result, the decisions of the council resulted from proper decree-making filling the gaps of the reconciliation decree. Its decisions were complementary to the regulations of the decree ratified by the *damos* and would have shaped the outcome of the reconciliation.

---

[38] I will also discuss a stronger case of stability of institutionalized divided power in Sparta in the next chapter.

[39] Müller (2014) envisages a similar mechanism of 'institutional memory' operating in the late Hellenistic Boeotian *koinon*.

[40] See Chapter 2 pp. 76–84.   [41] Dimopoulou-Piliouni (2015) 264–5.

DIVIDED POWER IN MYTILENE AND MEGALOPOLIS 107

What we can reconstruct about both the ideological and institutional contexts of fourth-century Mytilene confirms this picture. As Gray points out, the civic ideals shaping the Mytilenian reconciliation agreement were built on the association of individual advantages negotiated within the community through a process of bargaining in order to obtain reciprocal social stability.[42] By representing the Mytilenian *damos*, the council was the best institution to decide on matters left unregulated by the decree. In a newly established democracy, the council must have enjoyed a high level of democratic legitimacy according to the principles of divided power. The Mytilenians, as a result, could rely on the decisions of a proper democratic authority of the city, which had the power to deliberate by enacting new regulations about the reconciliation.

It is therefore important that the *damos* should opt for delegating this matter to a civic institution, rather than calling for the external arbitration of the Macedonian king. The important studies by Gauthier, Ma, O'Neil, and more recently Boffo demonstrated that royal instructions had legal force and both free and subject cities could not ignore royal regulations, yet these norms were to be applied in a given city according to the local laws.[43] The local adaptation of a royal order is remarkably displayed in way the Mytilenians dealt with their complicated civic reconciliation. Although the decree was the result of the external input of a royal *diagraphē*, the Mytilenians carefully distinguished between the previous verdicts on exile and death decided according to the laws of the city (lines 14–20) and unlawful convictions.[44] In this way, the implementation of the royal order was shaped by the local statutes, which granted the legal foundation for a universal reconciliation within the community. In this context, the council provided the ideal institutional setting to mediate between the legal frame of the *diagraphē* and the statutes of the city. Here, the council does not play a judicial role in adjudicating disputes about property—a task delegated to the special board of arbitrators—but it was empowered to make decisions about the normative procedures in the reconciliation process. The nature of the council's decisions, unsurprisingly, remained in the realm of deliberation. A large council that was ideologically and sociologically representative of the people in its deliberative capacity had a strong level of legitimacy, within the political and institutional

---

[42] For the general discussion on this model based on the example of Dikaia see B. D. Gray (2015) 42–57; for Mytilene cf. 80–3.

[43] Cf. Polyb. 21.41.2 and in particular Ma (1999) 106–74. Gauthier (1993) 41–55 with analysis of the case of Aegina, where the royal *epistatēs* adjudicated according to the royal *prostagmata* and the civic laws (*IG* IV² 2. 749); O'Neil (2000) 424–31. Boffo and Faraguna (2021) 375–6 n. 13 with full bibliography on this topic. Cf. *Syll*³ 283 (*diagramma* of Alexander for Chios); *Syll*³ 344 (decree of Antigonus I for the synoecism of Teos and Lebedus); *SEG* 9.1, 7–8 (law of Ptolemy I for Cyrene); in all these cases the local laws are kept valid. For the royal *prostagmata* see Bencivenni (2010) 149–78; Boffo (2013) 201; for an overview of kings and Hellenistic *poleis* see Ma (2005).

[44] Cf. Joyce (2016). In the Athenian amnesty of 403 BCE states that adjudications made during the former democracy were valid.

108   DIVIDED POWER IN ANCIENT GREECE

culture of the late Classical and Hellenistic 'democratic *koinē*'.[45] Building on this legitimacy, the delegation clause allowed for a division of deliberative power between the assembly and the council. The delegation allowed the latter institution to become the venue where foundational decisions were made. The role of the council in the reconciliation decree, ultimately, helped bridging the gaps between the reconciliation, the reintegration of property, and legal rights as well as anchoring the royal decision into the legitimacy system of the late Classical polis. The process of reconciliation and legitimacy-building in late Classical Mytilene were fostered by typical institution of the polis and through a legal institution of divided power, that is the delegated power to the council.

Another significant point in this complex picture is the local institutional tradition in Lesbos. Ellis-Evans has recently pointed out the tension between city sovereignty and cooperation among the cities of Lesbos, with Mytilene being highly integrated with the mainland, while the island identity remained strong among all the Lesbian cities. Even during the period of the Hellenistic Lesbian *koinon*, city identity and institutions remained strong and independent.[46] The co-existence between opposing drivers made possible competition and the parallel developed of similar, yet not identical institutional procedures.[47] A contemporary example from another Lesbian *polis* can provide a relevant point of comparison for our purposes.

A series of documents of the Lesbian city of Eresus, the so-called 'Tyrants Dossier', dated from between 332 and 306 BCE, casts light on the institutions of the city (RO 83).[48] Like Mytilene, Eresus had experienced a similar institutional intervention by Alexander, who enacted a *diagramma* abolishing the tyranny and setting up a democratic constitution. The inscriptions trace the relationship between the city and the Macedonian kings and reports a number of relevant documents: the proceedings of the trials against the two tyrants Eurysilaus and Agonippus, two royal *diagrammata*, respectively enacted by Alexander and by Philip III, and another *diagramma* of 306 BCE by Antigonus who attempted to resettle the dispute in favour of the tyrants' relatives.[49] In response to Antigonous' *diagramma*, the people of Eresus passed a decree reaffirming their verdict against the tyrants, who were tried according to the *diagraphē* of Alexander. This last decree is especially interesting for a reconstruction of the council's role and political legitimacy within a system of divided power. The prescript of the decree states: 'The *damos* resolved. Concerning the matters about which the council had made a *probouleuma*, or had made resolution or had revised a resolution [...]' (γ back 4–5: [ἔ]γν[ω δᾶμος· περὶ ὦν ἀ βό]λ[λα] προεβόλλε[υσε, ἠ

---

[45] Gauthier (1993).   [46] Ellis-Evans (2019) 156–97, 242–3.
[47] Labarre (1996) 40; Ellis-Evans (2019) 199–202.
[48] For an analysis of these documents see Bencivenni (2003) 55–77. For a discussion of the ideological implications of inscribing the 'Tyrants Dossier', see Ellis-Evans (2012) 183–212.
[49] On the trial against tyrants see Koch (2001) 193–5.

ἔδο]-|[ξ]ε ἦ [μ]ετέδ[οξε τᾶ βόλλα] [...]). The enactment formula reveals that the council of Eresus had wide deliberative powers: in addition to the usual probouleutic powers, the council enacted its own decrees as well as modify previous regulations, as the verb μεταδοκέω indicates.[50] There was an institutional tradition of divided power in Lesbos according to which democratic councils shared with the assembly the power of enacting and revising decrees. Even if not in the same identical fashion than in Eresus, it is not surprising that the Mytilenian council could also make its own decisions without referring back to the *damos*, as the council was perceived as a democratic, and more importantly, representative deliberative body, entrusted to complement the decisions approved by the assembly.[51] The Mytilenian procedure confirms also the decisive role of deliberation organized according to multi-level stages that is typical of Greek divided power. Multiple and different levels of deliberation were singled out by institutions and procedures: a motion was first discussed in the council during *probouleusis*, in the assembly and again in the council through the delegated powers. This articulation of divided power enhanced democratic participation and striked a balance between democratic power and constitutional commitment.[52]

To summarize, the epigraphical evidence provides a clear picture of divided power and the decree-making process in fourth-century Mytilene. The restoration of the democracy and the civic reconciliation offer the opportunity to analyse the workings of the city's institutions and of divided power in practice. The assembly, the council, and the magistrates are all involved in adapting the Macedonian *diagramma* into the Mytilenian context. The council performed a special role within the decision-making procedures, as it was ideologically legitimized and legally delegated to decide on matters of reconciliation policy after the enactment of the decree itself, and could enact further decrees, participating in the decision-making process at several levels. The Mytilenian example is therefore important for several reasons. First, it shows that there were common constitutional patterns of democracy across Greece. Like Athens, Mytilene had the relevant legal tools, which allowed the council to be given the power of filling gaps in the regulations, by adding a further level of policy-making after the assembly's approval. While in Mytilene a delegation clause appears in institutionally formative events, such a post-*stasis* reconciliation, in Athens delegation is more consistently attested

---

[50] Rhodes with Lewis (1997) 258; The verb literally means 'to change opinion' or 'to change plan' see *LSJ* s.v. μεταδοκέω, 1111 and Montanari s.v. μεταδοκέω, 1323; cf. e.g. Hdt. 5.92; Dem. 20.34.

[51] On representation see Cammack (2021) and Simonton (2021).

[52] This principle, in a way, is not too different from the multi-layered decision-taking of the *gnōmai tou dēmou* so frequently used in Hellenistic democracies as noted by Schuler and Zimmermann (2012); Ma (2018) 283–4. The *gnōmē tou dēmou* reflected repeated decision-taking moments through which a motion was converted into a decree of the assembly which was in turn put forward for a second decision-making cycle. This was another way of institutionalizing divided power through a sort of second reading of a bill, which allowed for a much stronger control of presiding officials and magistrates, rather than by the fluid system of delegation that we see in Athens and Mytilene.

110 DIVIDED POWER IN ANCIENT GREECE

throughout the Classical period for ad hoc purposes. Despite the superficial differences, this analysis shows that Greek constitutional law and institutional practices shared more in terms of patterns, tools and arrangements, as sometimes thought.[53] Like Athens, the decision-making institutions of Mytilene were designed according to similar substantive rules, which were embodied in a precise procedure to delegate ad hoc deliberative power to the democratic council, when the assembly required it. When it comes to tackling procedural norms in the constitutional framework, these often have substantive implications, as they aim to enforce or preserve the spirit of the constitution.[54] For example, the Athenian procedural norms for a *graphē paranomōn* lawsuit prescribed how to bring to court anyone who proposed an illegal decree, but this system of judicial review did not have only procedural implications. The *graphē paranomōn* was in fact embedded in democratic ideology and had important substantive implications for the stability of the democracy and the legal order in fourth-century Athens.[55] In the case of the delegation clauses, procedure shows a concern for the preservation of divided power and the rule of law, which is a fundamental principle in Greek institutional organization from the Archaic period onwards.[56] Such principles were so embedded in the institutional culture of the Greek *poleis* that even royal regulations had to adapt to the civic legal and institutional practices. The delegation procedure was a legal tool which made it possible to conduct an interactive policy-making process by concurrently avoiding the concentration of power in a single institution and enabling the city organically to exploit the expertise of each institution in the decision-making process. This helps us to understand the toolset and arrangements of democratic constitutions in a broader context, which is not only that of the Athenian model.[57]

Greek political communities kept using their own institutional practices to shape the implementations of the prescriptions of the monarchs, who in turn included the principles of local laws and legal practices when formulating royal political and judicial decisions. A significant difference can be identified in the role of council in the late Hellenistic period. Indeed, the use of delegation clauses to the council suggests a different ideological approach to decision-making, as the case of Megalopolis demonstrates.

---

[53] For the similarities in Constitutional Law across Greek *poleis* see Gagarin (2005) and especially Rhodes (2015). For the unity of Greek law see Wolff (1975); Biscardi (1982). For a detailed analysis of substance and procedure in the laws of Athens see Harris (2013c) 139–74.

[54] For the interrelation of substance and procedure in modern public law in common law systems see Bell, Elliott, Varuhas, and Murray (2016).

[55] On *graphē paranomōn* in Athens see a full discussion in Chapter 6. Cf. Tribe (1980) 1067–80 points to a similar approach concerning the American Constitution. Substantive legal values underline procedural rules in the U.S. Constitution, such as the voting procedure, based on the substantive norm 'one person, one vote'.

[56] Cf. the Dreros Law (Körner 1993 n. 90 = *Nomima* I 81), the earliest Greek law, which sets a limit of ten years for a man to hold the office of *kosmos*.

[57] For different views on Hellenistic democracies see the works by Grieb (2008); Carlsson (2010) with the important review article by Hamon (2009) 347–82; Mann (2012); Wiemer (2013); Ma (2018).

3.4 Megalopolis: The Institution of *Sunedrion*

Megalopolis was founded as the capital of the Arcadian Confederacy. The city was the result of synoecism by ten founders from five Peloponnesian *poleis* in 368 BCE: Mantinea, Tegea, Cleitor, the Mainalians, and the Parrhasians (Diod. 15.72.4).[58] The new city was founded with the precise purpose to serve as an anti-Spartan bulwark after the battle of Leuctra in 371 BCE. Megalopolis had a prominent role within the Arcadian *koinon*, as it appears that the city appointed ten *damiorgoi*, as federal officials, whereas Mantinea and Tegea elected only five members each.[59] Membership of the *koinon* in this period is attested for another fourteen Arcadian *poleis*.[60] The Arcadian Confederacy played a key role in the post-Classical period until it broke up into two factions. In the third century, after the dissolution of the Confederacy, Megalopolis, under the tyrant Lydiadas, joined the second Achaean League in 235 BCE, and remained within the League until 146 BCE, when the Romans dissolved the federation. Megalopolis was immediately a very influential member of the Achaean League. The tyrant Lydiadas was elected federal *stratēgos*, the most important office of the League, which he held several times (Polyb. 2.44.5).

In a famous passage, Polybius highlights the great level of political and cultural integration within the League. He affirms that the Achaeans shared the same weights, measures, laws, and institutions (Polyb. 2.37.10–11). Scholarship has long debated the actual level of integration of the league legal and political institutions.[61] Harter-Uibopuu has argued that arbitrations for disputes between cities of the League were frequent and several local procedures were applied by the cities without federal enforcement, which was optional. A recent inscription from Messene however draws a more complex picture. In an arbitration between Messene and Megalopolis, the federal institutions played a prominent role in shaping the various stages of arbitration between cities of the League. The procedure was started at the federal level and federal institutions supervised the adjudication made by a panel of Milesian judges.[62]

The federal institutions of the Achaean League represent the starting point for our analysis of the scarce sources concerning Megalopolis' council in the late Hellenistic period. Achaean political institutions were structured according to those of a standard Greek *polis*: a federal assembly, a federal council (*boulē*),

---

[58] For Arcadian *poleis* in the Classical period see Nielsen (2002). For a general overview see Hansen and Nielsen (2004) 520–1; Nielsen (2015) 250–68.

[59] Nielsen (2015) 261–2. There are very few pieces of evidence about the Arcadian federal institutions in the fourth century. There was a federal council (Βουλὴ τῶν Ἀρκάδων) and an assembly (Xen. *Hell.* 7.4.2, 33–9).

[60] See Nielsen (2002) 477–8. Only one decree of the Confederacy has survived: *IG* V2.1.

[61] Harter-Uibopuu (1998); Roy (2003) 83; Rizakis (2008); Mackil (2013) 328–9.

[62] Luraghi and Magnetto (2012); Thür (2012) 294–336 which anticipates a further stage of the dispute from an unpublished *proklēsis*.

112   DIVIDED POWER IN ANCIENT GREECE

and boards of federal magistrates.[63] Polybius provides us with a broad picture of these institutions. The federal *stratēgoi*—who became a single office in 255 BCE— were in charge of the common affairs. We do not know much more about the actual powers of the *stratēgoi*, which must have played a very influential role within federal decision-making institutions. In a recent article, Sizov revises all the relevant scholarship on the Achaean federal assemblies, and shows that the *sunodos* of the Achean League was a large assembly formed by delegates of all the cities of the League.[64] The exact size of the *sunodos* is unknown, but Sizov, based on the Polybian account of the federal meetings, estimated a number around several thousand members. An assembly of such a size indicates that the *sunodos* was formed by representatives of the cities of the League in proportion to the population of each *polis*. This system was in a way similar to arrangement used for appointing the board of *nomographoi*.[65] This system favoured the role of city-elites in the political process, but even if not genuinely democratic, it did not require a formal census threshold for access to the Achaean assembly.[66]

The sociological composition of the institutions of many federal states dramatically changed in the late Hellenistic period. In his seminal work, Gauthier identified in the late Hellenistic period a shift in the political culture and the nature of institutions of the Greek *poleis*, where wealthy elites played a pivotal role in political life through the control of formally democratic institutions.[67] Hamon has also emphasized that the Roman influence, and then the Roman gradual conquest and inclusion of Greece in their imperial system, had far reaching consequences in the participation of citizens in the federal and civic institutions alike.[68] During their progressive conquest of Greece, the Romans imposed reforms on the federal institutions in order to restrict political participation. Censitary requirements became necessary to be appointed to the federal council or to be elected as officials in Thessaly (194 BCE) and in Macedonia (167 BCE), where, according to Polybius, the Romans established a δημοκρατικὴ καὶ συνεδριακὴ πολιτεία (Polyb. 31.2.12).[69] When talking about Achaea, Polybius says that after the Achaean war he remained in Greece to answer to the requests of the Achaean cities arising from the new constitution (*politeia*) and the laws given to them by Mummius (Polyb. 39.5.2–3).[70] Pausanias makes clear that Mummius introduced a

---

[63] For the other federal officials see Larsen (1955) 220–1.

[64] Larsen (1955) 223–4; Rizakis (2015) 123–4. For a discussion of the nature of federal assemblies and councils see Roy (2003) 84–5. For the terminology of the primary assembly and council of the Achaean League see Sizov (2017) 383–5.

[65] For the system of representation based on the *nomographoi* see Rizakis (2008); Larsen (1955) 226. A similar criterion was also followed by the council of the Aetolian League; see Mackil (2013) 360.

[66] The assembly was not predominantly made up by elite members. Cf. the description of the Achaean assembly at Corinth as packed of common people and artisans cf. Polyb. 38.12.1–6.

[67] Gauthier (1985).   [68] Hamon (2005) 130–1.

[69] A mention to the Roman influence on the Achaean *koinon* is found in Polyb. 39.5.2.

[70] For a nuanced overview of interaction between Roman and local legislation in Achaea after the Roman conquest see now Girdvainyte (2020) esp. 225–35.

DIVIDED POWER IN MYTILENE AND MEGALOPOLIS   113

wealth qualification principle for all *archai* (ἐνταῦθα δημοκρατίας μὲν κατέπαυε, καθίστα δὲ ἀπὸ τιμημάτων τὰς ἀρχάς), which means that this was also a valid requirement for the appointment of citizens as councillors (Paus. 7.16.9).[71]

This constitutional reform has very important implications for our understanding of how delegation practices to the late Hellenistic council functioned. The close reading of an inscription from Megalopolis dated between 150 BCE and 100 BCE sheds light on this issue (*IpArk* 30 = *IG* V, 2 433).

[— — — — — — — — γ]ινέσθ[ω — — — — — — — — —]

. . . . .τω ὁ ἀγορασθεὶς περὶ δι [— — — —]

[. . . . . τὸ δὲ σ]υνέδριον κύριον ἔστω [φυλάσ]-

[σον ἐν τῶι γρ]αμματοφυλακίωι τὸ προ[ειρημένον]

5 [διάγραμμα].

[εἰ δέ τι δόξε]ι ἐνλείπειν ἐν τοῖς νόμοι[ς τοῖς προ]-

[γεγραμμέ]νοις, κύριον ἔστω τὸ ἐφ᾽ ἔτο[ς συνέδρι]-

[ον ὅσσα κα]ὶ δόξει τῶι συνεδρίωι ἀδιοίκει[τα προσθεῖ]-

[ναι. μηδέ] τις μήτε νομογράφος μήτε γ[ραμμα]-

10 [τοφύλαξ] ἀλλοτριωθῆναι τὰ βυβλία [ἐπιτρεπέτω].

[οἱ δὲ νόμ]οι οἱ γεγραμένοι περὶ τῶν [συγγραφῶν],

[ἐφ᾽ ὧι ἂν συ]ψευδοκείσωσι μεταθε[ῖναι, διορθω]-

[θέντων. {²($3)}² εἰ δέ τ]ις νόμον ἢ ψάφισμ[α γράψει παρὰ]

[ταῦτα, ...]ς καὶ ὃ βλάπτοι, διπ[λόον ἀποτι]-

15 [νέτω, εἰ μὴ ἔχει χ]ρείαν ὑπ᾽ ἀνάγκ[ας — — — — — —]

[— — — — — ἔστω το]ῦ ἐμφα[νίσαντος — — — — —]

[— — — — — — — — —]ιλ[— — — — — — — —]

The *sunedrion* shall have authority to preserve the prescribed decree in the archive. If there is anything left out in the written laws, the current *sunedrion* shall have authority as long as the *sunedrion* resolves to make an addition about what is unregulated. No *nomographos* or *grammatophulax* may allow the documents to be disposed of. The written laws about the agreements which they agreed to modify may be rectified. If a law or a decree will be drafted against these [...] and he who would damage (the decree?), he should pay double, unless he is in a state of necessity [...].

---

[71] See also Hamon (2005) 131: 'Cette pratique s'appliqua certainement aux membres des conseils civiques'.

114 DIVIDED POWER IN ANCIENT GREECE

The epigraphical evidence from Megalopolis is not abundant.[72] This inscription is also unfortunately very fragmentary, which makes it difficult to contextualize the epigraphical material in its broader historical and institutional context. This inscribed document, nonetheless, provides an important, even though incomplete, insight into Megalopolis' institutional practice.

According to the restoration at l. 6, this inscription reports a *diagramma*. The legal document should not be confused with the royal letter from the Hellenistic kings, as seen in the case of Mytilene. This use of the term *diagramma* differs from early Hellenistic practice, as it refers to a civic enactment, such as a decree or a law. In this text, thus, the word *diagramma* was interchangeable with words such as *nomos* and *psaphisma* (l. 13), which implies that there was no clear-cut hierarchy of the statutes like post-Euclidean Athens.[73] As Kantor points out, the lack of a systematic hierarchy of sources of law seems to be the rule rather than the exception in the Hellenistic *poleis*, even where some distinct procedure for passing laws and decrees were envisaged.[74] The term *diagramma* underlines the written nature of the statute, as opposed to *rhētra*,[75] and was quite widespread in Peloponnesian documentary practice of this period.[76] It is found in another very fragmentary decree from Megalopolis, also containing a clause for filling the gaps where the power is given to the assembly and the *sunedrion* (IG V, 2 433.8: [εἰ δὲ δόξῃ τῶι δάμωι ἢ τοῖς συνέδρ]οις ἐπιδιορθῶσαι τὸ διάγραμμα).[77] Similarly, a contemporary Messenian regulation about grain supply is called *diagramma* (18–19 καθὼς γέγραπται ἐν τῶι διαγραμ|[ματι]). The text of the sacred law of Andania (55 BCE) refers to the statute as *diagramma* at several points (lines 5, 25, 28, 113, 114, 181–2, 189–90, 192).[78] This inscribed document is doubtless an enactment of the civic authorities of Megalopolis. The *diagramma* has no pre-script; it is therefore impossible to identify for certain the enacting body.

A possible answer to this problem, however, can be provided by the delegation clause at lines 6–9. The *diagramma* delegates full power (*kurios*) to the council (*sunedrion*) in order for it to legislate if there is anything unregulated in the written laws (εἰ δέ τι δόξε]ι ἐνλείπειν ἐν τοῖς νόμοι[ς τοῖς προ]|[γεγραμμέ]νοις, κύριον ἔστω τὸ ἐφ᾽ ἔτο[ς συνέδρι]|[ον ὅσσα κα]ὶ δόξει τῶι συνεδρίωι ἀδιοίκει[τα προσθεῖ]|[ναι]).[79] The full power of the council is also marked by the second part of the clause, which states that the council will resolve to regulate what was 'not managed' (ἀδιοίκει[τα προσθεῖ]|[ναι]). The decree employs language that is peculiar of deliberative practice: the verb δοκέω implies an act of deliberation made by

---

[72] Achaean inscriptions from other *poleis* have been published by Rizakis (1998), (2008).

[73] The term was also used to refer to the *edictum* of Roman officials and emperors; see Mason (1974) 35–6, 127–31. On the blurred distinction between laws and decrees outside Athens see §6.3 below.

[74] Kantor (2012) 72–5. Cf. also Chapters 6 and 7 pp. 199–200 and p. 217 n. 1.

[75] See Chapter 4 on Sparta, pp. 136–7.   [76] Quass (1971); Hölkeskamp (2002).

[77] For the meaning of διορθόω see Bencivenni (2003) 34 n. 56. For διόρθωμα as rectificatory act see Hamon (2009) 380; *pace* Carlsson (2010) 178–9.

[78] Deshours (2006) 58; Gawlinski (2012) 1–2.   [79] Cf. Chapter 2 on *kurios* clauses, pp. 70–5.

DIVIDED POWER IN MYTILENE AND MEGALOPOLIS 115

the council, which had the power to enact a new decree to complement the *diagramma*. This practice is paralleled, in slightly different fashion, in a delegation clause to the council contained in another very fragmentary and undated *diagramma* from Megalopolis, where the councillors are instructed to rectify the decree (ἐπιδιορθῶσαι τὸ διάγραμμα), but the preserved text of the inscription does not allow us to draw any further conclusions (*IG* V, 2 434).[80] This is also confirmed by the provision at lines 4–5 giving the council the power to keep the records in the archive (*grammatophulakion*)—another clause at lines 9–10 forbade the *nomographoi* and the *grammatophulakes* from disposing of the written records, which were usually under their supervision.[81] The combination of these clauses gave the council a free hand in managing further stages of the decreemaking procedure after the enactment of the *diagramma*: the council could pass additional enactments to complete the *diagramma*'s text with new regulations as well as having sole supervisory power over the laws, by excluding other officials from this task. As Sickinger rightly argued, this document reveals the Greeks were 'unwilling to accept deficiencies, shortcomings, and weakness in their existing law', and therefore specific institutions were put in place to rectify and correct norms.[82]

The Megalopolitan council seems to have broad deliberative powers to add further regulations to the *diagramma*. The preserved text is too fragmentary to inform us about the exact content of the enactment, which would have helped to reconstruct the competences of the council. What the text makes clear, instead, is the fact that late Hellenistic Megalopolis had changed the nature of its council from a democratic *boulē* to an elitist *sunedrion*. Hamon has carefully studied this institutional development across the Greek world, and has convincingly shown that there was a connection between terminological change and the sociological composition of late Hellenistic councils.[83] During the Classical and early Hellenistic periods, the term *boulē* normally indicated a democratic council representing the whole citizen body. As I have emphasized in the discussion on the council of Mytilene, this kind of *boulē* was appointed by lot for a one-year term (or even shorter terms) and without censitary requirements.[84] Conversely, the term *sunedrion* was originally used for 'congresses' of leagues and federal

---

[80] Cf. *IG* IX 1² 583.75–6 (Olympia, 216 BCE): τοὺς δὲ ἱε[ρο]ὺς | νόμους ἐξέστω διορθοῖν, ἐπεί κα νομοθεσία καθίκῃ, μηθὲν ὑπεναντίον | τοῖς ἐν τᾶι στάλαι καταγράφοντας (it is allowed to rectify the sacred laws, when the *nomothesia* takes place, without recording anything contrary to those (laws) in the *stelai*). On nomothetic procedure outside Athens see Canevaro (2016a).

[81] Cf. *I.Magnesia* 38.45–50 from Megalopolis (208–7 BCE). The *nomographoi* are in charge of drafting the laws as well as to keep the records. Cf. Rhodes with Lewis (1997) 92.

[82] Sickinger (2008) 190–1; Boffo and Faraguna (2021) 562–3 for the role of the city magistrates in archiving state documents.

[83] Hamon (2005) 121–44, (2007) 79–100.

[84] e.g. the Council of Rhodes was in session for only six months of the year. See Gabrielsen (2000) 190–1 and esp. A. C. Thomsen (2020) 19–22 for an overview of the Hellenistic political institutions of

116   DIVIDED POWER IN ANCIENT GREECE

states, which were not necessarily a democratic body.[85] Hamon shows that during the second and first centuries BCE, the term *sunedrion* gradually replaced *boulē* as the term to define the councils of several *poleis* in continental Greece. The composition and political activity of such councils became predominantly the province of wealthy local elites, and the spread of the more neutral term *sunedrion* marked this shift in the sociological composition of the city councils and enshrined into the institutional and documentary terminology.

This was probably due to a twofold process of endogenous development of the Greek political culture in combination with imitation to the civic level of the new arrangements of federal institutions, which had been transformed by the census reforms imposed by the Romans. As a result, Roman influence could indirectly favour the establishment of elite-dominated councils in the Greek *poleis*, which was then formalized in proper requirements after 146 BCE. Such process of elite-capture of civic councils cannot only be attributed to Roman indirect or direct influence, which was definitely important. As Fabiani showed for the case of third-century Iasos, the phenomenon of elite-capture in key offices in charge of preparing the assembly agendas, such as the *prutaneis*, was first of all a Greek phenomenon that already in the making before the Roman conquest and paved the way to the later measures taken by the Roman magistrates after campaigns against Greek states.[86] Similarly, Thomsen has recently shown the important role of associations in Hellenistic Rhodes in bringing together a magisterial elites. Members of the Rhodian elites that played a key role in politics and regularly held political offices for more than one term. Especially the presiding board of the *prutaneis* exercised considerable influence in the agenda-setting and proposal-making of the Rhodian deliberative institutions.[87]

In the case of Megalopolis, the terminological and institutional shifts go hand in hand. The change from *boulai* to elitist *sunedria* was consolidated in the late Hellenistic period and during the early Imperial period, as is also confirmed by a bilingual inscription from Megalopolis dated under the reign of Augustus, in

---

Rhodes. C. A. Thomsen (2020) 21 n. 20 citing an unpublished decree of 168 BCE containing a delegation clause to the Rhodian council to enact an additional decrees in case there is something missing in the assembly's decree. As Thomsen rightly notes, the delegation clause does not in any way limited the power of the assembly. Cf. Wiemer (2002) 334 n. 35. Cf. the Rhodian association decree of Zenon of Selge (*Annuario* n.s. 1–2 [1938–9] 158 n. 18) that contains an almost identical clause and shows that delegation clauses were also common in associations' decree.

[85] On the *sunedrion* of the Second Athenian League see RO 22, 41–6; for a discussion of the *sunedria* of Greek federal states, see among other e.g. for the Aetolian League Funke (2015) 108–17; for the Thessalian League see Bouchon and Helly (2015) 241.

[86] Cf. e.g. Dio Chry. *Or.* 45.3–7, who says that one hundred councillors were enrolled in the council of Prusa that year (ἑκατὸν βουλευτῶν καταλεγέντων). The verb καταλέγω matches the Latin verb *adlegere*, which is the verb used for referring to the enrollment in the Roman senate; see Mason (1974) 59.

[87] C. A. Thomsen (2020) 22–48.

which the Latin expression *iubente senatu*, displayed in the prescript, is translated into Greek with κατὰ τὸ δόγμα τῶν συνέδρων.[88]

Endogenous and exogenous process of institutional change appeared to have characterized the shift in the nature of councils across Greece. The development of a civic *sunedrion* in Megalopolis is consistent with this trend. Müller demonstrates that city *sunedria* appeared in Boeotia around 170–167 BCE.[89] Knoepfler shows that in Chalcis and Eretria the local *boulai* were transformed into *sunedria* after the battle of Pydna.[90] Ismard has recently shown that in late Hellenistic Athens, the *genē* gradually underwent a gradual process of aristocratization from the second century BCE, which ended up with the creation of proper *ordines* with legal prerogatives in the Imperial period.[91] Yet, as Hamon points out, a similar change is also attested later in the Greek *poleis* of Asia Minor during the first century BCE, when *bouleutēria* gradually became the most important civic buildings marking the higher status of the councillors within the community.[92] The *sunedrion* in Megalopolis is to be contextualized within this historical trend. The new council of Megalopolis developed to work as an elitist institution with a higher prestige and social status than the average citizen which was reinforced by the appointment in the *sunedrion*.

Heller insightfully points out that this '*transfert culturelle*' was not unidirectional and was a more complex and nuanced historical process.[93] The progressive elitization of Greek deliberative institutions was part of a broader shift in the value system of Greek honour (*timē*), which impacted the way honours qua offices (*timai*) started to be allocated according to a different system of values. This new system accepted the use and display of individual private wealth in the public realm. The new social setting of the council did not completely replace the pre-existing set of ideological values embedded in the institutional role and practice of divided power.

On the contrary, the delegation clause to the council, typical of Greek democratic institutions, acquires a different colour and a new role vis-à-vis the social composition of the council, which exploits the routine mechanisms embedded in the institutional practice, but converts them to new purposes. Historical institutionalism defines this typology of institutional change as 'conversion'. It conceptualizes a framework in which the formal rules remain stable, but the political actors can interpret and re-enact the existing institution for a purpose different from the original one, encouraging different kinds of collective behaviour.[94]

---

[88] *IG* V, 2 456.1–2, 6.   [89] Müller (2005) 114–15.

[90] Knoepfler (1990) 497.   [91] Ismard (2013).

[92] Kockel (1995); Hamon (2005) 132–44, (2011) 315–22 esp. for the religious cults celebrated in late Hellenistic and Imperial *bouleutēria*.

[93] Heller (2009) 372.

[94] Conran and Thelen (2016) 63–5. This concept is closely associated to the concept of 'drift', according to which the formal rules are stable but the environment shifts by causing enforcement of the rules with effects different from the original institutional intent. See Streeck and Thelen (2005); Hacker and Pierson (2010).

118 DIVIDED POWER IN ANCIENT GREECE

Indeed, institutional design cannot foresee the long-term use of an institution, which can change its ideological underpinning at some point in its historical development. Change may happen for several reasons, such as opposition in the relevant governmental bodies to changing the formal rules or political inaction. Hacker, Pierson, and Thelen demonstrate that institutions are especially subject to conversion when formal rules have some ambiguous aspects, not precisely regulated and therefore open to interpretation.[95] This is the case of the delegation clause, whose purpose within the decision-making process could be differently interpreted within a political landscape where the sociological composition of the institutions was changing. Even though the legal formulation of the delegation remained the same within a system of divided power, the social milieu of the agents holding the part of the deliberative power was changing. This model allows us to shed light on the use of delegation clauses in late Hellenistic Megalopolis.

As discussed in Chapter 2, in fully democratic contexts, the delegation clauses regulated the role of the council in the decision-making process by transferring deliberative power from the *dēmos* to the council and created an extra deliberative level which benefitted from the expertise of the councillors in the field of administration. This procedure reflected the principle of divided power embedded in the relevant institutions. The democratic councils represented the *dēmos* as a whole and allowed empowerment of decree-making power into a single institution without undermining the legitimacy of the democratic process.

The council of late Hellenistic Megalopolis no longer fits this context and ideology, and yet we find here the use of delegation from the *dēmos* to the council, with formal features very similar to those of democratic Athens and Mytilene. The *dēmos* in the assembly still exercised a degree of control over public *timē* assigned to his officials by being the arbiter of the self-assertion of prominent leaders and granting the delegation to the council to enact further regulations. This ostensible discrepancy can be solved by highlighting the working of path dependence, and especially of conversion. Political institutions are meant to be steady and permanent, and as March and Olsen have shown, changing institutional rules and legal and deliberative practices is very hard once those practices have been internalized into the institutional order. This is the case of the delegation clauses in Megalopolis, which no longer denote a fully democratic system of divided power between deliberative bodies; nevertheless, continuity in the deliberative relationship between the council and the *dēmos* was preserved by delegating powers to the council. In this way, the city elites benefited from and were legitimized by the old institutional practice, shaped by democratic values, and

---

[95] Hacker, Pierson, and Thelen (2015) 189 build their theory on the legal concept of 'precision' and 'imprecision' in the formulation of rules and procedural norms.

were even more incisive in making political decisions in the council. Through the delegation clause, the city elites gathered in the council were legally empowered to enact decrees, which they could complement with further measures, as the democratic *boulai* did. The endurance of previous institutional practices is also stressed by the fact that the inscription shows that the council's tenure was still annual (7–8: τὸ ἐφ' ἔτο[ς συνέδρι|ον), not unlike the democratic Athenian council, demonstrating how the old practice was still formally respected, even though the social composition of the council had changed.[96]

The scarcity of other sources and the fragmentary preservation of the epigraphical evidence do not help to reconstruct a broader picture of the institutional development in Megalopolis in this important turning point in Greek history. The analysis of the inscription however casts light on the institutional interplay between deliberative bodies in late Hellenistic Megalopolis. This confirms that the divided power between the powers of the people's assembly and those of the councils in policy-making was not only a feature of Classical Athenian democracy, but this lively relationship is attested during the Hellenistic period in other *poleis*. The practice of distributing decree-making power among different deliberative bodies did not end with the Roman conquest. Even after the Romans set up a provincial government in Achaia, city *sunedria* kept being given the power of filling the gaps in local regulations, as in the case of the law of Andania of 55 BCE, displaying a persistence of the deliberative practices of the city-states even when the external context had deeply changed. Old practices persisted in line with a mechanism of path dependence although their role changed radically within the new political context. Their new roles were conceptualized and legitimized within the framework of longstanding institutional practices.

3.5 Path Dependence and Conversion in Greek Divided Power

The findings of this chapter demonstrate the complexity of deliberative practice in Mytilene and Megalopolis and the institutional continuity and changes in the Hellenistic period. Delegation clauses played an important role in implementing the concept of divided power by regulating the relationship between assemblies and councils. This happened not only in massive *poleis* like Athens, but also in smaller city-states, such as Mytilene and Megalopolis, located in different parts of the Greek world. Both these cases show that the civic institutions had to deal

---

[96] Hamon (2005) 132 points out that nothing forbade to old *sunedroi* from taking part to the meetings of the council after the expiration of their term of office, as it is attested in a first-century decree of Pagai.

somehow with higher levels of state sovereignty, such as the Macedonian monarchy or the Achaean League.

The analysis of the case study from fourth-century Mytilene show that the council was a key institution in the newly restored democracy which reenacted practices and procedures of the previous democratic moments of the Mytilenian history. Unlike other public officials of the city, the council played an active role in settling the deliberative matters concerning disputes left unresolved by the royal *diagraphē*. This is important because it demonstrates a more nuanced picture of decision-making in the Greek city-states, where the actual enactment and the implementation of decrees are often intertwined. In Mytilene, like Classical Athens, the council could take an interactive role on different institutional levels: preparation of the assembly's agenda, supervision over the implementation of the political decisions, and, like this case, actual policy- and decision-making. The delegation clause was precisely designed to regulate the interplay of deliberative institutions as well the different stages of decree-making.

The inscription from Megalopolis, even if very fragmentary, provides an insight into the workings of deliberation in the city in the late Hellenistic period. The *diagramma* preserved on stone shows that the city council turned from a *boulē* into a *sunedrion* by the end of the second century BCE. The establishment of *sunedria* provides evidence for a change in the composition of the councils across Greece. The civic councils are shifting from fully democratic bodies representing the people into deliberative institutions dominated by civic elites. This different sociological setting of the council did not change the deliberative practice, as we find delegation clauses to the *sunedrion*, which could fill the gaps in the *diagramma*. Despite the elitist composition of the council, the practice of delegation still reproduced the dynamics of divided power, which implies a well-regulated interplay between the assembly and the council. The latter could introduce a further deliberative stage, but within the boundaries of the people's will expressed by the delegation, which remained an ad hoc transfer of power. These practices however declined as the constitutions became oligarchic, with a different relationship between probouleutic bodies and the people. In Megalopolis, political actors partook in a larger process of institutional change that took place across the Greek world. This change of the nature of the civic councils *converted* the institutional purpose of delegation from a democratic rationale to an elitist purpose. Path-dependent practices made the institutional procedure stable, but political actors used delegation to concentrate power into a narrower and distinct part of the civic body. This shows how the interpretation of the procedural rules is built on the relevant substantive norms and political discourse underpinning the constitutional order. In non-democratic regimes, the balance between deliberative bodies does not envisage ad hoc delegation, which becomes unnecessary. In other words, the concept of divided power also informed decision-making, even when the *dēmos* was not fully in control of the ideological and institutional tenant of the system. The interaction between council, magistrates and assembly institutionalized a specific non-democratic version of divided power, with emphasis on control of legality in the hand of oligarchic and anti-egalitarian institutions. This will be the focus of the next chapter about divided power and decree-making in Sparta.

PART II
DIVIDED POWER AND CONTROL OF LEGALITY

4

Divided Power and *Eunomia*

Deliberative Procedures in Ancient Sparta

4.1 Spartan Political Institutions and the *Mirage Spartiate*

Spartan political power was institutionally grounded on the interplay between the council of elders (*gerousia*), the ephors, and the assembly. This interplay followed different ideological patterns from those found in the other Greek council-assembly relationships.[1] Unlike the Athenian assembly, the Spartan assembly did not possess the power to transfer decisions to another deliberative body. On the contrary, the character of the Spartan *politeia* gave the probouleutic bodies— the *gerousia* and the ephors—the power to play a direct and prominent role in political deliberation, by shaping policy-making through the powers of *probouleusis* and *nomophulakia* (guardianship of the law). Neither of these institutions, however, had exclusive control over these functions, which were in fact divided between ephors and *gerontes*. The study of the working of this constitutional mechanism shows the complexity of the Spartan institutional balance, and sheds light upon the features of divided power in practice in a non-democratic political system, where high officials and a powerful council were in charge of key functions of legal control. Through a systematic analysis of Spartan decision-making, this chapter introduces the discussion of the power of legal control in Greek divided power.[2] The Spartan instantiation of divided power had integrated, within the deliberative procedures, specific steps for controlling the legality of the assembly's decrees and the coherence of the decision with the traditional Spartan *nomos*.

Spartan institutions were pictured as a model of political stability from the Classical period onwards.[3] The so-called Spartan '*mirage*' involved not only its constitutional order but also its social and economic institutions.[4] Xenophon begins his *Constitution of the Lacedaemonians* by associating Spartan fame with the *politeia* set up by Lycurgus, which made the Laconian city the most powerful

---

[1] Cf. Chapter 2 and Chapter 3 pp. 61–92 and pp. 98–119.
[2] This important aspect of divided power will be further explored in Chapters 5 and 6 (pp. 154–76 and pp. 177–213) with reference to Classical Athens and other Hellenistic case studies.
[3] For Sparta as a model for modern republicanism see Nippel (1994).
[4] For the expression '*mirage spartiate*' see Ollier (1933).

Divided Power in Ancient Greece: Decision-Making and Institutions in the Classical and Hellenistic Polis. Alberto Esu, Oxford University Press. © Alberto Esu 2024. DOI: 10.1093/oso/9780198883951.003.0004

(δυνατωτάτη) and famous (ὀνομαστοτάτη) *polis* in Greece (Xen. *Lac.* 1.1).[5] In Aristotle's *Politics*, in which the assessment of Sparta is more complex and nuanced, one finds a critique of contemporary Spartan institutions, as well as praise for Lycurgus as a great lawgiver who established the laws of Sparta.[6] Most other ancient sources often remark upon the unchangeable features of some Spartan institutions as a key aspect of Spartan *eunomia*. Thucydides maintains that after a long period of war and *stasis*, the Dorians established excellent laws and Sparta employed the same constitution for more than four hundred years (Thuc. 1.18.1).[7]

This ancient invention of the ideal Spartan constitution and of its legendary lawgiver Lycurgus has been long recognized in scholarship.[8] Cartledge has pointed out how this 'partly distorted and partly invented' view of Sparta was due to non-Spartans.[9] Millender has demonstrated the Athenian ideological process of 'barbarization' of the Spartan social norms in Classical period.[10] Flower, however, showed that the Spartans themselves were not immune from inventing their own past during the Classical and Hellenistic periods.[11] This outcome was often reached by attributing contemporary institutional and social innovations to Lycurgus, according to an ideological attitude that is also well known with regard to Solon and the *patrios politeia* in fourth-century Athens.[12] Yet Hodkinson has shown in several important studies how this view of Sparta as an exceptional and static society within the Greek world during the Archaic and Classical periods is in need of revision.[13] In fact, most of the evidence about the institutions, the economy, and the society of Sparta does not reflect the actual Archaic and Classical Spartan *kosmos*, but results from later invention, aimed at shaping collective memory about the past, and consistent with reforms of the Hellenistic period.[14]

This is especially true when it comes to studying the Spartan political institutions and deliberative practices. The preservation of the Great Rhetra, the alleged 'founding' constitutional document of Sparta, has given rise to a long debate about

---

[5] On Xenophon's *Constitution of the Lacedaemonians* see Tuplin (1994); Rebenich (1998); Lipka (2002); V. Gray (2007); and the recent work by Humble (2021). On the Xenophon and Sparta see the important essays collected in Powell and Richer (2020).

[6] Arist. *Pol.* 1269a69; *Pol.* 1273b20; for a careful analysis of Sparta in Aristotle's works see Bertelli (2004).

[7] See also Lys. 33.7.

[8] For studies about the myth of Sparta see Tigerstedt (1965–78); Hodkinson and Powell (1994).

[9] Cartledge (1987) 118.   [10] Millender (1999).   [11] Flower (2002).

[12] For first lawgivers see Szegedy-Maszak (1978); Hölkeskamp (1999) 44–59; Camassa (2011a) 71–177; Canevaro (2015); Loddo (2018). For a nuanced treatment of the Spartan construction of the tradition about Lycurgus see Nafissi (2017).

[13] Hodkinson (1994), (2009b); Hansen and Hodkinson (2009). For a concise but effective history of modern scholarship about Sparta see in the same volume, Hodkinson (2009a) ix–xxxiii with bibliography.

[14] On collective memory, see the classic work by Halbwachs (1950); Giangiulio (2019); for a methodological analysis of the *mnemonic turn* in historical scholarship see Proietti (2021) 12–33.

DIVIDED POWER AND *EUNOMIA*   127

the origin of Spartan institutions. The text of the Great Rhetra, preserved in Plutarch's *Life of Lycurgus*, reports a document from the lost Aristotelian *Constitution of the Lacedaemonians* and an additional clause, the so-called 'rider', which Plutarch attributes to the kings Theopompus and Polydorus (Plut. *Lyc.* 6.1–10).[15] This document details the constitutional structure and the deliberative procedures of Sparta traditionally attributed to Lycurgus and based on the interaction between three institutions: the two kings, the council of elders (*gerousia*) and the *damos*. Nafissi has demonstrated that the rhētra does not, in fact, outline the original foundation of the Spartan constitution; rather it is a piece of retrospective history elaborated and accepted by Archaic Spartan society.[16] The Great Rhetra marks the moment of institutionalization of the Spartan community between the seventh century and the sixth century, and is itself a first attempt at dating back their institutions to a remote past.[17]

Although the Rhetra cannot be used for exploring the foundations of the Spartan political system, it gives important insights into the workings of Spartan institutions at the time when it was composed.[18] It provides a brief account of the three most important Spartan institutions, which are still attested during the Classical and Hellenistic periods, along with the fundamental office of the five ephors, not mentioned in the text of the Rhetra. Spartan deliberation was the result of a complex interaction between the council of elders (*gerousia*), the ephors, and the assembly. The *gerousia* and the ephors constituted the most important boards of officials in Sparta. They shared the probouleutic power and checked the legality of the enactments of the Spartan assembly, which ratified the proposals of *gerontes* and ephors.[19]

There is, however, no consensus amongst scholars about the actual workings and the balance of power among deliberative bodies of ancient Sparta. Some scholars have stressed the fundamental oligarchic features of Spartan deliberation, in which the assembly played a marginal role, whereas powerful officials made all

[15] The noun *rhētra* shows an oral origin of the Archaic text. The division of the text of the Great Rhetra and the rider is in fact a later antiquarian distinction; see Nafissi (1991) 67–71. For the Aristotelian *Constitution of the Lacedemonians* as a source for the Great Rhetra see Manfredini and Piccirilli (1980) 234. Cf. Hdt. 6.57; Xen. *Lac.* 15.5. As Nafissi (2010) 110 n. 110 points out, being a law based on an oracle, the Rhetra was not affected by the Lycurgan ban for written law. If Plutarch had consulted the Delphic archives, he would have mentioned it as in Plut. *Sol.* 11.2.

[16] Nafissi (2010) with full bibliography on the Great Rhetra at 93 n. 20; *contra* Schulz (2011) 154. For intentional history see Gehrke (2001), (2010). See also Maffi (2002); and Lupi (2014b), for the identification of the Great Rhetra with an Archaic procedure for the admission of new members in the Spartan civic body during the religious festival of the *Apellai*.

[17] Nafissi (2010) 127; on the relationship between the Great Rhetra and Tyrtaeus' *Eunomia* see van Wees (1999); van Wees (2002) argues against the identification of clear cross-references between the two texts; *contra* Raaflaub (2006).

[18] On the substantial level of social and economic inequality in Archaic Sparta see Hodkinson (2000) 76–80 and 399–441. The Rhetra may also be seen as reflecting this social inequality in the constitutionalization of divided power.

[19] See §4.3 below.

128 DIVIDED POWER IN ANCIENT GREECE

the decisions.[20] By contrast, Ruzé has argued that the text of the Great Rhetra already envisaged a right of free speech for the *damos*, which could actively shape Spartan policy-making.[21] In particular, Ruzé's approach plays down the role of the *gerousia* in the probouleutic procedure, by arguing for an informal *probouleusis* during which the *damos* debated preliminary proposals without however taking a formal vote. Conversely, Schulz has made the case for a prominent role of the *gerousia* in Sparta's institutional system, and has provided a picture of the legislative procedure in which the *gerontes* played a key role. Although Schulz recognizes that the decree-making process was achieved through interaction between the *gerousia* and the ephors, he argues that when there was no consensus amongst the *gerontes* about a motion to submit before the *damos*, the ephor did not introduce the bill to the assembly, instead an advisory assembly would be called to check the people's opinion on an informal basis, and only afterwards could the *gerousia* either submit or veto the draft through their probouleutic power before an actual vote of the assembly.[22] These approaches are, however, problematic, for several reasons. First, there is no evidence of informal or advisory meetings of the people's assembly in Greek deliberative practice *tout court*, including in non-democratic contexts, and this assumption is mainly based on the idea of Sparta's exceptionality. Second, assuming the existence of advisory meetings of the assembly fails to isolate the difference between the power of *probouleusis* and the power of *nomophulakia*, which was performed by the *gerousia*'s veto of decision after the debate in the assembly.[23]

This chapter argues that the Spartan decision-making process shared the principle of divided power with the other Greek case studies discussed in Chapters 2 and 3. This is clearly shown by the evidence regarding the role of the *gerousia* and the ephors in the deliberative procedures of Classical and Hellenistic Sparta. In Sparta, too, deliberation was the result of institutional interaction and envisaged a multi-layered decision-making system. This is particularly true in regard to the relationship between the *gerousia*, the ephors, and the *damos*, which was designed so that power was divided between these bodies in order to keep the deliberation within the framework of the traditional legal order.

The balance of power and a sound legal order were key features of the Greek *poleis* since the Archaic period. *Eunomia* is the term that Spartans and other Greek communities used to refer to this kind of political system, which preserved freedom under the laws, and was regarded as typical of the Greek *poleis* in opposition to tyranny (Hdt. 1.65, 7.104; Thuc. 1.18.1).[24] Indeed, during the process of institution-formation, Spartan political institutions were not conceptualized as

---

[20] Andrewes (1966) 5 n. 8; de Ste. Croix (1972) 127 n. 99; Jeffery (1976) 249.
[21] Ruzé (1997) 150–6.   [22] Schulz (2011) 196–201.
[23] On these two powers of the *gerousia* see also Cartledge (1987) 123.
[24] For Spartan *eunomia* and the spirit of Archaic law see Harris (2006) 3–28.

part of an *oligarchia* in opposition to a *dēmokratia*. The opposing pair oligarchy–democracy became prominent in Greek politics and political thought only from the second half of the fifth century, and Spartan understanding of their regime as non-democratic emerged later, after the Peloponnesian War, in the same way the Athenians started conceptualizing their political regime as a *demokratia* in opposition to the Spartan constitutional model, which granted more power to small bodies of officials and required property qualification for office.[25] Just as in the other Greek *poleis*, the rule of law and divided power were at the foundation of the Spartan constitution, defining the very aim of its institutions. These institutions and procedures, however, were marked—compared, for example, to those in Athens—by stronger devices and powerful offices to limit the power of the people, and to keep it in check, while, at the same time, recognizing its formal authority. It was, as at Athens, a case of divided power, but one with explicit protection of the deliberative power of the elite vis-à-vis that of the *damos*—a power that was maintained through complex procedures and institutional steps from the Archaic period to the Hellenistic period showing the path dependence of Spartan institutions.[26] Thus, the interplay between different governmental bodies followed these ideological patterns of the Spartan *politeia*, which gave the probouleutic bodies—the *gerousia* and the ephors—the power to shape the decree-making through the powers of *probouleusis* and *nomophulakia*. Neither of these two institutions, however, had exclusive control over these constitutional functions, which were in fact divided between ephors and *gerontes*. The study of the practical workings of this constitutional mechanism underscores the complexity of Sparta's institutional equilibrium and the features of divided power in practice in a non-democratic political system.

Unlike Classical Athens or other Hellenistic *poleis*, Sparta did not, however, show the same 'epigraphic habit' by inscribing state decrees and laws, which provide evidence for legal procedures regulating political deliberation, such as the delegation clauses discussed in Chapters 2 and 3. This chapter examines the two most detailed ancient literary accounts concerning the workings of Spartan deliberation reported by Diodorus and Plutarch (Diod. 11.50.2–7; Plut. *Agis* 11.1). It begins by sketching an overview of Spartan political institutions and their functions. I shall then focus on the analysis of the literary sources in order to reconstruct the interactive relationship between distinct governmental bodies, in particular the interplay between the two probouleutic bodies, the *gerousia* and the ephors, and the Spartan assembly in the process of deliberation. This will shed light on the constitutional workings as well as on the ideological features of Spartan deliberation by focusing on the powers of *probouleusis* and *nomophulakia* shared by *gerontes* and ephors.

---

[25] Harris (2016b) 1–13. On the fifth-century characterization of Sparta as an atypical oligarchy which was a model for other oligarchies see Simonton (2017) 54–8.

[26] Cf. de Ste. Croix (1972) 128 for Sparta as 'a strongly hierarchical society'.

130 DIVIDED POWER IN ANCIENT GREECE

4.2 Spartan Decision-Making Institutions: Kings, *Gerousia*, and Ephors

The two kings, the *gerousia*, and the ephors made up the three institutions that dominated Spartan political deliberation.[27] The text of the Great Rhetra alludes to two of these institutions: the *gerontes* and the founders (*archagetai*), a term interpreted by Plutarch as referring to the kings.[28] Although the Great Rhetra is a retrospective document, these references show that both the *gerousia* and the Spartan kingship were already fully institutionalized in the early Archaic period.

In order to understand the nature of deliberation and divided power in Sparta, an examination of the three major decision-making institutions is needed. During the Classical and Hellenistic periods, the Spartan kings were formally limited in their power. In Xenophon's *Constitution of the Lacedaemonians*, one reads that the kings had to take an oath in which they swore to reign according to the established laws (Xen. *Lac.* 15.7: ὁ δὲ ὅρκος ἐστὶ τῷ μὲν βασιλεῖ κατὰ τοὺς τῆς πόλεως κειμένους νόμους βασιλεύσειν). Aristotle, in the *Politics*'s discussion of good kingship, states that the Spartan constitution provides a kingship which is lawful and limited in its authority (Arist. *Pol.* 1285a7: ἡ γὰρ ἐν τῇ Λακωνικῇ πολιτείᾳ δοκεῖ μὲν εἶναι βασιλεία μάλιστα τῶν κατὰ νόμον, οὐκ ἔστι δὲ κυρία πάντων). He then defines the nature of Spartan kingship as a kind of supreme generalship for life (αὕτη μὲν οὖν ἡ βασιλεία οἷον στρατηγία τις αὐτοκρατόρων καὶ ἀΐδιός ἐστιν). As recent studies have pointed out, although the two kings were limited in their constitutional power, they could enjoy significant charisma-based authority grounded in the mythical origin of the Heraclid dyarchy, in their life-long tenure, as well as in their wealth and the broad powers granted to them during military campaigns.[29] Spartan military success was also due to the balance between legal controls over the kings and the need of a centralized military command. This institutional design prevented the kings from acquiring too much power without interfering with the unity of command necessary for military efficiency on campaign.[30]

Constitutional limits to the power of the kings were not only entrusted to laws and the balance with other powerful offices, that is, the *gerousia* and the ephors. The very same design of the double kingship is a remarkable paradigm of divided

---

[27] The incorrect identification of the ephors in the Rhetra and in Tyrtaeus' *dēmotai andres* is based on weak interpretations of literary evidence from Plut. *Lyc.* 6.10 and Diod. 7.12.6, and on arbitrary assumptions that Diodorus' lines come from Tyrtaeus' poem; cf. Nafissi (2010) 98–102; *contra* Richer (1998) 98–106; Link (2000) 19–30; Luther (2004) 44–59.

[28] See Plut. *Lyc.* 6.3. Nafissi (2010) 104–7 points out that this is a retrospective word, normally used for oikists and founders of cults.

[29] Nafissi (2007) 331–2; Millender (2009). On Spartan kingship see Carlier (1984) 274–87; Cartledge (2001) 55–67; Millender (2017a). See already de Ste. Croix (1972) 125 on the prestige of kings in political decision-making.

[30] Harris (2015a) 83–90.

DIVIDED POWER AND *EUNOMIA*   131

power where the *basileis* would control one another and ultimately limit the overall power of their joint office. Such peculiar arrangement of the double kingship (or 'divided' kingship) helps explain its extraordinary resilience of Spartan kingship in the political environment of the Classical *poleis* which was generally hostile to hereditary political offices and sole rulers. Luraghi convincingly suggests that limiting royal power by means of collegiality should be seen as the reason why this institutional formula was firstly introduced.[31] This institutionalization of a double kingship is consistent with the general pattern of Spartan constitutional thought and practice. The Spartan kingship should not be understood as the product of the fusion between two separate and independent institutions or of a residual office, but an institution that, just like the rest of the Spartan system, was devised to keep up with the notion of divided power and curb autocratic tendencies.[32] The frequent Homeric analogies concerning the Spartan kings, as Luraghi noted, would make the *Iliad* and the *Odyssey* forms of 'repositories of political tradition' that the Spartans used to legitimize this peculiar institution in the political landscape of the Classical Greek *poleis*.[33] This interpretation is also supported the connection between the kings and the institutions of the council of elders—a close relationship often found in the Homeric poems (e.g. Hom. *Od.* 6.53–5, 7.189, 8.41, 13.10–12).[34]

The *gerousia* was a cornerstone of Spartan political power and an examination of this institution is key for our understanding of Spartan divided power. As the text of the Great Rhetra shows, the two kings along with the twenty-eight *gerontes* constituted a collegial institution, the *gerousia*.[35] The *gerousia*, however, should not be interpreted as a 'royal council'. As several sources confirm, the kings' votes had the same weight as those of the other *gerontes*,[36] and, as I shall discuss in detail later, during the Hellenistic period the kings even needed the support of the ephors to introduce motions to the *gerousia*.

Unlike the Athenian council, made up of five hundred citizens appointed by lot every year, the Spartan *gerousia* was constituted of only thirty members appointed for life (Aesch. 1.180; Arist. *Pol.* 1270b39, 1272a36; Plut. *Lyc.* 6, 26.1; *Ages.* 4.2; Paus. 3.5.2).[37] Ancient evidence confirms that the *gerousia* was the most respected and prestigious Spartan institution, according to the typical values of aristocratic constitutions.[38] According to Aristotle's *Politics*, the *gerousia* represented the

---

[31] Luraghi (2013) 16–17; Carlier (1984) 240–319 and in particular 306–9 for the origin of the dyarchy.

[32] Carlier (1984) 299–309.   [33] Luraghi (2013) 16.

[34] On the connection between Homeric *basileis* and councils cf. Schulz (2011) 28–41.

[35] For a discussion about the Doric name of the *gerousia* see Schulz (2011) 95–6. The regular Doric word was γεροντία; cf. Xen. *Lac.* 10.1.

[36] See Nafissi (2007) 331; Schulz (2011) 237. For the voting powers and the status of the *gerontes* see Lupi (2014a) 38–41; and Schwartzberg (2014) 25–7. Cf. Hdt. 6.57; Thuc. 1.20.3; Plat. *Leg.* 692a2 (δύναμις ἰσόψηφος).

[37] For the life appointment see E. David (1991) 18; Ruzé (1997) 138–9.

[38] Schulz (2011) 106–8.

132   DIVIDED POWER IN ANCIENT GREECE

aristocratic element of the Spartan mixed constitution, and its members were the *kaloi kagathoi*.[39] As Aristotle states, in Sparta the different parts (*merē*) of the city kept their relevant roles allowing the endurance of the constitution: the kings received their honour (διὰ τὴν αὐτῶν τιμήν), the people held the ephorate (διὰ τὴν ἐφορείαν), and the *kaloi kagathoi* were entitled to the membership of the *gerousia* as an award for their individual merits and virtues (οἱ δὲ καλοὶ κἀγαθοὶ διὰ τὴν γερουσίαν, ἆθλον γὰρ ἡ ἀρχὴ αὕτη τῆς ἀρετῆς ἐστιν), which the Spartan civic community highly respected. Although it is worth noting that there no was no legal restriction for the access to the *gerousia* and the only formal requirement for appointment to the *gerousia* was that the candidate had reached the age of 60, the evidence implies that especially members of the social elites could reasonably expect to compete for such an important office.[40] This is also confirmed by Xenophon, who states that Lycurgus was a good lawgiver for having established the *gerousia*, which makes it possible for the *gerontes* to show off their virtues (Xen. *Lac.* 10.1–3). In *Against Leptines* (Dem. 20.107), Demosthenes employs an expression similar to that used in Aristotle's *Politics*, stating that the *gerousia* is the master of the Spartan *politeia* and a reward for merit (τῆς ἀρετῆς ἆθλον). Such values were embedded in the fundamental social and economic inequality of Spartan society, which was institutionalized in the formal offices and the relevant procedures of the political system.[41]

The Spartan elites manning the *gerousia* obtained a formalization of their claims for major political prestige and power in light of their wealth, birth, and age. The prestige of this office and the *gerontes*' awareness of the relevant values attached to it can be traced in a fourth-century epigram commemorating the election of one Hippansidas to the *gerousia* (*SEG* 46.400).[42] The *gerōn* dedicated a seat to Athena Alea as a memorial of his office (μνᾶμα γεροντείας) and made it available to anyone who wishes to use it to watch the rituals 'on the condition, however, that the young give up their seat to the elders'. Hippasindas' epigram is an important source for understanding the normative values informing the office of *gerōn* and the institutionalized rituals of deference at Sparta. The ritual of rising from one's own seat in the presence of high officials as a mark of deference for the office's *timē* is well attested in Sparta. When describing the prerogatives of the kings, Xenophon says that all rise in the presence of the king, expect ephors from the ephoral seats (Xen. *Lac.* 15.6). This episode signals that the two-way character

---

[39] For *kalokagathia* in Sparta see Wankel (1961); Ph. Davies (2013); *pace* Bourriot (1996) with review of Cairns (1997) 74–6.

[40] de Ste. Croix (1972) 353–4; Ph. Davies (2013) 269–70 and (forthcoming); Schulz (2011) 121–2 calculated that average office term for an elder was roughly 7.5 years, with a turnover of 3.73 new *gerontes* every year.

[41] For an accessible and important discussion of inequality in Spartan society see Ph. Davies (2017) esp. 489–93 about politics and the Spartan elites, see also Ph. Davies (forthcoming).

[42] Kourinou-Pikoula (1992–8); Cassio (2000); for an alternative reading see Lanérès (2012). On Athena Alea at Sparta cf. Xen. *Hell.* 6.5.27.

DIVIDED POWER AND *EUNOMIA*   133

of this deference ritual. While rising before the king shows deference for the institution of kingship, at the same time the ephors' prerogatives of remaining seated on their chairs mark their status as guardians of the laws and supervisors of the royal conduct.[43] Likewise, by dedicating a seat to Athena Alea, Hippansidas showed his demeanour as a pious citizen who is worthy of election to the *gerousia*, certainly one of highest honours for a Spartiate.[44] Consistently with his office, Hippansidas acts as an enforcer of the elders' authority when reminding the young to show deference to the elders and give up their seat.[45] This symbolic capital and ideology were ultimately enshrined in the institution of the *gerousia* and played a very important role in shaping the institutional task of the *gerontes* and the nature of their political decisions in the legislative and deliberative procedure.

This is also confirmed by the appointment procedure of the *gerontes*—described by Plutarch—in which the *damos* played an important role in the election of the candidates by shouting (Hdt. 9.28.1; Thuc. 1.87; Plut. *Lyc.* 26). Some chosen men were closed in a separate building, so that they could not see the candidate, but only hear the shouts. According to Plutarch's account, the judges had tablets on which they recorded the volume of each vote without knowing the candidates. They declared as elected whoever received the longest and loudest shouts (ὅτῳ δὲ πλείστη γένοιτο καὶ μεγίστη, τοῦτον ἀνηγόρευον). In the *Politics*, Aristotle disapproves of the voting procedure for electing the *gerontes* and defines it as 'childish' (παιδαριώδης), a term that he employs also for the appointment of the ephors (Arist. *Pol.* 1270b24–5).[46] Aristotle does not justify his severe judgement, but it is likely that he is referring to the same acclamatory procedure described by Plutarch. In spite of Aristotelian criticism, the acclamatory shouts of the Spartan *damos* reflected a voting procedure embedded with precise ideological features. Schwartzberg argues that, by voting through acclamation, the Spartans in the assembly secured a collective result for the election, in which the individual votes were not counted, because of the different levels of 'epistemic dignity' among the members of the civic community as a whole.[47] As already shown, the *gerousia* voted by majority rule, because the political and epistemic weight of each elder—including the two kings—was the same, but also higher than that of common citizen of the assembly. The *damos*, on the other hand, voted as a collective deliberative body, showing the will of the community through

---

[43] Cf. Tyrt. fr. 9.40 G–P; Hdt. 2.80 on the young giving precedence on the streets to the elders at Sparta. See E. David (1991) 64–9 for the symbols and non-verbal rituals of Spartan gerontocracy.

[44] On the religious zeal of the Spartans and its connection with orderliness see Parker (1989) 162; cf. Hdt. 5.63; Xen. *Ages.* 11.2; Richer (2007); and Flower (2018).

[45] I refer here to Erving Goffman's model of social interaction. In Goffman's terminology, demeanour is the strategy of self-representation of individuals in social interaction, while deference is the system of rituals and marks of respect that go from an individual to another. See Goffman (1967) 47–95.

[46] Schulz (2011) 114–15. For the election of the ephors see Richer (1998) 296–307.

[47] Schwartzberg (2014) 25–6.

134 DIVIDED POWER IN ANCIENT GREECE

acclamation. This different voting system also had relevant consequences for the legislative process. I will return to this later in this chapter when analysing the veto powers of the *gerousia*.

The collective vote of the whole citizen community in selecting the *gerontes* was an important acknowledgement of the moral and political virtues of the *gerontes*, as representatives of the *damos* within the council of elders. Once elected by the *damos*, the *gerontes* held several honours, which were broadly similar to those for the winners of athletic contests in other Greek *poleis*.[48] Plutarch's account of the ceremony of a newly elected elder offers a good picture of how the higher level of *timē* of this office was institutionalized and recognized by the Spartan *polis*. A new elder wore a crown and visited the temples followed by a procession of young men and women praising him with songs (Plut. *Lyc.* 26.3–6).[49] He then went to the common mess in which he received a double portion that he was expected offer to one of his female relatives whom he esteemed the most.[50] Such considerable honours for the new *gerontes* were appropriate to the broad powers of the *gerousia*. The council of elders, including the kings, had exclusive judicial powers in lawsuits in which the penalty was death, *atimia*, or exile (Xen. *Lac.* 10.1; Arist. *Pol.* 1294b29; Plut. *Lyc.* 26).[51] The *gerousia* was also involved in trials of the kings, but in this case, the lawcourt was composed of the twenty-eight *gerontes*, the other king, and the ephors.[52] Unlike democratic Athens, where trials lasted only one day, capital and royal trials in Sparta could last for several days (Plat. *Apol.* 37a; Plut. *Apoph. Lac.* 217a13). The legal procedure for capital trials began before the ephors, who brought the charge before the *gerousia* and notified the defendant through a written statement proposing the penalty. Fragment A of the Vatican palimpsest of Theophrastus' *De eligendis magistratibus* seems to envisage this judicial procedure by showing that the *anakrisis* was made by the ephors who referred the case to the *gerontes*.[53] According to MacDowell, it is likely that the ephors had the power to decide whether the case was to be transferred to the *gerousia*.[54] This seems to be what happened during the plot of Cinadon in 399 BCE: when the ephors discovered the conspiracy, they started an investigation of

[48] For the role of athletics at Sparta see Hodkinson (1999) esp. 170–3 on the limits to private commemorations of athletic victories in Archaic and Classical Sparta; Mann (2001) 121–63; Christesen (2013), (2018).
[49] For a nuanced assessment of the role and status of women in Spartan society see Millender (2017b). For Spartan women and the mirage see Millender (1999); Cartledge (2001); Hodkinson (2004).
[50] For an analysis of the ritual see B. Jordan (1990); E. David (1991) 18–19; Schulz (2011) 117–19; and now esp. Bernardo (2019) 286–90.
[51] For death penalty and exile convictions cf. Schulz (2011) 180–1.
[52] For instances of trials of Spartan kings see Hdt. 6.82; Paus. 3.6.8; Xen. *Hell.* 3.3. 8–11; Plut. *Agis.* 19.
[53] Vat. Gr. 2306 fr. A 1–30. The text is written in two *folia* (A and B). For the study of *folium* A see Keaney (1974). His interpretation is followed by MacDowell (1986) 138; Richer (1998) 441; Schulz (2011) 177.
[54] MacDowell (1986) 46.

DIVIDED POWER AND *EUNOMIA*   135

Cinadon and his supporters in order to prevent the conspiracy, after having consulted with some *gerontes* (Xen. *Hell.* 3.3.8–11).[55] Plutarch says that the ephors ordered King Agis IV to defend himself before the *gerontes* in a trial (ἐκέλευον ὑπὲρ τῶν πεπραγμένων ἀπολογεῖσθαι).[56] Thus, literary evidence shows an important interplay between the *gerousia* and the ephors in judicial decisions.

Despite the fact that they are not mentioned in the Great Rhetra, the ephors were fundamental to the Spartan decision-making process. The ephorate was established after the Rhetra was composed, by the creation of a board of five officials.[57] Evidence for the origin of the ephorate is lacking, and the story about their origin in connection with King Theopompus is a later tradition (Arist. *Pol.* 1313a25–33). As Nafissi suggests, it is likely that the office was instituted during the sixth century reflecting the institutional consolidation of the political community.[58] Its members were the highest magistrates of Sparta—one of whom was the eponymous—elected by the *damos* for one year, possibly with the same procedure used to elect the *gerontes*.[59] As their office's name suggests, the ephors had to oversee (ἐφορᾶν) the respect of *nomoi* as well as the behaviour of the individual citizens (Xen. *Lac.* 8.3). The kings were also subject to close control by the ephors. Two of the five ephors accompanied one of the kings during military campaigns (this is again another sign of divided power) or, as we saw, the board of ephors could prosecute them in a trial. They also had jurisdiction over areas that in Athens were supervised by the council, such as the mobilization of the army, public order, public finance, religion, and the supervision of other officials.[60]

The interaction between ephorate and *gerousia* was not limited only to the judicial sphere, but was particularly prominent in political deliberation. As was typical of Greek institutional practice, the council had probouleutic power, which in Sparta was shared between the council of elders (*gerousia*) and the ephors. If one compares Spartan *probouleusis* with its Athenian equivalent, it is immediately clear that Sparta shows a different constitutional pattern. In Athens, the probouleutic power was held by the council, which submitted *probouleumata* to the assembly. There were no other institutions entitled to prepare the agenda or to submit formal proposals to the *dēmos*.[61] The Athenian assembly could discuss only items put in the agenda by the council. For example, when Nicias tried to have the *prutaneis* put a motion to the vote about the expedition to Sicily, despite

---

[55] See Richer (1998) 353–6. For a comparison between Athenian and Spartan institutional means to deal with internal crisis see Esu (2021a) 169–72.

[56] Plut. *Agis* 19.3. Cf. also Hdt. 5.39–40 for the case of King Anaxandrias.

[57] Ephors are also called by sources as ἀρχή, ἄρχοντες, τὰ τέλη, οἱ ἐν τέλει. See Richer (1998) 265–70.

[58] Nafissi (2009) 130–1.

[59] It is possible that an ephor could be elected only once to that office.

[60] Arist. *Pol.* 1271a6–7; for mobilization see Richer (1998) 324–34, for the religious role 157–257, for finance 477–9, for *euthunai* 442–4 with Fröhlich (2004).

[61] For *probouleusis* in Athens cf. Dem. 22.5–7; [Arist.] *Ath. Pol.* 45.4. See Introduction §1.1 and Chapter 2 pp. 43–4.

136 DIVIDED POWER IN ANCIENT GREECE

its not being on the agenda of the assembly, he knew that he was doing something illegal, because his proposal did not follow the probouleutic procedure and was not in a *probouleuma* of the council (Thuc. 6.14). In Sparta, on the other hand, *probouleusis* was not exercised by a single institutional agency, but by both the *gerousia* and the ephors according to different procedures, which shows that this fundamental power was actually 'divided'. Unlike democratic contexts, however, the interplay between the deliberative institutions reflects different institutional values, embedded in the constitutional design and therefore in the non-democratic features of the Spartan *politeia*. Spartan institutions evolved from the Archaic arrangement shown by the Great Rhetra, for example, by introducing the board of five ephors. Nevertheless, political institutions changed incrementally and are path dependent and preserved, to an extent, functions, features, and values of the *eunomia* which originally shaped them. These values, enshrined in the relevant institutions, preserved the balance of powers as well as the stability of the legal order, and were still found in the workings of the deliberative institutions in the Classical and Hellenistic periods, with consequences for the workings of decision-making and the enactment of decrees. With this framework in mind, one can analyse the literary evidence from Diodorus and especially from Plutarch's *Life of Agis*. These sources offer an account of Spartan deliberation in practice in the Classical and Hellenistic periods, and a careful analysis will reveal the institutional and ideological patterns of the Spartan decision-making process.

4.3 Interaction between Ephors and *Gerousia*: 'Divided' *Probouleusis* and *Nomophulakia*

In Aristotle's *Politics*, one finds the theoretical description of the workings of *probouleusis* in oligarchic regimes. At 1298b26–35, he states that in oligarchies there are probouleutic magistrates, called *probouloi* or *nomophulakes*, who put forward proposals to the *dēmos*, which can discuss only these motions.[62] The *dēmos* cannot advance or debate proposals, except those already approved by these magistrates (ἔτι ἢ ταὐτὰ ψηφίζεσθαι τὸν δῆμον ἢ μηθὲν ἐναντίον τοῖς εἰσφερομένοις).[63] If one compares the Aristotelian account with the text of the Great Rhetra, it seems clear that the Aristotle's statement matches the procedures envisaged in the Great Rhetra as well as in Spartan institutional practice. The text of the Great Rhetra is the following:

---

[62] On *probouloi* and *nomophulakes* see Arist. *Pol.* 1323a; *probouloi* were elected in Athens soon after the defeat in the Sicilian expedition. See Thuc. 8.1.3; [Arist.] *Ath. Pol.* 29.2–31.3. Cf. Rhodes (1981) 362–415.

[63] Cf. Canevaro (2014) 314.

DIVIDED POWER AND *EUNOMIA* 137

Διὸς Συλλανίου καὶ Ἀθανᾶς Συλλανίας ἱερὸν ἱδρυσάμενον, φυλὰς φυλάξαντα καὶ ὠβὰς ὠβάξαντα, τριάκοντα γερουσίαν σὺν ἀρχαγέταις καταστήσαντα, ὥρας ἐξ ὥρας ἀπελλάζειν μεταξὺ Βαβύκας τε καὶ Κνακιῶνος, οὕτως εἰσφέρειν τε καὶ ἀφίστασθαι δάμῳ <...> καὶ κράτος. [...] αἰ δὲ σκολιὰν ὁ δᾶμος ἕλοιτο, τοὺς πρεσβυγενέας καὶ ἀρχαγέτας ἀποστατῆρας ἦμεν.

Having founded a cult of Zeus Syllanios and Athena Syllania, having divided the people [or: 'kept the divisions'] in tribes and having divided it in *obai*, having appointed a council of thirty members, including the founders, regularly cele-brate the *Apellai* between Babyka and Knakion. Bring forward and reject (pro-posals) as follows: to the people must go < ... > and final decision, [...] but if the people speaks crookedly [or: 'asks for something crooked'] the elders and the founders are to be rejecters. (trans. Nafissi)

The text of the Great Rhetra shows that, during the Archaic period, the *gerousia* and the kings had the power of putting proposals before the assembly (οὕτως εἰσφέρειν τε καὶ ἀφίστασθαι).[64] The so-called rider also implies that the *gerousia* could veto motions of the assembly in case the *damos* 'speaks crookedly', which means that the assembly could not pass an enactment different from the *gerousia*'s proposal without the possibility of it being vetoed—a clear example of the power of *nomophulakia* of the *gerontes* (Plut. *Lyc.* 6.3).

Evidence for the working of deliberation in Classical and Hellenistic Sparta is scanty. The very same terms *probouleusis* and *nomophulakia*, used in accordance with Aristotle's usage, are not found in Sparta. The former, in Aristotle, indicates the power of the council or of the probouleutic officials (or a collaboration between these two bodies) to set the agenda of the people's assemblies, in order to achieve efficient deliberation. The latter denotes the power to control the conformity of the motions of the assembly to the general laws which governed the life of the community. Both these powers were fundamental to preserving balance between popular power and rule of law typical of the Greek *poleis* from the Archaic period onwards. In Greek standard institutional terminology, the two terms *probouloi* or *nomophulakes* (and cognates) were often used interchangeably to indicate special magistrates (and functions) who had the power of drafting proposals and checking the legality of deliberations. For example, Plutarch uses the expression τὸ προβουλεύειν at *Agis* 11.1 to describe the powers of the Spartan *gerontes* when vetoing Agis' *rhētra*. In Plutarch's passage, the term indicates that the *gerontes* were acting as *probouloi* with their relevant powers of legislative review. In Aristotle's terminology, that would constitute an exercise of *nomophu-lakia*. Despite the occasional terminological overlap, the Aristotelian classification

---

[64] A late sixth-century probouleutic council of elders (*preiga*) is also attested in *IG* IX I² 609 from western Locris. It played a role along with the assembly (*polis*) and the *apoklesia* in overriding an entrenchment clause about division of the land. See the discussion at §5.2.

138   DIVIDED POWER IN ANCIENT GREECE

shows that the two procedures were conceptually different, and that they marked two different moments of deliberation (Arist. *Pol.* 1299b–1300a). Even though neither term is found in Spartan practice, however, just as in most of the Greek *poleis*, the Spartan deliberative bodies performed those functions through the relevant legal procedure, and therefore the use of this terminology has significant heuristic value within a Greek perspective.

The only piece of evidence for the probouleutic procedure in fifth-century Sparta is provided by a slightly obscure passage in Diodorus. He describes a debate in Sparta in 475/4 BCE, after the conflict between the Greek *poleis* and the Persians (Diod. 11.50.1–7). The historical authenticity of these events seems dubious, even though recent scholarship accepts Diodorus' account as trustworthy.[65] The historical events might be fictional, but it is hard to argue that the institutional framework is fictional.[66] Diodorus narrates that the *gerousia* was summoned (συναχθείσης δὲ τῆς γερουσίας) to deliberate on the possibility of making war against the Athenians (ἐβουλεύοντο περὶ τοῦ πολέμου), who had supremacy over the seas and had therefore become a threat to Sparta. Likewise, the assembly was summoned (ὁμοίως δὲ καὶ τῆς κοινῆς ἐκκλησίας συναχθείσης) and the majority of the citizens agreed that Sparta had to gain leadership of the seas. Diodorus' account seems at first glance to imply that a second meeting of the *gerousia* was held (τῆς γερουσίας συνεδρευούσης περὶ τούτων), in which the *gerontes* were about to make their decision by following the people's preference for war. Hetoimaridas, one of the *gerontes*, however persuaded both the *gerousia* and the *damos* with his eloquence to change their mind. The problem with this account is that it excludes the ephors from the procedure, whereas other evidence indicates that there was active interaction between the *gerousia* and the ephors. As I argue below, in cases where there was an absence of unanimity within the *gerousia*, the ephors could formally introduce a proposal to the *damos* for ratification, but this bill had then to be examined and voted again by the majority of *gerontes* in order to be passed.

This is shown by the most detailed account of the political decision-making procedure in Sparta, found in Plutarch's *Life of Agis*, which describes the legislative procedure during the Hellenistic period (Plut. *Agis.* 8–11). Plutarch's account is not immune from ideological bias, as it relies on the contemporary work of Phylarchus, who was fiercely criticized by Polybius for his dramatic historiographical style.[67] Yet, Polybius' critiques should not be overestimated, as he himself

---

[65] On the essential reliability of the event, even in presence of stereotypes such as young arrogance vs old wisdom see Vattuone (2008) 131–51. See also Green (2006) 111 n. 190; Zaccarini (2011) 291 n. 15, (2017) 55; *contra* Fornara and Samons, Jr (1991) 122–4.

[66] Griffith (1966) 134 n. 10; see also Kelly (1981) 59 n. 45.

[67] Gabba (1957) 3–55, esp. 15, 193–239; Africa (1961); cf. Polyb. 2.56; Pédech (1989) 403; for an overview on previous scholarship see Rebenich (1997); for a more recent study on Polybius and Phylarchus' dramatic historiography see Schepens (2005) 141–64. For Plutarch's cautious but not dismissive use of fragments of Duris and Phylarchus see Hau (2021) 248–51.

DIVIDED POWER AND *EUNOMIA* 139

adopted a biased perspective against Phylarchus because of his anti-Spartan attitude. In his analysis of the role of women in the *Lives of Agis and Cleomenes*, Powell shows how several details drawn from Phylarchus' work are indeed plausible pieces of information from contemporary Sparta.[68] According to Plutarch, in 243/2 BCE, King Agis IV proposed an ambitious plan of reforms— remission of debts, distribution of land, and extension of citizenship.[69] Agis succeeded in procuring the election of Lysander as ephor, and through him the bill was put forward before the *gerousia* (Plut. *Agis* 8.1: εὐθὺς εἰσέφερε δι' αὐτοῦ ῥήτραν εἰς τοὺς γέροντας). The new *rhētra*, however, did not receive the unanimous favour of the *gerontes*, who were divided in their opinions (γραφείσης δὲ τῆς ῥήτρας, καὶ τῶν γερόντων εἰς ταὐτὸ ταῖς γνώμαις οὐ συμφερομένων). Lysander therefore summoned the assembly (ἐκκλησίαν συναγαγὼν ὁ Λύσανδρος) to discuss the proposal (Plut. *Agis* 9.11). After a debate between the kings Agis and Leonidas, who supported the traditional *kosmos* against Agis' reforms, the Spartans backed Agis by passing his motion (τῷ μὲν Ἄγιδι τὸ πλῆθος ἐπηκολούθησεν). The *gerontes*, however, eventually vetoed the motion through a majority vote (τοὺς γέροντας, οἷς τὸ κράτος ἦν ἐν τῷ προβουλεύειν), so that the reforms never entered into force (Plut. *Agis* 11.1).

Building on these two literary accounts, several studies have reconstructed Spartan legislative procedures as characterized either by an unclear distribution of powers between ephors and *gerousia* or by an informal preparatory phase. Kelly, in his interpretation of the procedure in Diodorus, highlights that the meeting of the *gerousia* was held before the *damos*, which usually showed its mood through shouts, silence, and applause.[70] As Diodorus makes clear, the *gerousia* was still in session when the *damos* expressed favour for war (πάντων δὲ σχεδὸν τῶν πολιτῶν πρὸς ταύτην τὴν ὑπόθεσιν ὡρμημένων, καὶ τῆς γερουσίας συνεδρευούσης περὶ τούτων). For this reason, Kelly argues that when the *gerontes* and the ephors—not mentioned by Diodorus—did not agree on a motion, they put their case before the assembly and decided on the spot whether to put their motions to the vote in the assembly. Thus, during the same meeting, Hetoimaridas persuaded the *gerontes* to put his motion to the vote, which was passed by the *damos*. Kelly envisages the very same procedure in Plutarch's account of the reforms of Agis IV without clearly identifying the relevant roles of the ephors and of the *gerontes* in the decision-making procedure.[71] Other scholars have adopted views stressing the informality of Spartan deliberation. Following Ruzé,

---

[68] Powell (1999) 401–15; on the *Lives of Agis and Cleomenes* see Pelling (2023).

[69] For the reforms of Agis IV see Cartledge and Spawforth (1991) 68–72. For the increasing autocratic character of kingship in Hellenistic Sparta see Millender (2009) 31–5 and Walthall (2013) 123–59.

[70] Diodorus' text does not mention shouts and applauses but this practice is attested in Sparta. For voting by shouting see p. 133.

[71] Kelly (1981) 60.

140   DIVIDED POWER IN ANCIENT GREECE

Richer argues that the literary sources about both episodes show that both the *gerousia* and the assembly were not summoned to make an ultimate decision because the *gerontes* did not submit a formal proposal to the *damos*, so that the early stages of the procedure, that is the first meeting of the *gerousia* and the first meeting of the assembly, consisted of mere preparatory work before the final decision.[72] Schulz argues that these passages from Diodorus and Plutarch attest deliberative procedures in which the assembly played an advisory role when there was no unanimity among the *gerontes*.[73] According to Schulz, Plutarch's passage in particular illustrates a probouleutic procedure structured in two steps.[74] First, the *gerousia* prepared the motions to be submitted to the assembly. Second, the assembly was summoned and the motion was put to the vote. However, if the *gerousia* could not make a unanimous decision, a meeting of the *damos* could be held in order to gauge the people's opinion without taking a formal vote. After hearing that, the *gerousia* submitted a final *probouleuma* for the vote before the *damos*, approving it by majority rule.[75]

These studies, however, provide accounts of the probouleutic procedure that do not fit the historical evidence of deliberative practice in non-democratic constitutions.[76] In reconstructing the Spartan deliberative procedure, all these scholars have drawn a forced analogy between the Hetoimaridas' debate in Diodorus' *Library* and the Plutarchian account of Agis' reforms. The reconstructions also underestimate the role of the ephorate in the deliberative practice by implying that the assembly did not vote on a formal proposal. There are several problems with these accounts.

First of all, one should clearly identify the specific procedural features of the two historical accounts. The problem with any simple juxtaposition is that the episodes are substantially different from a procedural point of view—not in the nature of the procedure, but in how the procedure unfolds. We can see that Diodorus' account, structured in two parts, shows a decision-making process that is conditioned by a key difference from that summarized by Plutarch. Initially, the *gerousia* and the *damos* agreed on making war against Athens, then Hetoimaridas delivered his speech and persuaded both *gerontes* and citizens

---

[72] Richer (1998) 349–51; cf. Ruzé (1997) 150; Ruzé (2012) 5–15 has re-asserted her interpretation of the Great Rhetra. Cf. Gagarin's reply: Gagarin (2012) 17–20.

[73] Schulz (2011) 198–200. In particular the passages in Plut. *Agis* 5, 3–5 about the *rhētra* introduced by the ephor Epitadeus and those in Plut. *Lys.* 16–17 about the prohibition of silver and gold seems clearly to highlight the wide probouleutic power of the ephors, rather than the primacy of the *gerousia*. Yet, Schütrumpf and Hodkinson have clearly demonstrated that the Epitadeus episode in the *Life of Agis* is an unhistorical account, and is based on Plato's *Republic* (555c–e). See Schütrumpf (1994) 317; Hodkinson (2000) 90–4; Nafissi (2008) 72–84.

[74] For other previous reconstructions see Forrest (1967) 11–19.

[75] Schulz (2011) 196–201. Schulz singles out two distinct kinds of assemblies: an advisory assembly (*beratende Volksversammlung*) and a decision-making one (*entscheidende Volksversammlung*).

[76] Ruzé (1997) 154 argues that the '*spécificité*' of the Spartan *polis* made it difficult for the ancient author to describe the decision-making by using ordinary institutional terminology.

DIVIDED POWER AND *EUNOMIA*   141

to change their plans. Diodorus thus, makes clear that there was an initial general consensus among the *gerontes*, as well as among the citizens, and this is the reason why no one 'dared to advance any other proposal' (οὐδένα τολμήσειν συμβουλεῦσαι ἕτερόν τι). In contrast to the case of Agis described by Plutarch, there is no dispute within the *gerousia*, and this consensus in the *gerousia* determines the next procedural step: a vote of ratification by the assembly. Plutarch clearly shows that in the case of Agis' reforms there was instead political dissent, organized into two factions: Agis, the ephor Lysander, the majority of the citizens on one side, and the majority of the *gerontes* and King Leonidas on the other. This dissent was already expressed in the first meeting of the *gerousia* and later in the debate in the citizens' assembly. By contrast, in Diodorus' passage, there is no opposition at all. Everyone agreed about the proposal for making war and an assembly was ready to ratify the proposal of the *gerousia*. Hetoimaridas, at that point, delivered his speech persuading the *gerontes*, still in session, and the assembly not to take military action. The original proposal is rejected without any opposition from the *gerontes*. This shows a probouleutic procedure that follows the usual pattern common in the Greek world. The council of elders, and possibly the unmentioned ephors, reached an agreement about a proposal, which was then submitted to the assembly for ratification. In this case, the assembly, influenced by an elder who spoke against the bill approved by the *gerousia*, rejected the bill, with the endorsement of the rest of the *gerontes*, that had by then also changed their mind.

Moving from Diodorus to Plutarch's *Life of Agis*, we find a more detailed description of the procedure, whose steps are compatible with those identified in the case of Hetoimaridas. A close reading of the passage will help identifying the procedural similarities as well as the crucial role of the ephors in Spartan divided power. Plutarch gives an account of the way Agis' *rhētra* was put forward in the relevant institutional bodies. In order to proceed to a close an analysis of these two chapters, it is useful to report sections 8–9 of Plutarch's *Life of Agis*.

[8] Οὐ μὴν ἀλλὰ διαπραξάμενος ὁ Ἆγις ἔφορον γενέσθαι τὸν Λύσανδρον, εὐθὺς εἰσέφερε δι᾽ αὐτοῦ ῥήτραν εἰς τοὺς γέροντας, ἧς ἦν κεφάλαια χρεῶν μὲν ἀφεθῆναι τοὺς ὀφείλοντας, τῆς δὲ γῆς ἀναδασθείσης τὴν μὲν ἀπὸ τοῦ κατὰ Πελλήνην χαράδρου πρὸς τὸ Ταΰγετον καὶ Μαλέαν καὶ Σελασίαν κλήρους γενέσθαι τετρακισχιλίους πεντακοσίους, τὴν δ᾽ ἔξω μυρίους πεντακισχιλίους· [...] [9] Γραφείσης δὲ τῆς ῥήτρας, καὶ τῶν γερόντων εἰς ταὐτὸ ταῖς γνώμαις οὐ συμφερομένων, ἐκκλησίαν συναγαγὼν ὁ Λύσανδρος αὐτός τε διελέχθη τοῖς πολίταις, καὶ Μανδροκλείδας καὶ Ἀγησίλαος ἐδέοντο μὴ δι᾽ ὀλίγους ἐντρυφῶντας αὐτοῖς περιϊδεῖν ἐρριμμένον τὸ ἀξίωμα τῆς Σπάρτης, ἀλλὰ τῶν τε προτέρων χρησμῶν μνημονεῦσαι, τὴν φιλοχρημοσύνην ὡς ὀλέθριον τῇ Σπάρτῃ φυλάττεσθαι διακελευομένων, καὶ τῶν ἔναγχος ἐκ Πασιφάας κεκομισμένων αὐτοῖς.

142   DIVIDED POWER IN ANCIENT GREECE

[8] However, Agis procured Lysander's election as ephor, and at once employed him to introduce a proposal into the *gerousia*, the chief provisions of which were that debtors should be relieved of their debts, and that the land should be divided up, that which lay between the water-course at Pellene and Taÿgetus, Malea, and Sellasia, into forty-five hundred lots, and that which lay outside this into fifteen thousand [...]. [9] The *rhētra* was introduced in the *gerousia*, and the elders were divided in opinion. Lysander therefore called together an assembly and discussed the matter himself with the citizens, and Mandrocleidas and Agesilaus begged them not to suffer the insolent opposition of a few to blind them to the prostration of Sparta's dignity, but to call to mind the earlier oracles which bade them beware of the love of riches as a fatal thing for Sparta, as well as the oracles which had lately been brought to them from Pasiphaë.

(adapted trans. Perrin)

In Plutarch's account, the kings, the *gerousia*, the ephors, and the assembly are all involved. First, Plutarch makes it clear that it was the ephor Lysander who drafted a formal written proposal (γραφείσης δὲ τῆς ῥήτρας) in the *gerousia* (εὐθὺς εἰσέφερε δι' αὐτοῦ ῥήτραν εἰς τοὺς γέροντας).[77] The use of written documents in Spartan public life is not surprising. As Millender has convincingly shown, the Spartans made wide use of written documents for their diplomatic activities, and already in the Classical period, Sparta had an archive with copies of state documents, such as international treaties, and lists of eponymous ephors and athletic victories.[78] This means that there was an official document containing the provisions of the bill, and only after the presentation of the formal proposal, as expressed by the aorist participle, did the legislative procedure begin. The *gerontes* did not reach a unanimous decision about the provisions of the proposal, which means that a proper draft had to be prepared after a discussion in the *gerousia*. The two genitive absolute clauses are key here. The former genitive absolute (γραφείσης δὲ τῆς ῥήτρας)[79] shows a causal connection between the presentation of the *rhētra* by Lysander and the subsequent dissent of the *gerontes* (καὶ τῶν γερόντων εἰς ταὐτὸ ταῖς γνώμαις οὐ συμφερομένων),[80] which presupposes a formal debate in the *gerousia* on the relevant written proposal presented by the ephor. The following sentence (ἐκκλησίαν συναγαγὼν ὁ Λύσανδρος αὐτός τε διελέχθη τοῖς πολίταις)[81] is logically coordinated and implies that Lysander, in force of his ephoral power, summoned the assembly to discuss the same written motion. After a debate in the assembly between kings Agis and Leonidas, who supported the traditional *kosmos*

---

[77] Schulz (2011) 200. For the use of writing by the ephors see Richer (1998) 436–7, 446–7, 479–80; for the Spartan *skytale* see Richer (1998) 483–90; on literacy in Sparta see Boring (1979).

[78] Millender (2001) 127–41.   [79] 'The *rhētra* was introduced in the *gerousia*'.

[80] '...and the elders were divided in opinion'.

[81] 'Lysander therefore called together an assembly and discussed the matter himself with the citizens.'

DIVIDED POWER AND *EUNOMIA* 143

against Agis' reforms, the Spartans backed Agis by passing his motion (τῷ μὲν Ἅγιδι τὸ πλῆθος ἐπηκολούθησεν).

The role of the ephor Lysander in starting the decision-making process highlights a key feature: *probouleusis* was not the exclusive province of the *gerousia*; rather the power was actually divided between ephorate and *gerousia*.[82] Even without the unanimous vote of the elders in the *gerousia*, the ephor Lysander was able to summon an assembly and to put the motion to the vote. This is also supported by the fact that Agis IV was very concerned with procuring the election of Lysander before presenting his bill to the *gerousia*, in order to have a political ally for his revolutionary reforms. In a system when elections where often favoured by patronage and personal ties, it is not surprising that Agis promoted the election of a close friend as ephor.[83] This details also shows that the king clearly had no power to introduce his *rhētra* to the assembly without the fundamental support of the ephor who could bypass the *gerontes* when initiating the deliberative process.[84]

The ephors took part in the *gerousia* meetings, and the eponymous ephor was in charge of presiding over the assembly and supervising the voting of the *damos*.[85] This is consistent with the evidence concerning the power of the ephors to initiate legislation. In the *Hellenica* (Xen. *Hell.* 3.2.23), Xenophon says that in 400 BCE the Spartan ephors and the assembly resolved (ἔδοξε τοῖς ἐφόροις καὶ τῇ ἐκκλησίᾳ) to send ambassadors to Elis. He employs the same expression when Sparta decides to go to war with the Achaeans against the Acarnanians (Xen. *Hell.* 4.6.3: ἔδοξε τοῖς τ' ἐφόροις καὶ τῇ ἐκκλησίᾳ).[86] Ruzé rightly points out that this formula resembles the Athenian enactment formula, which shows a parallel between the probouleutic function of the Athenian council and that of the Spartan ephors.[87] The *edoxe*-formula in deliberative practice is not only similar to the Athenian version, but was widespread across the Greek world.[88] Thucydides reports the Spartan enactment formula by quoting two treaties in Doric dialect between Sparta and Argos. The first

[82] The power of agenda-setting was divided between the two most important boards of officials. On a theoretically informed analysis of agenda power in democratic regimes see Landauer (2023).

[83] On patronage and political appointments in Sparta see Cartledge (1987); Hodkinson (2002); Maehle (2018) 263–6.

[84] For the *boulē–dēmos* opposition in the narrative of Plutarch's *Lives* see Pelling (2009) 211–17.

[85] Kennell (2010) 169. Cf. Xen. *Hell.* 2.3.34; the decisions of the board of ephors were binding for all its members.

[86] Cf. Plut. *Lys.* 14.4 which reports a decree of the ephors stating 'This is resolved by the authorities of the Lacedaemonians' (τὸ δ' ἀληθινὸν δόγμα τῶν ἐφόρων οὕτως εἶχε: τάδε τὰ τέλη τῶν Λακεδαιμονίων ἔγνω).

[87] Schulz (2011) 212 explains that the formula mentions only the ephors and the assembly, because of an ellipsis of the term *gerousia*, since it was in between these two institutions in the decision-making. The ephors started the legislative procedure by putting forward the motion in the *gerousia* and the assembly ratified it. However, the enactment formula usually shows the enactment bodies of a decree or a law or indicate general entities such as the assembly, the people or the *polis*.

[88] There are 3,692 occurrences of this clause on the PHI database of Greek inscriptions. Cf. Rhodes with Lewis (1997) for an overview of the enactment formulas in Greek decrees.

144   DIVIDED POWER IN ANCIENT GREECE

text (Thuc. 5.77.1) is a Spartan peace treaty draft with the preliminary proposal to Argos (κατ τάδε δοκεῖ τᾷ ἐκκλησίᾳ τῶν Λακεδαιμονίων), the second (Thuc. 5.79.1) document provides the final text of the alliance between the Spartans and Argives (ἔδοξε τοῖς Λακεδαιμονίοις καὶ Ἀργείοις).[89] In both cases, the formula shows patterns similar to those found in Xenophon's *Hellenica*, even if the ephors are not mentioned.[90] These formulas are not in contradiction with each other. Indeed, Xenophon had direct access to Spartan institutional practice and the formulas he cited can therefore be taken to represent the normal decree-making practice in Classical Sparta. Thucydides instead reports the draft and the final version of a copy of an international treaty, which he perhaps consulted during the period of his exile.[91] In the Spartan proposal only the assembly is mentioned, but it is clear that some unmentioned probouleutic body—in all probability the ephors— must have introduced the motion to the assembly. It is interesting to note that in early fifth-century Athens too, decrees could have only ἔδοχσεν τὸι δέμοι without mentioning the council in the enactment formula (e.g. *IG* I³ 1). In this case, Thucydides might have consulted an archival copy. On the other hand, the second formula underlines the agreement procedure between the two communities, without mentioning the respective deliberative bodies of the two cities. Another famous Thucydidean passage shows that the ephors were in charge of putting a matter to the vote even without the unanimous consensus of the *gerousia*. When the Spartans were discussing whether they should declare war against Athens in 432 BCE, King Archidamus delivered a speech against war, while the ephor Sthenelaidas spoke forcefully in favour of war, and he himself put the question to the vote of the assembly (Thuc. 1.79–87: τοιαῦτα λέξας ἐπεψήφιζεν αὐτὸς ἔφορος ὢν ἐς τὴν ἐκκλησίαν τῶν Λακεδαιμονίων), which passed it.[92] Yet, a comparison with other Hellenistic cities demonstrates that the role of the Spartan ephors in the decision-making process also has a contemporary parallel in the function of the Iasian *prutaneis* in the decree-making. Decrees from Hellenistic Iasos attest that, after the third century's reform, the Iasian assembly could only examine motions passed by the council after prior consideration of the *prutaneis* acting as *probouloi*.[93] Likewise, in Hellenistic Kyme, the *stratēgoi* summoned the council and intro- duced the *probouleumata* to the assembly.[94]

---

[89] On the treaty in Thucydides see Canfora (1990) 193–216.   [90] Richer (1998) 339.

[91] On Thucydides' autopsy of these documents see Schepens (1980) 184.

[92] For this episode and the controversial use of split voting imposed by Sthenelaidas see Simonton (2017) 126–7; for oligarchic assemblies see Simonton (forthcoming); Schulz (2011) 206–7 interprets this passage as evidence for the lack of *probouleusis* between the two speeches and the vote of the assembly. It is possible that no written draft was discussed, but it is clear that the ephor was legally empowered to use his probouleutic power by putting the item to the vote of the *damos*. Similarly, in Polyb. 4.34–5 the ephors allowed the Aetolian ambassador to address the assembly and to discuss the alliance, even if there was no unanimity among the *gerontes*.

[93] Fabiani (2012) 156.   [94] Hamon (2007) 70.

DIVIDED POWER AND *EUNOMIA*   145

The probouleutic power of the ephors and their relevant role in the deliberative procedure shows that there is no need to hypothesize any *contio*-like or advisory meeting of the Spartan assembly. As Nafissi rightly notes, the Great Rhetra does not mention any informal meeting of the *damos*.[95] An examination of the probouleutic practice in the Greek *poleis* provides no evidence of such advisory meetings of an assembly before or during *probouleusis*. Instead, Greek deliberative procedure shows that the people's assemblies were always gathered either to discuss a well-defined proposal drafted by the relevant probouleutic body—a council or a board of officials—or to discuss an open *probouleuma*, which implies broad deliberative powers of the people's assembly.[96] The Spartan assembly had only the first of these prerogatives, and could enact or reject a proposal submitted by *gerousia* or ephors, but could not deliberate on an open *probouleuma*.[97] In the passage from Diodorus, the assembly is asked to vote on the *gerousia*'s proposal for war, already approved by the *gerontes* unanimously. Conversely, in the passage from Plutarch, Lysander opens the formal discussion in the assembly about Agis' reforms, which are then passed by the *damos*, but the bill had not been previously approved unanimously by the *gerousia*. The text shows that if the *gerousia* had not passed unanimously the bill, even after the assembly's approval, it could be vetoed by the *gerontes* with a simple majority vote.[98] This point should be stressed: it appears that the vote of the *damos* on a decree not pre-approved unanimously by the *gerontes*, was not final; but it was not meaningless either, as it gave the proposal the chance to be approved by a simple majority of *gerontes*, whereas if the proposal was approved unanimously at probouleumatic stage by the *gerousia*, the vote of the *damos* was final.

Thus, a procedure structured in these three stages fits both the so-called rider of the Great Rhetra and the Aristotelian account of oligarchic *probouleusis*, already mentioned. At *Pol.* 1272a10–12, Aristotle describes the similarities between the Cretan and the Spartan constitutions by drawing analogies between the roles of the Cretan *kosmoi* and the Spartan ephors as well as between the role of the councils of elders.[99] He then states that in both constitutions every citizen attends

[95] Nafissi (1991) 364.

[96] Rhodes with Lewis (1997) 484–91 with many examples of *probouleusis* in practice in the Greek *poleis*.

[97] Nafissi (2007) 335; *pace* Ruzé (1997). For the prohibition on emending proposals drafted by magistrates in the Spartan assembly see Arist. *Pol.* 1272a10–12 below; *pace* Andrewes (1966) 4, who drew an analogy with Athenian practice of open *probouleumata*. It is worth noting that even in fourth-century Athens, where the assembly had broad powers, in the period 403/2 BCE–323/2 BCE the number of preserved decrees on stone that were *verbatim* ratifications of the council's *probouleumata* is higher than non-probouleumatic decrees amended by the *dēmos* (52 per cent to 48 per cent), see Oliver (2003) 46. For a different proportion, more leaning towards non-probouleumatic decrees, see Lambert (2017) 227–74 who studies the decrees of the period 352/1 BCE–323/2 BCE.

[98] Kennell (2010) 110.

[99] For oligarchic *probouleusis* see Simonton (2017) 122–4; for Cretan council of elders see Youni (2015) 103–26 with an answer of Maffi (2015) 127–30. Against a view of powerful councils of elders in Crete see Gagarin and Perlman (2016) 62–4.

146 DIVIDED POWER IN ANCIENT GREECE

the meetings of the assembly, which has no authority (κυρία δ' οὐδενός ἐστιν)[100] except in ratifying the proposals (συνεπιψηφίσαι τὰ δόξαντα) of the elders and of the *kosmoi*.[101] Yet at 1298b, when describing the institutional powers of *probouloi* and *nomophulakes*, Aristotle states that in the *politeia* regimes—such as Sparta and Crete—the few have the authority to reject (οἱ γὰρ ὀλίγοι ἀποψηφισάμενοι μὲν κύριοι), but not to pass proposals (καταψηφισάμενοι δὲ οὐ κύριοι), which are always referred to the *dēmos* (ἀλλ' ἐπανάγεται εἰς τοὺς πλείους αἰεί). The verb ἀποψηφίζεσθαι is the very same term that Plutarch employs to describe the vote of rejection by the *gerousia*. As the literary evidence shows, this verb is often used in Athenian forensic speeches for penalties that needed to be approved, therefore of proposals that had already been formally presented (Antiph. 1.12, 5.96; Lys. 10.31, 12.90; Lyc. 1.149). In the case of Sparta the verb marks the fact that the proposal had already been passed by the *damos*.[102] To push the parallel with the Athenian usage of the verb, the *apepsēphismenoi* were those Athenian citizens who lost their civic rights for not fulfilling the legal requirements and were therefore 'rejected' from the *lexiarchika grammateia*, the civic registers of the demes.[103] Thus, according to the Aristotelian account, in some oligarchic constitutions legislation needs to be ratified by assemblies, but the probouleutic bodies can make them invalid a posteriori. In addition to the probouleutic power, which is used before a proposal reaches the assembly, they have a veto power that can be used after the approval of a bill by the assembly. This matches closely the powers of the Spartan *gerontes*: they had probouleutic powers setting the agenda of the assembly, but also the power of *nomophulakia* through which they could stop the legislative procedure by invalidating those motions that contradicted the *nomoi*, which were therefore 'skolion' as the Great Rhetra states.[104] A similar view is found in Aeschines' *Against Timarchus* (Aeschin. 1.180–1).[105] When praising Sparta, Aeschines states that, during a debate, a dissolute but skilful speaker addressed the assembly which was persuaded by his argument. An elder, however, stood up and said that they should not listen to the speaker, and asked a virtuous man to give the same advice, so that the Spartans could act according to the suggestions of a distinguished citizen. This anecdote is unlikely to be historically accurate, but it clarifies the Athenian understanding of political decision-making in Sparta, and of the role of the *gerousia*. An elder could stop the debate in the assembly, if some

[100] For an analysis of the term *kurios* see Chapter 2 pp. 70–5. Cf. Miller (2007) 106–7.

[101] Cf. Nafissi (1991) 363–5; Bertelli (2004) 40–3; cf. the use of the same expression in Polyb. 21.32.1 to indicate the ratification vote of the *sunedrion*'s motion by the *dēmos* (δόξαντος δὲ τῷ συνεδρίῳ, καὶ τοῦ δήμου συνεπιψηφίσαντος, ἐκυρώθη τὰ κατὰ τὰς διαλύσεις).

[102] Canevaro (2014) 315–17. Cf. also *IG* II² 1237.31, 38, 90, 95, 98, 101–3.

[103] Poddighe (2006) 16.

[104] E. David (1991) 33; *contra* Schulz (2011) 155–7 does recognize that the *gerousia* was empowered of *nomophulakia* as *cura morum*, but does not include it in his reconstruction of the probouleutic and deliberative procedure.

[105] Cf. Fisher (2001) 329.

DIVIDED POWER AND *EUNOMIA*   147

basic principles embedded in the *eunomia* were not respected, performing therefore a *nomophulakia* role.

Finally, a comparison between Plutarch's account and other non-democratic deliberative practices may also shed some light on this issue. Demetrius of Phalerum introduced magistrates called *nomophulakes* in Athens between 317 and 307 BCE, during the oligarchic government following the peace between the Athenians and the Macedonian king Cassander.[106] The powers of the Athenian *nomophulakes* are described in an entry of *Lexicon Rhetoricum Cantabrigense* (s.v. νομοφυλάκες), based on Philochorus' evidence, which states that the *nomophulakes* sat at the meetings of the council and the assembly next to the *proedroi* charged with the task of stopping inexpedient deliberations.[107] This shows a clear analogy with the role of the *gerontes* in Spartan decision-making procedures. The *gerousia* indeed was present and gathered during the assemblies of the *damos*,[108] like the Athenian *nomophulakes*, but not to gauge informally the *damos*; rather their role involved checking the legality of deliberation and potentially vetoing illegal enactments. This is the reason for which, after Agis' *rhētra* had been enacted by the assembly, a simple majority vote of the *gerontes* would have sufficed for the bill to be carried, instead of the unanimity required at the probouleutic stage. Agis must have known that he could not obtain a unanimous vote from the *gerontes*, but must have hoped that, faced with the overwhelming favour of the *damos*, at least a simple majority of *gerontes* would decide to let the bill stand. Agis claimed to represent the Lycurgan tradition, but similarly his opponents among the *gerontes* could maintain that his *rhētra* was contrary to the established *nomoi*. The *gerousia* therefore exercised its prerogative to halt the legislative procedure safeguarding the traditional order—the majority vote at *nomophulakia* stage sank his reform.

What was the ideological rationale of this decision-making procedure? Chapters 2 and 3 have shown how in Classical Athens as well as in fourth-century Mytilene and Hellenistic Megalopolis, the delegation clauses provided legal tools designed to transfer some decisions to the council in order to complement the decision-making by exploiting expertise of the councillors in particular matters and displaying a 'divided power' in deliberation between council and assembly. The origin of that procedure was rooted in the democratic ideological framework according to which, the deliberative power did not belong exclusively to one institutional agency. Democratic ideology was alien to Sparta, but one can

---

[106] For the legislation of Demetrius of Phalerum see O'Sullivan (2009); Banfi (2010); Canevaro (2013c) 66–9.

[107] Bearzot (2007) 43–68, (2012) 29–47; Canevaro (2014) 315–17; for *nomophulakes* in Athens see Canevaro (2013c) 66–7; Faraguna (2015a) 141–55; cf. also Harpocration s.v. νομοφύλακες; Pollux 8.94 confirms the information in the *Lexicon Rhetoricum Cantabrigense*; *pace* Morrow (1960) 199, n. 108 who argues that there is no evidence of *nomophulakes* acting as probouleutic officials apart from Aristotle's statement.

[108] Kelly (1981) 60.

148 DIVIDED POWER IN ANCIENT GREECE

nevertheless find patterns of divided power, though non-democratic in its nature. The *ethos* of the Spartan deliberative procedures was to constrain deliberation within the boundaries of the traditional *nomos*. As the evidence has shown, the probouleutic procedure in Sparta limited free debate in the assembly. *Probouleusis* therefore assumes a prominent role in the constitutional equilibrium, since every matter discussed in the assembly was put forward through this procedure without allowing further changes. The Spartan institutional system, however, shows that this power was shared between ephors and *gerousia*, because neither of these two bodies had an exclusive role in bringing motions before the *damos*. A *probouleuma* thus needed the unanimous vote of the *gerousia* in order to be submitted for ratification before the assembly, but the ephors, being in charge of initiating the legislative process, could also present a motion directly to the *damos*. This institutional mechanism allowed the ephors to run the legislative process by giving voice to the people, in the case of opposition by the *gerontes*. In other words, the Spartan system gave a prominent role to the voice of the assembly in case of dissent between the *gerontes* and the ephors or when the *gerontes* could not reach a unanimous decision. The standard legislative procedure was therefore based on the need for general consensus within and between those institutions that held the probouleutic powers. No single institution had a more prominent role in the decision-making process, as the constitutional system was designed to achieve balance and stability. Ephors and *gerontes*, therefore, had to play a joint role in managing an effective *probouleusis*, in order for a decree to be finally enacted by the assembly.

On the other hand, when there was no consensus between the two probouleutic bodies, or within the *gerousia*, a bill could go to the assembly anyway, but with the proviso that it would still need to be ratified by the *gerontes* by simple majority. The alleged rider of the rhētra provided the legal foundation and the necessary source of legitimacy for this practice by allowing a decision of the *gerontes* after a vote of the assembly was taken. In Athens, the council could be legally empowered through a delegation clause to enact a new decree to integrate the decision passed by the assembly. Just as in Athens, therefore, in Sparta a probouleutic body could reconsider a decision, but there was no need of ad hoc delegation, because the *gerontes* were in charge of checking whether the decrees of the assembly conformed to the *nomoi*, rather than integrating the people's decisions with new enactments. The *gerousia* played the role of a legislative-review body that in Classical Athens was performed by the law courts. Athenian lawcourts democratically scrutinized the legality of assembly's decrees through the *graphē paranomōn*, which could be brought by any Athenian citizen (*ho boulomenos*). By contrast, in Sparta, the same institutional task was performed by a restricted body according to different procedures, but addressing the same need to conform to the laws.

In order to be performed, this *nomophulakia* did not require the unanimity of the elders, who rejected the *rhētra* of Agis with a vote by simple majority. The

DIVIDED POWER AND *EUNOMIA*   149

different voting procedure adopted by the *gerousia* at the two different stages reflects the different roles it was called to perform—in one case *probouleusis*, in the other *nomophulakia*. Through its use of majority vote in the veto procedure, the council of elders was able to render invalid a decree of the *damos*, which was voted by acclamation, because of their higher status in the community in terms of *timē* and prestige that the office of elder carried.[109] More remarkably, it is worth stressing that the *gerousia* itself employed two different voting systems in performing *probouleusis* and *nomophulakia*, which had relevant implications for the nature of decree-making. The difference in voting system is not only a matter of institutional technique, but was supported by strong connections with two distinct ideological approaches. When voting a draft to be sent for ratification to the assembly, the *gerousia* did not use majority rule, but a unanimous vote which was a deliberative mechanism favouring the creation of consensus within the political body, in this case the narrow gathering of the elders. This consensus-based mechanism was typical of deliberative settings in the Greek world and tried to shape decision-making through the inclusion, rather than the exclusion of dissent.[110] By contrast, when the *gerontes* acted as guardians of the laws, performing a legislative review, they adopted the principle of majority rule.[111] In this case, the task required by the decision-making procedure was different. When vetoing a decree of the *damos*, the *gerontes* were checking the consistency of that decree with the traditional Spartan *nomos*. What was at stake was not a political decision and the creation of consensus, but rather the safeguarding of the laws. Again, this is consistent with the practice of other Greek *poleis* in which legislative or judicial review is attested. In democratic Athens, most of the time, the council and the assembly passed their decrees with overwhelming consensus or unanimity, very rarely by a bare majority (e.g. Thuc. 3.37.3–4 during the Mytilenian debate).[112] The lawcourts, however, when adjudicating the legality of decrees and laws through the *graphē paranomōn* and *graphē nomon mē epitēdeion theinai*, voted by majority rule because of their distinct institutional function. Each voting procedure was thus designed to foster different collective behaviour and to answer the distinctive ideological and institutional goals of *probouleusis* and *nomophulakia*.

In addition to this, it is important to underscore that the features of 'divided power' applied not only to *probouleusis*, but also to the practice of *nomophulakia*, which was also shared between *gerontes* and ephors. The *nomophulakes*, as we find them attested in other *poleis* and as their function is described by Aristotle, did not

---

[109] For the institutional values of the office of *gerontes* cf. above pp. 132–3.

[110] Cf. a list of forty-one epigraphical examples of voting figures in Todd (2012) 33–48. Consensus was also used by boards of officials cf. Thuc. 6.46.5–50.1; Plut. *Nic.* 14.3; *Alc.* 20.2–3. For consensus in Greek deliberative practice see now Canevaro (2018a). For consensus-building in oligarchic councils and boards of magistrates, see Simonton (2017) 84–6.

[111] For a similar distinction in voting procedures see §6.2 on Athenian *graphē paranomōn*.

[112] Cf. Canevaro (2018a).

150 DIVIDED POWER IN ANCIENT GREECE

only exercise control over deliberation, but they also supervised the application of the rule of law. While the *gerousia* was in charge of supervising the legality of the debate in the assembly, the ephors had the task of overseeing the observance of the laws by public officials as well as the individual behaviour of citizens according to the laws. Like the Athenian *nomophulakes* during the Demetrian oligarchy, the ephors had broad powers over the other magistrates, who had to perform their duties according to the laws, in order not to be subject to the severe sanctions of the five ephors.[113] Xenophon states that the ephors did not, as in other *poleis*, leave the elected magistrates to rule as they liked throughout the year (τοὺς αἱρεθέντας ἀεὶ ἄρχειν τὸ ἔτος), but immediately punished those who broke the laws (τινα αἰσθάνωνται παρανομοῦντά τι, εὐθὺς παραχρῆμα κολάζουσι), in the manner of tyrants and supervisors of athletic games (Xen. *Lac.* 8.4). Aristotle says that the ephors have the power to perform the *euthunai* over the other magistrates (Arist. *Pol.* 1271a4–6). The kings themselves were supervised by the ephors during their military campaigns, and every month the kings and the ephors took an oath. The kings swore to rule respecting the established *nomoi* (κειμένους νόμους βασιλεύσειν) and the ephors swore to preserve the kingship (Xen. *Lac.* 15.7).[114] The ancient sources therefore illustrate that both the powers of *nomophulakia* and *probouleusis* were shared between the *gerousia* and the ephors who worked jointly in running the deliberative process as well as in preserving Spartan laws according to the ideology of the Spartan *politeia*. This conservative ideology required a permanent control of the elected magistrates regarding deliberation, which was strictly constrained within the limits of the traditional *nomoi*. Institutions and legal procedures were therefore shaped according to these ideological values, which, in the institutional sphere, favoured in practice the dominant role of the elites within the restricted group of Spartan citizens.

4.4 Non-Democratic Divided Power

The analysis of ancient evidence about deliberative procedure in Sparta shows the working of a sophisticated form of non-democratic divided power in action. Such a system was gradually designed and shaped to perpetuate and preserve the political control and social capital of a socio-economic elite. As a result, in the institutional practice a decree ratified by the Spartans in the assembly could go back to the *gerousia* because of the permanent legal and political control of its officials over the *damos*, which regulated the decision-making interplay

---

[113] Fröhlich (2004) 294–7: in other constitutional regimes, *ho boulomenos* could bring a charge against magistrates, who were usually supervised by larger bodies, such as the council or the assembly. Cf. Rubinstein (2003) 87–113, (2016) 419–50 with a response of Arnaoutoglou (2016) 451–60.

[114] Lipka (2002) 246; cf. Plut. *Cleom.* 9.2 who, reporting Aristotle, says that the ephors taking office told the citizens 'to shave their moustaches and to obey the laws' if they wanted to avoid their sanctions.

DIVIDED POWER AND *EUNOMIA*   151

between *gerousia*, ephors, and assembly. As in the rest of the Greek world, the assembly in Sparta played an important role in the political decision-making, but the people's deliberation was strictly controlled and influenced by probouleutic officials. The *gerousia* and the ephors shared the role of probouleutic bodies, as well as that of *nomophulakes* within the Spartan decision-making process, according to the patterns of divided power. As literary evidence from Plutarch demonstrates, the ephors had the power of initiating the legislative procedure, both in the *gerousia* and in the assembly, but a unanimous vote of the *gerontes* was needed in order to submit a *probouleuma* to the *damos* for final ratification. The ephor could introduce a motion in the assembly with no need of unanimity among the *gerontes*, but in this case, the procedure required the bill to be revised by the *gerousia*, which could veto the motion with a majority vote by employing the power of *nomophulakia* granted by the Great Rhetra. The deliberative procedure therefore required a third passage in the council of elders when there was a lack of consensus among the probouleutic bodies (or even within the *gerousia* alone). The ideology of Spartan institutions granted a higher level of *timē* to officials vis-à-vis the assembly, and this recognition was institutionalized in the divided powers of *probouleusis* and *nomophulakia*. The aim was to avoid innovation in legislation and institutional practice, as well as to maintain balance in the decision-making process, even if Spartan society was remarkably unequal even with its very narrow citizen body.[115] Such a decision-making process combines the need to gain popular consent with a strict control over legislation in accordance with conservative values and practices.

---

[115] For the standard analysis of property and wealth in Sparta see Hodkinson (2000).

5

Divided Power in the Athenian Assembly

Adeia and Fifth-Century Deliberative Ideology

5.1 Institutional Complexity in the Athenian Assembly

The previous chapters have shown that political decision-making and the enactment of decrees in the Greek *poleis* were practised as divided power with different levels of institutional involvement by the people's assemblies and by probouleutic bodies. The dynamic of divided power could happen through democratic delegation of deliberative authority from the assembly to the council in order to exploit the council's expertise and discursive practices in the decree-making, as the analysis of epigraphical evidence has shown for Athens, Mytilene, and, with different mechanism, for Megalopolis.[1] The complex deliberative procedures at Sparta, on the other hand, show that the divided power in assembly-council interactions could also aim to ensure legal stability in the people's enactments through the permanent control of the probouleutic bodies over the assembly.[2] Reconciling popular power and legal consistency in deliberation was also a major concern in Classical Athens. The Athenians, however, adopted a different approach to achieve a balance between the people's deliberation and legal stability. As a result, distinct institutions were designed to address this issue throughout the fifth and the fourth centuries.[3]

This chapter explores the fifth-century attempt to design legal tools that favoured consistency between the people's decrees and the established laws in the assembly's political decision-making. This chapter discusses the institutional complexity and the sequencing of deliberative moments that the procedure of *adeia* introduced within the framework of fifth-century Athenian deliberative practice.[4] In Athenian law, *adeia* was an institution for granting immunity

---

[1] For delegation from the assembly to the council in Classical Athens see pp. 71–92. For the delegation clauses beyond Athens see pp. 98–119.

[2] For deliberative procedures in Sparta see pp. 125–51.

[3] The main tools used by the Athenian to achieve this goal were the *graphē paranomōn* and the *graphē nomon mē epitēdeion theinai*. For a detailed discussion on these procedures see pp. 177–213.

[4] This chapter only analyses *adeia* in the Athenian deliberative institution of Athenian divided power. For a comprehensive analysis of the procedure with its implications as emergency power in fifth-century Athens, see Esu (2021a).

Divided Power in Ancient Greece: Decision-Making and Institutions in the Classical and Hellenistic Polis. Alberto Esu,
Oxford University Press. © Alberto Esu 2024. DOI: 10.1093/oso/9780198883951.003.0005

DIVIDED POWER IN THE ATHENIAN ASSEMBLY   153

from legal prosecution or exemption from a legal procedure without danger of sanctions. The assembly conferred *adeia* through a voting process requiring a quorum of 6,000 votes, as one can extrapolate from a reliable document inserted in Demosthenes' *Against Timocrates* (Dem. 24.45).[5] This represented a traditional figure symbolizing the whole *dēmos* of the Athenians since the fifth century, and continued unmodified in fourth-century practice.[6] The institution of *adeia* had important implications for the working of the Athenian legal system and for our understanding of its deliberative procedures. In order to understand the role of *adeia* in Athenian fifth-century deliberation and how this legal procedure created a sort of divided power within the assembly, it is first necessary to provide a picture of Athenian attitudes to legislation as well as the relevant deliberative practices during the Archaic and Classical periods.

It has long been recognized in scholarship that the Greeks used several terms to indicate laws, norms, and regulations. For example, the term *rhētra* referred to the oral enactment of the rule, whereas terms such as *grammata* and *graphos* stressed the written dimension of statutes. In Classical Athens, the most common word referring to a general and unchangeable law was *nomos* (from *nemein* 'to share', 'to allocate', or 'to distribute'), as opposed to *psēphisma* (from *psēphos* 'pebble'), an ad hoc decision of the council and of the assembly.[7] As Hansen has demonstrated, in fifth-century sources before 403 BCE the two terms could often be used interchangeably to indicate the same regulation either as *nomos* or *psēphisma* (e.g. in Xenophon's *Hellenica* the Law of Cannonus is called *psēphisma* at 1.7.20 and *nomos* at 1.7.23).[8] Normally, the assembly only passed decrees, but these enactments often had the features of laws, which were approved without any explicit and restrictive rule of change. As a result, legislative activity was often incoherent. Only after the restoration of democracy, the principle of a hierarchy between laws and decrees was finally formalized and enforced by public action against illegal decrees (*graphē paranomōn*)[9] and by the public action against inexpedient laws (*graphē nomon mē epitēdeion theinai*).[10] A standard procedure for law-making (*nomothesia*) was set up; new laws were, therefore, enacted by the *nomothetai* according to a distinct procedure different from decree-making (e.g. *IG* II² 140.7–8).[11]

---

[5] For a discussion of the authenticity of the document see Canevaro (2013b) 127–31.

[6] Gauthier (1990). Cf. pp. 166–71 for a detailed discussion.

[7] On *nomos* and *psēphisma* see in general §1.3 and Quass (1971) 14–15; Hansen (1978); Hölkeskamp (2002) 115–46. On the different forms of decrees and local terminology across the Greek world see Rhodes with Lewis (1997) 550–6.

[8] Hansen (1978) 315–30, (1979a) 27–53, (1991) 161–77, 256–7; Rhodes (1987) 5–26.

[9] For fifth-century *graphai paranomōn* cf. Andoc. 1.17, 22; Antiph. fr. 13.47; see MacDowell (1962) 76–7; Wolff (1970); Hansen (1987b) 63–73; Canevaro (2015) 25; Canevaro (2016b). For the use of the *graphē paranomōn* as a political weapon see Hansen (1974); Harris (2013c) 307–44. For the role of *graphē paranomōn* in the deliberative system in Classical Athens cf. Chapter 6 pp. 177–99.

[10] On the procedure of the *graphē nomon mē epitēdeion theinai* see Kremmydas (2012) 24–33; Canevaro (2016a) 12–31, (2016b), (2019).

[11] On *nomothesia* in fourth-century Athens see Canevaro (2013a); *pace* MacDowell (1975) 62–74; Rhodes (1984); Hansen (1985a). On legislation cf. also Introduction §1.3. and Canevaro (2018b).

154 DIVIDED POWER IN ANCIENT GREECE

All these legal innovations were the product of reforms started at the end of the fifth century with the revision of all Athenian statutes by the *anagrapheis*, who then republished them.[12] Canevaro shows that during the fifth century, Athenian legislation was based on the ideological assumption that the real laws of the city had been created by Draco and Solon, who were the first lawgivers (*nomothetai*), able make new laws because of their higher authority in the community.[13] This attitude is consistent with the Greek distinction between ordinary administration and legislation, in which the latter was not undertaken by the institutions of the *polis*, but by special lawgivers at exceptional times.[14] In the fifth century Draco's and Solon's statutes were still called *thesmoi* (from *tithēmi* 'to set'), a term that highlights the establishment of laws from on high.[15] Since the authority of the statutes does not derive from the people's legitimate deliberation, but from the personal prestige of the lawgiver, the laws were conceived and made in order to be kept unmodified through the entrenchment clauses which did not allow any legal change. This principle is clearly found in the fifth-century sources (e.g. the Mytilenian debate in Thuc. 3.37.3–4;[16] Ar. *Thesm.* 352–71), and has key implications for Athenian legislative practice before 403 BCE. As Canevaro demonstrates, the institutional ideology of the *polis* did not in fact allow for any form of legal change, as far as the real laws of Draco and Solon were concerned. Yet, fifth-century Athenians did legislate in the assembly, but never acknowledged that they were creating statutes on a par with those of Draco and Solon and potentially contradicting them. They legislated through 'tacit legal change' which means that new laws were actually enacted without changing or repealing previous statutes even if those enactments were contradictory. There was no explicit recognition that what was being done was a form of nomothetic activity.[17]

The procedure of *adeia* is, in my interpretation, closely linked to fifth-century tacit legislation. The procedure of immunity enabled two important goals to be achieved without formally challenging the nomothetic tradition and the belief in the immutability of the laws. First, *adeia* was a tool for authorizing new laws or modifications without providing a proper and comprehensive rule of change.[18] *Adeia* created a double-level system to enact special decrees, which would be illegal otherwise due to entrenchment clauses. This was a first attempt introduced within the standard decree-making process according to which the *dēmos* in the

---

[12] On the fifth-century revision of the Athenian laws see Canevaro and Harris (2012), Canevaro (2015).

[13] Hansen (1989b); Canevaro (2015); Loddo (2018); on Solon's laws see the new edition with commentary by Leão and Rhodes (2015). For a discussion of *kurbeis* and *axones* see Davis (2011).

[14] Harris (2006) 3–28; Canevaro (2015).

[15] The term *thesmos* became rare in Classical Athens, but it was still widespread in other contemporary Greek *poleis* (e.g. Delphi [400 BCE] *CIG* 1.9 C 19; Kos [270 BCE]; *HGK* 8.17; Thessaly *Nomima* I, 102); see Quass (1971) 11–12; Papakonstantinou (2008) 133–5. For the change in Athens see Hölkeskamp (2002) 123–6.

[16] For an analysis of this debate see Harris (2013c) 94–109.   [17] Canevaro (2015).

[18] For institutionalization of the rules to allow for the exception to the law see Esu (2021a) 153–4.

DIVIDED POWER IN THE ATHENIAN ASSEMBLY   155

assembly controlled itself through a double mechanism of vote, and divided the decision-making power in two stages of deliberation. Second, the required quorum of 6,000 votes envisaged the registration, through *psēphophoria*, the consensus reached by the community through deliberation, through which the will of the whole citizen-body, thanks to the quorum, was explicitly expressed. Despite the importance of this procedure, *adeia* has received little attention from modern scholarship.[19] The most comprehensive nineteenth-century treatment of *adeia* is now outdated and does not place the legal institution in its full historical perspective.[20] The understanding of the nature of Athenian institutional and legislative practices during the Classical period has developed in recent years with new discoveries of epigraphical evidence and new studies on documentary practice. For example, Goldstaub does not distinguish *adeia* from the procedure for enacting a *nomos ep' andri*[21] described in the provisions of a document in Demosthenes' *Against Timocrates*, which has been shown to be inauthentic and consequently unreliable as a source for Athenian Law.[22] A more recent but less exhaustive work by McElwee traces the history of the word *adeia*. Yet, McElwee fails to reconstruct the word's legal use in Classical Athens. McElwee confuses *adeia* with the institution of amnesty by building once again on documents in Andocides' *On the Mysteries*, such as the decree of Patrocleides.[23] These documents have recently been revealed to be later forgeries and are untrustworthy sources for Athenian Law and legal procedure.[24] Furthermore, as Paoli pointed out, *adeia* cannot be confused with amnesty, since the institution of immunity works in advance by preventing the breaking of the law.[25] This chapter provides a new comprehensive study of *adeia* and its function in Athenian political decision-making and legislation and insert this procedure within the institutional mechanism of Athenian divided power.

---

[19] For brief studies of *adeia* see Paoli (1933) 122 n. 2, (1953) 139; Biscardi (1982) 70; Miller (2007) 307–9; later authors (Cic. *Phil.* 1.1; Dio Cass. 60.3.5) glossed *adeia* with the Roman *abolitio*, and this juxtaposition was formalized by Mommsen in his *Römisches Strafrecht* (1899) 458, but the identification of these two institutions is incorrect. The Roman *abolitio publica* was granted during festivals or joyful public events, and suspended a charge presented to a magistrate for thirty days. When the prescribed period of time elapsed, the accuser could bring forward another charge. For a recent study of *abolitio* in Roman law see Gamauf (2013).

[20] Goldstaub (1889) 1–8 for the definition of *adeia*, 10–87 for *adeia* as general immunity, and 88–110 for *adeia* as immunity from prosecution.

[21] There could be no νόμοι ἐπ' ἀνδρί in Athens; see Canevaro (2019b).

[22] Goldstaub (1889) 109–10; Dem. 24.59; cf. Andoc. 1.89; see Canevaro and Harris (2012); Canevaro (2013b) 145–50.

[23] McElwee (Diss. Albany University 1975) 19–62. Most of McElwee's dissertation deals with amnesty in Classical Athens.

[24] Canevaro and Harris (2012) 98–129; Canevaro and Harris (2017). All the documents of §§78–96 in Andocides' *On the Mysteries* are forgeries (i.e. the decree of Patrocleides, the decree of Teisamenus, the law establishing the hierarchy of *nomoi* and *psēphismata*, the law about private suits and arbitrations, and the decree of Demophantus) *pace* Sommerstein (2014); Hansen (2015) 34–48.

[25] Paoli (1933) 122 n. 2; For remission of convictions in Classical Athens see Pecorella Longo (2004).

156   DIVIDED POWER IN ANCIENT GREECE

This chapter shall first explore the origin of the terminology of *adeia* by connecting it with the dominant nomothetic ideology and fifth-century deliberative practice and political culture. The chapter will then reconstruct the details of legal procedure of *adeia*. Finally, this chapter will discuss the rationale of *adeia* in Athenia divided power and the limits of this tool for political decision-making.

5.2 'Absence of Fear': The Expressive Terminology of Immunity

In the *Nicomachean Ethics* Aristotle discusses the economic concepts of profit and loss. Aristotle explains that to have more than one's own is profit, while the opposite is loss, in what concerns buying and selling and the other transactions allowed by the law (Arist. *Eth. Nic.* 1132b15–16; lit. for which the law gives immunity, ἄδειαν δέδωκεν ὁ νόμος). This use of the word *adeia* has been interpreted as expressing the right of free trade by which merchants could gain profits and establish prices.[26] Aristotle also uses the term *adeia* in the *Politics*, and states that some constitutions envisage a fine for those rich citizens who do not perform their dikastic duty, but poor people enjoy immunity (τοῖς δ' ἀπόροις ἄδειαν) from these fines, as we see in the law of Charondas (Arist. *Pol.* 1297a21–4). These few instances show that the term *adeia* generically indicated 'license' or 'permission', which could be employed with different meanings and was context-dependant.[27] Since the earliest fifth-century occurrences of the word, the term *adeia* shows a number of meanings stemming from the semantic field of emotions which was institutionalized in the legal terminology. In order to understand the relationship between the legal institution of *adeia* and the practices of legislation in fifth-century Athens, it is important to identify the actual meaning of the term and the role played by *adeia* in Greek legal terminology within the broader context of legislation and emotions in ancient Greek culture.

The noun *adeia*, the literal meaning of which is the 'absence of fear', is a relatively recent occurrence, as the word is not attested before the fifth century BCE. However, cognate words such as the adjective ἀδειής are found in the Homeric poems.[28] In *Iliad* 8.117, during a discussion with his brother Menelaus, Agamemnon

---

[26]   See Miller (1997) 105.

[27]   Miller (1997) 94–108, (2007) 102–9; identifies *adeia* qua immunity as a key term for the ancient Greek theory of legal rights. The other three legal rights are just claim (*dikaion*), liberty (*exeinai*), and authority (*kurios*). On the Athenian conceptualizations of rights as *timē* see now Canevaro (2020); Canevaro and Rocchi (forthcoming).

[28]   Chantraine (1970) s.v. δείδω; McElwee (1975) 130. *Adeia* is the only abstract noun derived from the stem *δϜει-/δϜοι-. Other words from the same stem are e.g. δείδω (to fear), δεινός (fearful), δειλός (worthless). For a study of -ια suffixes in noun formation see Petersen (1922) 72–3 'it seems that the words in -ια were more popular and free from the frigid learned tone which characterized most of those in -της (e.g. μεσότης)'.

DIVIDED POWER IN THE ATHENIAN ASSEMBLY   157

refers to Hector as a fearless man (ἀδειής). The same adjective is used twice with a negative connotation later in the poem in the insulting expression 'impudent dog' (κύον ἀδεές) (Hom. Il. 8.423, 21.481).[29] Herodotus provides the first literary attestation of term *adeia* and uses the term with the prevalent meaning of 'security' or 'safety'. At 8.120, describing the Persian withdrawal from Greece, he announces that Xerxes was safe (ὡς ἐν ἀδείῃ ἐών) only when he reached Abdera.[30] The term *adeia* with the meaning of safety is paralleled in fifth-century tragedy. In Sophocles' *Oedipus at Colonus* (447), Oedipus affirms that Antigone and Ismene supplied his daily food as well as the concession of a safe place to stay (γῆς ἄδειαν). The process of lexicalization of the 'lack of fear' is more evident in Antiphon's *On the Murder of Herodes*, where the speaker switches from the meaning 'safety' to 'license' when defending his father, tells the judges that they allowed the Mytilenians to live in their land (Antiph. 5.77: τοῖς δ' ἄλλοις Μυτιληναίοις ἄδειαν ἐδώκατε οἰκεῖν).[31] The lack of fear produces security and consequently the license to live there. Thucydides employs it with a more nuanced meaning, including both general and technical connotations of the word (Thuc. 3.58.3, 8.91.3). For example, he says that a group of Thasians exiled by the Athenians were plotting along with their supporters in the city to cause a revolt in Thasos with 'security about their acts' (8.64.5: ἄδειαν τῶν πρασσομένων). In another passage (8.76.7), Thucydides says that Thrasybulus persuaded the Athenians in Samos to grant immunity and the right to return to Alcibiades (ἦν αὐτῷ ἄδειάν τε καὶ κάθοδον). All fifth-century literary occurrences unanimously show that the term is closely related to the semantic field of individual or communal security and safety.[32]

But why did the Athenians name a legal institution with a term stemming from the semantic field of security? What are the implications of this particular etymology for the legal term? The Athenians, in fact, often employed ordinary terminology to indicate specific legal institutions, but when used in a legal context this terminology assumed a distinctive legal colouring. It does not follow from the fact that legal terminology was often overlapping with ordinary language that

---

[29] Zaborowski (2002).   [30] See also Hdt. 2.121, 9.42.

[31] Similar uses are also quite frequent in fourth-century forensic speeches; cf. e.g. Lys. 1.36; Dem. 19.190.

[32] *Adeia* occurrences in Classical literary sources: Hdt. (ἄδειη) 2.121, 8.120, 9.42; Thuc. 3.58.3, 4.92.6, 4.108.4, 6.60.3, 6.60.4, 7.29.3, 8.64.5, 8.76.7, 8.81.1, 8.92.1; Soph. *Oed. Col.* 447; Antiph. 5.77.3; Andoc. 1.11–12, 1.15, 1.20, 1.34, 1.77, 2.22, 2.23, 2.27; Hellan. (*FGrH* 31); Xen. *Mem.* 2.1.5; Isocr. 3.56, 14.24; Plat. *Leg.* 701; Lys. 1.36, 1.48, 2.15, 6.23, 6.36, 6.43, 12.85, 13.55, 16.13, 22.19, 25.28, 29.13, 30.24; Dem. 5.6, 5.8, 7.15, 8.64, 10.66, 13.17, 16.5, 18.222, 18.286, 19.149, 19.191, 19.272, 19.289, 21.33, 21.210, 22.25, 22.42, 23.12, 23.94, 23.125, 23.128, 23.133, 23.159, 23.192, 24.9, 24.31, 24.45–7, 24.88, 24.102–3, 24.106, 24.205, 44.63, 51.15, 54.21, 58.6, 58.65, 59.111, 59.113; Aesch. 1.108, 2.183, 3.162; Hyp. 5.8; Lyc. 1.104; Arist. *Eth. Nic.* 1132b15; *Pol.* 1297a22; *De virt.* 1250b9. *Adeia* occurrences in Athenian epigraphical sources: *IG* I³ 52B.16–17 (see pp. 163–4); *IG* I³ 370.15, 28, 30, 33, 64. For extra-Athenian epigraphical evidence, see *IG* IX.1.119.7 (Elateia, fourth century BCE); Schmitt, *SdA* 429.6, 12, 14 (Theangela, 310 BCE); *IG* XII 9.211.23, 212.16, 231.10 (Eretria, third century BCE); *Milet* 148.62 (Miletus, 196/175 BCE).

158   DIVIDED POWER IN ANCIENT GREECE

the Athenians were unable to distinguish between legal and non-legal uses of the same terms.[33]

That *adeia* was not exclusively a technical legal term is not surprising. A clear-cut distinction between extra-legal and legal terminology is not useful to understand the actual ancient usage of this word, and it does not describe correctly the development of the institution of *adeia*. The word in fact occurs both with a clear legal meaning and as a general term, without for this reason being used incoherently and misunderstood. This is the use of Thucydides in Book 8. At 8.91, when recounting the end of the Four Hundred, Thucydides reports that the oligarchs were only concerned with securing their personal safety (τοῖς γε σώμασι σφῶν ἄδεια ἔσται). This passage comes after the section in 8.77, mentioned above, wherein Thucydides uses *adeia* to refer to the immunity of Alcibiades. The term functioned as both a legal and extra-legal term depending on context. In other words, *adeia* acquired different meanings, both legal and extra-legal, predicated on the basic emotional concept.[34] The emotional notion underpinning the word *adeia* is what unified the various meanings, and allowed the user to recognize the differences between them while at the same time not finding them incoherent, but rather understanding them as members of one semantic family.

From Homer to Thucydides, *adeia* and its cognate words shared their origin in the emotional language of fear and apprehension. The use of emotional and psychological terms in Greek legal language is not new and is paralleled in other institutions of Greek law. For instance, the Greek noun for amnesty (ἀμνηστία) appears for the first time in two later Hellenistic inscriptions dated to 196–180 BCE (*Milet* 148.62, 150.36). Throughout the Classical and most of the Hellenistic periods the Greeks referred to the institution of amnesty with expressions such as *mē mnēsikakein* (not to begrudge) which describe a legal act of the civic community through emotional and psychological language.[35] In the case of the word *adeia*, the basic meaning of the term is linked to the emotion of fear, which bears important implications for the meaning of the word as a legal term.[36]

Like other human emotions, fear is the product of many factors at the biological, psychological, and cultural levels, which jointly shape our emotional responses.[37] This rich complexity is also displayed in the ancient Greek vocabulary of fear. The Homeric poems, for example, already contain a surprisingly high

[33] Harris (2006) 211.

[34] For a similar mechanism for *timōria* in fourth-century forensic speeches see Cairns (2013a).

[35] Cf., for example, Thuc. 8.73; *IG* I³ 76.15, 21; *IG* II² 111.58, 281.3; *IPArk* 5.59. See also the expression μὴ μνασιχολῆσαι ('not to remember with hate') in *IPArk* 24.5. On amnesty and emotions see Chaniotis (2013).

[36] For law and emotions see Deigh (2008) and the essays in Sellers (2017). For ancient emotions see Konstan (2006); and the essays in Chaniotis (2012); Chaniotis and Ducrey (2013); Cairns and Fulkerson (2015); Cairns and Nelis (2017); and Cairns (2019b) 1–15 with survey of different methods and approaches.

[37] See the concept of 'heterogenous construction of emotions' in Griffiths (1997) 132.

DIVIDED POWER IN THE ATHENIAN ASSEMBLY 159

number of terms referring to fear, with different connotations, such as *tarbos* (terror), *oknos* (alarm), *kēdos* (anxiety), *phrikē* (shudder).[38] In more general terms, the two of the most common Greek words referring to fear are *phobos* and *deos*.[39] While this distinction is found in many sources, the two terms can also be used interchangeably, especially in regard to fear towards authority and laws. This is found in much evidence from the Classical and Hellenistic periods. The same concept is found in the *Laches* when Socrates explains that *deos* is caused by neither the past nor the present, but by the expectation of evil (Plat. *Lach.* 198b: τὰ προσδοκώμενα· δέος γὰρ εἶναι προσδοκίαν μέλλοντος κακοῦ). This is also the use of the *deos*-cognates found in Thucydides described above, where he reports the antidemocratic plot of the Thasian exiles. Similarly, Thucydides employs the verb δείδω to convey Themistocles' psychological attitude in Book 1 (Thuc. 1.137.1). When Themistocles was fleeing from Argos to Persia, his ship was about to be captured by the Athenians, but fearing this (*deisas*), he was able to conceive a plan to escape the danger. Yet, in Aristotle's *Politics*, when talking about the institution of *gumnasia*, Aristotle says that the presence of magistrates (the law-enforcing authorities) among the youth creates *aidōs* and *phobos* in the free citizens (Arist. *Pol.* 1331a41).

The fact that the word for the legal institution of immunity is conceptualized by directly referring to the emotion of fear cannot be a coincidence.[40] The term *adeia* conveys through the institutionalization of emotional language, the multi-faceted relationship between fear, law, and political community. The word *adeia* communicated fear for the established laws into official legal terminology. This is in a way similar to other expressive and emotional elements, such as the concern for pollution (*miasma*) in homicide cases and the procedure of supplication, which combined legal and religious elements.[41] Such arrangements were created in the Archaic period, but were then formalized and enshrined in the legal system of the *polis* and kept throughout the Classical and Hellenistic periods.[42] Through the lexicalization of the 'absence of fear', the Athenians connected a broad value system about legislation with the actual practice. This was an ideological feature of many Greek communities that is clearly confirmed by an analysis of the ancient evidence from Classical Athens and other Greek *poleis*. In Aeschylus' *Eumenides*, when establishing the new council of the Areopagus, Athena declares: 'Upon this

---

[38] For a lexicographical survey on fear terminology in Homer see Zaborowski (2002) 71–239. On *phrikē* see Cairns (2013).

[39] Patera (2013) 110 who sees a too stark opposition in the meanings of *phobos* and *deos* while Greek sources show a good degree of overlap between the two terms.

[40] *Adeia* can be defined as an institution according to MacCormick's definition of 'institution-arrangement' (for example, contracts, trust, property, or marriage). These are institutions that are the result of acts of persons or agencies. See MacCormick (2007) 35–6.

[41] On supplication see Naiden (2006) and p. 164 n. 63 below.

[42] For the role of pollution in homicide cases see Harris (2015d) 22–8; *contra* Parker (1983) 104–43. Other studies on pollution see Chaniotis (2012) 123–39 and the recent study on purity in early Greek religion by Petrovic and Petrovic (2016) with a review by Cairns (2019a).

160   DIVIDED POWER IN ANCIENT GREECE

hill, the respect (*sebas*) and inborn fear (*phobos*) of the citizens will prevent any wrong be done, alike by day and night' (tr. Sommerstein [2008], adapted). The goddess then invites the Athenians not to drive fear wholly out of the city (καὶ μὴ τὸ δεινὸν πᾶν πόλεως ἔξω βαλεῖν) because no mortal acts justly without fear (Aesch. *Eum.* 698).[43] There is a similar usage in Sophocles' *Ajax*, when Menelaus explains why Ajax is a *hubristēs*. He says that the laws could never rule a city without the presence of fear (*deos*), which promotes *aischunē* within the community.[44] In one of the most famous passages of his *Histories* (7.104.4), Herodotus describes the discussion between the Spartan Demaratus and Xerxes during the Great King's invasion of Greece. Speaking about the Spartans, Demaratus states that they are free men having the law as their master, which they fear (ὑποδειμαίνουσι) more than the king's subjects fear him. This is also confirmed by Plutarch, who explains that Sparta erected shrines to several abstractions (*pathēmata*) such as Death (*Thanatos*), Laughter (*Gelos*), and Fear (*Phobos*). The latter plays a particular role in Spartan civic religion, as it was worshipped at the *ephoreion*, the official building of the ephors (Plut. *Cleom.* 9.1–4).[45] As guardians of the *nomos*, the ephors preserved and enforced the established laws of the *polis*. Thus, when commenting on the cult of Fear in Sparta, Plutarch makes clear the link between the cult of Fear and the *nomophulakia* of the ephors.[46] In the funeral speech, Pericles affirms that the Athenians do not break the laws in the public sphere most of all owning to fear of the penalties (Thuc. 2.37.3: τὰ δημόσια διὰ δέος μάλιστα οὐ παρανομοῦμεν).[47] Similarly, Plato's *Laws* once more associate fear and *aidōs* (*Leg.* 647a). In the dialogue, the Athenian speaker draws an analogy between fear, honour, and the role of the legislator by saying that the lawgiver (*nomothetēs*) should hold fear in high consideration by naming it *aidōs*, which encourages honourable and just disposition in the citizens.[48]

This picture of a close connection between fear and the laws drawn by the ancient sources is consistent with the legislative practices of fifth-century Athens. During the Archaic and Classical periods the Athenians, like all the other Greeks, conceived of their laws as enacted by authoritative *nomothetai* whose statutes, once established, were unchangeable. The legal remedies used by Archaic and Classical legislation to ensure the immutability of laws and their perpetual implementation have been termed by scholars as 'entrenchment clauses'.[49]

---

[43] On the relationship between fear, *sebas*, and *aidōs* see Cairns (1993) 213–14.

[44] Soph. *Ajax* 1074–6 with Cairns (1993) 228–41.

[45] Plutarch quotes three verses; cf. also the fragment of the elegy by Tyrtaeus in Lyc. 1.107.

[46] For the temple of *Phobos* in Sparta see Richer (1998) 91–115 and 219–24. On the proximity of *aidōs* and fear in Sparta see Richer (1999) 91–111. For *nomophulakia* in Spartan deliberation see Chapter 4.

[47] The passage is important because it shows no dichotomy between formal penalties expressed by the laws and emotional response of citizens *pace* Lanni (2016).

[48] For the association of *aidōs* and fear in Plato see Cairns (1993) 373–5.

[49] D.M. Lewis (1997) 136–49.

DIVIDED POWER IN THE ATHENIAN ASSEMBLY   161

Lewis defines an entrenchment clause as a provision inserted in a piece of legislation for the purpose of preventing any change to the law. These clauses included provisions stating that the decree or the law should be valid for all time, and envisaged very serious penalties or threats. The emotion of fear plays a fundamental role in implementing the immutability of the laws implied by the nomothetic tradition. These laws envisaged heavy penalties and curses, sometimes sealed by a solemn oath to the gods, for those who would amend or repeal the measure.[50] Epigraphical evidence shows that this kind of clause was widespread in the legislative documents of several *poleis* across the Greek world. A sixth-century law (*tethmos*) from a city of western Locris, perhaps Naupactus, regulates land division, and its provisions are entrenched by listing several penalties and a curse (*IG* IX 1² 3, 609).[51] Whoever proposes a change in the law is cursed for all time, he and his family, his properties should be confiscated, and his house demolished. The law is sacred to Apollo, who supervises the observance of the law. A law of 575–550 BCE from Argos punishes those who will erase the law with exile, with confiscation of his property, and casts curses on them (*IG* IV 506).[52] Similarly, a fifth-century law from Teos (*c.*475 BCE) known as *Dirae Teiae* confirms the wide use of public curses to entrench legislative texts (OR 102).[53] The curse envisions the destruction of the wrongdoer and his descendants as well as providing penalties against several different typologies of crimes against individuals (for example, poisoning a Teian), but especially against the community and its leader, the *aisumnetes* (e.g. treason).[54] The law ends by addressing this curse to anyone who removes or breaks the stele with the entrenchment clause.[55] In the case of Athenian Archaic legislation, we know from a quotation in Demosthenes' *Against Aristocrates* that Draco's homicide law was entrenched by prescribing *atimia* (loss of right) for whoever violated or modified the law (Dem. 23.42).[56] It appears that a similar entrenchment clause existed for the laws of Solon. According to

---

[50] For a general treatment of curses in the Greek world see Eidinow (2007) 139–55; for the role of curses in oaths see Konstantinidou (2014). For curses in the Athenian assembly, see Dem. 19.70. This practice is also well attested in some fourth-century lead cursing tablets against opponents in Athenian lawsuits; see D. R. Jordan (1995); Rubinstein (2007).

[51] Camassa (2009) 82–3, who argues that the first instance of this legislative practice might be already found in the first Greek law from the Cretan *polis* of Dreros (*Nomima* I, 48). The law contains regulations for the office of *kosmos*, which could not be iterated before a period of ten years. The ending formula θιὸς ὄλοι ὄν can be interpreted as 'may the god destroy him', therefore a curse against anyone who modifies the written statute. Cf. Seelentag (2015) 139–63; Gagarin and Perlman (2016) 203–5.

[52] For a discussion on this law, see Körner (1993).

[53] For the analogies between the law of Teos and the biblical Deuteronomy see Hagerdon (2005) 127–50. For a study of legislative practice in the Near East and Archaic and Classical Greece, see Harris (2006) 5–16; Camassa (2011a).

[54] For the *aisumnetes* in the Greek *poleis*, see Faraguna (2005) 321–38. For religious imprecations and curses in Greek legislative texts, see Rubinstein (2007) with a list of the epigraphical evidence from late Classical and Hellenistic *poleis*. For continuity of religious features in Greek law see Parker (1997) 256–81, (2005) 76–7. For further epigraphical evidence for penalties about the breaking of entrenchment clauses see B. D. Gray (2015) 117.

[55] On this epigraphical document see Youni (2011).   [56] Canevaro (2013b) 38–46.

162 DIVIDED POWER IN ANCIENT GREECE

Dio Chrysostom, the Athenians established a curse for those who attempted to overthrow the laws of Solon (Dio Chrys. *Or.* 80.6; Aul. Gell. *Noc. Att.* 2.12.1).[57] A fifth-century Athenian example is found in the Brea decree which orders the foundation of a colony (445 BCE).[58] The text of the decree includes a provision (OR 142.24–9) prescribing *atimia* for the wrongdoer and his descendants and confiscating his property, if anyone would put to the vote or propose a change in the decree. At the beginning of each assembly meeting, moreover, deterrent curses were cast against those who would try to change the democratic constitution.[59]

It is within this cultural and ideological context that one should place the origin of *adeia* as a legal institution. The possibility of calling it 'absence of fear', when referring to a legal institution, demonstrates that the Athenians labelled a legal procedure by associating it with an emotional experience, such as fear towards the laws. Nevertheless, what is important to stress is that *adeia* did not indicate the absence of respect for the authority of the law, but rather the temporary absence of fear for the legal penalty as granted by the community.

This enabled the conceptualization of immunity in terms of emotional language. Just as with many other Athenian legal expressions, there was no actual dichotomy between the extra-legal and legal meanings of *adeia*.[60] The term *adeia* was both a state of personal security and a lexicalization for legal security against penalties. The latter had a decisive ideological meaning, since the legal context institutionalized the emotional state through a formal act of the *dēmos*, which managed this civic control of fear by giving democratic assent to immunity. Only the *dēmos* could enable someone to be unafraid of the laws: the normal and expected state was one of fear and respect for the laws. The linguistic mechanism, by which the term immunity is expressed, clearly shows that the Athenians recognized that this new legal institution (for the fifth century) was specifically designed to convey the relationship between the law and the fear of incurring the penalties and curses imposed in the entrenchment clauses grounded on the nomothetic tradition. This was possibly the best way of describing expressively an institutional tool conceived in opposition to the fear raised by a legislative ideology and practice which was adverse to legal change. The legal procedure of *adeia* allowed an Athenian citizen to prevail over the fear of legal constraints and penalties integral to the nomothetic tradition, and to put forward legislative innovations to the established legal framework. Nevertheless, as the analysis of

---

[57] For a commentary see Leão and Rhodes (2015) 149–50. For Solon's nomothetic tradition in Classical Athens, see Canevaro (2015); Loddo (2019) 18–37 with discussion of previous bibliography. For the reception of Solon in the fifth and fourth centuries, see Nagy and Noussia Fantuzzi (2015).

[58] For the date of the Brea decree see Psoma (2009); (2016).

[59] For ritual *arai* (curses) in the Athenian assembly cf. Dem. 18.282; 20.107; and 23.97; Ar. *Thesm.* 331–51; Dem. 24.107.

[60] The overlap between ethical and legal level also applies to Greek *atimia* that was both a social sanction based on ethical principles and an institutionalized legal penalty, see the important discussion in Rocchi (2023c).

DIVIDED POWER IN THE ATHENIAN ASSEMBLY   163

the procedure will show, *adeia* did not represent a coherent and systematic rule of change, as *nomothesia*, established only in 403 BCE, did. *Adeia* was one of the first, limited, and imperfect, yet innovative attempts made by fifth-century Athenians to balance the need for preserving the immutability of their laws with democratic control over legislation. It is not a surprise that the first occurrence of *adeia* as a legal term is found in an entrenched decree: the financial decrees of Callias, which help in reconstructing the procedural features of the *adeia* and its rationale within the development of the Athenian attitude towards legal change.

5.3 Procedure: Legal Change and Divided Power in Fifth-Century Decision-Making

In 434/3 BCE Callias proposed two financial decrees in close succession (*IG* I³ 52).[61] The first decree establishes the new treasury of the Other Gods, which unified several other religious funds under the supervision of a single board (*IG* I³ 52A).[62] The second decree reports regulations passed by the Athenian assembly instructing the magistrates to supervise the works for the gateways of the Acropolis (*IG* I³ 52B). The decree prescribes at lines 12–17 that the money of Athena should only be used for this purpose, with 10,000 drachmas as a spending threshold, and adds an entrenchment clause. I reproduce the relevant section of the decree:

τοῖς δ]ὲ ἄλλοις χρέμα[σιν τοῖ]ς τὲς Ἀθεναίας το[ῖς τε νῦν ὄσι]-
[ν ἐμ πόλει κ]αὶ hάττ' ἂν τ[ὸ] λο[ιπὸν ἀν]αφέρεται μὲ χρέσ[θ]α[ι μεδὲ δαν]-
[είζεσθαι ἀ]π' αὐτôν ἐ[ς] ἄλλο μ[εδὲν ἒ] ἐς ταῦτα hυπὲρ μυ[ρ]ί[ας δραχμὰ]-
15   [ς ἒ ἐς ἐπισκ]ευὲν ἐάν τι δέε[ι· ἐς ἄλλ]ο δὲ μεδὲν χρέσ[θ]α[ι τοῖς χρέμα]-
[σιν ἐὰμ μὲ τ]ὲν ἄδειαν φσεφ[ίσεται] ὁ δῆμος καθάπερ ἐ[ὰμ φσεφίσετ]-
[αι περὶ ἐσφ]ορᾶς· ἐὰν δέ τις [εἴπει ἒ] ἐπιφσεφί[σ]ει μὲ ἐ[φσεφισμένε]-
[ς πο τὲς ἀδεί]ας χρὲσθαι το[ῖς χρέμ]ασιν τοῖ[ς] τὲς Ἀθε[ναίας, ἐνεχέ]-
[σθο τοῖς α]ὑτοῖς hοῖσπερ ἐά[ν τι ἐσ]φέρεν εἴπει ἒ ἐπιφ[σεφίσει.[...]

The other monies of Athena, what is now on the Acropolis and whatever may be brought up in future, shall not be used or [have expenditure made] from them for any other purpose other than these, above ten thousand drachmas, or for repairs or completions or fittings out if any are needed. The monies shall not be used for

---

[61] For an early date of the decree see Samons (2000) 129–33; *contra* Kallet-Marx (1994) 94–113, who argues for a later enactment in 431 BCE. Mattingly (1996) 215–22 made the case for dating the decree at 422/1 BCE. Scholarship on the two decrees of Callias was entangled in the diatribe about the use of three-bar sigma in fifth-century Attic epigraphical practice, which has been now resolved in Chambers, Gallucci, and Spanos (1990). Cf. Rhodes (2003b); Papazarkadas (2009).
[62] Linders (1975); Rhodes (2013) 213–14.

164   DIVIDED POWER IN ANCIENT GREECE

anything else unless the People vote immunity (*adeia*) as when they vote about capital tax (*eisphora*). If anybody proposes or puts to the vote when immunity has not been voted that the monies of Athena shall be used, let him be liable to the same penalties as when somebody proposes or puts to the vote that there shall be a capital tax.

(trans. Lambert and Rhodes, https://www.atticinscriptions.com/)

As the text of the second decree of Callias shows at lines 16–17, the spending limit provision is entrenched. In order to override the entrenched 10,000 drachmas bar, the decree orders a vote of *adeia*,[63] similar to the vote taken for the levy of *eisphora*, providing the same penalty in case of failure to secure a vote for *adeia*.[64] We do not know what kind of penalty was envisaged in case of violation of *eisphora* levy procedure.[65] Thucydides affirms that in 431 BCE the Athenians set new protections for the treasury of Athena by establishing a new separate fund for war expenditures, as well as the death penalty for those who used money from this treasury for other purposes (Thuc. 2.24). Building on this passage, Lewis argues that a lesser penalty was possibly envisioned for those who failed to follow the procedure of *adeia*.[66] This kind of entrenchment clause was designed to make legislative change more difficult, rather than impossible. As a result, the decree of Callias represents a typical example of what Canevaro defines as fifth-century tacit legislation.[67] Even if the legal text takes the form of a decree (*psēphisma*), its provisions are not concerned with the daily administration of the *polis* but rather establish permanent norms, which shall be applied to the whole community in the future.[68] The decree of Callias is therefore an entrenched law passed by the assembly. Remarkably, the second decree of Callias is evidence for the ambiguous

---

[63] Goldstaub (1889) 7–8 argues that the origin of *adeia* was a secular development of the religious institution of supplication. Yet Naiden (2006) 171–218 demonstrates that there was no clear-cut distinction between the religious and legal aspects of supplication in Athenian law. Supplication bridged the religious and the civic spheres and was enforced by the relevant political bodies of the *polis*. *Adeia* was rather an institution that emerged according to a logic of path dependence from the nomothetic ideology. Second, even the supposed procedural similarities between the two institutions are superficial. The Aristotelian *Athenaion Politeia* clearly states that supplications were part of the regular business of the Athenian assembly, which held specific meetings for discussing supplications ([Arist.] *Ath. Pol.* 43.6). Conversely, the request of *adeia* was not a standard item on the agenda of the assembly, but an extraordinary procedure.

[64] For archaic *eisphora* see van Wees (2013) 44–56. For a study of *eisphora* see R. Thomsen (1964); Brun (1983); Christ (2007) 53–69; *adeia* and *eisphora* see Poddighe (2010); Migeotte (2014); Canevaro (2016b) 50–2. On the ideology of *eisphora* in Classical Athens see Liddel (2007) 276; cf. e.g. Isae. 7.39–40; Dem. 28.4; Lys. 19.43, 20.23, 21.3.

[65] For penalties in fifth-century decrees see Scafuro (2014a).

[66] D. M. Lewis (1997) 137–8; Schwartzberg (2004).

[67] Canevaro (2015); for a definition of law see Pospisil (1974) 11.

[68] A similar fifth-century example is the so-called Standards Decree (*IG* I³ 1453) which establishes a general norm about coinage, weights, and measures by decree to be applied across the Athenian Empire (and it even amends the bouleutic oath at line 10). The inscription is very fragmentary, but it is mocked in Aristophanes' *Birds* (1040–5) where is called *psēphisma* by the Decree-seller, but *nomos* by Pisetaerus. For the relationship between Athenian legislation and empire see Liddel (2010).

DIVIDED POWER IN THE ATHENIAN ASSEMBLY   165

law-making practices of fifth-century Athens. On the one hand, the Athenians followed the nomothetic ideology of legislation by safeguarding the decree with an entrenchment clause, given its law-like contents. On the other hand, the entrenchment clause itself described the legal procedure that made it possible to modify the relevant regulations. The procedure of *adeia* was already institutionalized when Callias proposed his decree, as the reference to *adeia* for the levy of *eisphora* suggests. Yet, in the extant epigraphical attestation, this is the first time in Athenian legislative practice that a procedure for authorizing legal change, even if imperfect and incomplete, can be seen in an entrenched piece of legislation. A vote of *adeia* authorized the proposal of new regulations that would modify the content of the entrenched decree by acknowledging the power of the *dēmos* to introduce legislative changes to the existing statute. *Adeia* played an innovative role in fifth-century deliberative practice, as this procedure could override the ban imposed by the entrenchment clause, a device in keeping with the nomothetic tradition that underpinned Athenian legislative ideology.

It is important to stress that the *adeia* procedure was not retroactive. There is no evidence that *adeia* was understood as a general principle also to be applicable to other Athenian statutes for which it was not explicitly prescribed. For example, the assembly could not change the old entrenched laws of Draco and Solon by voting *adeia*, as the source of legitimacy for those statutes was the lawgivers' authority and not popular power, and no derogation to the entrenchment clause was contemplated in them. Conversely, the decree of Callias shows one of the first attempts to create a rule of change as well as some form of hierarchy in the enactments of the assembly, and in this way provides a compromise in the clash between nomothetic immutability and the people's law-making power. The novelty of *adeia* within the Greek legislative tradition is clear when one compares the *adeia* clause in the decree of Callias with the law about land tenure of sixth-century Naupactus mentioned above. There the law clearly forbids any motion or vote to change the statute to be held in the political bodies of the cities, the assembly (*polis*), the council of elders (*preiga*), and the *apoklēsia* (lines 9–14: ℎόστ|ις δὲ δαιθμὸν ἐνφέροι ἒ ψᾶφον διαφέροι ἐν πρείγαι, ἐν πόλι, ἐν ἀποκλεσίαι | ἒ στάσιν ποιέοι περὶ γαδαισίας αὐτὸς μὲ|ν ϝερρέτο καὶ γενεὰ ἅματα πάντα, χρέματα δὲ δαμευόσθον | καὶ ϝοικία κατασκαπτέσθο κὰτ τὸν ἀνδρεφονικὸν τετμ|όν).[69] The people of Naupactus strictly followed the nomothetic ideology, and their entrenchment clause is very thorough in forbidding any attempt within their civic institutions to change the relevant statute. All forms of legislative activity tampering with this law are completely banned.[70]

---

[69] 'Should anyone request a land redistribution or cast a vote in favour of this matter in the council of elders (*preiga*), in the assembly (*polis*), in the *apoklēsia* or instigate discord for the purpose of land redistribution, he and his progeny shall perish forever, his property shall be confiscated and his house shall be demolished according to the homicide law.'

[70] Camassa (2011a) 110–2.

166 DIVIDED POWER IN ANCIENT GREECE

The use of *adeia* in deliberative procedure during the years following the second decree of Callias is attested by the records of the treasurers of Athena in 418/17 BCE (*IG* I³ 370). This epigraphical document is fragmentary; nevertheless, three occurrences of *adeia* are clearly readable on the stone (15, 30, 63–4), whereas another two occurrences are restored (28, 33). The formulaic expression φσεφισαμένο τô δέμο τὲν ἄδειαν is consistent with the wording found in the entrenchment clause of the second decree of Callias, and it records the exact day of the prytany in which the vote was taken by the assembly.[71] The figure of 6,000 votes as quorum is not mentioned in the inscription, but this is not surprising. A vote of *adeia* was therefore taken and carefully recorded, probably in the archival copies, to authorize changes in the financial regulations after the enactment of the second financial decree of Callias. Similarly, in the speech *On his Return*, a speech delivered between 410 and 405 BCE, Andocides reminds the Athenians that the decree granting him *adeia* in 415 BCE was still valid, and a copy of the relevant decree was kept in the archive of the *bouleutērion* (Andoc. 2.23).[72] This is important in showing that the Athenians carefully followed this legal procedure. During their final *euthunai*, financial officials could provide written evidence that the payments were made in accordance with the law.[73] Extra payments made by the treasurers of Athena had to be instructed by a decree of the assembly which was passed after a vote of *adeia* and provisionally overrode the entrenched spending limit of the second decree of Callias.

The *adeia* clause in the second decree of Callias, however, does not give any detail about the procedural steps for voting the immunity. The only reference within the text of the decree is that *adeia* is to be voted according to the same procedure employed for the levy of the *eisphora*. Despite its vagueness, the clause implies that *adeia* was to be voted on according to a distinct and more complex procedure, which was different from that normally used for votes in the assembly. This is also consistent with the excerpt of the law about deliberations on *atimoi* and public debtors quoted in Demosthenes' *Against Timocrates* (24.45).[74] According to this law, there could be no discussion of matters pertaining to an *atimos* without a preliminary vote of *adeia* taken by 6,000 Athenians by secret ballot (ἐὰν μὴ ψηφισαμένων Ἀθηναίων τὴν ἄδειαν πρῶτον μὴ ἔλαττον ἑξακισχιλίων,

---

[71] At line 64 it is stated that the vote of *adeia* took place during the third prytany of the tribe Aiantis, but the day is missing.

[72] Andoc. 2.23. On the archival practices of the fifth-century see Sickinger (1999) 62–91. For archival and legal practice in Athens see Faraguna (2007) 89–102, (2016). For a study of archival practice in the Greek world, see now the monumental Boffo and Faraguna (2021).

[73] For *euthunai* in Classical Athens see Oranges (2021). For *euthunai* and building accounts see Epstein (2013) 127–41; on *euthunai* and archives, see Boffo and Faraguna (2021) 237–64. For prosecution for financial offences in *euthunai* cf. [Arist.] *Ath. Pol.* 48.3–5, 54.2 with Rhodes (1981) 560–4, 597–9; Migeotte (2014) 449–52.

[74] This law seems to be an authentic document inserted in the *Urexemplar* of the Demosthenic speech; see Canevaro (2013b) 127–32 for an analysis of the document.

οἷς ἂν δόξῃ κρύβδην ψηφιζομένοις).[75] The information extrapolated from this document—as mentioned in the opening section of this chapter—seems to confirm that a successful grant of *adeia* required a vote by *psēphophoria* (secret ballot) in order to record a quorum of 6,000 votes. The same quorum was also prescribed for naturalization decrees, and the fact that this is not mentioned in the second decree of Callias and in *IG* I³ 370 is not surprising. The example of grants of citizenship provides a good epigraphic term of comparison. In his analysis of inscribed citizenship decrees in the fourth century, Osborne shows that naturalization decrees never mention the quorum required to ratify the grant, even though the law doubtless prescribed it.[76] In addition, voting by secret ballot (*psēphophoria*) was not the standard voting system employed by deliberative bodies in Classical Athens.[77] The council and the assembly normally made their decisions by show of hands (*cheirotonia*) rather than by secret ballot, which was the system commonly used in judicial settings.[78] As Hansen has demonstrated, when the Athenian assembly voted by show of hands, these votes were never counted, but they were roughly assessed by the *prutaneis* in the fifth century and then by the *proedroi* in the fourth.[79] By contrast, Hansen shows that the use of *psēphophoria* was not intended to guarantee the secrecy of the vote. The votes were counted when a quorum was required by the voting procedure.[80]

A formal quorum of 6,000 votes by secret ballot was needed not only for *adeia*. Two other procedures demonstrate the same requirement: (1) the fifth-century procedure of ostracism[81] ([Arist.] *Ath. Pol.* 43.5; Philoch. *FGrH* 328 F30; Diod. 11.55; Plut. *Arist.* 7.6); and (2) grants of citizenship ([Dem.] 59.89).[82] By analysing the epigraphical evidence from several Greek city-states, Gauthier demonstrates that the quorum was designed to register formally the consensus of the whole

---

[75] 'If immunity (*adeia*) is not granted by no less than 6,000 Athenians, who so resolve voting by secret ballot.'

[76] Osborne (1981–3) 4.162 n. 30; see the epigraphical instances in Osborne (1981–3) vol. 1, with commentary in Osborne (1981–3) vol. 2.

[77] Staveley (1972) 93–5.

[78] For a diachronic study of the voting systems in the lawcourts see Boegehold (1963), (1995) 21–41.

[79] Hansen (2004); cf. [Arist.] *Ath. Pol.* 44.3 (τὰς χειροτονίας κρίνουσιν); Rhodes (1980) 535. For the *prutaneis*' role in the assembly see Harris (2014); Canevaro (2019d).

[80] Hansen (1987a) 48–50; for a more recent discussion see Canevaro (2018a).

[81] Evidence about a formal quorum for the ostracism is ambiguous. The figure 6,000 votes is mentioned in Plutarch's *Life of Aristides*. When describing the procedure, Plutarch says that the archons counted first the whole number of *ostraka* cast (οἱ δ' ἄρχοντες πρῶτον μὲν διηρίθμουν τὸ σύμπαν ἐν ταὐτῷ τῶν ὀστράκων πλῆθος), and if there were less than 6,000 voters, the ostracism was invalid (εἰ γὰρ ἑξακισχιλίων ἐλάττονες οἱ φέροντες εἶεν, ἀτελὴς ἦν ὁ ἐξοστρακισμός). That the figure of 6,000 votes for ostracism was a quorum was first proposed by Jacoby, followed by many other scholars. Cf. R. Thomsen (1964) 66 n. 3; Rhodes (1981) 270–1; Hansen (1983) 26 n. 6. For the role of ostracism in policing claims to *timē* and elite behaviour in fifth-century Athens see Barbato (2021).

[82] Osborne (1981–3) 3/4.155–68. Traditional accounts about the quorum also include the νόμος ἐπ' ἀνδρί based on an unreliable document in Dem. 24.59. For the lack of rationale of the νόμος ἐπ' ἀνδρί in the context of fourth-century Athenian legislation and the problems with this document see Canevaro (2013b) 145–51.

168   DIVIDED POWER IN ANCIENT GREECE

civic body.[83] In the case of *adeia* and naturalization, the ancient evidence shows that the required quorum is well attested throughout the fourth century, whereas a parallel for a fifth-century quorum is provided by ostracism.[84] Hansen' shows that in the fifth century a formal quorum was already required and was verified through a very simple mechanism. The so-called Pnyx I, the fifth-century meeting place of the assembly, could contain 6,000 participants; therefore, when the Pnyx was full, this showed that the quorum was reached.[85] Preserved *ostraka* show that in a single *ostrakophoria* the Athenian preferences were usually very fragmented, which also points out that the Athenians did not concentrate 6,000 votes on one candidate, but the number was a quorum prescribed by law to make the ostracism valid.[86] The figure of 6,000 was therefore a formal quorum already in force in fifth-century voting procedures and constitutes a contemporary parallel for the quorum necessary for *adeia*.

It should be highlighted that the Athenian notion of quorum did not conform to the modern parliamentary concept. According to the *Concise Oxford Dictionary of Politics*, a quorum is the 'minimum number of members that must be present to make proceedings of a political body valid.'[87] In the case of Greek democratic assemblies, the number of members was not fixed by a constitutional law, but rather coincided with the notional, symbolic, and idealized number of citizens of the whole *dēmos*, since all enfranchised male citizens were members of the assembly. As Gauthier has rightly highlighted in his study of the quorum in Greek *poleis*, the figure of 6,000 symbolized the whole civic body of all the Athenians, and was preserved over time regardless of the actual number of citizens.[88] The figure of 6,000 is consistent with the number of citizens that were selected every year by lot to serve as judges in the Athenian courts during both the fifth and the fourth centuries, and this panel embodied the Athenian *dēmos* in its judicial capacity (Andoc. 1.17; Ar. *Vesp.* 662; [Arist.] *Ath. Pol.* 24.3; Suid. s.v. πρυτανεία). The figure of 6,000 is strongly symbolic with important ideological implications for the vote of *adeia*. The quorum of 6,000 votes necessary to pass a vote of *adeia* was designed formally to record the fact that the virtual totality of the

---

[83] Gauthier (1990) 73–99.

[84] For the different stages of the Pnyx, see Hansen (1996) 25–9. For different figures for the Pnyx I, see Stanton (1996) 18–19, who sees a correlation between the quorum and the capacity of the Pnyx, although it is difficult to say when an open auditorium is full and his arguments on this specific point are mainly based on comparison with modern people's attitude to cramming together in trains and buses during peak hours. This interpretation also underestimates the power of *prutaneis* to check the attendance and to keep people in and out of the Pnyx as attested in Aristophanes' *Acharnanians* (19–20) and *Ecclesiazousae* (379). For the powers of the presiding magistrates during meetings of the assembly, cf. Aeschin. 2.84; Dem. 22.5, 9; *contra* Epstein (2009).

[85] Hansen (1987b) 48–50; Canevaro (2018a).

[86] On ostracism, see Brenne (2001) 23; Siewert (2002); Forsdyke (2005) 149 n. 20, 283. For the regional distribution of ostracized citizens and *ostraka*, see Gouschin (2009) 233–45; see Brenne (2018) for an in-depth study of the *ostraka* of the Kerameikos.

[87] McLean and McMillan (2009), s.v. quorum.   [88] Gauthier (1990) 81–2.

DIVIDED POWER IN THE ATHENIAN ASSEMBLY   169

Athenians were present and agreed to discuss the matter and participated in the deliberation which led later, in the same assembly, to a vote by show of hands presumably expressing the consensus of the community to change an entrenched decree.[89]

In order to modify an entrenched decree with *adeia*, many institutional stages were needed. First, a vote of *adeia* was to be included in the assembly's agenda by a *probouleuma* of the council. As mentioned above, *adeia* was not a standard item in the assembly's agenda since the Aristotelian *Athenaion Politeia* does not mention immunity among the regular items discussed during assembly meetings. As we know that no motion could be introduced to the assembly without the preliminary approval of the council, a *probouleuma* was therefore needed in order for the *dēmos* to put to the vote a grant of *adeia* ([Arist.] *Ath. Pol.* 45.4).[90] A preliminary discussion on whether *adeia* should be voted was thus held in the council, which voted a *probouleuma* by *cheirotonia*. Second, the *prutaneis* introduced the vote of *adeia* to the next meeting of the assembly. There was no preliminary discussion in the assembly, but the Athenians voted by secret ballot when entering the Pnyx. Yet the vote did not enact any particular measure: it simply made debating the modification of the entrenched provision possible, at the same time certifying that the virtual totality of the Athenians is present for the ensuing deliberation and the resulting vote by show of hand. The fourth-century vote for granting citizenship provides a basis for comparison with the vote of *adeia*. In *Against Neaera*, Apollodorus paraphrases the procedure prescribed by the law for granting Athenian citizenship. Apollodorus makes clear that a decree of citizenship passed by the assembly was not valid until it was ratified by a quorum of 6,000 secret votes in the next assembly meeting. The law instructed the *prutaneis* to place the ballot urns outside the assembly in order that the Athenians could cast their secret ballot when entering the assembly place ([Dem.] 59.89–90).[91]

The vote for the *adeia* procedure would have, in all probability, followed a very similar process. Yet, the vote of *adeia* was not a ratification and occurred before the normal vote of the assembly, not afterwards as in the case of naturalization. As both the decree of Callias and the law at Dem. 24.35 show, *adeia* was to be voted before the discussion of the decree in the assembly, otherwise the proposer could not have enjoyed legal immunity; his proposal would have been unlawful and he would have been punished according to the penalties envisaged by the entrenchment clause. This procedural detail is very important, and sheds light on the rationale of *adeia* in fifth-century decision-making. The text of the *Against*

---

[89] For votes by show of hands encouraging consensus see Canevaro (2018a).

[90] Rhodes (1981) 543–4.

[91] For the ratification vote in inscriptions cf. *IG* II[2] 103.34–5, the first epigraphical instance. For the procedure see Osborne (1981–3) 3/4.155–70 and esp. 161–4.

170   DIVIDED POWER IN ANCIENT GREECE

Neaera clearly reports that the ratification vote for a grant of citizenship was aimed at confirming that the candidate was worthy of receiving Athenian citizenship (εἰ ἄξιός ἐστι τῆς δωρεᾶς), on which the assembly had already deliberated ([Dem.] 59.90).[92] When voting on *adeia*, the assembly instead gave legal authority to a citizen to put forward a proposal for changes to entrenched, and therefore supposedly unchangeable, legislation. Without previous debate, the assembly must have, in the vote on *adeia*, taken into account primarily the legal reasons that justified overriding the entrenchment clauses, aggregating the unmediated opinions and preferences of the individual Athenians on the opportunity to do so, as was normal with *psephophoriai* in the lawcourts: this in itself stresses the quasi-legal dimension of this vote. Deliberation and consensus-building came next: the assembly debated the motions and took a vote by show of hands in that very assembly meeting. In this way, the vote of *adeia* played the role of framing the deliberation on the relevant entrenched decree within the respect of the established laws of Athens and the hegemonic nomothetic ideology.[93]

As shown in the previous chapter on Spartan deliberation, voting systems are not just technicalities but are embedded in the form of deliberation performed by the relevant body and shaped the collective behaviour of decision-makers.[94] The use of the *psephophoria*, a system usually employed by the courts, in the assembly had a precise ideological goal. Beside the functional need to count a quorum, the *psephophoria* has also important ideological implications distinguish two different types of the collective behaviour of the Athenians in the assembly. As mentioned above, the Athenians usually voted by show of hands in the council and in the assembly.[95] By contrast, voting by secret ballot was standard practice in the lawcourts where the judges had to apply the decrees and written statutes, and there was no room for deliberation about public policy.[96] The constitutional role of the law courts is also reflected in the distinct voting system which applied strict majority rule made possible by the *psephophoria*.[97] Similarly, when voting *adeia*, the Athenian assembly adopted a voting system enhancing the rule of law in deliberation and pursuing the goal of providing a strong legal framework for the discussion of the relevant decree. In the assembly meetings involving the vote of *adeia*, the Athenians combined the voting practice of the deliberative (*cheirotonia*)

---

[92] [Dem.] 59.90.

[93] I use the term 'hegemonic' according to Gramsci's definition. As we have seen in Chapter 4, the nomothetic ideology in Sparta became also (but not exclusively) instrumental to preserve the power of the elites.

[94] Cf. Chapter 4 for the difference in voting between the Spartan *gerousia* and assembly.

[95] For the implication of *cheirotonia* in Athenian deliberation see Schwartzberg (2014); Canevaro (2018a), (2020b).

[96] This difference also applies to the arguments used in deliberative speeches and forensic oratory see Harris (2013a) 95–6. Cf. Arist. *Rhet.* 1359b; Dem. 24.36; Lyc. 1.4.

[97] The *psephophoria* in the lawcourts was regulated by a law see Aeschin. 1.79; the procedure is fully described by [Arist.] *Ath. Pol.* 68–9 with Rhodes (1981) 730–5 and Boegehold (1995) 82–6, 209–22. Cf. Chapter 6 on *graphe paranomon*.

DIVIDED POWER IN THE ATHENIAN ASSEMBLY   171

and the judicial settings (*psēphophoria*) since *adeia* was designed to provide the legal basis within which deliberation about an entrenched decree could be performed. The rule of the established laws is respected, and the *dēmos* designed the relevant voting procedure to ensure that the civic body applied the procedure when changing legislation. This shows the very nature of *adeia* as a procedure negotiating between accepted ideology and actual institutional practice. These institutional values will be preserved and finally formalized in a logic of path dependence in the more sophisticated procedure of *nomothesia* at the end of the fifth century.[98]

It is possible to draw further procedural analogies between *adeia* and fourth-century *nomothesia*. In Demosthenes' *Against Timocrates* (24.25), we read that the Athenians performed, to start the *nomothesia* procedure, a preliminary *diacheirotonia*: a vote by show of the hands in the assembly on whether new laws could be proposed or not. Canevaro demonstrates that *diacheirotonia* initiated the law-making procedure by authorizing the introduction of new legislative proposals.[99] As in the case of *adeia*, a preliminary vote was taken, and it was only after this vote that the legislative procedure started. The grant of *adeia* represented the fundamental step to be undertaken in order to override an entrenchment bar, but further procedural stages were required. After having obtained the immunity, the proposal could be introduced and discussed in that meeting or in another meeting of assembly. The matter of *adeia* was introduced with an open *probouleuma* of the council, after which the relevant modification authorized by the grant of *adeia* could be discussed by the *dēmos* in the assembly.

The institutional complexity of the procedural arrangements aimed to implementing the concept of divided power within the assembly decree-making, and complemented the differed mechanisms, such as delegation, discussed in the previous chapters. The double voting fostered distinctive behaviours of the *dēmos* when passing a decree requiring a preliminary vote of *adeia*. In the first stage, the presence of a quorum and the *psēphophoria* favoured deliberation on matters of law and about the opportunity to override an entrenchment clause. It was a way to give the assembly the power to control and to check itself with particular procedural set ups and mechanisms that allowed the *dēmos* to perform different kinds of deliberation and distinctive discursive protocols within the same institution.

To summarize, the Athenian assembly could vote *adeia* in order to authorize ad hoc derogation to an entrenched norm. The *adeia* procedure differed from the normal votes in decree-making procedure and consisted of three stages: (1) after debate, the council passed an open *probouleuma* allowing a vote of *adeia* to be

---

[98] Cf. on this development Chapter 7 p. 217. *Adeia* will remain in use in the fourth century for authorizing deliberation about *atimoi* in the assembly. I will return on this topic in another publication.

[99] Canevaro (2013a) 146.

taken in the assembly (Dem. 22.5–7; [Arist.] *Ath. Pol.* 45.8); (2) the *prutaneis* introduced the vote to the following assembly meeting, at which the Athenians voted by *psēphophoria* requiring a quorum of 6,000 votes (*IG* I³ 52B; inferred from Dem. 24.45); (3) if *adeia* was successfully granted, the relevant topics 'authorized' by the vote of *adeia* were introduced and discussed in the same assembly (*IG* I³ 370). In this way, the vote of *adeia* played the role of framing the deliberation with respect to the established laws of Athens. The grant of *adeia* allowed for a temporary suspension of the law in order to introduce an ad hoc measure without repealing the norms.

5.4 *Adeia*: An Incomplete Rule of Legal Change

This institutionalization of legal change through the procedure of *adeia* should not be overestimated. Despite some important similarities, *adeia* did not constitute a comprehensive rule of change similar to the fourth-century *nomothesia* procedure. While providing a procedure for overriding the entrenchment clause, and therefore dividing the power of creating binding norms, the provision of the decree of Callias does not provide a way for automatically repealing old contradictory statutes (*lex posterior derogat priori*). A vote of *adeia* paved the way for changing or bypassing the provisions of an entrenched statute, but it did not envisage a systematic set of rules to ensure legislative coherence. In other words, new and old regulations could simultaneously be enforced with the same legal validity. Fourth-century *nomothesia* also required a preliminary vote to be taken in the assembly in order to authorize the process of legislation. When this preliminary vote was taken, however, it did not authorize the enactment of a law through the normal procedure for enacting decrees, but rather began a distinct law-making procedure, which included the publication of the bills, the prior repeal of potential opposing laws, and the summoning of *nomothetai* to pass new statutes.[100]

By contrast, the vote of *adeia* allowed the discussion of a normally unlawful matter through the usual decree-making procedure and the standard institutional tools of administration, through which the assembly rejected or passed the relevant motion without necessarily repealing opposing regulations. It was an ad hoc provision that modified only the entrenchment of the particular decree that prescribed it. The *dēmos* was not officially empowered to change the laws through a systematic procedure, but the institutional and ideological

---

[100] Canevaro (2013a) 146–7. For the identity of *nomothetai* and the puzzling absence of this institution in the Aristotelian *Athenaion Politeia* see Canevaro and Esu (2018) 130–6 who explain Aristotle's omission of the *nomothetai* in light of his philosophical methodology and show that the *nomothetai* were a special law-making session of the assembly labelled as such.

DIVIDED POWER IN THE ATHENIAN ASSEMBLY   173

implications of *adeia* are nevertheless important for Athenian divided power.[101] *Adeia* clearly shows the attempt of the Athenians to design a procedure which made the relationship between democracy and nomothetic concerns less problematic. In this way, the *adeia* procedure allowed ad hoc changes in the laws or temporary suspensions of the entrenchment clauses prescribed in the legislation. The text of previous statutes was formally unmodified, as *adeia* did not authorize the repealing of laws. This configures *adeia* as a typology of 'law of exception'.[102]

This point is further confirmed by the fact that the very same procedure was used to grant immunity from prosecution. In this case, immunity was not employed for a deliberative purpose, but the procedure had the same legal implications. A vote of *adeia* authorized ad hoc suspension of the legal force of a statute. As a result, the *adeia*-holder was not subjected to prosecution under the relevant laws. As Andocides' speech *On the Mysteries* demonstrates, *adeia* was extensively used to obtain information during the investigation following the profanation of the Eleusinian Mysteries and the mutilation of the Herms in 415 BCE. When speaking in his defence for a charge of impiety, Andocides reconstructs the dramatic events of the profanation at the eve of the Sicilian expedition. According to Andocides' account, the assembly was gathered in order to appoint the generals to send to Sicily, when Pythonicus accused Alcibiades of having performed the Mysteries in a private house and asked the assembly to grant *adeia* to a slave who could witness it (Andoc. 1.11: ἐὰν ψηφίσησθε ἄδειαν ᾧ ἐγὼ κελεύω, θεράπων ὑμῖν ἑνὸς τῶν ἐνθάδε ἀνδρῶν ἀμύητος ὢν ἐρεῖ τὰ μυστήρια).[103] Only after *adeia* was voted, the slave Andronicus reported that the Mysteries were performed at Polytion's house by Alcibiades, Nicides, Meletus, and others who were present, including himself, his brother, and Meletus' slave. Other informers provided pieces of information under the protection of *adeia*. A metic, Teucrus, had fled to Megara, but he offered to be a witness to the council in return for *adeia*. The council, which had full authority (*autokratōr*) in the investigation, gave *adeia* to Teucrus, who accused several people for the profanation of the Mysteries as well as for the mutilation of the Herms.[104] Similarly, Andocides himself was granted *adeia* by the council for

---

[101] For the record of the vote of *adeia* in the accounts of the treasurers of Athena in 418/17 BCE showing that *adeia* was effectively used see above pp. 166–7.

[102] For a detailed discussion of this concept and its application to Classical Athens see Esu (2021a) 169–72.

[103] 'If you vote to give immunity to the person to whom I tell you to, a servant of one of the men present here, though he is uninitiated, will tell you about the Mysteries' (trans. MacDowell in Gagarin and MacDowell [1998], adapted).

[104] For *autokratōr* in Athenian legal terminology see Chapter 2. The term is here used as a technical term. As I have shown in Chapter 2, when the council was made *autokratōr*, the term refers to the power to act without referring back to the assembly. The council acted in this case with judicial powers rather than performing a deliberative role.

174 DIVIDED POWER IN ANCIENT GREECE

revealing then what he knew about the facts (Andoc. 1.60).[105] In all these three cases, however, the normal *adeia* procedure was completely overridden. The vote was taken in the council, which normally had no power to grant *adeia*, and therefore no quorum of 6,000 votes was required. The council could bestow *adeia* only because of the full powers that the assembly had previously delegated to the council, a key institutional stage that Andocides takes as understood in his account.[106] It was the assembly that normally voted *adeia*, and these instances are only justified by the emergency followed by the mutilation of the Herms on the eve of the Sicilian expedition. This is confirmed by the only other piece of evidence for *adeia* for witnesses and informers in Lysias' *Against Agoratus*.[107] Agoratus and Menestratus acted as informers for the Thirty during their tyrannical rule. At 55–6, while accusing Menestratus of collaboration with the Thirty, Lysias gives an account of how *adeia* for informers was voted and provided the relevant decree of *adeia* at the trial. Hagnodorus of Amphitrope proposed to grant immunity to Menestratus, and the assembly at Munichia granted him *adeia*, after which he provided information against some citizens (Lys. 13.55–6).[108]

These instances do not provide evidence for different typologies of procedure. The legal procedure reported in the decree of Callias and the *adeia* described in the accounts by Andocides and Lysias are in fact the same institution. *Adeia* could be employed with different legal purposes, as the procedure was generally designed to suspend the effects of legal norms without repealing the statutes. The case of immunity in judicial cases and the *adeia* for changing entrenched decrees shares the basic principle of the 'exception to the rule'. It is important to stress, however, the *adeia* voted for the informants during the investigation of the Eleusinian Mysteries is retrospective as it stops prosecution for a crime in the past. On the other hand, *adeia* voted for superseding an entrenchment clause is prospective because it prevents the violation of the relevant legal provision. The common principle behind all these instances is the common interest of the community, which might allow a degree of flexibility in the application of the law (in the case of the profanation of the Mysteries) or of nomothetic ideology (in the case of entrenchment clauses). This is confirmed by the fact that it is the assembly's prerogative—not the council or the lawcourts or any magistrate—to grant *adeia*, as the temporary suspension of the law must be confirmed by the

---

[105] Cf. Esu (2021a) 164–72 where I analyse in detail the use of *adeia* in the investigation following the profanation of the Mysteries and the mutilation of the Herms within a broader analysis of emergency power in Classical Athens with comparisons with Classical Sparta and the Roman Republic.

[106] This is also confirmed by Thucydides (6.27.2) who does not detail the procedure either. He only reports that it was voted that anyone who knew of the impiety could give information without fear of consequences (μηνύειν ἀδεῶς τὸν βουλόμενον). This clearly implies a vote of *adeia*.

[107] On this speech, see Todd (2000), (2020).

[108] On the Thirty abusing the procedure of *adeia*, see Esu (2021a) 168. For the Thirty's abuse of other public procedures for political reasons, see Esu in Harris with Esu (2021) 84–5.

community. The range of application of the procedure was not precisely defined, however, marking a clear difference with fourth-century *nomothesia*.[109] Unlike fourth-century law-making, the *adeia* procedure did not specify clearly every institutional circumstance in which it could be applied. Thus, the procedure could be used for purposes other than changing an entrenched decree, like the case of immunity from prosecution. Nevertheless, the fact that Athenians employed the same procedure as *adeia*, in its various manifestations, displays unitary substantive values allowing for temporary derogation from the established laws.

5.5 Dividing Deliberation in the Athenian Assembly

The findings of this chapter shed light on *adeia* and on how this procedure worked in fifth-century decree-making practice. The procedure of *adeia* applied the concept of divided power to the assembly procedures and constituted one of the first attempts pursued by the Athenians during the fifth century to combine legal stability and democratic decision-making in their deliberative institutions. *Adeia* added an additional decision-making layer in Athenian special legislation and in the attempt to institutionalize a democratic system of control of legal coherence.

The function of *adeia* within fifth-century legislative ideology is clear from its expressive terminology. The word shared its etymology with the semantic field of fear and apprehension and was therefore linked to Greek nomothetic ideology which we have already seen in Spartan deliberation, according to which the laws were not drafted by the *dēmos* but enacted by authoritative lawgivers in extraordinary times. In fifth-century ideology, the Athenians implemented the nomothetic ideology with the use of entrenchment clauses attempting to avoid legal change to democratic decrees, while at the same time enacting tacit legislation.

Adeia, as envisaged in the second decree of Callias, provided a distinct democratic procedure to change a piece of legislation without reneging the nomothetic ideology. The procedure required an explicit quorum of 6,000 votes, usually not necessary in Athenian decree-making, which certified that the symbolic totality of the Athenians was involved in changing an entrenched decree and introduced for the first time a procedure to change an unchangeable rule. The procedure established two distinct steps that divided the decree-making power of the assembly. In doing so, the procedure established two different institutional

---

[109] I borrow the concept of 'precision' from the legal theorists Abbott, Keohane, Moravcsik, Slaughter, and Snidal (2000) 412–15. Precision 'specifies clearly and unambiguously what is expected of a state or other actor (in terms of both the intended objective and the means of achieving it) in a particular set of circumstances'. In their words, precision 'implies not just that each rule in the set is unambiguous, but that the rules are related to one another in a non-contradictory way, creating a framework within which case-by-base interpretation can be coherently carried out'.

176   DIVIDED POWER IN ANCIENT GREECE

constraints upon the assembly activity. In the first step, the assembly took into account the legal dimension or the exceptional circumstances to grant immunity and therefore to allow legislative change; in the second step, the assembly performed its usual deliberative role of discussing a decree. The institutional design of *adeia* provided for distinctive behaviour within the same institution, rather than delegating it to a separate body. This rule of change, however, was not precisely defined and comprehensive. A vote of *adeia* granted permission to override an entrenchment clause, but it did not prescribe a distinct and retroactive law-making procedure ensuring the consistency of the legal order as a whole. The institution of *adeia* was therefore an innovative experiment which managed to create a kind of rule of change, even though incomplete and not entirely effective. It is not surprising then that *adeia* was introduced and implemented a generation before the first attested mention of a *graphē paranomōn* in 415 BCE, an institution sharing with *adeia* the same concern for legal consistency between permanent laws and the people's decrees, enforcing the principles of the rule of law and of divided power. This is the subject of my next chapter.

6

Divided Power and Judicial Review

Graphē Paranomōn in the Decision-Making
of Greek *Poleis*

6.1 Divided Power and Legal Hierarchy in Ancient Athens

The Athenians considered the public action against illegal decrees (*graphē paranomōn*) one of the most important defences of their constitutional system and a symbol of their democracy. In Demosthenes' *Against Timocrates*, Diodorus recalls the time when democracy was overthrown, the *graphē paranomōn* was abolished, and the power of the lawcourts was wiped out (Dem. 24.154).[1] Similarly, in *Against Ctesiphon*, Aeschines reminds the judges of his father's memories of the suppression of the *graphē paranomōn* by the Thirty in 404 BCE.[2] Thucydides and the Aristotelian *Athenaion Politeia* also confirm that, during the oligarchic revolution of 411 BCE, the oligarchs suspended the *graphē paranomōn* (Thuc. 8.67.2; [Arist.] *Ath. Pol.* 29.4).[3] When Demosthenes and Aeschines delivered their forensic speeches, the institution of the *graphē paranomōn* had been in consistent usage for less than a century, since the first documented instance dates to 415 BCE.[4] In that year, according to Andocides, Leagoras of Cydathenaeum brought a *graphē paranomōn* against a decree of Speusippus; a court of 6,000 judges then repealed the decree (Andoc. 1.17–22). This trial was not a standalone occurrence in the fifth century. Other pieces of evidence show that *graphai paranomōn* were brought in at least two other cases. In 414 BCE, Antiphon indicted an honorary decree of Demosthenes of Aphidna, whereas in 406 BCE, Euryptolemus of Alopeke brought a *graphē paranomōn*

---

[1] Cf. also [Dem] 58.34: 'when the *graphai paranomōn* are cancelled, it is the end of democracy' (ὅταν αἱ τῶν παρανόμων γραφαὶ ἀναιρεθῶσιν, ὁ δῆμος καταλύεται).

[2] Aeschin. 3.191. Both Aeschines and Dem. 24 rely on oral traditions and they represent the fourth-century Athenian view on the purpose of the *graphē paranomōn* as a paramount institution for the working of the democracy. For other examples cf. e.g. Dem. 4.24, 19.227, 20.52. On the use of ancestors in Attic oratory see especially Steinbock (2013); Barbato (2017), (2020); Canevaro (2018c); Westwood (2020).

[3] Rhodes (1981) 378.

[4] Wolff (1970) 21 argues that the procedure was likely established between 427 and 415 BCE. MacDowell (1962) 76 also maintains that it was a 'new kind of prosecution' at that time. Rhodes (1972) 62, (1981) 315–16 argues for an earlier date after the reform of Ephialtes, but see now Zaccarini (2018); Harris (2019a).

Divided Power in Ancient Greece: Decision-Making and Institutions in the Classical and Hellenistic Polis. Alberto Esu, Oxford University Press. © Alberto Esu 2024. DOI: 10.1093/oso/9780198883951.003.0006

178 DIVIDED POWER IN ANCIENT GREECE

against Callixenus for his decree instructing the assembly to vote to punish the generals of the battle of Arginusae collectively and without trial.[5]

The procedure is much more extensively attested in the fourth century, when the *graphē paranomōn* became one of the symbols of the democratic constitution and established a system of judicial review by enforcing the legal principle of the hierarchical superiority of the *nomoi* over the *psēphismata*. The legal recognition of this notion was part of substantial legal reforms that the Athenians introduced in 403 BCE, after the restoration of the democracy. The distinction between *nomoi* and *psēphismata* was formalized in the legal system and, as a result, laws and decrees became two separate and unblurred sources of legal authority (Andoc. 1.89). A *nomos* was a permanent and general norm enacted by the *nomothetai*, while a *psēphisma* was an ordinary decision of the council or the assembly.[6] Decrees were subordinated to and could not overrule the laws, and more importantly decrees could not be converted into a law. After the restoration of the democracy, the Athenians in fact decided to create two different and non-overlapping decision-making procedures for the decrees and the laws (*nomothesia*). This means that the authority of a decree could not be expanded and transformed into a law.[7]

In Chapter 5, I have discussed these substantial reforms to Athenian law and legal procedure that took place in the last decade of the fifth century when the *anagrapheis* were instructed to carry out the revision of the Athenian statutes. In this period, the Athenians became increasingly aware of tensions between their public ideology, which forbade any legal change, and their actual deliberative practice, which allowed for decrees to be passed by the assembly as if they were laws.[8] I have argued that the institution of *adeia* was one of the very first attempts to reconcile the immutability of the statutes with democratic deliberation by creating a procedure to enable the assembly to perform the special role of overriding an entrenchment clause, and thus to modify legislation. The procedure of *adeia* was created within an ideological framework and public discourse that did not officially conceive of legal change. Nevertheless, the Athenians designed a rule of change that established different procedures for different enactments of the assembly. In his 1971 volume, Quass argues that a grant of *adeia* safeguarded a citizen from prosecution for illegality (*Paranomieprozess*), drawing a connection

---

[5] On this trial see Harris (2013c) 242–3.

[6] Greek philosophy also theorizes this concept; see [Plat.] *Def.* 415b; Arist. *Pol.* 1292a32–7; *Eth. Nic.* 1137b13–14; cf. On Plato see Stalley 2007, 57–76 and on Aristotle see Miller (2007) 80–108. In Aristotle's *Politics* (1292a4–38), the distinction between laws and decrees is key in distinguishing between radical democracy, where the *plēthos* rules over the laws through decrees, and a democracy that respects the rule of law. On this see also Canevaro and Esu (2018).

[7] This is the case outlined in an inscription from second-century Kyme (*I.Kyme* 12) where a decree is referred to a lawmaking court (*nomothetikon dikastērion*) which is asked to give higher legal validity to the decree. Cf. §6.2 below.

[8] For a summary of these reforms with the relevant bibliography cf. Introduction §1.3 and Chapter 5.

DIVIDED POWER AND JUDICIAL REVIEW   179

with the *graphē paranomōn*.[9] Quass's argument is important, yet it needs to be better qualified to frame these two procedures within a larger picture of Athenian divided power.

In the previous chapter I argue that the fifth-century procedure of *adeia* was designed, in the first place, to override an entrenchment clause and its relevant penalties or to pass extraordinary measures like the *eisphora*, which were legal tools that put the nomothetic ideology into practice. This happened at least twenty years before the first instance of *graphē paranomōn* is attested. The safeguard granted by *adeia*, in fact, did not initially operate within the hierarchy between laws and decrees, formalized in 403 BCE, which the *graphē paranomōn* came to enforce and protect in the fourth century. Yet, after the introduction of the *graphē paranomōn*, a decree enacted under the protection of *adeia* could not be charged of illegality before a lawcourt.

Thus, the procedures of *adeia* and the *graphē paranomōn* were the product of the same legal and political culture of the end of the fifth century, when there was an on-going discussion in Athens about their laws and the constitutional system. The two institutions were very different from a procedural point of view, but they shared the same concern for legal coherence and consistency in the enactments of democratic bodies. *Adeia*, on the one hand, was a procedure working within the assembly creating a series of distinct institutional steps that the Athenians in the council and in the assembly had to follow in order to override an entrenchment clause without penalty. This made it possible to change an otherwise unchangeable piece of legislation, while respecting the constitutional order. *Adeia*, therefore, did not rely on delegation of power from one institutional body to another. The procedure prescribed several distinct institutional arrangements, such as the double vote, that encouraged distinctive practices and behaviours within the assembly with the aim of combining democratic deliberation and legal consistency. By developing the *graphē paranomōn*, on the other hand, the Athenians set up another more sophisticated institution to ensure the predictability and stability as sources of legitimacy for their enactments. The differences are striking: first, judicial review through the *graphē paranomōn* was achieved by delegating this task to the lawcourts, a different body which did not perform political decision-making through deliberation. Second, the *graphē paranomōn* introduced the juridical concept of *lex superior derogat inferiori* (the higher norm repeals the lower one), a principle that a grant of *adeia* suspended.

The *graphē paranomōn* was a key innovation for Athenian democracy. The importance of this institution has long been recognized in scholarship in a series of important studies, but there is no consensus on the overall rationale of the *graphē paranomōn* in the Athenian democracy. Scholarship has long been divided

---

[9] Quass (1971) 42–4.

180   DIVIDED POWER IN ANCIENT GREECE

between juridical understanding of the *graphē paranomōn* and socio-political view of this procedure. Wolff's classic treatment provides the fullest study of the legal aspects of the procedures of the *graphē paranomōn* and of what he defines the 'parallel institution' (*das Parallelinstitut*), the *graphē nomon mē epitēdeion theinai*.[10] Wolff argued that in both the *graphē paranomōn* and the *graphē nomon mē epitēdeion theinai*, legal interpretation was key to the arguments of the litigants and the decisions of the judges. Conversely, Hansen set the discussion of the *graphē paranomōn* within the broader institutional and political context of fourth-century Athenian democracy. In a series of classic studies, Hansen made the case for the sovereignty of lawcourts in fourth-century Athenian democracy—a concept that I have challenged throughout this study.[11] Unlike Wolff, however, Hansen downplayed the role of legal arguments in *graphē paranomōn* trials and stressed instead the political nature of this kind of litigation and the primacy of political argumentation in the decision of the courts. In his view, through the *graphē paranomōn*, the courts, along with the council and the assembly, became a third deliberative forum of the Athenian democracy, but one enjoying ultimate sovereignty. Yunis takes a halfway position, recently reaffirmed by Lanni—they argue that both legal and political pleas played a role in shaping the judges' decisions in prosecutions against illegal decrees.[12] Lanni, however, highlights that the main purpose of *graphē paranomōn* was to protect the 'basic democratic decision-making structures' (the assembly and the lawcourts) from decrees that could pose a threat to their power.[13] Lanni does not see a proper judicial review in the institution of the *graphē paranomōn* (i.e. mainly conceived on the model of the American judicial review), but rather a form akin to bicameralism, in which the lawcourts worked as a second chamber along with the assembly.[14] This approach, reliant on Hansen's reconstruction, has also been reaffirmed by other scholars, though with different nuances. More recently, Schwartzberg has also rejected the idea that the *graphē paranomōn* performed a proper judicial review on decrees because of the lack of legal expertise of the judges.[15] In a series of stimulating works, Cammack has further reaffirmed Hansen's view on the superiority of the lawcourts by arguing that because of the *graphē paranomōn* and the other powers of the courts, Athenian democracy was

---

[10] Wolff (1970) 12–22 on *graphē paranomōn*; 28–37 on the *graphē nomon mē epitēdeion theinai*. For the role of the public action against unsuitable laws see Canevaro (2016b), (2016c).

[11] Hansen (1974) esp. 15–18 and 28–65, (1991) 205–12. Ostwald (1986) follows Hansen in distinguishing between fifth-century popular sovereignty and an alleged fourth-century sovereignty of the law. For a review of these arguments see Introduction §1.1.

[12] Yunis (1988); Lanni (2010) 240–1.   [13] Lanni (2010) 242.

[14] Lanni (2010) 258: 'It has the effect that the assembly and the court are comparable to some extent with a bicameral system in which the court is the controlling chamber'. Cf. Hansen (1974) 50. Hansen reaffirms the same point in the discussion following Lanni's essay at 268. Cf. Lanni (2016) 56 n. 47.

[15] Schwartzberg (2013) 1060–1. Cf. also the view of Banfi (2012) 61–2.

DIVIDED POWER AND JUDICIAL REVIEW   181

in fact a dikastic democracy.[16] In the most recent book-length treatment of the subject of legal control in Classical Athens, Carawan reaffirmed the view of a marginal role of the laws in adjudication of *graphē paranomōn* cases. In Carawan's view, the *graphē paranomōn* was designed as a remedy against official's misconduct and abuse; the procedural design of *graphē paranomōn* was therefore an ineffective form of legal control, and the courts took a 'second decision' and represented the 'will of the people reconsidered'.[17] There are several problems with these approaches.[18]

Many of these important studies overestimated the political dimension of public actions against illegal decrees while downplaying the basic and crucial function of the procedure: the protection of the hierarchy between *nomoi* and *psēphismata* and the enforcement of the law. Building on the political role of the courts, these studies draw a picture of the constitutional superiority of the law-courts that does not consider the fundamental procedural, discursive, and ideological difference between deliberation in law-making and decree-making in the assembly and adjudication in court. The lawcourts never had any constitutional superiority over the assembly in Classical Athens, and the assembly could change a decision from the lawcourts.[19] This is a point to which I shall return later in this chapter. The studies take a procedural and minimalist view of Athenian law which reduces the substantive character of Athenian law as well as the institutional constraints under which the judges performed their role in the lawcourts.[20]

This chapter offers a new study of the rationale of the *graphē paranomōn* within the political decision-making of Classical Athens and other *poleis*, where a similar procedure is attested. By focusing on the institutional design of the legal procedure and of the judicial decision-making, this chapter argues that the *graphē paranomōn* was a democratic and participative form of judicial review and a fundamental feature of divided power, preserving the legal consistency of popular enactments, that is, the decrees of the council and the assembly with the *nomoi*. This purpose is clearly evident in the very institutional design of the legal procedure, which did not make the lawcourts a deliberative forum or a 'second legislative chamber'. As a result, political arguments played little role in assessing the *paranomia* of the decrees. From a systemic perspective, the procedure was designed to create a majoritarian stage to protect the rule of law within a

---

[16] Cammack (2013) 132–73; Cammack (2022a) also sees the role of the judges as a more genuine representation of democratic power.

[17] Carawan (2020) 244. For a discussion of Carawan's view on judicial reviews and lawmaking in Classical Athens, see Esu (2021c).

[18] For a discussion of these approaches with a focus on the *graphē nomon mē epitēdeion theinai* see Canevaro (2016c) 71–7, (2019a). Cf. also Straumann (2016) 227–37 who sees a typology of *formal* constitutionalism in fourth-century Athenian trials for *graphē paranomōn* and *graphē nomon mē epitēdeion theinai*.

[19] Pecorella Longo (2004); Harris (2016a) 80–1.

[20] On legal expertise see Harris (1991) 133–8.

182 DIVIDED POWER IN ANCIENT GREECE

larger deliberative and consensual political decision-making. A similar purpose of judicial review procedures is not only valid for Classical Athens, but can also be noted in other *poleis* of the Greek world which adopted similar institutions to safeguard the legality of the people's enactments. This chapter is structured into two sections. It first provides a discussion of the *graphē paranomōn* in Athens against the political and legal cultural of the Athenain democracy. Then, it offers a systematic analysis of the historical evidence concerning judicial review institutions attested different Greek *poleis* and in the Achaean League in the Hellenistic and Imperial periods.

6.2 *Graphē Paranomōn* in Classical Athens: The Role of Judicial Review in Democratic Decision-Making

The *graphē paranomōn* was a public suit.[21] This means that, as in the case of all *graphai*, any Athenian citizen (*ho boulomenos*) could bring a charge against an illegal decree and its proposer (Dem. 23.4, 45.4; Din. 1.100–1; [Dem.] 59.16, 59.66).[22] Every year, 6,000 Athenians selected by lot took the judicial oath and served in the courts for one year ([Arist.] *Ath. Pol.* 63–5).[23] A *graphē paranomōn* trial took place before a panel of at least 501 judges who could uphold or repeal the *psēphisma*. The *paranomia* of a decree was considered an offence against the community, and the relevant legal procedure was designed to tackle this issue, since legal consistency was at the foundation of the rule of law on which the democracy was based.[24] Through this procedure and the *graphē nomon mē epitēdeion theinai*, the lawcourts checked and balanced the political decision-making in the council and the assembly and were foundational in the creation of Athenian democratic divided power.[25] Pasquino has noted that the Athenian interaction between lawcourts and assembly should not be compared to a form of bicameralism and the lawcourts did not hold sovereign power. This would have meant that Athenian lawcourts could autonomously start the decision-making process and make independent decisions, like second chambers—senates or upper-houses—in modern parliaments.[26] In fact, the parallel drawn with modern systems of judicial review is much more appropriate, but Pasquino also noted a

---

[21] This section develops and expands in greater detail the argument in Esu (2020) 75–85.

[22] Hansen (1991) 205. For resident aliens bringing a *graphē* see MacDowell (1978) 221–4. For an overview on volunteer prosecutors in the Greek world see Rubinstein (2003). On metics engaging in public prosecution see [Arist.] *Ath. Pol.* 43.5.

[23] For the allotment machine (*klērōtērion*) see Rhodes (1981) 705–9; Boegehold (1995) 31–4. On the judicial oath see Harris (2013c) 101–37; Mirhady (2007) 48–59, 228–33.

[24] The crime of *paranomia* could only be prosecuted through the *graphē paranomōn*. The offences were prosecuted through the relevant legal procedure; see Carey (2004) 114–5.

[25] See Chapter 4 for a comparison with Spartan non-democratic divided power.

[26] Pasquino (2010) 12–4.

DIVIDED POWER AND JUDICIAL REVIEW 183

stark difference between the strictly majoritarian decision-making process in *graphē paranomōn* trials and the consensus-based decision-making of modern constitutional courts in Europe, for example in France, Germany, and Italy.[27] Modern judicial review courts also play a deliberative role and, as Pasquino and Ferejohn argue, there are relevant 'deliberative expectations' in the judicial review process. These expectations are given substance through the necessity for modern judges performing legislative reviews to provide legal reasoning as legitimation of their decisions.[28] Regardless of the kind of judicial review put in place—European or American-style—modern constitutional courts offer, to use Pasquino and Ferejohn's words, a 'counter-majoritarian opportunity'.[29] Judicial review courts can push the majority of the legislative to re-think and revise a political choice and, if necessary, to re-enact a new law. As a result, courts play an indirect, yet meaningful, deliberative role.

In Classical Athens, the *graphē paranomōn*, however, provided for a different judicial procedure which was inserted into a radically different political decision-making system. In modern democracies, legislative and executive bodies make decisions by majority rule, whereas judicial bodies such as constitutional courts— with the notable exception of the Common Law system and the U.S. Supreme Court—make decisions by consensus. Athenian decision-making procedures worked in the opposite way;[30] the council and the assembly usually passed their decisions through consensus-aimed deliberation, while the courts applied strict majority rule. Within the Athenian institutional framework, the argument of 'counter-majoritarianism' does not apply because the majority of the judges selected by lot could repeal a decision by the whole *dēmos* in the assembly. In fact, the *graphē paranomōn* introduced a strictly majoritarian and counter-deliberative practice within a decision-making process that was generally structured according to deliberative and consensual parameters.

These premises open a number of questions about the institutional design of Athenian divided power. Should we agree that Athenian lawcourts enjoyed superiority over deliberative decision-making in the assembly and the council? How could the majoritarian procedure of the *graphē paranomōn* fit in a deliberative democracy like Athens? Could one also envisage 'deliberative expectations' in the *graphē paranomōn*? A closer analysis of the procedural steps and the

---

[27] This argument does not apply to the United States Supreme Court and Common Law courts which make decisions by majority.

[28] Ferejohn and Pasquino (2002) 21–3. Their view is based on Rawls's justification of judicial review. See also Zurn (2007) 163–220 offers a compelling justification of judicial review in light of deliberative democratic theory.

[29] Ferejohn and Pasquino (2010). This expression echoes the label 'counter-majoritarian difficulty' coined by Bickel (1986, originally 1962) to describe the tension between judicial review and democratic decision-making in the United States.

[30] This was also the case in Sparta and in most other *poleis*. Cf. Chapter 4 on Spartan deliberation and legislative review performed by the *gerousia*.

184　DIVIDED POWER IN ANCIENT GREECE

institutional design of *graphē paranomōn* trials will shed light on the overall rationale of this legal procedure in the decree-making system. To appreciate the rationale of the *graphē paranomōn* procedure within the Athenian deliberative system, it is important to discuss the various institutional steps of the procedure. This legal procedure is well documented and scholars have long agreed on the main patterns of this legal institution. I shall first give a brief summary of the procedure, and I shall then move to a closer analysis of the institutional design behind it, with examples from the attested cases in fourth-century forensic speeches.

The Athenian council and the assembly deliberated on and passed several decrees during each meeting.[31] If a decree did not conform to any written law, a *graphē paranomōn* could be initiated at any moment as follows. (1) A decree could be charged both during the preliminary discussion in the council or during the debate in assembly or after it had been approved by the council and the assembly (Xen. *Hell.* 1.7.12–14; Dem. 22.5, 9–10).[32] (2) The plaintiff had to take the *hupōmosia*, an oath swearing that the indicted decree was illegal. (3) The procedure then prescribed that the accuser presented a formal written document (*graphē*) providing evidence of the illegality of the decree to the *thesmothetai*, who introduced the case to court ([Arist.] *Ath. Pol.* 59.2);[33] at this point the case could still be dropped before it was brought forward to the next stage. (4) The trial was held before a panel of at least 501 judges. (5) The judges could repeal the decree or uphold it, if the decree had already been enacted by the assembly. (6) If the assembly had not yet voted in favour of the decree, but it was upheld by the court, it went back to the assembly where it was discussed again and finally enacted. Otherwise, a decree not yet enacted by the assembly, which was considered *paranomōn*, was never enacted. (7) In the case of a successful charge, not only was the decree rescinded, but if less than one year had elapsed between the approval of the decree and the loading of the charge (*prothesmia*),[34] the proposer of the decree could also be punished with a penalty, decided at the *timēsis*, ranging from a fine to *atimia*.[35]

---

[31] Hansen (1987b) 110 counts that the assembly passed no fewer than nine decrees at each meeting. The council met every day, so *probouleumata* were not drafted at every meeting. The council enacted several of its own decrees that were often not inscribed. Hansen counts 13,000 decrees enacted by the assembly in the period 355–322 BCE. See also Liddel (2020b) 15 n. 10.

[32] Decrees of the council could also be indicted; see [Dem.] 47.34 and cf. Chapter 2 pp. 53–4.

[33] On *enklēma* see Thür (2008) 51–74; and esp. Harris (2013a) 143–60. On the penalties for frivolous prosecutions and failing to show up at the *anakrisis* see Harris (2006) 405–22.

[34] Giannadaki (2014), (2020) 11.

[35] Rocchi (2023a) demonstrates that *atimia* was often the consequence of heavy fines that the defendant was not able to pay which resulted in total *atimia* (cf. Dem. 21.182). See also Rocchi (2023b). Harris (2006) and (2017c) demonstrate that, after three convictions in a *graphē paranomōn*, the defendant would become partially *atimos*, losing his right to speak in the assembly (i.e. proposing decrees).

DIVIDED POWER AND JUDICIAL REVIEW   185

It is important now to understand how the *graphē paranomōn* impacted on democratic deliberation in practice. When the assembly passed a decree, this became immediately valid. The assembly could decide to inscribe a copy on stone and display it in a public space, while in any case a copy was written on papyrus or *sanides* and was stored in the *Metroon*, where everyone could consult it.[36] The magistrates and the courts were then bound to enforce the decree, unless this was stopped by a charge of illegality. A good example of this is provided by the case described in Demosthenes' speech *Against Androtion* (Dem. 22).[37] In 356/5 Androtion had served in the council for the second time.[38] At the end of his term, Androtion put forward a motion in the assembly to honour the councillors with a crown for their good service to the *polis*. The assembly enacted the decree, but its validity was challenged by Euctemon, who immediately charged the decree with illegality.[39] The decree was stopped on four legal grounds, around which the entire Demosthenic speech is structured. First, the decree did not receive the prior approval of the council (Dem. 22.5–6). Second, the decree violated the law forbidding the council to be crowned without having the legal number of ships built during its term (Dem. 22.8). Third, Androtion had been a prostitute and was not permitted to address the assembly (Dem. 22.21–4). Fourth, his father was a public debtor and he had inherited the debt, so he could not address the assembly (Dem. 22.33–4). As a case study in this chapter I will follow the institutional steps that brought this honorary decree from the approval of the assembly to court.[40]

A *graphē paranomōn* against an honorary decree should not come as a surprise. All the preserved fourth-century speeches delivered for a *graphē paranomōn* deal with honorary decrees. In Hansen's catalogue of documented *graphai paranomōn*, eighteen cases out of thirty-nine are public actions against illegal honorary decrees.[41] The case of Androtion's decree is paradigmatic in showing the apparent contrast between deliberative decision-making and majority decision-making in the Athenian system. One cannot know precisely how many votes were cast in favour of Androtion's decree in the assembly, but the tone of the Demosthenic speech seems to imply that the decree was approved by large consensus in the assembly. Indeed, when anticipating Androtion's argument, Diodorus says that Androtion will argue that there is a law allowing his decree and he briefly singles out how the voting procedure unfolds: 'the chairman asked this question, the assembly cast its vote and the motion is passed' (Dem. 22.5: φησίν ὁ ἐπιστάτης, διεχειροτόνησεν ὁ δῆμος, ἔδοξεν). This is consistent with the usual practice in

---

[36] On archives in Classical Athens see Sickinger (1999); Faraguna (2007), (2015b); and now Boffo and Faraguna (2021).

[37] On this speech see now the commentary by Giannadaki (2020); see also Harris (2008) 167–70.

[38] For the career of Androtion see Harding (1994) 13–25, 53–9; and now Giannadaki (2020) 29–32.

[39] The speech was delivered by Diodorus as Euctemon's *sunegoros* (supporting speaker); cf. Dem. 22.1.

[40] On the legal arguments of this speech see Giannadaki (2020) 114–392; Esu (forthcoming).

[41] Hansen (1974) 28–42.

186 DIVIDED POWER IN ANCIENT GREECE

Classical Athens and in other Greek *poleis*. Canevaro makes a strong case against the common belief that majority rule was the usual voting practice in Greek political bodies, arguing for the widespread practice of consensus deliberation in councils and assemblies.[42] Such a practice was fostered by the relevant voting procedures in the assembly. In Classical Athens, bills were passed by *diacheirotonia*, a procedure that allowed for a free discussion, open to everyone, with several speeches and the possibility to include amendments from the floor. This consensus deliberation resulted in a vote by a show of hands, assessing first the ayes and then nays on a single proposal. Votes were not counted, but only broadly assessed, but the *proedroi* called the vote when wide consensus was clearly evident on a proposal.[43] Thus, it is not surprising that the enactments of the assembly and the council were passed with unanimous or almost unanimous votes. This was a widespread practice across the Greek world. For example, Aeschines states that when Ctesiphon returned to Athens after his embassy to Macedonia, he reported back to the assembly. After his report, the *dēmos* accepted his account and praised him (τὸν Κτησιφῶντα ἐπαινέσαντος), and because nobody spoke in opposition, Philocrates put forward a decree, which the assembly passed unanimously (ὁ δῆμος ἅπας ὁμογνωμονῶν ἐχειροτόνησεν), to allow Philip to send envoys to Athens (Aeschin. 2.13). This is important because it shows that decrees on other matters than honours were also passed by consensus. The point that Aeschines is trying to make in these sections (2.11–14) is an opposition between the decree of Philocrates, voted by all the Athenians as standard practice, and the attempt to block it through a *graphē paranomōn* by a small group of political opponents. The accuser Lycinus did not even obtain one-fifth of the votes in court against the decree of Philocrates.[44] We find a comparable picture in the inscribed decrees of other Greek *poleis*. A third-century inscription from Iasos records that an honorary decree for Hekatomnus was passed by secret ballot with eighty-three votes in favour in the council—probably on a plenum of more than 100 members—and 1,011 in favour in the assembly.[45] A first-century honorific decree for Arconidas from Anaphe records that the decision was unanimous and all ninety-five votes were in favour (*IG* XII 3, 249.39). Similarly, a decree of Colophon dated at 120/19 BCE shows the voting figures of the assembly that honoured Menippus, with 1,326 votes in favour and only sixteen against (*SEG* 39.1244 col. III, 48–51).

---

[42] See Canevaro (2018a) for a detailed analysis of consensus practices in Athenian deliberation and outside Athens. Cf. also Chapter 4 for an example of consensus in an oligarchic polity.

[43] See Canevaro (2018a), (2020b); *contra* Hansen (1987b) 41–2.   [44] See Harris (1995) 47.

[45] Maddoli (2007) 306–20 B. There are seven other decrees from Iasos, mostly honorary decrees for foreign judges. When the votes are recorded, they always show overwhelming majorities in the council and in the assembly: e.g. *SEG* 41.932, 10–12 (council: sixty-eight; assembly: 841); Blümel (2007) 2 II, 40–1 (council: 111; assembly [102]2/[110]2). See Fabiani (2015) 118 for a systematic study on the honorific decrees from Iasos. For the Iasian deliberative institutions see Fabiani (2012) 109–63 and (forthcoming). On this cf. also §3.3 above.

DIVIDED POWER AND JUDICIAL REVIEW   187

This is very much consistent with a deliberative democracy in which consensus was highly valued and a necessary decision-making practice to legitimize the approval of a binding decision. Yet the *graphē paranomōn*'s design appears at odds with this system. When Euctemon indicted Androtion's decree and brought it to court, the decree was suspended and it was put under review according to a procedure whose design and rationale did not foster deliberative goals and consensus. After swearing the *hupōmosia* which suspended the validity of the decree, Euctemon must have brought his indictment to the *thesmothetai*. The indictment took the form of an official document (*graphē*) that followed a standard format. Harris demonstrates that the *graphē* is a key document for understanding the *graphē paranomōn* and the use of legal evidence in Athenian trials more generally.[46] The plaint included the names of the accuser and the defendant, the relevant offence, and the proposal of a penalty.[47] In plaints for *graphai paranomōn*, all laws broken by the decree were listed and attached to the written document (Aeschin. 3.200). In the case of Androtion's decree, these were the law on *probouleusis*, the law on the awards for the council, and the law forbidding prostitutes and public debtors from addressing the assembly. If the magistrate accepted the indictment, the plaint was published in the agora at the monument of the Eponymous Heroes.

After denunciation to the magistrate, litigants attended the preliminary hearings. This stage was the first part of an Athenian trial: the preliminary hearings were called *anakrisis* in public charges and *diaita* in private charges and were presided by the relevant magistrate. During the *anakrisis*, the magistrate oversaw the litigants as they debated the case and posed inquiries to one another.[48] It is during this stage of the procedure that litigants could learn their opponents' strategy and arguments. For our purpose, the *anakrisis* is especially meaningful. One could say that the *anakrisis* was the only part of a *graphē paranomōn* in which an open debate was allowed, as the litigants could question one another; this could last for several meetings before the actual trial (Isae. 6.12; Dem. 53.22). Litigants were requested to answer to the magistrate's questions, and if he deemed that the written indictment was insufficiently formulated, the magistrate could compel the litigants to incorporate key legal terms (Isae. 10.2; Lys. 13.85–7).[49]

The debate between the magistrate and litigants is very important and its nature should be clearly analysed. Although the *anakrisis* involved a debate between the parties, it was not intended as a deliberative process and did not seek to reach a

---

[46] Harris (2013a) 143–5 with examples of *enklēmata*: Dem. 21.103, 45.46; Scheibelreiter (2018) 214–31; and the discussion by Faraguna in Boffo and Faraguna (2021) 272–7.

[47] Penalties were not always included, as in some cases the *timēsis* would be concerned with deciding that. But it was included in some cases, see e.g. [Dem.] 58.43; Aeschin. 2.14.

[48] Faraguna (2007) 95–7; Thür (2007) 131–49; Harris (2013a) 211.

[49] For magistrates requiring litigants to correct their written indictment see Harris (2006) 373; Kremmydas (2018) 110–31. For the importance of the correct names on the indictment see Antiph. 6.49; Dem. 39.15.

188 DIVIDED POWER IN ANCIENT GREECE

compromise between litigants—unlike its equivalent in private trials which involved public arbitration.[50] In the case of a *graphē paranomōn* like that brought against Androtion's decree, at the *anakrisis*, litigants' debates could not tackle public policies and political matters and the magistrate could not suggest a political compromise, such as, for example, an emendation of the text of the decree. This stage was not a further policy-making moment which reduplicated the formulation of a decree in the assembly. This rationale is further proved by the law that set a penalty of 1,000 drachmas and forbids bringing any public charges in the future for a prosecutor who dropped the case after the *anakrisis*. Harris shows that this was primarily a powerful incentive against frivolous prosecutions, but also demonstrates that, although the *anakrisis* was characterized by discussion and debate, the relevant law clearly did not favour a compromise and an open deliberative discussion between litigants, but provided regulations to constrain the debate to stick to matters of law.[51] The magistrate also had the power to reject the indictment, in case it did not conform to the law, which also points to a strictly judicial and adversarial setup (Lys. 10.10, 13.86). The procedure was specifically designed to produce sound legal evidence to be brought to court, frame the litigants' arguments on the relevant laws, and preclude the introduction of irrelevant material at the trial (*exō tou pragmatos*). The orators knew the arguments of their counterpart, and in the case of *Against Androtion*, the supporting speaker Diodorus was able to anticipate the arguments of Androtion and his supporting speakers several times in the speech (Dem. 22.5–8, 10, 17, 21, 23, 33, 35, 38, 40, 42, 70).

All documents—decree, laws, and witness statements—produced at the *anakrisis* were put into a sealed jar (*echinos*).[52] The clerk in court would then open the jar and read out the relevant documents to the judges. The role of secretaries during a legal procedure, like the *graphē paranomōn*, is particularly important to understand the use of the laws in court. Filias noted that by reading aloud copies of the laws and the decrees attached to the written indictment, the clerk complemented the judges' knowledge of the laws and helped them in comparing the text of the laws and the provisions of the indicted decree.[53] In other words, the written documents produced at the *anakrisis* served the purpose of framing the judicial debate within the relevant laws so that both litigants and judges could perform their role according to the values enshrined in their oaths and in the institution of the lawcourt.[54]

---

[50] Thür (1977) 156, 313, (2007) 134 has defined this part of the procedure '*dialektisch*'. We have no direct evidence of speeches or proceedings of an *anakrisis*. The best evidence is Aesch. *Eum.* 408–90 where the goddess Athena acts as a magistrate.

[51] Harris (2006) 408–16.

[52] The seal of an *echinos* for a *diamarturia* has survived see *SEG* 32.329; cf. also Boegehold (1995) 79–81.

[53] Filias (2020) 201 with Aeschin. 3.192.

[54] Thür (2007) 131–50, (2008) 51–74; Harris (2013b).

DIVIDED POWER AND JUDICIAL REVIEW 189

After discussing the rationale of the *anakrisis* in the procedure of *graphē paranomōn*, I now turn to the proper judicial hearing. The second stage of a *graphē paranomōn* took place in court before the judges and the structure of the trial is well known. It was judged by a broad panel of judges and lasted an entire day. The prosecutor and the supporting speakers spoke first, followed by the defendant and his supporting speakers. In the case of the *graphē paranomōn* against Androtion's decree, we have one of the accusation speeches written by Demosthenes and delivered in court by Diodorus. This speech attests to the allegations put forward against Androtion, but also makes it possible to reconstruct some of the arguments of the defendants. His arguments are straightforward and he consistently tries to represent the decree as illegal and Androtion as a criminal. In the first part of the speech, Demosthenes concentrates on discussing the legal allegations in order to demonstrate that the decree was *paranomōn*, which is the substantive offence put forward in that trial (Dem. 22.1–46). In the second part of the speech, he shows that Androtion had done this before and had *mens rea* when he proposed his decree (Dem. 22.47–8).[55]

This stage of the trial was the most adversarial part. Litigants were not allowed to interact either with the court or with their counterpart. Deliberation and discussion were excluded, and the procedure was designed to adhere to the point of the legal charge as it had been defined in the *graphē* and at the *anakrisis*. Both litigants had to tackle the legal issue and try to demonstrate with speeches and legal evidence that their decree had or had not broken the law.

The decision-making procedures and rules of the court are consistent with this aim and foster an anti-deliberative behaviour. The judges did not deliberate on the legal case and the panel could only hear the speeches and cast their secret ballot after the litigants' speeches ([Arist.] *Ath. Pol.* 68.5–15).[56] The whole procedure before the court aimed at finding a solution with no compromise. This unfolding of the judicial procedure shows that when considering a case of *graphē paranomōn*, the court was not acting as a 'second chamber', as the very same decision-making process did not favour a revision of the political decisions taken in the council and in the assembly. The formal procedures and rules (e.g. voting system, rules of debate in court, number of actors involved in the judicial process) and the discursive standards of the actors[57] in a trial for a *graphē paranomōn* are the opposite of what happened in the assembly, and the court therefore cannot be a third deliberative forum besides the council and the assembly. This constitutional role of the lawcourt and of the *graphē paranomōn* is clearly illustrated in another Demosthenic speech for a *graphē paranomōn*, *Against Aristocrates*

---

[55] *Pace* MacDowell (2009) 180; Lanni (2010) 254–5. The second part of the speech is relevant to the charge against the decree. Cf. Rhodes (2004) 137–58; Esu (forthcoming).

[56] Cf. Arist. *Pol.* 2.1268b10. Aristotle says that most legislators make rules to prevent consultation among the judges (οἱ δικασταὶ μὴ κοινολογῶνται πρὸς ἀλλήλους).

[57] Harris (2017a) 223–42.

190 DIVIDED POWER IN ANCIENT GREECE

(Dem. 23). At 100–1, having demonstrated with several legal documents the illegality of Aristocrates' decree, the speaker examines the rationale for the procedure of *graphē paranomōn*.[58] He cites an example that he had recently seen in a *graphē paranomon* trial. A man was unable to defend the legality of his decree at the trial and was clearly guilty according to the law (τοῖς νόμοις μὲν ἁλισκόμενον), but he made the case before the judges for upholding his decree because it was in their interest (ὡς δὲ συμφέρονθ' ὑμῖν γέγραφεν λέγειν ἐπιχειροῦντα). Demosthenes, by contrast, stresses that this line of argument is 'silly and shameless' (εὐήθη μέν, οἶμαι, μᾶλλον δ' ἀναιδῆ λόγον) because even if the decree was in the *dēmos*' interest in all other respects (εἰ γὰρ καὶ κατὰ τἄλλα πάντα συμφέρει τὰ εἰρημένα), it would have been inconvenient (ἀσύμφορ' ἂν εἴη) to ask the judges to vote against their oath and the laws, which is their most important duty.

This passage is key to demonstrating that the aim of the *graphē paranomōn* was not to reconsider the political expediency of a decree or rethink matters of public policy enacted by decree, but to enforce the principle of the superiority of the laws over the decrees. If a decree was illegal, there could be no compromise, and the lawcourt simply had to enforce the statutes.[59] This is also echoed in another Demosthenic speech, *Against Timocrates* (incidentally a *graphē nomon mē epitēdeion theinai*) in which Demosthenes refers to the judges as the guardians of the laws (φύλακας ὑμᾶς τῶν νόμων), confirming that the application of the laws was the purpose of the courts (Dem. 24.36).[60] Similarly, in Lycurgus' *Against Leocrates*, a speech delivered in an *eisangelia*, the speaker recalls in broader terms what the three most important pillars are for the protection of democracy: first, the system of the laws (πρῶτον μὲν ἡ τῶν νόμων τάξις); second, the vote of the judges (δεύτερον δ' ἡ τῶν δικαστῶν ψῆφος); and third, the trial that brings crimes under control (τρίτον δ' ἡ τούτοις τἀδικήματα παραδιδοῦσα κρίσις) (Lyc. 1.3–4). This idea was rooted in Athenian culture and survived in later official language as well. The only mention of the term παράνομον in Attic epigraphical evidence is found in a later fragmentary inscription from the first century BCE. At lines 8–10, the decree instructs the treasurer to provide the money for the expenditure which must be made in a fashion that is neither παράνομον nor ἀσύμφορον (IG II² 1062). In a decree of the assembly, a deliberative act of the *dēmos*, these two concepts are equally displayed and valued, while in a lawcourt, τὸ συμφέρον is subordinated to τὸ δίκαιον.

---

[58] This speech is rich in laws and decrees, which are generally reliable documents. See the analysis of Canevaro (2013b) 37–45. For a commentary on the speech see Zajonz (2022). For an analysis of the speech's legal arguments and their impact on Athenian diplomatic discourse see Esu (2020).

[59] This does not mean that the orators only used arguments that were strictly fitting to the wording of written statutes. Rather it means that the laws provided in the *graphē* framed the relevant arguments in the speech, and that arguments about public service and expediency were always built on principles extracted by the laws, and not in opposition to written statutes. On this issue see Sundahl (2000) 86–7; Harris (2013c) 121–2; Canevaro (2016a) 71–6, (2019a).

[60] See the same expression in Din. 3.16.

The charges brought by litigants in other attested cases of *graphē paranomōn* in fourth-century Athens provide further evidence for the view that lawcourts did not carry out a deliberative role when adjudicating legal cases. When discussing occurrences of *graphē paranomōn* before the court, the orators provide a detailed interpretation of the relevant laws broken by the indicted decree. The legal charge, moreover, shapes arguments about personal conduct and character, as the plaintiff aims to demonstrate that the author of the decree had broken both the letter and the spirit of the law. These charges do not show concern for the protection of democratic deliberation, but for safeguarding key tenets of the rule of law, such as protection of the hierarchy of the sources of law to secure consistency, the safeguard of individual rights and accountability for officials.

A brief survey of the *graphē paranomōn* speeches confirms that the trials against illegal decrees aimed to enforce legal consistency. The Demosthenic speech *Against Aristocrates* was written for an indictment in a *graphē paranomōn* brought forward by Euthycles against a decree of Aristocrates prescribing that anyone who killed Charidemus could be arrested anywhere and extradited (*agōgimos*) to Attica for trial. Euthycles brought his charge on several legal grounds. Demosthenes' main charge is based on a different interpretation of the word *agōgimos*. He claims that the decree deprives the person of the right to a fair trial, as anyone could seize them and do whatever they wanted. Building on this, Euthycles claims that the decree breaks many provisions of the homicide laws. First, the law that prescribes that those accused of deliberate homicide are to be tried by the Areopagus (22–7). Second, the decree violates the law forbidding setting a ransom for someone who is accused of homicide (28–36). Third, Aristocrates' *psēphisma* is against the law that protects from violence those convicted of murder who went into exile (37–43). Fourth, it violates a similar law that protects those convicted of homicide from enslavement and confiscation of property if they went to exile (44–50). In addition, the decree breaks the provision of the law protecting from prosecution those who report a convicted murderers returning to Attica (51–2). The decree, moreover, contravenes the law that absolves from the accuse of homicide those who kill during athletic games against their will, or during war in ignorance, or those who kill a *moichos* for having intercourse with their wives, sisters, daughters, mothers, or concubines (53–8). Finally, Euthycles argues that Aristocrates' decree violates the law forbidding ad hominem legislation. Euthycles, thus, did not base his charge on deliberative reasons, but tried to demonstrate that the decree broke the relevant laws because he knew that the judges would have made their decisions on legal ground and protected individual rights.[61]

---

[61] On this speech see Esu (2020) with comprehensive bibliography.

192   DIVIDED POWER IN ANCIENT GREECE

Similarly, in *Against Ctesiphon*, Aeschines indicted of illegality the decree of Ctesiphon to award a golden crown to Demosthenes on three main legal charges. The first allegation claims that Ctesophon's decree violates the law that forbids the awarding of a crown for a magistrate in office before he had passed his *euthunai* (3.9–31). Aeschines also charges Ctesiphon's decree of breaking the law on the announcement of awards in the assembly (3.32–48). Finally, Aeschines accuses Ctesiphon of including false statements about Demosthenes' career into the decree, which contravenes the law against introducing false information into laws and decrees (3.49). In this case, the indictment was brought according to the laws that regulated the principle of accountability for magistrates and the way civic honours bestowed for their performance should be awarded. It is important to stress that the principle of accountability was not a democratic feature, but was a principle shared by all Greek *poleis* as a key aspect of the rule of law. Aeschines' main legal argument was based on a broad interpretation of the first charge, meaning that the law applied to all magistrates in office before their *euthunai*.[62] Ctesiphon's proposal was legal as he had added a specific legal clause in the decree which awarded the crown 'after he had given his account and passed his examination' (ἐπειδὰν λόγον καὶ εὐθύνας τῆς ἀρχῆς δῶι).[63] Demosthenes, on the other hand, in his defence speech *On the Crown* (Dem. 18), maintains that Ctesiphon's decree is legal by taking a different and narrower interpretation of the law which was based on several precedents. Ctesiphon's decree honoured Demosthenes for that single act of generosity and not for the whole performance as magistrate, and had not violated the relevant law (Dem. 18.117). Demosthenes supported his case with several legal precedents, leading the judges to acquit Ctesiphon and consider his honorary decree legal. Once again, the charges by Aeschines and the defence arguments of Demosthenes in a trial for a *graphē paranomōn* show that this procedure was not designed to create another deliberative or legislative forum or to protect democratic deliberation. Litigants concentrated on legal issues and the court made its decision on the soundest legal interpretation.

The last surviving speech delivered for a *graphē paranomōn* is Hyperides' *Against Philippides*.[64] The extant parts of the speech are fragmentary and Hyperides spoke as supporting-speaker for only thirty-six minutes, but we can nevertheless identify the legal charges against the indicted decree (Hyp. 2.13). After Chaeronea in 338 BCE, Philippides and other citizens proposed honorary decrees for the Macedonians in the assembly. The motion was put forward in the assembly without a prior *probouleuma* of the council and was procedurally illegal (cf. one of the charges against Androtion's decree), but the *proedroi* put it to the vote anyway, possibly out of fear and intimidation. In spite of that, Philippides

---

[62] For a detailed analysis of the legal arguments of Aeschines and Demosthenes see Harris (2013c) 225–33, (2019b) Westwood (forthcoming).

[63] On this formula see Harris (2017b).   [64] Whitehead (2000).

DIVIDED POWER AND JUDICIAL REVIEW   193

later put forward a decree to crown the *proedroi* for having carried out their office according to laws. As Hyperides makes clear, the main charge was against the *proedroi* and the decree which granted them public honours for their performance even if these magistrates had acted against the laws (Hyp. 2.4). Hyperides paraphrases the decree of Philippides to show before the court that the decree was illegal, and once again, a few paragraphs after recalling the judicial oath, he reminds the judges that arguments on expediency of Philippides' policies would undermine the legitimacy of the court (Hyp. 2.10).

All the charges in the surviving speeches delivered in court for *graphai paranomōn* cases show that this procedure was undoubtedly a form of judicial review to secure the rule of law.[65] Litigants' charges demonstrate that they had to prove that a decree violated the relevant laws; the debate in court was focused on legal issues according to the proper discourse of the lawcourt. The decision of the judges had an impact in the overall decision-making in the case of the repeal of an illegal decree, but this did not mean that the lawcourts worked as a second chamber alongside the assembly.

This very purpose of the *graphē paranomōn* is also apparent if one examines the voting procedures used by the Athenian judges closely. Unlike other institutional settings, such as the council, the assembly, and arbitrations, the lawcourts applied strict majority rule. As a result, a decree passed by the assembly with wide consensus (unanimously or close-to-unanimously, as was probably the case with Androtion's decree) could be repealed by a simple majority in the lawcourts. Such a voting system bears important ideological and constitutional implications. We know the details of the voting procedure from the abundant archaeological findings as well as from the detailed account found in the final chapters of the Aristotelian *Athenaion Politeia* ([Arist.] *Ath. Pol.* 68–9).[66] Each judge received two ballots after the end of the litigants' speeches. These two bronze ballots were identical, but the ballot in favour of the prosecution had a hollow peg, while the one against the prosecution had a solid peg in the centre. These ballots allowed the judges to keep their vote secret by covering the central peg until they had cast their vote in a bronze urn. The votes were carefully counted and put into a wooden box. In public cases like the *graphē paranomōn*, the same procedure was followed at the *timēsis* in order to set the penalty.[67]

The procedure confirms that what was at stake in a *graphē paranomōn* was the preservation of legal coherence. From an Athenian perspective, the legality of a decree could not be established through deliberation and consensus. While

---

[65] Modern scepticism towards the nature of the *graphē paranomōn* as a form of judicial review has also concentrated on the passive role of Athenian courts which could not automatically review all decrees. Cf. Giannadaki (2020) 26 n. 157. However, modern constitutional courts do not initiate the judicial review process and do not systematically check all laws of the legislative, but only a small number of cases of laws and executive acts are reviewed.

[66] Rhodes (1981) 730–5.   [67] For the time of *timēsis* see Aeschin. 3.197–8; Plat. *Apol.* 35e1–38.

194 DIVIDED POWER IN ANCIENT GREECE

the statutes could be interpreted and the law could be debated, as in modern jurisdictions, there could be no political negotiation on the laws or on the lawgiver's intention behind a written statute.[68] The rationale of this judicial procedure, in line with the features of Athenian trials, is diametrically opposite to that of the arbitration procedure.[69] While both private and public arbitrators tried to solve litigation through compromise and deliberative techniques that fostered an inclusive solution with no winners and losers, the judicial procedure before a court did exactly the opposite by singling out a clear winner and a clear loser. Aristotle notes this opposition in the *Rhetoric*, when he contrasts the arbitrator who considers matters of fairness with the role of the judge who looks at matters of law (Arist. *Rhet.* 1.13: ὁ γὰρ διαιτητὴς τὸ ἐπιεικὲς ὁρᾷ, ὁ δὲ δικαστὴς τὸν νόμον). It is also important to stress that no public offence, such as the *paranomia* of a decree, could be brought before a public arbitrator. There could be no mediation on a matter that affected the constitution and the community, and the relevant procedure and the voting mechanism were designed accordingly.

The *graphē paranomōn* (and the *graphē nomon mē epitēdeion theinai*) introduced a strong anti-deliberative and majoritarian arrangement in the political decision-making process of Classical Athens. For example, according to the scholia on Aeschines, in 363/2 BCE, a decree of Aristophon of Azenia was indicted with a *graphē paranomōn* and repealed by a court with a majority of only two votes.[70] Yet, how could the Athenians envisage a deliberative democracy in which a popular decree could ultimately be scrapped by a narrow majority of two votes if it was considered illegal? Could this system pave the way for social division or even *stasis*?[71] As we have already seen, the ancient evidence points to a very different scenario in which the *graphē paranomōn* was unanimously considered to protect the integrity and stability of the democracy. The ostensible 'contradictory' attitude between decision-taking in the assembly and in the lawcourts was instead underpinned by a sophisticated institutional rationale. This clear-cut division of labour between the institutional design and the majoritarian procedures in the lawcourts and the consensus-based procedures of the council and the assembly were grounded in the same fundamental value: the superiority of the laws, on which the *politeia* was founded.[72] As I have pointed out, this principle is not only found in the speeches of the Attic orators but is also consistent with the

---

[68] See MacCormick (2005) showing the 'arguable character' of rule of law in modern Common Law.
[69] Harris (2018a).   [70] *Scholia in Aeschinem* (Dilts 145) see Hansen (1974) 31.
[71] On classical *stasis* see the fundamental work by Gehrke (1985) esp. 251–7. Cf. also van Wees (2008) for *stasis* in the Archaic period; Loraux (2002); and Hansen and Nielsen (2004) 124–9. For the late Classical and Hellenistic *stasis* see B. D. Gray (2015); Börm (2019).
[72] The term *politeia* is usually translated as 'constitution' or 'way of life of a community'. The *politeia* was not limited to the laws, but it also includes the customs and values of a community. These principles of the *politeia* were, however, enshrined in the system of the laws of a Greek *polis* and constituted a coherent whole. Cf. Arist. *Pol.* 1291a31–2; *Eth. Nic.* 1181b15–23. See Bordes (1982); Schofield (1999); Harte and Lane (2013); Canevaro (2019a).

DIVIDED POWER AND JUDICIAL REVIEW   195

Aristotelian theorization in *Politics* 4, where the philosopher highlights that when the laws are not sovereign, there is no constitution at all.[73] Thus, the different decision-making bodies performed different roles and the lawcourts upheld the superiority of the laws on which the democratic decisions of the council and the assembly were based. This foundational concept unified and made coherent the whole decision-making process where power was institutionally divided.

The concept of the rule of law in Classical Athens has drawn the attention of scholars in the last forty years. On the one hand, many scholars have argued that the Athenians failed to achieve the rule of law in their legal institutions consistently, while stressing with different nuances the extra-legal notions of justice in Athenian legal practice.[74] On the other hand, another strand of scholars has demonstrated that the Athenians conceptualized the rule of law in their laws and put this concept into practice through their institutions.[75] The notion of the rule of law was one of the main ideological principles at the foundations of Greek political culture and identity and it was the most important source of ideological legitimization for a political regime and its institutions in Archaic and Classical Greece.[76] Since the Archaic period, the Greeks shared a common identity based on the idea of the rule of *nomos*, typical of their political communities, as opposed to the rule of a single man, understood as tyranny. This general principle was enforced by several institutional arrangements such as the collegiality and accountability of officials, limits to the magistrates' power and tenure, the exclusive validity of written statutes, and equality before the laws.[77] As I have argued in Chapter 4, this strong ideological concept was embedded across the Greek *poleis* in different kinds of constitutional systems, in democracies such as Classical Athens and also in oligarchies such as Sparta.

This basic ideal is crucial to our understanding of the ideological rationale of the majoritarian judicial review within consensus-based political decision-making. The concept of rule of law involves several requirements; legal scholars have provided different definitions.[78] According to Fuller's formal definition of rule of law, there are eight key aspects identifying the rule of law: (1) the generality of the law, (2) public promulgation, (3) laws cannot be retroactive, (4) clarity of

---

[73] Arist. *Pol.* 1292a4.

[74] See Osborne (1985); Ober (1989a); Todd (1993); Cohen (1995); Christ (1998); Lanni (2006), (2016).

[75] For comprehensive studies on the rule of law in Classical Athens see especially Harris (2006), (2013c); for studies recognizing the rule of law in Classical Athens but with different nuances and approaches, see Ostwald (1986); Sealey (1987); Hansen (1991) (these three scholars see the rule of law as a way to temper democracy in the fourth century); Rubinstein (2000); Rhodes (2004); Herman (2006); Sickinger (2008); Canevaro (2016c), (2017b); Forsdyke (2018) acknowledges that Athens had a form of rule of law, but underestimates the capacity of Athenian institutions in assuring legal certainty.

[76] Canevaro (2017b).

[77] Cf. also Introduction §1.1.

[78] There is no unanimous definition of the rule of law. For a review of different approaches and 'thick' and 'thin' definitions of this idea see Tamanaha (2004); Møller and Skaaning (2014) 13–27.

196 DIVIDED POWER IN ANCIENT GREECE

the laws, (5) no contradiction between the existing laws, (6) laws cannot require the impossible, (7) constancy of the laws through time, and (8) consistency between action and formal requirements.[79] As we have already seen, at the end of the fifth century, the Athenians enforced many legal reforms whose purpose matches many of these requirements. The institution of the *graphē paranomōn* tackles points (4) and (5) precisely, as it avoids inconsistency between legal sources and fosters clarity in the legal system. These are two crucial aspects of the rule of law, and it is not surprising that the Athenians designed a very effective procedure to preserve them. Thus, the majoritarian principle of the *graphē paranomōn* is explained as a counterbalance mechanism enhancing the superiority of the laws without altering the consensus-based deliberation of Athenian democracy.[80] Such a layered decision-making process provided for a system in which decisions went through different bodies, but there was no reduplication of functions between what the council, the assembly, and the lawcourts decided, as every institution added its own expertise and distinct concerns to the decree-making process. By preparing *probouleumata* for discussion in the assembly, the council added its relevant expertise on matters of public administration, the assembly enriched the decree through wide deliberation (a decision-making practice shared with the council), and finally the lawcourts secured the legality of the deliberative process by adding legal expertise and a focus on the consistency and predictability of the decisions enacted by the council and the assembly.

In this way, different parts of the decision-making system interacted and complemented other parts with their expertise and institutional values, creating a balanced and mutually productive relationship. This interaction brought together the civic consensus created in the council and in the assembly with the check on legality guaranteed by the majoritarian vote of the lawcourts. The democratic power is thus divided, but coherent at the same time. It was shared by different institutions which contributed variously through a complex system of inter-institutional relations to the working of the Athenian decision-making.

Furthermore, a technical detail of the procedure of *graphē paranomōn* corroborates this point. In his classic study on *graphē paranomōn*, Hansen argues that in case a *probouleuma* or a decree not yet passed by the assembly was stopped by a charge of illegality, the court could repeal or enact the decree. According to this reconstruction based on three passages from the Attic orators (Aeschin. 3.8, 213,

---

[79] Fuller (1969) 39.

[80] This is also valid for a broader discussion of deliberative democracies. Non-deliberative moments of the decision-making process can contribute to the general rationale of the deliberative system. For an overview see Elstub, Ercan, and Mendoça (2016) 144–5. Cf. in particular Dryzek (2011); Bohman (2012); Mansbridge et al. (2012). For a broader discussion of the systemic dimension of Athenian democracy see Canevaro (2018a), (2020b).

DIVIDED POWER AND JUDICIAL REVIEW   197

230; Dem. 24.9–14), if a decree was considered constitutional by a lawcourt, there was no need for another vote in the assembly to enact the *psēphisma*.[81] This reconstruction was criticized with strong arguments by Hannick and again defended with further arguments in a second essay by Hansen.[82] I will review the evidence in order to prove that a decree always needed a vote of approval in the assembly. The first instance is from Aeschines' *Against Ctesiphon*, a speech delivered against a decree honouring Demosthenes with a crown.[83] Aeschines claimed the *probouleuma* put forward by Ctesiphon was illegal but the trial took place only six years later. We know that Aeschines lost at the trial, but this case cannot provide enough evidence to understand whether the *probouleuma* could be actually enacted directly by the court or not because a *probouleuma* elapsed one year after the enactment (Dem. 23.92–3).

The second and most meaningful case is a dense account of a *graphē paranomōn* against Euctemon preserved in the Demosthenic speech *Against Timocrates* (Dem. 24.9–14). In this part of the speech, Demosthenes tries to demonstrate that Timocrates' law violates previous norms that were properly passed by the *dēmos* in the relevant bodies of government. This is the background: Aristophon put forward a decree appointing a commission of inquiry to collect information from anyone who knew of any public money held in private hands. Euctemon gave information to the commission and pointed out the names of two trierarchs Archebius and Lysitheides, who had kept nine talents and thirty minas from a captured ship from Naucratis (Dem. 24.11). As a result, Euctemon approached the council, which passed a *probouleuma*, and the assembly passed it by *procheirotonia* (προσῆλθε τῇ βουλῇ, προβούλευμ᾽ ἐγράφη. μετὰ ταῦτα γενομένης ἐκκλησίας προύχειροτόνησεν ὁ δῆμος). As Hansen correctly suggests, this must have been an open *probouleuma* that opened the debate, during which Euctemon addressed the assembly and put forward a proposal from the floor (ἔδωκε γνώμην Εὐκτήμων) demanding the sum be paid back by the trierarchs and that any dispute should be adjudicated and the loser be indebted to the state. Until this point, Demosthenes' account is very accurate and does not miss any part of the procedure in the council and in the assembly. He then only concludes by saying that Euctemon's decree was charged by Androtion, Glaucetes, and Melanopus and was brought before a court which found it to be legal (γράφονται τὸ ψήφισμα· εἰς ὑμᾶς εἰσῆλθεν· ἵνα συντέμω, κατὰ τοὺς νόμους ἔδοξεν εἰρῆσθαι καὶ ἀπέφυγεν).

---

[81] Surprisingly, Hansen (1985a) 360–70 does not envisage the same automatic mechanism in a *graphē nomon mē epitēdeion theinai*, which was procedurally identical to the *graphē paranomōn*. According to Hansen, in case the judges upheld a *nomos*, this had to be referred back to the *nomothetai* for approval. This reconstruction is necessary to support Hansen's point of the sovereignty of the judges/nomothetai. On the identity of *nomothetai* as the assembly see now Canevaro and Esu (2018).

[82] Hannick (1981); *contra* Hansen (1974), (1989a).

[83] For the arguments of this speech and the law for crowning magistrates see Harris (2013c) 225–33, and (2017b).

198   DIVIDED POWER IN ANCIENT GREECE

Because Demosthenes does not say whether the assembly voted in favour of Euctemon's proposal, Hansen has argued that the decree was upheld by the lawcourt without a vote in the assembly. By contrast, Hannick has brought strong arguments against this interpretation. In particular, the use of *psēphisma* to denote Euctemon's proposal is at odds with Hansen's reconstruction. Even if it is true, as Hansen points out, that the word *psēphisma* can mean both 'bill' and 'act', it seems more logical that after having defined Euctemon's proposal with the standard term *gnōmē* in the previous paragraph (13), when Demosthenes is referring to it as *psēphisma* at 14, he means a voted decree which has resulted from the approval in the assembly of Euctemon's *gnōmē*. In this part of the speech, Demosthenes explicitly cuts short his account of the procedure (ἵνα συντέμω), and takes for granted that the audience understands that the assembly had voted on the proposal and that what the accusers indicted was a fully valid decree.[84] Demosthenes, moreover, accuses the law of Timocrates of aiming to make the decisions of the council, the assembly, and the lawcourts invalid (ἄκυρα), which stresses again that the decree had been passed by the council and the assembly and was finally reviewed by the court.

One can thus conclude that the account at 9–14 of *Against Timocrates* does not provide evidence for a *probouleuma* that was upheld by a court. This is rather a standard account of an indictment in a *graphē paranomōn* of a decree that was enacted by the assembly, and was later considered constitutional by a court. In the case that a *probouleuma* was stopped before a vote in the assembly, there is no evidence that the court had the power to uphold the decree, as this would be inconsistent with the aim of the procedure of *graphē paranomōn* as well as with the rationale of Athenian decree-making. Through the *graphē paranomōn*, the Athenian courts performed a fundamental role in the decision-making process. They secured the necessary consistency of legal sources and respect of the superiority of the laws over the decrees. The lawcourts did not reduplicate the institutional functions of the council and the assembly when examining a decree, but rather judges added their own legal expertise, shaped by their participation in many trials during the year, to the decree-making without overlapping with the other institutions.

Although the power of judicial review of the courts was a cornerstone of democracy, this should not be overestimated or improperly assimilated to that of modern constitutional courts. While the *graphē paranomōn* allowed Athenians to preserve legal consistency between laws and decrees, the decisions of the courts, even though important, did not constitute a binding precedent with force of law.[85]

---

[84] *Pace* Hansen (1989a) 70, who argues that Demosthenes would have said that a vote was taken, if this had actually happened.

[85] On this see Canevaro (2019a); see also Harris (2013c) 246–73, (2018b) 43–6, who shows that precedents, even if not binding, were used to achieve consistency in the verdicts. In case of *graphē paranomōn*, written copies of decrees that had been indicted were kept and could be used as precedents.

DIVIDED POWER AND JUDICIAL REVIEW   199

Thus, the Athenian lawcourts were not an *entgrenztes Gericht* ('boundary expanding court'), as some legal scholars have called the German constitutional court, since they did not form a jurisprudence which shaped the laws of Athens and its constitution.[86]

The introduction of the *graphē paranomōn* in the fifth century created a virtuous relationship within the procedure of enacting decrees. The procedure empowered the lawcourts to enforce the separation between *nomoi* and *psēphismata* of the council and of the assembly, a principle which was foundational to Athenian decision-making and divided power until 322 BCE.[87] Judicial control over the enactments of the people's assembly was not only limited to Classical Athens and there is evidence for similar institutions from other *poleis* in the Hellenistic and Imperial periods. In the next section, the analysis of this material sheds light on the differences and similarities of this institutional practice beyond the Athenian model.

6.3 Judicial Review outside Athens

As the previous section of this chapter has demonstrated, the basic concept underlying the institution of *graphē paranomōn* was a distinction between laws and decrees. This clear-cut distinction, as it was formalized in fourth-century Athens, was not a widespread feature among post-Classical Greek cities.[88] Occasional attempts to achieve consistency between legal sources are attested outside Attica in the Hellenistic period. For example, the hierarchical superiority of the laws over decrees is attested in three decrees from Hellenistic Cos, which prescribe that if part of the decree is in conflict with a law, the law should prevail.[89] More broadly, the terminological distinction between general and permanent laws (e.g. *nomoi, thesmoi, rhētrai*) and decrees (e.g. *psēphismata/psaphismata, dogmata, diagrammata*) is found in many *poleis* of the Greek world. For instance, a second-century decree from Aegiale orders the recording of the laws on tablets for the city archive (*IG* XII 7, 515.131–2). Another contemporary decree from Imbros mentions 'the written decrees and the written laws', showing that the two terms were not considered equivalent (*IG* XII 8, 51.5–6). Yet, one must be careful with this evidence, as the terminological differentiation did not always envisage two neat legal categories and separate procedures to enforce this principle as it did in fourth-century Athens.[90] On the one hand, this can be explained by the fact that the Athenian model was an extraordinary one, which deviated from the

---

[86] Jestaedt, Lepsius, Möllers, and Schönberger (2011).
[87] On the post-322 mechanism of legislative review see Canevaro (2013c).
[88] Velissaropoulos-Karakostas (2011) 60–3; Kantor (2012) 69–70.
[89] See the text in Hallof, Hallof and Habicht (1998) 110, n. 7; Parker and Obbink (2001) 266, n. 3.
[90] Canevaro (2016a).

200   DIVIDED POWER IN ANCIENT GREECE

nomothetic tradition widespread in the rest of the Greek world.[91] On the other hand, Hellenistic cities also dealt with other legal sources above the level of civic legislation, such as the laws enacted by the Hellenistic kings, laws of federal leagues, and later by Roman officials.[92] As the separation between laws and decrees was often unclear, this meant that the juridical hierarchy was not consistently respected. As Chaniotis and Kantor note, a second-century CE decree from Chersonesus in Tauris shows an important reform of the judicial courts enacted by decree with the force of a law (*SEG* 55.838), in a way similar to what happened in fifth-century Athens.[93] In some other cases, a decree could be turned into a law through a special procedure. For example, a second-century inscription from Kyme reports an honorific decree which was to be referred by the proposer to a *nomothetikon dikastērion* (legislative court) for ratification, which shows that in this context the two categories of decree and law were not as clear-cut as in fourth-century Athens (*I.Kyme* 12).[94] Similarly, a second-century decree from Elaea honouring the deified king orders the inclusion of the decree itself in the sacred laws of the city (*IvP* 246, 59–61). Yet, the lack of a comprehensive system of law-making separated by that of decree-making according to the Athenian model does not necessarily entail the absence of a system of judicial review beyond the major example of fourth-century Athens. As I have discussed in the first section of this chapter, in Athens the *graphē paranomōn* was established before the introduction of the *nomothesia* procedure in 403 BCE. Scattered evidence for the *graphē paranomōn* is found in other Greek *poleis*, mainly in inscriptions of the Hellenistic period. This evidence does not indicate that the procedural details and the overall legal system followed the Athenian model, but that these *poleis* also envisaged a system that tried to reconcile democratic deliberation with judicial control over the consistency of people's enactments. Thus, the concept of divided power in the realm of judicial review can also be seen at work in *poleis* beyond Athens, in a way similar to the concept of delegation as discussed in Chapter 3. This is also important to show the common Greek concern for the consistency of norms, their predictability and applicability, which points to a unity of Greek legal principles.

However, very few literary sources report evidence for the procedure of *graphē paranomōn* outside Athens, and there is no attestation of a non-Athenian judicial speech on this matter. Some of them are clearly anecdotal, and no sound historical reconstruction can be built on these pieces of evidence. Yet, they do show that the concept of judicial review was known in other *poleis*. For example, in the *Life of Pelopidas*, Plutarch mentions an episode in which Pelopidas claimed a decree

---

[91] Canevaro (2015).
[92] Velissaropoulos-Karakostas (2011) 63–6; on Greek law under the Romans see Kantor (2015).
[93] Kantor (2013) 72–4.
[94] See other examples at Rhodes with Lewis (1997) 497–9; Canevaro (2016a).

DIVIDED POWER AND JUDICIAL REVIEW 201

of Menecleidas honouring Charon (τοῦτο τὸ ψήφισμα γράφεται Πελοπίδας παρανόμων), one of his political opponents, was unconstitutional. At the trial, Menecleidas was heavily fined and was unable to pay the sum (Plut. *Pelop.* 25.7).[95] The evidence from Plutarch is very likely a fiction alluding to the later sources that Plutarch used to compose this life.[96] However, we do know that in Boeotia there were *nomoi* and *psēphismata* enacted by both the federal *koinon* and the cities of the league. This might imply a hierarchy between laws and decrees or that this procedure was similar to what happened in fifth-century Athens, where the distinction between *nomoi* and *psēphismata* was blurred, but the *graphē paranomōn* was still operative.[97] In this case, a decree could undergo judicial review if in conflict with other decrees, as is also attested in four Hellenistic decrees from Magnesia where it is said that the provisions of any decree contrary to those of a new decree were to be invalid (*I.Magnesia* 92 a.13–14; b.18–19, 94: λελύσθαι δὲ καὶ εἴ τι ψήφισμα ἐναντίον ἐστὶ τῶιδε τῶι ψηφίσματι κατ᾽ αὐτὸ τοῦτο καθ᾽ ὅ ἐστιν ἐναντίον). Another later anecdotal attestation of a system of legislative review outside Athens is found in Lucian. In his dialogue *Toxaris, or Friendship*, a man called Mnesippus tells the story of a citizen of Massalia, Menecrates. He was a rich member of the elites who put forward an unconstitutional proposal which was repealed by the Six Hundred.[98] This institution was traditionally understood as an oligarchic council, but Giangiulio has persuasively shown that the body of the Six Hundred conforms more to an assembly.[99] Menecrates himself became *atimos* and his property was confiscated (Luc. *Tox.* 24). The penalties envisaged, such as *atimia* and confiscation of property, are consistent with those of Classical Athens for the same crime. In this case, however, we do not know anything about the unfolding of the legal procedure. What is interesting in Lucian's account is that confirms that Greek political culture considers it normal that the principle of legal consistency was not limited to democracies, and that a form of legislative review could exist in different constitutional regimes such as the oligarchic government of Massalia, albeit in a fictional account.

---

[95] See discussion in Rhodes (2016a) 62.

[96] For the several sources of Plutarch in the *Life of Pelopidas* see Georgiadou (1997) 15–28.

[97] Von Fritz (1968) 98–107 and Triantaphyllopoulos (1985) argued that a procedure similar to *graphē paranomōn* might be found in Syracuse. This argument is based on a passage in Plutarch's *Life of Dion* (48.3), in which the Syracusan assembly voted to make invalid (ἀκυρώσας) a previous decree voted by the assembly itself. This procedure recalls the Athenian *anapsēphisis*, with which the assembly could vote against a previous decree (Thuc. 6.14), rather than the *graphē paranomōn*. On *anapsēphisis* in Athens, see Harris (2014) *pace* Dover (1955).

[98] The anecdote is inserted in a philosophical work influenced by the contemporary Greek novel. This indicates that the anecdote is in all probability a classicizing invention and does not give an insight into real politics of contemporary Massalia, see ní Mheallaigh (2014) 39–71. In the *Politics*, Aristotle says that Massalia was first an oligarchy and then a moderate regime closer to *politeia* (*Pol.* 1305b4, 1320b18, 1321a30). Later, according to Strabo (4.1.5), Massalia had an oligarchic council (called *senatus* by Val. Max. 2.6.7) whose members served for life and were called *timouchoi*. For a discussion of these sources see Domínguez (2004) 165–7.

[99] Giangiulio (2018) 287–8.

202 DIVIDED POWER IN ANCIENT GREECE

Some Greek states in the post-Classical period decided not to use a civic judicial body for reviewing legislation. The decision to not administer justice through civic courts in many Hellenistic and Imperial cities is not uncommon, and is strictly linked to the practice of summoning courts manned by foreign judges from other *poleis*.[100] The institution that modern scholars have labelled 'foreign judges' (usually called in ancient sources *metapemptoi* or *apostalentes dikastai* or *xenikon dikastērion*) is attested in literary and especially epigraphical sources.[101] The epigraphical evidence that mentions foreign judges is abundant. Foreign judges started to be extensively used in Asia Minor, but then they spread across the Greek world.[102] There are around 280 inscriptions attesting to the activity of foreign courts judging mainly private lawsuits (*enklēmata*), commercial disputes (*sumbolaia*), as well as cases for unpaid debts.[103] Yet, it is striking that the epigraphical sources show that foreign judges were also called upon to decide the illegality of a decree in procedures that closely resemble the Athenian *graphē paranomōn*. This means that a political community could ask a court of foreign *dikastai* to judge an enactment of the city according to the local laws. Unlike Athens, there was no conformity between the people passing decrees in the assembly and the judges reviewing them in court. The power was still divided, and the ideological preconditions were still based on the principle of the rule of law, in particular the principle of fairness and impartiality which contributed to build legitimacy around a court of non-citizens. The use of a court made up of foreign citizens in cases of *graphē paranomōn* has implications for understanding the rationale of this procedure from a diachronic perspective across different constitutional arrangements.

Triantaphyllopoulos and Habicht have collected the epigraphical evidence for extra-Athenian judicial review.[104] The procedure is clearly attested in three inscribed decrees from respectively Demetrias, Mylasa, and, in a more controversial case, from Priene. It is useful to review all the evidence before providing an analysis of the procedure in light of the epigraphical material. The decree of the Thessalian city of Demetrias is the first occurrence of a judicial review procedure outside Athens preserved in an inscribed decree.[105] Habicht dates the decree to the last third of the second century BCE for prosopographical reasons.[106] The text of the decree is the following:

---

[100] The institution of foreign courts did not mean that civic courts were not still often summoned in the Hellenistic cities, see Walser (2012).

[101] The first piece of evidence concerning foreign judges is a fourth-century decree from Kyme honouring foreign judges sent by King Antigonus (*I.Kyme* 1). See Robert (1973); Crowther (2006).

[102] The practice to summon outsiders to settles internal disputes goes back into the Archaic period and is not a complete innovation (Hdt. 4.161). For foreign judges in continental Greece see Helly (1973) 116–19; Knoepfler (2001) 407–21; Crowther (2006) 34–5 (for the case of Thessaly).

[103] Magnetto (2016). For *sumbolaion* in Greek law see Harris (2015c).

[104] Triantaphyllopoulos (1985); Habicht (2008).   [105] *BCH* 95 (1971) 554.

[106] Habicht (2008) 17. I report the text by Helly (1971) 555–6 (with commentary) with emendation by Habicht (2008) line 10.

DIVIDED POWER AND JUDICIAL REVIEW 203

ἡ πόλις ἡ Δημητριέων τὴν πόλιν τὴν

Ἡρακλειωτῶν καὶ τοὺς δικασ-

τὰς Φῦρον Μελάντα, Κλέω-

να Ἐπιστράτου, Φιλόχωρον

5 Μοσχίωνος καὶ τὸν γραμ-

ματέα Σωκράτη Νίκωνος.

{²coronae quinque}²

Ἀρίσταρχος Ἀριστοκράτους Ἰώλκιος στρατηγὸς Μαγνήτ[ων καὶ οἱ κα]-

τὰ πόλιν στρατηγοὶ Θεσσαλὸς Φιλίσκου Γλαφυρεύς, [Ἀλέξανδρος Με]-

νίσκου Σπαλαυθρεύς, Εὔβουλος Ὀλυμπίχου Γλα[φυρεὺς εἶπαν· ἐ]-

10 πεί, αἱρεθείσης ἐν τῆι ἐκκλησίαι <τῆς> πόλεως Ἡρακ[λει— — — —]

μεταπέμψασθαι δικαστήριον ἐπὶ τὴν [δίκην τὴν ἐνεστηκυῖαν]

ὑπὲρ ψηφίσματος ὡς παρανόμου κεκ[ριμένου...c.13....]

καὶ ἐκκλησίας κατακολουθ[........c.20.......]

δικασταγωγου[............c.30........... ἡ πό]-

15 λις τῶν Ἡρακλειω[τῶν ἀπέστειλεν πρὸς ἡμᾶς δικαστὰς ἄνδρας]

καλοὺς καὶ [ἀγαθοὺς — — — — — — — — — — — — — — — —]

[— —]

The city of Demetrias (honours) the city of Herecleia and the judges Phyron son of Melas, Cleon son of Epistratus, Philochorus son of Moschion, and the secretary Socrates son of Nikon. When Aristarchus son of Aristocrates from Iolkos was general of the Magnesians and Thessalus son of Philiscus from Glaphyrai and Alexander son of Meniscus from Spalauthra were generals of the city (*kata polin*), Eubulus son of Olympicus from Glaphyrai put forward the motion. As, having been elected in the assembly of Heraclea [...] to send a court in charge of establishing a trial on a decree considered illegal [...] and the following assemblies [...] *dikastagōgoi* [...] the city of Heracleia sent to us excellent and virtuous judges ....

The decree honours three judges from Heraclea Trachinia who were sent to Demetrias. The decree makes clear at line 12 that the judges were called to adjudicate a case of *paranomia* of a decree. Unfortunately, the text does not specify the content of the decree under review. The wording of the honorific decree is very clear in singling out the task of the judges by using language resembling the Athenian procedure of *graphē paranomōn*. The existence of such a procedure in Demetrias suggests that either the decrees of Demetrias were to conform to previous decrees or in accordance with the laws, and a proper

204 DIVIDED POWER IN ANCIENT GREECE

legal hierarchy was in place. Similarly, as Habicht points out, the procedure envisaged in the decree of Demetrias seems to be consistent with the phrasing of a decree from the Carian city of Mylasa dated to the early Imperial period (*I.Labraunda* 56).

[— μηδείς]

[τὰς εἰσαγομένας? δ]ίκας [π]ερὶ τ[ο]ύτων εἰς τὸ[ν δῆμ]ο[ν ἐνγραφέ]-

[σθ]ω? τῆι τῶν ἐνκλημάτων τάξει, καθ' ὃ ἔτι εἰσάγοντα[ι] v. αἱ ἐ[κ τοῦ]

τ̣αρανόμου ψηφίσματος δίκαι, v ἐξεῖναι δὲ τοῖς ἄρχουσι [καὶ]

The decree concerns the administration of a shrine in Labraunda and reports at lines 1–3: 'the lawsuits brought forward about these matters shall enter the register of the *dēmos* (. . .) according to which the lawsuits for an illegal decree are brought forward'. The fragmentary state of preservation of the Mylasian decree does not allow us to understand whether foreign judges were in charge of the trial like in Demetrias or whether a civic court was active at the time in Mylasa. Despite the large chronological gap between the two inscriptions, there is no doubt that the procedure mentioned in the two decrees is one requesting a judicial review of a decree.

A third occurrence comes from Alexandria Troas.[107] Here, a court of foreign judges was summoned to decide on public cases according to an honorific decree from Priene (*I.Priene²* 119). The decree is well preserved and seems to follow the usual conventions of dikastic decrees. The good performance of the judges is honoured at lines 15–18 'because they judged equally and justly all the cases both those about illegal proposals and those about violence'

ἐπήνεκεν ἐπί τε τῶι σωφρόνως καὶ ἀνεγκλήτως παρεπιδημῆσαι καὶ διότι τὰς δίκας ἴσως καὶ δικαίως ἁπάσας ἔκριναν τάς τε τῶμ παρανόμων καὶ τὰς τῶμ βιαίων, τὸν δὲ δῆμον ἐστεφάνωκεν ἀρετῆς ἕνεκεν καὶ εὐνοίας τῆς εἰς τὴμ πόλιν καὶ διότι ἄνδρας καλοὺς καὶ ἀγαθοὺς ἀπέστειλεν· [. . .]

They agreed wisely and blamelessly to reside in a foreign city and because they judged fairly and justly all the lawsuits about illegal decrees and violence, the people has crowned (them) for their virtue and goodwill towards the city and because they sent good and virtuous men [. . .]

Scholars commenting on this decree have included it among those showing a *graphē paranomōn* procedure by pointing out the similarities with the content of

---

[107] For Alexandria Troas see Hansen and Nielsen (2004) 1000.

DIVIDED POWER AND JUDICIAL REVIEW   205

the decrees of Mylasa, and especially of Demetrias.[108] In his essay on judicial review in Greek states, Habicht argued that the case of Alexandria Troas is a distinct one because the foreign judges were not called to judge a public action for an illegal decree since there is no textual reference to a decree or a proposal under review. According to Habicht, the court was instructed 'to judge cases of *acts* that were unlawful and violent'.[109] However, this argument is problematic. First, the two genitive plurals τῶν παρανόμων and τῶν βιαίων are clearly governed by τὰς δίκας ... ἁπάσας. They specify and limit the scope of the judges' action by singling out two distinct legal procedures regulated by their relevant laws: a *dikē paranomōn* and a *dikē biaiōn*.[110] The former is, in all probability, a procedure substantially similar to the Athenian *graphē paranomōn*, and the latter is an action against violence. The fact that the action is called *dikē* instead of *graphē* is not surprising, as there is no evidence of *graphai* outside Athens in the Classical and Hellenistic periods. Thus, the foreign court was in charge of deciding only on those two kinds of lawsuits. Second, if one accepts Habicht's interpretation, the decree would contain a very odd expression. The term *paranomōn*, if left unqualified, is very general and indicates any unlawful act. This also encompasses acts of violence and de facto any crime sanctioned by a statute, which would not need to be specified separately. Yet, such an arrangement would mean that the city of Alexandria Troas had delegated its whole judicial activity to the foreign judges from Priene. It seems much more plausible and consistent with the rest of the evidence that the group of foreign judges was called to Alexandria with precise instructions and a well-defined judicial task.[111]

A close examination of the relevant epigraphical material shows that a judicial review procedure is attested in three different *poleis* at different times over a long chronological span dating between the second century BCE and the Imperial age. The epigraphical evidence provides very few details about the procedural features of these charges, yet important elements and comparison with other inscriptions can allow some level of historical reconstruction. In particular, the presence of courts with judicial review powers manned by foreign judges, instead of citizens, raises different questions about the relationship between democratic deliberation, divided power, and judicial review that are not found in the institutional context of Classical Athens. As discussed in the first part of the chapter, the *graphē paranomōn* in Athens was a legal procedure that complemented democratic deliberation with a majoritarian and non-deliberative step meant to secure the legality and coherence of decrees. Yet, this happened in a system of civic lawcourts manned by the very same men who attended the council, the assembly, and served

---

[108] Robert and Robert (1960) *BE* 94; Robert (1973) 445; Triantaphyllopoulos (1985) 219–20 n. 5.
[109] Habicht (2008) 20.   [110] For *dikē biaiōn* in Classical Athens see Harris (2006) 321.
[111] On the role of foreign judges as well-defined by the decrees of the inviting city see Walser (2012) 98–100.

206   DIVIDED POWER IN ANCIENT GREECE

as officials. In the case of extra-Athenian judicial review, it must be clarified why a community decided to delegate such an important decision to a court of foreign judges and how the procedure was designed in order to foster the rule of law. This can be accomplished with an analysis of the institutional design and social composition of these courts in order to understand the legal and institutional rationale of this procedure in the institutional environments of Hellenistic *poleis*.

In the attempt to reconstruct the judicial review procedures beyond Athens, my starting point is offered by the decree from Demetrias for the foreign judges of Heraclea, which mentions the *dikastagōgoi* at line 14. Unfortunately, the inscription for Demetrias does not preserve any information about the *dikastagōgoi* in the context of that decree. Yet, the presence of *dikastagōgoi* is meaningful, and understanding the role of these officials in the judicial procedure is key for reconstructing judicial review outside Athens. The *dikastagōgoi* were special officials chosen by a city requesting foreign judges (for any kind of trial) with the task of delivering the request and escorting the judges.[112] The appointment of a *dikastagōgos* coincided with the beginning of the judicial procedure which was initiated in the assembly. Hamon notes that the remaining epigraphical sources do not preserve an account of the deliberations in the council and in the assembly, which must have taken place in order to elect a *dikastagōgos*. Several factors were most likely discussed before appointing a *dikastagōgos*, including legal aspects and the expertise of the candidates, alongside more prominently political reasons such as international relations between the community and the city sending foreign judges.[113]

Three Coan decrees for *dikastagōgoi* of the second half of the second century BCE, published by Crowther, Habicht, and Luise Hallof, and Klaus Hallof, provide a valuable point of comparison for our purposes and shed light on the public service carried out by these officials.[114] The first step for a *dikastagōgos* was to address the council and the assembly of the foreign community in order to convince them to send judges. For example, the best preserved of the three decrees from Cos (*IG* XII 4, 1 59) honours Theugenes son of Hermogenes who was sent as *dikastagōgos* to Smyrna and addressed the council and the assembly with a detailed speech to ask for two judges and a secretary. The decree specifies that the chosen men were excellent and virtuous people, as the men mentioned in the decree of Demetrias (16) and of Priene (19–20), and the selection was delegated to the foreign community, as these were men they trusted (11–12: ἄνδρας καλοὺς καὶ ἀγαθοὺς καὶ πιστευομένους παρ' αὐτοῖς). As Crowther notes, this formula begins to appear in the second century when foreign judges start being defined as *pisteuomenoi* or *timoumenoi* in order to highlight their special standing in their homeland; their *pistis* and their *timē* are also recognized in the honorific decrees of the

---

[112] Magnetto (2016).   [113] Hamon (2012) 198–9.
[114] Crowther, Habicht, L. Hallof, and K. Hallof (1998) 87–100; Gauthier (1999).

DIVIDED POWER AND JUDICIAL REVIEW   207

hosting city.[115] A second-century decree from Peparethus honouring judges from Larisa shows that the relationship of trust and honour was reciprocal, and encompassed the trustworthiness of the judges as recognized by both their home city and the foreign city.[116] The decree honours the judges for being '*kaloi kai agathoi* of those honourable and trustworthy men, worthy of their homeland and of our city' (*SEG* 26.677 23–4: ἄνδρας καλοὺς καὶ ἀγαθοὺς τῶν τι-[μωμένων παρ' αὐτοῖς κ]αὶ πιστευομένων, ἀξίους τῆς τε | [ἐ]α[υτῶ]ν πατρ[ίδος καὶ τῆ]ς ἡμετέρας πόλεως).

The role of the *dikastagōgoi* was not limited to leading the embassy. Once the *dikastagōgos* returned home with the foreign envoy, he changed from a diplomat to a civic magistrate in charge of presiding over the judicial procedure. This is clearly shown by the decree, as Theugenes is also honoured for his *dikastophula-kia*. This term includes all activities required for the successful administration of justice. It is said that he carried out the guardianship of the judges by making arrangements for public and private *sumbolaia* according to his oath (20–3 τᾶι δικαστοφυλακίαι ἐκτενῶς | καὶ δικαίως ἀκολούθως τῶι ὅρκωι, ἕως οὗ | διεξάχθη τά τε δαμόσια καὶ ἰδιωτικὰ | συμβόλαια).

This clause of the decree clarifies that the *dikastagōgos* played the role of a judicial magistrate in charge of summoning the court and assisting the judges during the trial, in a manner similar to that of the *thesmothetai* and the *archontes* in Classical Athens. The text of the oath is not preserved, but we can read the text of another oath taken by *dikastagōgoi* for the arbitration between Halai and Boumelita in Boeotia. As Robert commented, the *dikastagōgoi* swore to carry out their office piously and justly (*FD* III 1, 362.26–35: πεποιῆ-|σθαι τὴν δικασταγωγίαν ὁσίως καὶ δικαίως) without bearing grudges against the judges and avoiding any attempt at bribery. The oath bound the *dikastagōgos* to be impartial and to follow the laws, as the expression ὁσίως καὶ δικαίως highlights. The *dikastagōgos* had to supervise the proper conduct of the judges by preventing cases of bribery, a not impossible event in a panel of only a few judges (usually up to ten). Finally, he also provided the money to fund the expenses for the judges' stay and for the civic festivals in their honour.[117] From an institutional perspective, therefore, the *dikastagōgos* was an official that fulfilled the role of ambassador, judicial magistrate, and liturgist. The status of the evidence, unfor-tunately, does not allow us to reconstruct whether a preliminary phase, like the Athenian *anakrisis*, preceded a debate before the foreign court, and whether the

---

[115] Crowther (1997) 356–7.

[116] On *pistis* and foreign judges see p. 208. For *pistis* in honorific language see Canevaro (2016c) 91–2.

[117] Hamon (2012) 205–6. Gauthier (1999) n. 405 and Hamon point out that the decree uses the term *parousia* (at line 27), instead of the most common *parepidēmia*, to indicate the judges' visit. This term is also attested for royal visits and seems to cover all the necessary acts to provide a good stay for important visitors.

208   DIVIDED POWER IN ANCIENT GREECE

dikastagōgos or some other official was responsible for receiving the evidence from the litigants. The surviving epigraphical material seems to indicate that the procedure envisioned (1) a decree of the assembly appointing a *dikastagōgos* with instructions to ask for foreign judges; (2) a diplomatic envoy, and (3) the summoning of a foreign court to review the decree.

The language of the decree reflects standard honorary terminology and this is important to understand how honorary language and institutional concern interact. It is said that Theugenes carried out his office with *philotimia* and *ekteneia* (line 9), but a special function is played by the value of *pistis*. The term *pistis* is key and entails the trustworthiness of the *dikastagōgos* and trust granted to him by the Coan community.[118] Moreover, *pistis* underpins the relationship between the community sending the foreign judges and the community requesting them (12). The decree specifies twice (25, 39) that the *dikastagōgia* was given to Theugenes with the trust of the whole community (τὰν ἐνχειρισθεῖσαν αὐτῶι πίστιν ὑπὸ τοῦ σύμπαντος δάμου). As Faraguna notes, *pistis* (and the opposite notion of deception) is central in Greek discussion on social, legal, and economic cooperation from the Archaic period onwards.[119] We have already noted the foreign judges are defined as 'trustworthy men in their own community' and this expression, far from being only a standard decree formula, indicates the Coan concern to avoid deception and build trust by appointing cooperative judges which would uphold the laws with impartiality and respect of the legal procedures, and would in turn deserve the relevant honours. The decree therefore creates a narrative of trust built on all the steps that the *dikastagōgos* has honourably performed to summon the courts of foreign judges, as detailed in particular in lines 13–25 of the decree:

> τάν τε παρεπιδαμίαν ἐποιήσα{ν}το
> ἀξίαν ἀμφοτερᾶν τᾶν πολίων ὑπὲρ
> ὧν ἁπάντων διαμεμαρτυρήκαντι Ζμυρ-
> ναῖοι διὰ τᾶς δοθείσας αὐτῶι ἀποκρίσι-
> ος, παραλαβών τε τὸς ἄνδρας καὶ παρα-
> γενόμενος ἐς τὰν πόλιν πᾶσαν κακοπα-
> θίαν καὶ ἐπιμέλειαν πεποίηται ποτικαρτε-
> ρήσας καὶ τᾶι δικαστοφυλακίαι ἐκτενῶς
> καὶ δικαίως ἀκολούθως τῶι ὅρκωι, ἕως οὗ
> διεξάχθη τά τε δαμόσια καὶ ἰδιωτικὰ
> συμβόλαια, διαφυλάξας ἴσως καὶ δικαίως
> καὶ μισοπονήρως πᾶσι τὰν ἐνχειρισθεῖσαν
> αὐτῶι πίστιν ὑπὸ τοῦ σύμπαντος δάμου.

---

[118] For an attempt to bribe some foreign judges cf. *Gonnoi* II 91, 20–5; *I.Mylasa* 134, 4–5.

[119] Faraguna (2012). On trust in modern societies see Luhmann (1979). For a study of trust in ancient Greece and Rome see Johnstone (2011).

and the rest of his visit he conducted
in a manner worthy of both cities; about
all of which the Smyrnaeans have testified
through the answer given to him;
and having gathered the men and come
to the city he has exerted every effort
and care, persisting in his guardianship of the judges strenuously
and justly, in keeping with his oath, up to the day
the public and private cases were settled,
preserving fairly and justly
and righteously toward all the trust
invested in him by the entire people.
(trans. Rigsby)

The reputation of the *dikastagōgos* Theugenes and of the foreign judges ultimately depends on the respect of the bond of trust that the Coan community granted through the decree. Theugenes' honourable conduct is not only a matter of his self-representation but his trustworthy demeanour was also confirmed by witness statements of the Smyrneans. The public display of *pistis* is necessary to represent that all the institutional actors involved were not deceptive, a behaviour which would otherwise undermine the system of divided power. In the case of a court of foreign judges, the legitimacy of the judicial panel could not stem from the popular composition of the court. It needed to be legitimized through the institutionalization of process of impersonal trust and the decree gives us an insight in the steps that the community took to create this relationship of trust. In this way, the value of *pistis* regulates a complex system of diplomatic relationships between two cities as well as the institutional working of the court operating for the judicial system of another *polis*.

If the example from Cos can also be applied to the decrees attesting to a form of *graphē paranomōn* decided by foreign courts, one can see that this marks a stark departure from the procedure of judicial review in Classical Athens. As noted in the first part of this chapter, the Athenian *graphē paranomōn* was a highly majoritarian procedure right from its initial steps. In the case of Athens, no decree of the assembly was needed to start the procedure, but the procedure was regulated by the relevant law, which delegated the judicial review to the lawcourts, and the volunteer initiative was demanded from public prosecutors. By contrast, when a city decided to turn to foreign judges, the volunteer prosecutors initiated the procedure by proposing a decree in the assembly and having it approved. We have no evidence of anything resembling the Athenian *hupōmosia*, but the procedure might have envisaged a sort of suspension of the legal validity of the decree. In order to start the judicial review, the accuser had to make a case in

210 DIVIDED POWER IN ANCIENT GREECE

the assembly which passed a decree and set the guidelines for the appointment of the *dikastagōgos* to enlist judges, as well as the relevant powers defining their judicial task.

This seems to be confirmed by an interesting account of *graphē paranomōn* in Polybius (Polyb. 28.7.1–15), as noted by Habicht.[120] In 172 BCE, the Achaean League had conferred honours on the king Eumenes II of Pergamon, but two years later, the decree was charged with illegality and judged by an ad hoc court of foreign judges from Rhodes, who repealed the decree. Yet, Attalus claimed back his brother's honours, and a debate arose in the Achaean assembly about whether the honours should be restored or not. Polybius was serving as hipparch, one of the main magistrates of the League. His speech in favour of Attalus' request sheds some light on the procedure of judicial review in the Achaean League. First, Polybius says that the procedure was initiated by a decree of the Achaeans, which set the legal guidelines for the judges to perform a judicial review. This decree stated that the honours that were unsuitable or illegal should be repealed, but not all of them (τὸ γεγονὸς ἐξ ἀρχῆς ψήφισμα τῶν Ἀχαιῶν ὑπὲρ τῶν τιμῶν, ἐν ᾧ γεγραμμένον ἦν ὅτι δεῖ τὰς ἀπρεπεῖς ἀρθῆναι τιμὰς καὶ τὰς παρανόμους, οὐ μὰ Δί' ἁπάσας). Here, the Polybian account does not say whether the procedure was started as a general review of the honours or as a charge brought by an individual. In any case, a citizen must have started the procedure either by putting forward the decree or by bringing forward the accusation of illegality before the decree was actually discussed. Moreover, Polybius accused the judges, Sosigenes and Diopeithes,[121] of having personal hostile motivations against Eumenes when they abolished the honours. For this reason, they went beyond the power the Achaeans had entrusted them and did not judge in accordance with justice and honour (τοῦτο πεποιηκέναι παρὰ τὸ τῶν Ἀχαιῶν δόγμα καὶ παρὰ τὴν δοθεῖσαν αὐτοῖς ἐξουσίαν, καὶ τὸ μέγιστον, παρὰ τὸ δίκαιον καὶ τὸ καλῶς ἔχον). The assembly passed a new decree enforcing part of the verdict from the foreign judges, but restoring the other honours, which were consistent with the Achaeans' laws and customs (τοῦ δὲ πλήθους εὐδοκήσαντος τοῖς λεγομένοις, ἐγράφη δόγμα προστάττον τοῖς ἄρχουσι πάσας ἀποκαταστῆσαι τὰς Εὐμένους τοῦ βασιλέως τιμάς, πλὴν εἴ τινες ἀπρεπές τι περιέχουσι τῷ κοινῷ τῶν Ἀχαιῶν ἢ παράνομον).

This Polybian passage is interesting in many respects. First, in his speech to the Achaean assembly, Polybius attacks the judges for abusing their judicial powers by repealing all the honours. This is an important piece of evidence as it shows that, similarly to Athens, the Achaean legal procedure was designed normatively to stick to the matter of law. When a court was suspected of having taken decisions for personal enmity or political reasons, such decisions did not have legitimacy

---

[120] F. W. Walbank (1979) 333–6; Habicht (2008) 22–3.

[121] For the identity of the two foreign judges see Dixon (2001). The names of the two judges also appear in an inscription recording the arbitration between Epidaurus and Hermion (*IG* IV, 2 1.75).

DIVIDED POWER AND JUDICIAL REVIEW   211

and were not admitted. The judges were called to express an impartial judgement according to the laws of city. The decree empowered them to cancel only those honours that were illegal (*paranomōn*) and unsuitable (*aprepēs*). This last term closely resembles the Athenian terminology used in the *graphē nomon mē epitēdeion theinai*. In Athens, a law had to be *epitēdeios* (suitable), which means that the statute should not be in contradiction with other laws or with the general *ethos* of the system of the laws and the reciprocity of the honorific system.[122] Here, similarly, Polybius underlines that the honours granted by the Achaeans should conform to the written statutes and to the morality of the Achaeans enshrined in their legal system. Thus, only the honours that did not respect these requirements and were unworthy of the Achaeans and the honorand were to be repealed by the judges. Second, as in the case of Demetrias and Alexandria Troas, the judicial review was carried out by a court of foreign judges.[123] Polybius makes very clear that the foreign judges were appointed by decree and their powers and prerogatives were clearly set out in this decree of appointment which was passed by the Achaean assembly (τὸ τῶν Ἀχαιῶν δόγμα). Unfortunately, no copies of these decrees survive, but, as Magnetto suggests, they presumably played the same role as the *enklēma* in the Athenian judicial procedure, stating the reasons for the dispute and the relevant powers delegated to the judges by the assembly.[124] Robert suggested that the *poleis* could also draft additional regulation (*diorthōma*) to guide the judicial activity of the foreign court.[125] One might argue that the decree would also have appointed a *dikastagōgos* to be sent to Rhodes and to supervise the judicial procedure. The literary account in Polybius is consistent with the epigraphical evidence and shows a substantial unity across the Hellenistic world regarding the use of foreign judges to review decrees.

In summary, the few pieces for evidence of judicial review outside Athens do not allow us to reconstruct a comprehensive picture of the use of institutions akin to the *graphē paranomōn* which is valid for the whole Greek world. What seems to be shared by all the *poleis* in which this institution is attested is the need to appoint

---

[122] See Canevaro (2016b), (2016c). The mechanism of *timē* (honour) are clearly embedded in the legal procedure of revision of the decree. The term ἀπρεπής encompasses the moral meaning of 'improper' and 'indecent' and bears on the bidirectionality of *timē* (cf. Thuc. 5.46). These means that the Achaeans only aimed to cancel the honours that were unworthy of the honorand as well as below the standards of community bestowing the relevant honours. Conversely, failing to honour King Eumenes properly would in turn impact negatively on the honour of the Achaeans. This is confirmed by the rest of Polybius' speech when he says that the Rhodian judges had acted against the authority given by the Achaean decree and consequently also against the principles of justice and honour (παρὰ τὸ δίκαιον καὶ τὸ καλῶς ἔχον). The decree restoring the honours to Eumenes specified that all previous honours were to be restored 'except those that are dishonourable to the Achaean *koinon* or contrary to the laws' (Polyb. 28.7.15).

[123] Holleaux rightly proved that the court was manned by Rhodian judges. The word Ῥοδίους had been deleted by the editors Ursinus and Büttner-Wobst see F. W. Walbank (1979) 335–6.

[124] Robert (1973); Hamon (2012); Magnetto (2016).

[125] Two *diorthōmata* are mentioned in *I.Erythrai* 116 and *I.Magnesia* 90. Walser (2008) 258–60 convincingly suggests that the so-called Ephesian law on debt is the only preserved *diorthōma*.

212 DIVIDED POWER IN ANCIENT GREECE

a foreign court to review local decrees passed by the relevant civic bodies. This phenomenon stresses a difference in arrangement, in terms of divided power, between Classical Athens and these cities, which chose to delegate the important task of maintaining legal consistency in their deliberations to a small group of judges from another community. The issue of the widespread use of foreign judges in Hellenistic cities has not been completely resolved yet. Building on Robert's argument, Magnetto has pointed out that the Macedonian kings after Alexander encouraged the use of foreign courts to keep or to restore *homonoia* in the *poleis* of their kingdoms and to respect their autonomy by avoiding direct involvement of royal authorities. This practice then became a habit of the Greek *poleis* in the Hellenistic and Imperial periods.[126] Nevertheless, the use of foreign judges in judicial review procedures did not curtail the divided power of their constitutional set-ups, as people's enactments were revised by a judicial body, whose role and powers were democratically defined by a decree of the assembly. Moreover, the use of a foreign court shows that the very aim of judicial review was to check the legality of decrees, and not to take into account political reasons regarding the community, which cities would have not delegated to a small group of foreigners. The relevant procedures attached to this task tried to pursue the specific purpose of checking decrees for legality, and to draw on legal expertise and impartiality, which were considered key to preserving the rule of law within the community.

6.4 Courts as Part of Divided Power in Ancient Greece

This chapter has examined the rationale of the institution of judicial review in the decision-making of Classical Athens and of other Greek *poleis*. Athenian democracy provides the most extensive example of the use of this practice. The *graphē paranomōn* was a key tool in instituting a divided power within the constitution, regulating the relationship between democratic and consensus-based decision-making and the stability and coherence of the norms. Through this procedure, the lawcourts play an important role in general decision-making by supplying the necessary legal control over the enactments of the *dēmos*, which granted the permanent enforcement of the principle of the superiority of laws over decrees. The Athenians achieved this by establishing a formal procedure regulated by the law to favour an independent and law-based decision of the court which never had a deliberative role in the decision-making process. On the other hand, the Athenian lawcourts did not become the 'master of the constitution', as the verdicts of *graphai paranomōn* were not enshrined in the legal system as superior norms and did not change the nature of the constitutional system. The decision-

---

[126] Magnetto (2016).

making of Classical Athens was multi-layered, and every institution had its own role and added its own expertise to the process of deliberation, enactment, and revision of decrees. The *graphē paranomōn* was part of those procedures, as I have argued throughout this book, that regulated this complex institutional relationship.

The findings of this chapter have also shown that similar institutions existed in other city-states and even in the federal states of the Greek world across a long chronological period. Regardless of the procedural differences between the Athenian *graphē paranomōn* and judicial review institutions in other *poleis*, the substantive purpose of the legal procedure (i.e. checking the legality of decrees) is shared and present in all the available historical sources. When a Greek *polis* instituted a procedure for the judicial review of a decree by a court of foreign judges, the city required a small group of judges to check the legality of a decree in the same way a court of citizens was manned in Athens to judge a case of *graphē paranomōn*. The fact that a court of foreigners could review decrees of another community shows that they were able to understand and to interpret the local laws on which their decision was to be based. Whether a city decided to use a civic court, like Athens, or foreign courts, like Demetrias or the Achaean League, the procedure of judicial review enhanced the rule of law and fostered the divided power of the constitution. Courts of law, as institutions, and the political actors who manned such institutions were thus part of the divided power, and not masters of the constitution.

7

Epilogue

This book explored the institutional design of Greek divided power in the decree-making of the Classical and Hellenistic *poleis*. Through a detailed analysis of some historical case studies, this book has demonstrated that Greek political decision-making was the result of a multi-layered and dynamic deliberative system of delegation and interaction between several institutions, which enshrined different rules, practices, forms of expertise, and informal discursive norms. Each institution and procedure played a specific role in decree-making and fostered different collective behaviours in the political actors acting within them. This book's approach has therefore combined a renewed attention to institutional design with the study of the normative and discursive aspects of institutions. In other words, institutions not only are the basic organizational structures of political life but also underpin values and norms informing political action.

It is now time to draw together the themes and arguments of this volume and to set out some conclusions. This book has renewed the paradigm for an institution-based study of ancient Greek decision-making and has challenged the culturalist and extra-institutionalist approaches which assign a relatively marginal role to political and legal institutions in shaping political and social behaviour. It has therefore attempted to bridge the gap between the formal reconstruction of constitutional procedures and the ideological interpretation of political activity in the *poleis* of ancient Greece. There is no gulf between these two kinds of investigation. Ideologies and practices were enshrined in the institutional arrangements and legal procedures that defined the nature of a political system. As a result, studying the institutions of collective decision-making has proven a viable method to reconstruct the general political values and discourse in the civic life of the Greek *poleis* of the Classical and Hellenistic periods.

By adopting a comparative approach to the institutional design of different Greek decree-making procedures, this book has also helped make a case for the substantial unity of Greek constitutional law. In political decision-making, both democratic and non-democratic constitutional regimes shared a common institutional toolset, which included the principle of *probouleusis* performed by councils or officials, a civic assembly, and legislative-review procedures. The substance of these constitutional functions was common to all the Greek city-states, but the institutional architecture and the procedural mechanisms for the preparation and enactment of decrees varied according to the specific features of each political regime. The different ways in which this basic Greek institutional toolset was

Divided Power in Ancient Greece: Decision-Making and Institutions in the Classical and Hellenistic Polis. Alberto Esu, Oxford University Press. © Alberto Esu 2024. DOI: 10.1093/oso/9780198883951.003.0007

EPILOGUE   215

applied are a clear manifestation of the different natures of various constitutional regimes, and shaped the way decision-making unfolded through the various institutions of each regime. The arrangement of institutions was key in shaping the political ideas of each Greek community. Understanding institutional design is therefore not a matter of antiquarian interest, and taking institutional design seriously does not mean falling into the so-called 'constitutional law trap'. It means understanding the fundamental factors sustaining and implementing the political ideologies in the varied political landscape of Classical and Hellenistic Greece.

The comparative analysis of the decree-making institutions of different *poleis* has uncovered different institutional manifestations of divided power and the flexible and adaptable nature of this political and legal notion. Two intertwined aspects have emerged as key components of Greek divided power: the institutionalized practice of delegation of authority between different decree-making bodies and the legal control of the enactments of councils and assemblies as a systemic part of the political decision-making.

Divided power between councils or probouleutic officials and assemblies went beyond *probouleusis* and the agenda-setting function and also encompassed a system of delegation of deliberative authority, which went back to the council for specific purposes. As shown in Chapter 2, this was most notably in display in Classical Athenian decree-making. The Athenians delegated decision-making authority to the council through specific clauses inserted in decrees, which consistently attest to this practice throughout the fifth and the fourth centuries. As a paramount institution of Athenian divided power, the council was often granted full powers to enact decrees, and, as a result, this institution could complement the decisions of the assembly through additional decrees. I have argued that this system of delegation was specifically designed to divide the decree-making power in a flexible and dynamic fashion so that a decree was the result of multiple deliberative stages which started with the preliminary deliberation in the council, continued in the assembly, and finally went back again in the council, when necessary. Moreover, by sitting every day in the council, the Athenian councillors acquired a thorough knowledge of the technical aspects of administration in several areas ranging from the navy, cult administration, diplomacy, and public finances. This system therefore allowed dividing power as well as creating legitimacy and consensus around a decision, thanks to the expertise of different institutions. If Classical Athens offers the best evidence for the delegation to the council, this practice was in no way limited to the Athenian democracy. This book has shown that delegation was a widespread feature of Greek divided power in Classical and Hellenistic decree-making in *poleis* with demographics, social compositions, and political cultures different from Athens, such as late Classical Mytilene and Hellenistic Megalopolis, which offer two case studies for continuities and changes in institutional practice in the first half of the Hellenistic

216   DIVIDED POWER IN ANCIENT GREECE

period. The case of Megalopolis, in particular, has illustrated the use of delegation from the assembly to an elitist council in which delegation served the purpose of transferring power to an institution representative of the city elites.

In fact, the notion of divided power was not only typical of democracies but was also foundational for the legitimation of power in Greek oligarchies. The relationship between council, officials, and assembly in Sparta underscores the importance in Greek political decision-making of combining decree-making and respect for the laws. While ad hoc delegation granted by a decree of the assembly is attested as a typical feature of democratic divided power in Athens, Mytilene, and Megalopolis, Spartan divided power was structured in such a way as to share systematically the functions of agenda-setting (*probouleusis*) and legal control (*nomophulakia*) between the *gerousia* and the ephors. The strong empowerment of the Spartan magistrates vis-à-vis the popular assembly had two important implications. First, this set-up meant that there was no need to delegate power from the assembly, as *gerontes* and ephors were already given by the Great Rhetra the power of keeping the decision-making in balance. As a result, institutional interaction between powerful offices preparing the bills and controlling their legal validity was constitutionalized and made permanent. Second, it offered a clear example of how different procedures fostered distinctive collective decision-making behaviours. While deliberation at the probouleutic stage enhanced consensus-oriented practices between *gerontes*, ephors, and citizens in the assembly, the guardianship of the laws was carried out according to majority procedure in the *gerousia* in order to safeguard legal stability. The Spartan system of deliberation highlights the effort made by the Spartans to institutionalize divided power in such a way that no institutions could claim hegemony of the system. This was achieved by means of sophisticated procedures of mutual control between magistracies, but without creating popular institutions with the role of reviewing legislation.

Legal control over popular enactments is another fundamental component of Greek divided power. As the analysis of the Spartan deliberative procedure highlights, Sparta's political institutions represent a local variation of divided power, which fitted into a broader Greek understanding of divided power as striking a balance between popular deliberation and respect of the established laws. The tension between these two aspects of divided power is also well illustrated by the innovative role of the procedure of *adeia* in fifth-century Athenian political decision-making. The institution of *adeia* for changing an entrenched decree was the first Athenian attempt to introduce a more sophisticated system of legal control of the enactments of the *dēmos*, in which the *dēmos* itself was in charge. This was obtained by means of different procedural stages which divided the deliberative power within the same institution. As in Sparta, different voting procedures fostered distinctive collective behaviours in decree-making. While the first vote to grant *adeia* by ballot recorded the civic consensus to change a piece

EPILOGUE 217

of entrenched legislation, the second vote on the decree envisaged standard deliberation in the assembly with different proposals and amendments from the floor. The rationale of *adeia* was to allow the *dēmos* to modify existing decrees without undermining the nomothetic ideology of the immutability of the laws and of entrenched enactments. The institution of *adeia* was a first step towards the democratization of law-making in the Athenian democracy, which will acquire a systematic and coherent form with the fourth-century *nomothesia*. The new procedures of law-making will be central to Athenian divided power for both its institutional complexity involving deliberative and judicial institutions and legal and political implications. Athenian *nomothesia* represented the highest point of ancient Greek constitutionalism for its capacity to combine popular power with legal coherence and consistency. Yet, the institutional balance designed in fourth-century Athens emerged as a unique experience in Greek history. Unlike other institutions and cultural products of Classical Athens, the sophisticated law-making procedure did not survive the end of the Classical democracy after the Lamian War, and has no real parallel in the political history of other Greek communities.[1]

The institutional complexity that underpinned Greek divided power did not only involve deliberative bodies. Courts of law played a key role in keeping together popular power and the rule of law. This is especially evident from the Athenian procedure of *graphē paranomōn* which was designed to protect primarily the hierarchy between laws and decrees. Both the institutional design and the discursive practices attested in the *graphē paranomōn* speeches show that the Athenian judges did not act as policy-makers, but the courts were normatively committed to provide *judicial* decisions about the indicted decree. As a result, the *graphē paranomōn* fostered a counter-deliberative behaviour in the judges which was different from that of citizens sitting in the council and in the assembly. The lawcourts, thus, were not sovereign in the Athenian *politeia*, but through the relevant procedures of judicial review they protected the *nomoi* and assured that the decree-making process abided by the constitutional order. Despite being at odds with the consensus-based working of Athenian political decision-making, this form of majoritarian judicial review complements the more deliberative aspects of Athenian democratic decision-making by safeguarding the constitutional superiority of the laws without diminishing popular power. Similarly, other judicial review procedures were in force in other Greek *poleis* in the Hellenistic

---

[1] There is evidence of several decrees that were upgraded to the level of laws by *nomographoi* in Aegiale on Amorgus (*IG* XII, 7 515), as well as in Hermione (*IG* IV 679), Megalopolis (*I.Magnesia* 38), and Samos of Caphaellenia (*I.Magnesia* 35). These cases suggest that, unlike in the Athenian *nomothesia*, the hierarchy between decrees and laws was blurred and a decree could simply become a law by a special vote of a body (cf. §6.3). Hellenistic cases of laws distinguishing more clearly the procedure of law-making from those of decree-making may be glimpsed in some decrees of Cnidus (*I.Magnesia* 56), the Acarnanian League (*IG* IX, I² 583), and Corcyra (*IG* IX, I 694) with Canevaro (2016a).

218   DIVIDED POWER IN ANCIENT GREECE

period, in which small courts of foreign judges performed the same function of checking that decrees passed by deliberative bodies were consistent with the laws.[2]

This book has proposed a more nuanced and multi-faceted view of Greek decree-making and has placed it within current debates about political institutions and sovereignty in the political sciences and constitutional theory. The authority to decide on a decree was not limited to procedures of approval in the assembly, but could be transferred to other institutions through specifically designed clauses or other procedures. This shows that no institution was the single holder of political sovereignty. Greek political institutions were designed to avoid concentration of power in the realm of deliberation (as in most other realms of political power), and this becomes even more evident if we try to apply the modern concept of 'sovereignty of an institution' to the context of Greek *poleis*. In an important contribution to the concept of sovereignty, the constitutional theorist Troper singles out three types of 'sovereignty', using German terminology: (1) *Souveränität* indicates the supreme legal personality of a state, (2) *Staatsgewalt* expresses the exclusive powers of the state (e.g. power of coercion), and (3) *Herrschaft* is the 'power of domination of an organ' of the state.[3] According to the third definition, the institutional persona that holds the *Herrschaft* is one who 'is not only habitually obeyed, but who does not obey anyone or rather who is not subject to any legal limits'.[4] While the notions of sovereignty behind definitions (1) and (2) are found in ancient Greece,[5] identifying in the political decision-making practices an institution possessing a permanent *Herrschaft* to make political decisions has proven problematic. This investigation has demonstrated that Greek decision-making institutions not only had to obey the laws and follow the proper legal procedures, but there were no institutions that could work, and therefore be 'sovereign', without the joint contribution of another constitutional body.

The workings of the institutions of Classical Athens in the deliberative process clearly demonstrate the non-applicability of the concept of sovereignty as *Herrschaft*. In fourth-century Athens, the assembly was the central institution in the decree-making process as the approval of the *dēmos* was always necessary. Yet, unlike modern legislative assemblies, the Athenian assembly could not summon itself and could not discuss any matter without the preliminary deliberation of the council. The interaction with the council was necessary to start the decree-making process. In fact, the council could be made *kurios* to enact decrees and yet, as my

---

[2] This is also a point recently reaffirmed by Ma (2018) 283.   [3] Troper (2012) 353.

[4] Troper (2012) 364. The second definition of sovereignty was formulated on the British model of 'sovereignty of parliament'. Hart (1961) criticized this conception and pointed out that in many other political regimes the authority of the parliament is limited by the constitution and the constitutional courts. Kelsen (1961), on the other hand, noted that parliaments could be considered sovereign even when limited by a written constitution, as they can change the constitution through constituent procedures.

[5] See Harris (2013c) 21–59 and 60–98; see also important points on sovereignty raised by Lundgreen (2022); Smith (2022).

EPILOGUE   219

study of the *kurios*-related terminology within its institutional context shows, this does not mean that the council became 'sovereign' over the other institutions. In these cases, the council still had to apply the laws and to respect the constitutional limits of other institutions such as the assembly, the officials, and the lawcourts. The delegation of decree-making authority highlighted that the deliberative power was transferrable and never held exclusively by one single agency. Indeed, even if the powers delegated to the council were ad hoc powers, these went beyond the normal enforcement of regulations passed by the assembly. When the Athenian council was empowered to fill the gaps in a decree, this was real decree-making authority, and the council did not need to refer back to the assembly. Similarly, a decree passed by the council and ratified by the assembly could also be indicted through the *graphē paranomōn* and repealed by the lawcourts on legal grounds in order to ensure the legality of all enactments. Again, when judging a case of *graphē paranomōn*, the lawcourts did not hold *Herrschaft* over the Athenian *politeia*. The Athenian lawcourts were 'passive organs' that could not autonomously block the decision-making process, like a proper 'sovereign' of the constitution.[6] More importantly, Athenian courts were not meant to consider the merit of policies in decrees. The close connection between institutional design and discursive and informal practices in the Athenian decision-making shows that political actors acted differently in the deliberative bodies (i.e. the council and the assembly) and in court. The Athenian judges were not expected to make political decisions and modify or replace decrees of the council and the assembly; they could only decide whether the decree was legal or not. This is important from a new institutionalist perspective. As North explains, it is necessary to distinguish between the rules and the players to build an effective theory of institutions.[7] While we cannot completely rule out that an individual Athenian judge voted to repeal or confirm the legality of decrees on political or personal grounds, the prescriptive rationale of the judicial review of decrees that I reconstructed from both the procedures and discursive norms did not support such behaviour.

The widespread view that we know nothing about how the Athenian judges made up their mind in court does not fully consider some important contemporary sources about verdicts. In fact, when mentioning unjust verdicts of the courts, Athenian litigants never cite political expediency as the reason for losing a case. A good and relevant example is given in the opening of Apollodorus' *Against Neaera*, when Theomnestus says that Apollodorus was charged with having proposed an illegal decree about the use of the stratiotic fund and his opponent Stephanus won the case because he had provided false witnesses in court ([Dem.] 59.6–8). In the *Against Ctesiphon*, Aeschines recalls an episode in which the prominent leader Thrasybulus was brought to court by Archinus and convicted

---

[6] Pasquino (2010) 32–3.   [7] North (1990) 4–5.

220 DIVIDED POWER IN ANCIENT GREECE

of proposing an illegal decree despite his record of public service (Aeschin. 3.195). In *On the Crown*, Demosthenes affirms that he was accused of proposing illegal decrees, but he says that he was acquitted because his decrees were considered legal (Dem. 18.249–50: τὰς γραφὰς ἀπέφευγον, ἔννομα καὶ γράφειν καὶ λέγειν ἀπεδεικνύμην). Athenian judicial review was primarily concerned with maintaining the legal consistency and coherence of the written laws, and behaviour by citizens and judges within this institution that did not abide by this basic concern is to be considered an exception to the normative expectations of the relevant institution rather than the rule.[8]

When we move beyond the Athenian model of divided power, this analysis is further confirmed. The reconstruction of the Spartan deliberative process demonstrates that in Sparta there was no single sovereign institution but an oligarchic form of divided power. Although in Sparta boards of magistrates, such as the *gerousia* and the five ephors, enjoyed wide powers, ratification in the assembly was always necessary for passing a decree. The *gerontes* could block a decision approved by the assembly, but similarly to the Athenian lawcourts, they could not impose a political decision on the *damos*. Despite Demosthenes' harsh criticism in *Against Leptines*, in which the *gerousia* is called 'master of the many' (δεσπότης ἐστὶ τῶν πολλῶν) and 'with authority over the *politeia*' (τῆς πολιτείας κυρίωι γενέσθαι), the *gerontes* could not pass decisions without the consent of the assembly and the ephors (Dem. 20.107). The collaboration between the two boards of officials was always needed in order to enact decrees.

The modern concept of sovereignty of an institution has thus proven inadequate to describe the deliberative power of the Greek *poleis* of the Classical and Hellenistic periods. Both in democracies and in non-democratic regimes, power was conceptualized as the power of the citizens (the whole people in democracies and mostly those who met the property qualifications in oligarchies) who made decisions according to the laws and within the official institutions of the *polis*. Such decision-making institutions of the Greek *poleis* were organized in such a way as to implement a form of divided power. This underpinned a complex multi-level system in which a plurality of institutional actors, each with their own expertise, practices, and rules, interacted to enact political decisions in the form of decrees. The flexible nature of Greek divided power could accommodate different and sometimes contrasting needs. As the evidence has shown, deliberation and vote on a decree in the assembly followed formal rules and discursive practices that promoted consensus on a policy, whereas legal procedures and the voting system in civic and foreign courts or in boards of officials judging the

---

[8] Cf. also Dem. 21.218; Hyp. *Eux.* 15–18. Evidence for the verdicts of Athenian trials is collected and discussed in Harris (2018c) and Siron (2020) and confirm this picture. See also the similar views of Rubinstein (2008); Sickinger (2008). Cf. also Ismard (2012a) discussing the '*perimetré de la legalitè*' in Classical Athens.

EPILOGUE 221

legality of a decree produced a yes-or-no alternative without room for deliberation and for the creation of consensus on the matter regulated by the decree. Political decisions made by decrees of the council and of the assembly enshrined these distinct values and discursive practices. Each institutional level contributed a different facet to the overall process, through formal procedures enlisting 'deliberative' or 'judicial' expertise interacting with each other. This interaction was designed to combine the decision-making power of the people with the respect of the laws and of legal procedure, but was also meant to promote horizontal expertise, which citizens acquired by acting within the formal institutions of the state.

This book has emphasized the ways in which political institutions were designed and worked in practice, as well as the normative relevance of divided power in regulating political life. Yet it is also important to point out that the institutions of divided power did not always lived up to their normative standards. In order for divided power to be effective, the rule of law should not be undermined by internal or external factors. Athens at the end of the fifth century provides a good example. Cleon's abuse of the lawcourts for engaging in political strife against his opponents shows that political actors could employ an institutional setting for the wrong purpose.[9] In this case, Cleon introduced the practice of attacking enemies for political reasons in the lawcourts, which, as shown in Chapter 6, were not conceived as deliberative bodies. On the other hand, Cleon used judicial discourse and tactics in assembly debates, as is clearly shown in Thucydides' Mytilenian debate.[10] Cleon's misuse of Athenian political institutions and the crossing of the proper institutional boundaries therefore undermined divided power and the rule of law.

A similar dynamic of social conflict which started through an abuse of the institutions of divided power is exemplified in another and more disruptive case: the famous fifth-century *stasis* at Corcyra (Thuc. 3.70–81).[11] In 427 BCE, a group of prisoners from Corcyra were released by Corinth on the condition that they would convince the Corcyreans to break their alliance with Athens and side with the Peloponnesians.[12] However, the Corcyreans in the assembly voted to remain allies of the Athenians, but to be friends with the Peloponnesians (ἐψηφίσαντο Κερκυραῖοι Ἀθηναίοις μὲν ξύμμαχοι εἶναι κατὰ τὰ ξυγκείμενα,

---

[9] Harris (2013c) 305–44; Saldutti (2014). On the role of demagogues in Classical Athens and political communication in the fifth century, see Mann (2007). For demagogic leaders in the Hellenistic period see Simonton (2022).

[10] Thuc. 3.37–50 with Harris (2013c) 94–109. The trend set by Cleon eventually led to dramatic results such as the trial of the generals of the battle of Arginousai in 405 BCE. Cf. Xen. *Hell.* 1.7.34.

[11] Thucydides states that many other *staseis* broke out in the Greek world as a consequence of the ideological polarization between pro-Athenian democrats and pro-Spartan oligarchs (Thuc. 3.82.1). For this social and ideological division in Greek interstate relations in the Peloponnesian War see Low (2007) 54.

[12] On the moral values in the debate between Corinthians and Corcyreans see Wilson (1987); Low (2007) 176.

Πελοποννησίοις δὲ φίλοι ὥσπερ καὶ πρότερον). The former prisoners then brought Peithias, a democrat and *proxenos* of the Athenians, into court with a charge of trying to enslave the city to Athens (3.70.3). After being acquitted, Peithias retaliated by prosecuting the five wealthiest among the former prisoners on the charge of cutting vine-poles from the sanctuaries of Zeus and Alcinous. The court convicted them to pay a fine of one stater, but being unable to pay, the convicted men went to the temples as suppliants and asked to pay in instalments. When Peithias convinced the council, of which he was a member (ἐτύγχανε γὰρ καὶ βουλῆς ὤν), to enforce the penalty, the convicted men armed with daggers entered into the council and killed Peithias and sixty others among the councillors and private citizens (3.70.6). The killing of Peithias led to the beginning of a violent *stasis* and shows how the political and social conflict was initially channelled through the institutions of the *polis*, which proved unable to normalize it. As I noted throughout the book, Greek divided power worked when each institution performed its role correctly according to a set of formal norms, shared practices, and ideas embedded in the institutions themselves, on which the legitimacy of the *polis*'s decisions was ultimately based. The illegitimate use of the judicial and deliberative institutions at Corcyra was one (but certainly not the only) factor that contributed to the outbreak of the conflict. Both the supporters of the oligarchy and the democrats abused the role of the courts, which consisted in applying the laws and trying individuals according to fair procedures. This failure inevitably provoked a breakdown of the overall system, because it undermined the legitimizing function of divided power.

High-level social conflict and mistrust could lead to improper use of trials for political reasons.[13] The case of Corcyra shows that local constitutional conflict rooted in socio-political polarization unfolded in the judicial institutions as well as in the council and in the assembly. While the abuse of the judiciary by both the oligarchs and Peithias undermined the legitimacy of the courts' verdicts, Peithias also tried crushing the oligarchs in the council and in the assembly. According to Thucydides, the convicted men acted upon the pressure of the legal conviction and because of Peithias' intention to persuade the assembly to pass an offensive military alliance with Athens (3.70.6).[14] Peithias' move would have reversed the previous decision of the Corcyrean assembly and the consensus reached in the community to remain friends of the Peloponnesians.[15] This would have obviously

---

[13] This is not only a matter of personal mistrust between individuals, but also of the breakdown of the impersonal trust between social groups of the institutions of the city.

[14] By using the adverb ἅμα, Thucydides stresses the connection of the two causes of *stasis*, that is, the court's conviction and the oligarchs' concern for a new decision in the assembly (Thuc. 3.70.6: οἱ δ' ἐπειδὴ τῷ τε νόμῳ ἐξείργοντο καὶ ἅμα ἐπυνθάνοντο τὸν Πειθίαν, ἕως ἔτι βουλῆς ἐστί, μέλλειν τὸ πλῆθος ἀναπείσειν τοὺς αὐτοὺς Ἀθηναίοις φίλους τε καὶ ἐχθροὺς νομίζειν).

[15] Cf. the split vote in the Athenian assembly that reversed the previous decision of the Athenians about Mytilene after Cleon's aggressive speech (Thuc. 3.49.1). Cf. Budelmann (2018) 198, who shows from a cognitive perspective that the *dēmos* was understood normally as a unitary and unanimous entity and the internal division was portrayed as 'deviations from the norm'.

EPILOGUE   223

excluded the pro-Corinthian citizens and split the community in the assembly. The normative features of divided power and the two different types of behaviour expected in courts (i.e. fair application of the laws by majority rule) and in the council and assembly (i.e. political decision-making by consensus to create *homonoia*) were disrespected and marked the outbreak of a violent *stasis*.[16]

A series of inscribed decrees from fourth-century Telos relating to the events of a *stasis* and the following reconciliation (*IG* XII 4.132) are also evidence of a breakdown of a system of divided power as a consequence of judicial decisions considered illegitimate by part of the community.[17] In the reconciliation clause (Face A, fr. b, 40–3), the reasons for *stasis* are clearly identified. It is stated that there should be a reconciliation between the people and 'those at odds with the people of the Telians (τοὺς διαφερομένους Τηλί[ων]) about the cases, both sacred and public, which were lost in court (ὀφλόντες ἐν τοῖς δικαστηρίοις) and the defendants were protesting that they had lost unjustly ([μὴ δικ]αίως ὀφλῆκεν)'. These resulted in confiscations of properties to pay the fines (48–51). Civil conflict broke out because some wealthy members of the community protested against the decisions of the courts, which, as we have seen, were a key institution of Greek divided power. The contested legitimacy of the court verdicts led to the breakdown of the system of divided power.

The Telos dossier also offers important insights into Greek political terminology of conflict and its connection with institutional practice. The Telian reconciliation documents consistently refer to those who initiated the internal unrest with the expression *diapheromenoi* ('those at odds with the Telians').[18] The term is closely related with the word *diaphora*, which is a recurring expression in contexts of *stasis* to describe a deep disagreement in the community and the rupture of the normal political dialectic and institutionalized decision-making.[19] The Nakone reconciliation agreement periphrastically defines *stasis* as a division among citizens competing about the common affairs (10–11: ἁ διαφορὰ τῶμ πολιτᾶν). The term even recurs at the beginning of Greek historiography, when Herodotus calls *diaphorē* the ancestral division between Persians and Greeks (Hdt. 1.1). The term *diaphora* and the conceptually connected notion of *stasis* are inconsistent with normal political competition and dissent, and point to Greek conceptualizations of civic conflict as a disfunction of society, institutions, and a disease of the body politic.[20]

[16] Price (2001) 11–22 for an analysis of the *stasis* at Corcyra as paradigmatic of the pathology of *stasis* in Thucydides' narrative.

[17] For an analysis of this important document see Thür (2011); B. D. Gray (2013) 393–5, (2015) 94–8; Scafuro (2014b) 368–9; Börm (2019) 183–8 with review of Fabiani (2021); Simonton (2019) 187–209.

[18] Simonton (2019) 195 n. 36 with epigraphical examples.

[19] See the text with translation and in-depth discussion in B. D. Gray (2015) 37–41.

[20] van Wees (2008); Brock (2013) 69–82 for the Greek image of the political community as a body and *stasis* as the disease of the body politic, e.g. Polyb. 2.39.1–4.

Preserving the divided power which keeps the institutions of the community together goes hand in hand with a general desire for *homonoia* ('same-mindedness').[21] Mentions of *homonoia* in the *polis* occur as frequently as mentions of *stasis* and show that on a normative level *stasis* was not considered a normal form of political and social conflict.[22] Concerning the role of the decision-making institutions and procedures, one major argument of this book is that divided power institutions are not only descriptive categories useful to reconstruct Greek political activity, but they also have a prescriptive role in shaping the behaviours and expectations of political actors in different institutions. The principle of divided power was normatively sustained by the idea of creating social cohesion according to some basic tenets of Greek civic culture, such as the primacy of the laws and the need to preserve *homonoia* (e.g. Xen. *Mem.* 4.4.16; *IvO* 260).[23] In terms of institutional design, these social norms created different, yet integrated layers in the decision-making both geared towards legitimacy. While a decision-making layer in the councils and assemblies attempted systematically to create legitimacy about policies through consensus and *homonoia*, another layer in the judicial institution created a complementary level of legitimacy by applying the laws. The necessity of institutions which combined these two distinct levels of legitimacy, it is at the origin of the development of divided power, spread across several institutions that collaborated for creating and integrating consensus, legality, and legitimacy about communal decisions. The creation of complex procedures to avoid the breakdown of the institutional system shows that the pursuit of *homonoia* within a system of divided power was not only an ideological construction, evidenced by oratory, inscriptions, and philosophy, which the Greek communities revered; it was also part of the political *Realien* of Greek political life.[24]

In conclusion, this book has contributed to bridging the gap between ancient history, legal history, and political science. The use of methodologies from political science and legal theory has suggested how interdisciplinary research between classical scholarship and the modern social sciences can provide valuable tools to renew the traditional field of Greek political and institutional history. The legal and political concept of divided power, employed within a historical institutionalist framework, has also allowed us to appreciate the 'unity' of Greek decision-

---

[21] For the cult of *homonoia* across the cities of the entire Greek world see Thériault (1996) 6–70 which sets out all the evidence and remarks the desire of the Greek communities of the Classical and Hellenistic periods to preserve harmony in the city.

[22] The most recent treatment of Hellenistic *staseis* by Börm (2019) views *stasis* not as an extraordinary breakdown of the political system but as a structural aspect of Greek civic life, and interprets civic conflict in terms of a Greek agonistic mentality and intra-elite competition for power. Consequently, amnesty agreements were a matter of reconciling conflicting elites. For views connecting moral norms of justice and lawfulness and reconciliation, see B. D. Gray (2015); Joyce (2022).

[23] Roy (2008).

[24] In general, on the Hellenistic intellectual and civic debates about civic solidarity, cosmopolitanism, and elite power see B. D. Gray (2018a) 68–92, (2018b) 187–225.

EPILOGUE 225

making, showing how the Greek *poleis* shared the same institutional toolset with which they organized their systems of political deliberation.

Behind this book's claim that institutions matter as the basic organizational forms of political action there is the idea that Greek decision-making institutions are closely connected with the values and ideas framing the civic morality of a *polis*. Throughout the book, my argument has been that deliberative institutions and other constitutional bodies involved in decree-making should not be analysed only descriptively, or treated as normatively and culturally irrelevant—considered merely arenas for elite competition. Political culture and social behaviour do not develop in an institutional vacuum. Institutions are key elements which shaped the way deliberation and political decisions were made and assessed by political actors in the different decision-making institutions. The dynamic picture of the interaction between institutions in the decree-making process goes beyond functionalist views and constitutional description of the workings of Greek political systems. Divided power was a constitutional ideal as well as a practice enshrined in the laws and institutions, and its application required a constant effort to live up to its standards from the Greek communities of the Classical and Hellenistic periods. In this sense, studying divided power in ancient Greece represents a way to understand how ideas and institutions are relevant to any constitutional regime and its society. It was a system that merged and combined different procedures and distinct social and ideological concerns, such as the usefulness of good deliberation with considerations of legality, in order to create a decision-making system coherent and consistent with the *ethos* of the constitution.

Bibliography

Abbott, K. W., Keohane R. O., Moravcsik, A., Slaughter, A.-M., and Snidal, D. (2000), 'The Concept of Legalization', *International Organization* 54.3, 401–19.

Accattino, P. (1986), *L'anatomia della città nella Politica di Aristotele*. Turin.

Accattino, P. and Curnis, M. (eds) (2013), *Aristotele. La Politica. Libro III*. Rome.

Africa, T. W. (1961), *Phylarchus and the Spartan Revolution*. Berkeley and Cambridge.

Ampolo, C. (1983), 'La *boule demosie* di Chio: un consiglio "popolare"', *PdP* 38, 401–16.

Anderson, G. (2009), 'The Personality of the Greek State', *JHS* 129, 1–22.

Ando, C. (2018), 'The Political Economy of the Hellenistic Polis: Comparative and Modern Perspectives', in N. Luraghi and H. Börm (eds), *The Polis in the Hellenistic World*. Stuttgart, 9–26.

Andrewes, A. (1956), *The Greek Tyrants*. London.

Andrewes, A. (1966), 'The Government of Classical Sparta', in E. Badian (ed.), *Ancient Society and Institutions. Studies Presented to Victor Ehrenberg on His 75th Birthday*. Oxford, 1–20.

Arato, A. (2017), *The Adventures of Constituent Power: Beyond Revolutions?* Cambridge.

Arena, V. and Prag, J. (eds) (2022), *A Companion to the Political Culture of the Roman Republic*. Hoboken.

Arnaoutoglou, I. (2015), 'Cult Associations and Politics: Worshipping Bendis in Classical and Hellenistic Athens', in V. Gabrielsen and C. A. Thomsen (eds), *Private Associations and the Public Sphere. Proceedings of a Symposium Held at the Royal Danish Academy of Sciences and Letters, 9–11 September 2010*. Copenhagen, 25–56.

Arnaoutoglou, I. (2016), 'Rewards to Informers: Response to Lene Rubinstein', in D. F. Leão and G. Thür (eds), *Symposion 2015: Vorträge zur griechischen und hellenistischen Rechtgeschicht*. Vienna, 451–9.

Arvidsson, M., Brännström, L., and Minkkinen, P. (eds) (2020), *Constituent Power: Law, Popular Rule and Politics*. Edinburgh.

Azoulay, V. (forthcoming), 'Athenian Democracy, Honours, and Punishments: Towards a Connected History', in D. Cairns, M. Canevaro, K. Mantzouranis and M. Zaccarini (eds), *Aspects of Honour in the Ancient Greek World*, Edinburgh.

Azoulay, V. and Ismard, P. (2007), 'Les lieux du politique dans l'Athènes classique: entre structures institutionnelles, idéologie civique et pratiques sociales', in P. Schmitt Pantel and F. de Polignac (eds), *Athènes et le politique. dans le sillage de Claude Mossé*. Paris, 271–309.

Azoulay, V. and Ismard, P. (2011), *Clisthène et Lycurgue d'Athènes : autour du politique dans la cité classique*, Paris.

Balot, R. K. (2017), 'Was Thucydides a Political Philosopher?', in R. K. Balot, S. Forsdyke, and E. Forster (eds), *The Oxford Handbook of Thucydides*. Oxford, 319–38.

Banfi, A. (2010), *La sovranità della legge: la legislazione di Demetrio Falereo ad Atene (317–307 a.C.)*. Milan.

Banfi, A. (2012), 'Qualche considerazione intorno al controllo di legittimità a Atene', in B. Legras and G. Thür (eds), *Symposion 2011: études d'histoire du droit grec et hellénistique*. Vienna, 49–76.

228 BIBLIOGRAPHY

Barbato, M. (2017), 'Using the Past to Shape the Future: Ancestors, Institutions and Ideology in Aeschin. 2.74–8', in E. Franchi and G. Proietti (eds), *Conflict in Communities: Forward-Looking Memories in Classical Athens*. Trento, 213–53.

Barbato, M. (2020), *The Ideology of Democratic Athens: Institutions, Orators and the Mythical Past*. Edinburgh.

Barbato, M. (2021), 'For Themistocles of Phrearrhioi, on Account of Honour": Ostracism, Honour and the Nature of Athenian Politics', *CQ* 71.2, 500–19.

Barbato, M. (2023), 'Elite Politicians or Ordinary Citizens? Decree Making and Political Friendship in Fifth-Century Athens', *Klio* 105.2, 403–48.

Barker, E. T. E. (2009), *Entering the Agon: Dissent and Authority in Homer, Historiography and Tragedy*. Oxford.

Bartels, M. (2017), *Plato's Pragmatic Project: A Reading of Plato's Laws*. Stuttgart.

Bearzot, C. (2003), 'L'uso dei documenti in Tucidide', in A. M. Biraschi, P. Desideri, S. Roda, and G. Zecchini (eds), *L'uso dei documenti nella storiografia antica*, Naples, 265–314.

Bearzot, C. (2007), 'I *nomophylakes* in due lemmi di Polluce (VIII 94 νομοφύλακες VIII 102 οἱ ἔνδεκα)', in C. Bearzot, F. Landucci Gattinoni, and G. Zecchini (eds), *L'Onomasticon di Giulio Polluce. Tra lessicografia e antiquaria*. Milan, 43–67.

Bearzot, C. (2012), '*Nomophylakes* e *nomophylakia* nella *Politica* di Aristotele', in M. Polito and C. Talamo (eds), *Istituzioni e costituzioni in Aristotele tra storiografia e pensiero politico*. Rome, 29–47.

Beck, H. (2013), *A Companion to Ancient Greek Government*. Chichester.

Beck, H. and Smith, P. J. (2018), *Megarian Moments: The Local World of an Ancient Greek City-State*. Montreal.

Bell, J., Elliott, M., Varuhas, J., and Murray, P. (2016), *Public Law Adjudication in Common Law Systems: Process and Substance*. London.

Bencivenni, A. (2003), *Progetti di riforme costituzionali nelle epigrafi greche dei secoli IV–II a.C.* Bologna.

Bencivenni, A. (2010), 'Il re scrive, la città iscrive: la pubblicazione su pietra delle epistole regie nell'Asia ellenistica', *Studi Ellenistici* 24, 149–78.

Bencivenni, A. (2014), 'The King's World: Hellenistic Royal Letters in Inscriptions', in K. Radner (ed.), *State Correspondence in the Ancient World: From the New Kingdom to the Roman Empire*. Oxford, 141–64.

Berent, M. (2000), 'Anthropology and the Classics: War, Violence and the Stateless *Polis*'. *CQ* 50, 257–89.

Bernardo, G. (2019), *Comandantes e Covardes: Honra e Mérito em Sparta*. São Paulo.

Bers, V. (1986), 'Dikastic Thorubos', in P. Cartledge and F. D. Harvey (eds), *Crux: Essays in Greek History Presented to G. E. M. de Ste. Croix on His 75 Birthday*. London, 1–15.

Bers, V. (2003), *Demosthenes, Speeches 50–59*. Austin.

Bertelli, L. (1994), 'Modelli costituzionali e analisi politica prima di Platone', in L. Bertelli and P. Donini (eds), *Filosofia, Politica, Retorica: intersezioni possibili*. Milan, 27–83.

Bertelli, L. (2004), 'La Sparta di Aristotele: un ambiguo paradigma o la crisi di un modello?', *RSA* 34, 9–71.

Bertelli, L. (2017), '*Metabole politeion*', in G. Besso and F. Pezzoli (eds), *Politeia en logois: studi sul pensiero politico greco*. Alessandria, 67–116.

Bertelli, L. (2018), 'The *Athenaion Politeia* and Aristotle's Political Thought', in C. Bearzot, M. Canevaro, T. Gargiulo, and E. Poddighe (eds), *Athenaion Politeiai tra storia, politica e sociologia: Aristotle e Ps. Senofonte*. Milan, 71–86.

BIBLIOGRAPHY 229

Bertelli, L. (Besso, G. and Pezzoli F. eds) (2017), *Politeia en logois: studi sul pensiero politico greco*. Alessandria.

Biagi, C. (1785), *Tractatus de decretis Atheniensium in quo illustrator singulare decretum Atheniense ex Museo Equitis ac Senatoris Iacobi Nanii Veneti*. Rome.

Bickel, A. M. (1986), *Least Dangerous Branch: The Supreme Court at the Bar of Politics*. New Haven (2nd edition).

Bingham, T. (2010), *The Rule of Law*. London.

Biscardi, A. (1982), *Diritto greco antico*. Varese.

Blamire, A. (2001), 'Athenian Finance 454–404 BCE', *Hesperia* 70, 99–106.

Blanshard, A. J. (2004), 'What Counts as the Demos? Some Notes about the Relationship between the Jury and the "People" in Classical Athens', *Phoenix* 58, 28–48.

Blok, J. (2017), *Citizenship in Classical Athens*. Cambridge.

Blok, J. (2021), 'Greek Numerals and Numeracy', in Y. Suto (ed.), *Transmission and Organization of Knowledge in the Ancient Mediterranean World*. Vienna, 21–40.

Blyth, M., Helgadottir, O., and Kring, W. (2016), 'Ideas and Historical Institutionalism', in O. Fioretos, T. Falleti, and A. Sheingate (eds), *The Oxford Handbook of Historical Institutionalism*. Oxford, 143–59.

Blümel, W. (2007), 'Neue Inschriften aus Karien III', *EA* 40, 41–8.

Bodin, J. (1606), *The Six Bookes of a Commonweale*. K. D. MacRae (ed.), R. Knolles (trans.), 1962. Cambridge, MA.

Boegehold, A. (1963), 'Toward a Study of Athenian Voting Procedure', *Hesperia* 32.4, 366–74.

Boegehold, A. (1995), *The Lawcourts at Athens*. Princeton.

Boffo, L. (2013), 'La "presenza" dei re negli archivi delle *poleis* ellenistiche', in M. Faraguna (ed.), *Legal Documents in Ancient Societies*, Vol. IV: *Archives and Archival Documents in Ancient Societies*. Trieste, 201–44.

Boffo, L. and Faraguna, M. (2021), *Le poleis and i loro archivi: studi su pratiche documentarie, istituzioni e società nell'antichità greca*. Trieste.

Bohman, J. (2012), 'Representation in the Deliberative System', in J. Mansbridge and J. Parkinson (eds), *Deliberative Systems—Deliberative Democracy at the Large Scale*. Cambridge, 72–94.

Bordes, J. (1982), *Politeia dans la pensée d' Aristote*. Paris.

Boring, T. (1979), *Literacy in Ancient Sparta*. Leiden.

Börm, H. (2019), *Mordende Mitbürger: Stasis und Bürgerkrieg in griechischen Poleis des Hellenismus*. Stuttgart.

Bouchon, R. and Helly, B. (2015), 'The Thessalian League', in H. Beck and P. Funke (eds), *Federalism in Greek Antiquity*. Cambridge, 213–49.

Bourke, R. (2016), 'Introduction', in R. Bourke and Q. Skinner (eds) (2016), *Popular Sovereignty in Historical Perspective*. Cambridge, 1–14.

Bourke, R. and Skinner, Q. (eds) (2016), *Popular Sovereignty in Historical Perspective*. Cambridge.

Bourriot, F. (1996), '*Kaloi kagathoi, kalokagathia* à Sparte aux époques archaïque et classique', *Historia* 45.2, 129–40.

Bovens, M., Goodin, R., and Schillemans, T. (2014), *The Oxford Handbook of Public Accountability*. Oxford.

Bowden, H. (2005), *Classical Athens and the Delphic Oracle: Divination and Democracy*. Cambridge.

Brennan, G. and Pettit, P. (2004), *The Economy of Esteem: An Essay on Civil and Political Society*. Oxford.

230 BIBLIOGRAPHY

Brenne, S. (2001), *Ostrakismos und Prominenz in Athen. Attische Bürger des 5. Jhs v. Ch. auf den Ostraka*. Vienna.

Brenne, S. (2018), *Die Ostraka vom Kerameikos*, vols 1–2. Wiesbaden.

Brock, R. (2013), *Greek Political Imagery from Homer to Aristotle*. London.

Brock, R. (2015), 'Law and Citizenship in the Greek *Poleis*', in E. M. Harris and M. Canevaro (eds), *The Oxford Handbook of Ancient Greek Law*. Oxford, https://doi.org/10.1093/oxfordhb/9780199599257.013.15

Brown, M. B. (2008), 'Expertise and Deliberative Democracy', in S. Elstub and P. McLaverty (eds), *Deliberative Democracy: Issues and Cases*. Edinburgh, 50–68.

Brun, P. (1983), *Eisphora, Syntaxis, Stratiotika. Recherches sur le finances militaires d'Athènes au IVe siècle av. J.-C.* Paris.

Brun, P. (1988), 'Mytilène et Athènes au IVe siècle av. J. C.', *REA* 90, 373–84.

Brun, P. (2005), *Impérialisme et démocratie à Athènes: inscriptions de l'époque classique (c.500–317 av. J-C)*. Paris.

Budelmann, F. (2018), 'Groups Minds in Classical Athens? Chorus and *Dēmos* as Cases Studies of Collective Action', in M. Anderson, D. Cairns, and M. Sprevak (eds), *Distributed Cognition in Classical Antiquity*. Edinburgh, 190–208.

Burke, E. M. (2010), 'Finances and the Operation of the Athenian Democracy in the "Lycurgan Era"', *AJPh* 10, 393–423.

Byrne, S. (2004), 'Proposers of Athenian State Decrees 286–61 BCE', in A. Matthaiou and G. Malachou (eds), *ΑΤΤΙΚΑΙ ΕΠΙΓΡΑΦΑΙ*. Athens, 141–54.

Cairns, D. L. (1993), *Aidōs: the Psychology and Ethics of Honour and Shame in Ancient Greek Literature*. Oxford.

Cairns, D. L. (1996), 'Hybris, Dishonour, and Thinking Big', *JHS* 124, 1–32.

Cairns, D. L. (1997), 'Review of F. Bourriot, Kalos Kagathos—Kalokagathia: *D'un terme de propagande de sophistes à une notion sociale et philosophique: étude d'histoire athénienne*', *CR* 47, 74–6.

Cairns, D. L. (2011), 'Honour and Shame: Modern Controversies and Ancient Values', *Critical Quarterly* 53.1, 23–41.

Cairns, D. L. (2013a), 'Revenge, Punishment and Justice in Athenian Homicide Law', *Journal of Value Inquiry* 49.4, 645–65.

Cairns, D. L. (2013b), 'Introduction', in D. L. Cairns (ed.) *Tragedy and Archaic Thought*, Swansea, ix–liv.

Cairns, D. L. (2015), 'A Short History of Shudder', in A. Chaniotis and P. Ducrey (eds), *Unveiling Emotions*, Vol. II: *Emotions in Greece and Rome: Texts, Images, and Material Culture*. Stuttgart, 85–107.

Cairns, D. L. (2019a), 'Review of A. Petrovic and I. Petrovic, Inner Purity and Pollution in Greek Religion. Volume I: Early Greek Religion', *Gnomon* 91.6, 481–8.

Cairns, D. L. (ed.) (2019b), *A Cultural History of Emotions in Antiquity*. London.

Cairns, D. L. (2019c), 'Honour and Kingship in Herodotus: Status, Role, and the Limits of Self-Assertion', *Frontiers of Philosophy in China* 14, 75–93.

Cairns, D. L. (2021), 'Anchoring the Tripartite Soul', in E. Poddighe and T. Pontillo (eds), *Resisting and Justifying Changes: How to Make the New Acceptable in the Ancient, Medieval and Early Modern World*. Pisa, 193–221.

Cairns, D. L., Canevaro, M., and Mantzouranis, K. (2020), 'Aristotle on the Causes of Civil Strife: Subjective Dispositions, Proportional Justice and the "Occasions" of *Stasis*', *Maia* 20, 551–70.

Cairns, D. L., Canevaro, M., and Mantzouranis, K. (2022), 'Recognition and Redistribution in Aristotle's Account of *Stasis*', *Polis* 38, 1–34.

BIBLIOGRAPHY 231

Cairns, D. L. and Fulkerson, L. (eds) (2015), *Emotions between Greece and Rome*. London.

Cairns, D. L. and Nelis, D. (eds) (2017), *Emotions in the Classical World: Methods, Approaches, and Directions*. Stuttgart.

Camassa, G. (2009), 'Scrittura e mutamento delle leggi in quattro culture del mondo antico (Mesopotamia, Anatolia ittita, Israele, Grecia)', *Mythos* 3, 67–92.

Camassa, G. (2011a), *Scrittura e mutamento delle leggi nel mondo antico: dal Vicino Oriente alla Grecia di età arcaica e classica*. Rome.

Camassa, G. (2011b), 'Les (nouvelles) lois de Clisthène et leur histoire', in V. Azoulay and P. Ismard (eds), *Clisthène et Lycurgue d'Athenes: autour de la politique dans la cité classique*. Paris, 43–58.

Cammack, D. (2013), *Rethinking Athenian Democracy*. PhD Diss. Harvard.

Cammack, D. (2020a), 'Deliberation and Discussion in Classical Athens', *Journal of Political Philosophy* 29.2, 135–66.

Cammack, D. (2020b), 'Deliberation in Ancient Greek Assembly', *CPh* 115, 486–522.

Cammack, D. (2021), 'Representation in Ancient Greek Democracy', *History of Political Thought* 42.4, 567–601.

Cammack, D. (2022a), 'The Popular Courts in Athenian Democracy', *Journal of Politics* 84.4, 1997–2010.

Cammack, D. (2022b), '*Kratos* and Other Forms of Power in the Two *Athenaion Politeiai*', *Polis* 39, 466–97.

Canevaro, M. (2013a), '*Nomothesia* in Classical Athens: What Sources Should We Believe?', *CQ* 63, 139–60.

Canevaro, M. (2013b), *The Documents in the Attic Orators: Laws and Decrees in the Public Speeches of the Demosthenic Corpus*. Oxford.

Canevaro, M. (2013c), 'The Twilight of *Nomothesia*: Legislation in Early Hellenistic Athens (322–301)', *Dike* 14, 55–85.

Canevaro, M. (2014), 'Commento a Arist. *Pol.* IV 14, 15, 16', in L. Bertelli and M. Moggi (eds), *Aristotele, Politica IV. Introduzione, traduzione e commento*. Rome, 279–377.

Canevaro, M. (2015), 'Making and Changing Laws in Ancient Athens', in E. M. Harris and M. Canevaro, M. (eds), *Oxford Handbook of Ancient Greek Law*. Oxford, https://doi.org/10.1093/oxfordhb/9780199599257.013.4

Canevaro, M. (2016a), 'Lawmaking (*nomothesia*)', in S. M. Goldberg (ed.), *Oxford Classical Dictionary*. Oxford (4th edition).

Canevaro, M. (2016b), 'The Procedure of Demosthenes' *Against Leptines*: How to Repeal (and Replace) an Existing Law', *JHS* 136, 39–58.

Canevaro, M. (2016c), *Demostene*, Contro Leptine: *introduzione, traduzione e commento storico*. Berlin and Boston.

Canevaro, M. (2017a), 'How to Cast a Criminal Out of Athens: Law and Territory in Archaic Attica', in Y. Xydopoulos, K. Vlassopoulos, and E. Tounta (eds), *Violence and the City: Law, Territory and Civic Identity in Ancient and Medieval Times*. London and New York, 50–71.

Canevaro, M. (2017b), 'The Rule of Law as the Measure for Political Legitimacy in the Greek City States', *Hague Journal on the Rule of Law* 9.2, 211–36.

Canevaro, M. (2017c), 'The Popular Culture of Athenian Institutions: "Authorized" Popular Culture and "Unauthorized" Elite Culture in Classical Athens', in L. Grig (ed.), *Popular Culture in the Ancient World*. Cambridge, 39–65.

Canevaro, M. (2018a), 'Majority Rule vs. Consensus: The Practice of Deliberation in the Greek *Poleis*', in M. Canevaro, A. Erskine, B. Gray, and J. Ober (eds), *Ancient Greek History and the Contemporary Social Sciences*. Edinburgh, 101–56.

232 BIBLIOGRAPHY

Canevaro, M. (2018b), 'The Authenticity of the Document at Dem. 24.20–3, the Procedures of *Nomothesia* and the So-Called ἐπιχειροτονία τῶν νόμων', *Klio* 100.1, 1–55.

Canevaro, M. (2018c), 'Memory, the Rhetors and the Public in Attic Oratory', in L. Castagnoli and P. Ceccarelli (eds), *Greek Memories: Theories and Practices*. Oxford, 136–57.

Canevaro, M. (2018d), 'What Was the Law of Leptines Really About? Reflections on Athenian Public Economy and Legislation in the Fourth Century BCE'. *Constitutional Political Economy* 29.4, 440–64.

Canevaro, M. (2018e), 'The Public Charge for *Hubris* against Slaves: The Honour of the Victim and the Honour for the *Hubristēs*', *JHS* 138, 100–26.

Canevaro, M. (2019a), 'Athenian Constitutionalism: *Nomothesia* and Judicial Review', in G. Thür and U. Yiftach-Firanko (eds), *Symposion 2017: Vorträge zur griechischen und hellenistischen Rechtsgeschichte*. Vienna, 65–98.

Canevaro, M. (2019b), 'Honorary Decrees and νόμοι ἐπ' ἀνδρί: on *IG* II3 1 327; 355; 452', in L. Gagliardi and L. Pepe (eds), *Dike: Essays in Honour of Alberto Maffi*. Milan, 71–86.

Canevaro, M. (2019c), '*Nomothesia* e amministrazione finanziaria: frammenti epigrafici di "costitutionalizzazione" e sviluppo istituzionale nell'Atene di IV secolo', *Historiká* 9, 485–524.

Canevaro, M. (2019d), 'La deliberation démocratique à l'Assemblée athénienne: procédures et strategies de légitimation', *Annales HSS* 74.2, 339–81.

Canevaro, M. (2020), 'I diritti come spazio di socialità: la *timē* tra diritti e doveri', in A. Camerotto and F. Pontani (eds), *Dike: ovvero della Giustizia tra l'Olimpo e la Terra*. Milan, 157–77.

Canevaro, M. (2021), 'Upside-Down Hegemony? Ideology and Power in Ancient Athens', in E. Zucchetti and A. Cimino (eds), *Gramsci and the Ancient World*. London, 63–85.

Canevaro, M. (2022), 'Social Mobility vs. Societal Stability: Once Again on the Aims and Meaning of Solon's Reforms', in J. Berhardt and M. Canevaro (eds), *From Homer to Solon: Continuity and Change in Archaic Greece*. Leiden, 363–413.

Canevaro, M. (forthcoming a), '*Timē*, Athenian Citizenship and 'Falling Short'', in L. Cecchet and C. Lasagni (eds), *Citizenship Imagined, Citizenship Practiced: Citizens and non-citizens in the ancient Greek World*, Stuttgart.

Canevaro, M. (forthcoming b), 'Recognition, Imbalance of Power and Agency: Honour Relations ans Slaves' Claims vis-à-vis their Masters', in D.M. Lewis, M. Canevaro and D. Cairns (eds) *Slavery and Honour in the Ancient Greek World*, Edinburgh.

Canevaro, M. and Esu, A. (2018), 'Extreme Democracy in Theory and Practice: *Nomophylakia* and Fourth-Century *Nomothesia* in the Aristotelian *Athenaion Politeia*', in C. Bearzot, M. Canevaro, T. Gargiulo, and E. Poddighe (eds), *Athenaion Politeiai tra storia, sociologia e politica: Aristotele e Ps. Senofonte*. Milan, 105–45.

Canevaro, M. and Harris, E. M. (2012), 'The Documents in Andocides' *On the Mysteries*', *CQ* 63.1, 98–129.

Canevaro, M. and Harris, E. M. (2017), 'The Authenticity of the Documents at Andocides' On the Mysteries 77–79 and 83–84', *Dike* 19, 9–49.

Canevaro, M. and Rocchi, L. (forthcoming), 'Greek Subjective Rights? Legal Discourse and Legal Institutions', in C. Ando, M. Canevaro, and B. Straumann (eds), *The Cambridge History of Rights*, Vol. 1: *Antiquity*. Cambridge.

Canfora, L. (1990), 'Trattati in Tucidide', in L. Canfora, M. Liverani, and C. Zaccagnini (eds), *I trattati nel mondo antico: forma, ideologia, funzione*. Rome, 193–216.

Carawan, E. (2013), *The Athenian Amnesty and Reconstructing the Law*. Oxford.

Carawan, E. (2020), *Control of the Laws in the Ancient Democracy at Athens*. Baltimore.

BIBLIOGRAPHY 233

Carey, C. (2004), 'Offence and Procedure in Athenian Law', in E. M. Harris and L. Rubinstein (eds), *The Law and the Courts in Ancient Greece*. London, 111–56.

Carlier, P. (1984), *La royauté en Grece avant Alexandre*. Strasbourg.

Carlier, P. (2004), 'La nozione di *arché* nella *Politica* di Aristotele', in S. Cataldi (ed.), *Poleis e Politeiai. Esperienze politiche, tradizioni letterarie e progetti costituzionali*. Alessandria, 393–401.

Carlsson, S. (2010), *Hellenistic Democracies: Freedom, Independence and Political Procedure in Some East Greek City-States*. Stuttgart.

Cartledge, P. (1987), *Agesilaos and the Crisis of Sparta*. London and Baltimore.

Cartledge, P. (2001), *Spartan Reflections*. London and Berkeley.

Cartledge, P. and Spawforth, A. (1991), *Hellenistic and Roman Sparta: A Tale of Two Cities*. London and New York.

Cassio, A. C. (2000), 'Un epigramma votivo spartano per Atena Alea', *RFIC* 128, 129–34.

Ceccarelli, P. (2014), *Ancient Greek Letter Writing: A Cultural History (600–150 BCE)*. Oxford.

Chambers, M. H., Gallucci, R., and Spanos P. (1990), 'Athens' Alliance with Egesta in the Year of Antiphon', *ZPE* 83, 38–63.

Chaniotis, A. (2009), 'The Dynamics of Ritual Norms in Greek Cult', in P. Brulé (ed.), *La norme en matière religieuse en Grèce antique* (= *Kernos* Supplement 21). Liége, 91–105.

Chaniotis, A. (ed.) (2012), *Unveiling Emotions: Sources and Methods for the Study of Emotions in the Greek World*. Stuttgart.

Chaniotis, A. (2013), 'Normen stärker als Emotionen? Der kulturhistorische Kontext der griechischen Amnestie', in K. Harter-Uibopuu and F. Mitthof (eds), *Vergeben und Vergessen? Amnestie in der Antike*. Vienna, 47–70.

Chaniotis, A. and Ducrey, P. (eds) (2013), *Unveiling Emotions*, Vol. II: *Emotions in Greece and Rome: Texts, Images, Material Culture*. Stuttgart.

Chantraine, P. (1977), *Dictionnaire étymologique de la langue grecque*, vol. 1. Paris.

Christ, M. R. (1998), *The Litigious Athenian*. Baltimore.

Christ, M. R. (2006), *The Bad Citizen in Classical Athens*. Cambridge.

Christ, M. R. (2007), 'The Evolution of *Eisphora* in Classical Athens', *CQ* 57.1, 53–69.

Christ, M. R. (2012), *The Limits of Altruism in Democratic Athens*. Cambridge.

Christesen, P. (2013), 'Sport and Society in Sparta', in P. Christesen and D. G. Kyle (eds), *A Companion to Sport and Spectacle in Greek and Roman Antiquity*. Chichester, 146–58.

Christesen, P. (2018), 'Sparta and Athletics', in A. Powell (ed.), *A Companion to Sparta*, vol. 2. Chichester, 543–64.

Clavaud, R. (1974), *Demosthene, Prologues*. Paris.

Clinton, K. (2008), *Eleusis. The Inscriptions on Stone. Documents of the Sanctuary of the Two Goddesses and the Public Documents of the Deme*. Vol. IA: *Text*, Vol. IB: *Plates*, Vol. II: *Commentary*. Athens.

Cohen, D. (1995), *Law, Violence and Community in Classical Athens*. Cambridge.

Cohen, E. (1973), *Ancient Athenian Maritime Courts*. Princeton.

Colón-Ríos, J. (2020), *Constituent Power and the Law*. Oxford.

Conran, J. and Thelen, K. (2016), 'Institutional Change', in O. Fioretos, T. Falleti, and A. Sheingate (eds), *The Oxford Handbook of Historical Institutionalism*. Oxford, 51–70.

Constantakopoulou, C. (2017), *Aegean Interactions: Delos and Its Networks in the Third Century*. Oxford.

Cooley, A. E. (ed.) (2000), *The Afterlife of Inscriptions: Reusing, Rediscovering, Reinventing & Revitalizing Ancient Inscriptions* (= *BICS* Supplement 75). London.

234 BIBLIOGRAPHY

Cornell, T. (2022), 'Roman Political Assemblies', in V. Arena and J. Prag (eds), *A Companion to the Political Culture of the Roman Republic*. London, 220–32.

Crowther, C. (1997), 'Inscriptions from Sparta and Larissa Museums', *ABSA* 92, 345–58.

Crowther, C. (2006), 'Foreign Judges in Thessaly in the Hellenistic Period: A Second Century Phenomenon?', in A. G. Pikoulas (ed.), *Inscriptions and History of Thessaly: New Evidence. Proceedings of the International Symposium in Honor of the Professor Christian Habicht*. Volos, 31–48.

Crowther, C., Habicht, C., Hallof, L., and Hallof, K. (1998), 'Aus der Arbeit der «Inscriptiones Graecae» I. Drei Dekrete aus Kos für δικασταγωγοί', *Chiron* 28, 87–100.

Culasso Gastaldi, E. (2003), 'Abbattere la stele. Riscrittura epigrafica e revisione storica ad Atene', *CCG* 14, 241–62.

Cuomo, S. (2001), *Ancient Mathematics*. London.

Cuomo, S. (2012), 'Exploring Ancient Greek and Roman Numeracy', *Journal of the British Society for the History of Mathematics* 27.1, 1–12.

Cuomo, S. (2013), 'Accounts, Numeracy and Democracy in Classical Athens', in M. Asper (ed.), *Writing Science: Medical and Mathematical Authorship in Ancient Greece*. Berlin, 255–78.

Daverio Rocchi, G. (1987), *Frontiera e Confini nella Grecia Antica*. Rome.

David, E. (1991), *Old Age in Sparta*. Amsterdam.

David, M. (1954), *La souveraineté et les limites juridiques du pouvoir monarchique du IXe au XVe siècle*. Paris.

Davies, J. K. (1994), 'On the Non-usability of the Concept of Sovereignty in an Ancient Greek Context', in L. Aigner Foresti (ed.), *Federazioni e federalismo nell'Europa antica*. Milan, 51–65.

Davies, J. K. (2004), 'Athenian Fiscal Expertise and Its Influence', *Mediterraneo Antico. Economie, Società e Culture* 7.2, 491–512.

Davies, Ph. (2013), '*Kalos Kagathos* and Scholarly Perception of Spartan Society'. *Historia* 62.3, 259–79.

Davies, Ph. (2017), 'Equality and Distinction within the Spartiate Community', in A. Powell (ed.), *A Companion to Sparta*, vol. 2. Chichester, 480–99.

Davies, Ph. (forthcoming), *Standing among the Spartans: Institutions and Status within the Spartiate Community*. London.

Davis, G. (2011), '*Axones* and *Kurbeis*: A New Answer to an Old Problem', *Historia* 60.1, 1–35.

De Laix, R. A. (1973), *Probouleusis at Athens. A Study of a Political Decision-Making*. Berkeley and Los Angeles.

De Polignac, F. (2012), 'Entré privé, public, civique: à propos de l'intégration de cultes extérieurs dans l'Athènes classique', in E. Cantarella, M. Gagarin, J. M. Modrzejewski, and G. Thür (eds), *Symposion 2011, Akten der Gesellschaft für griechische und hellenistische Rechtgeschichte*. Vienna, 199–210.

de Ste. Croix, G. E. M. (1963), 'The Alleged Secret between Athens and Philip II Concerning Amphipolis and Pydna', *CQ* 13, 110–19.

de Ste. Croix, G. E. M. (1972), *The Origins of the Peloponnesian War*. London.

Deigh, J. (2008), *Emotions, Values and the Law*. New York.

Dennert, J. (1964), *Ursprung und Begriff der Souveränität*. Stuttgart.

Denniston, J. D. (1996), *The Greek Particles*. Oxford (2nd edition revised by K. J. Dover).

Deshours, N. (2004), 'Les institutions civiques de Messène à l'époque hellénistique tardive', *ZPE* 150, 134–46.

Deshours, N. (2006), *Les mystères d'Andania: étude d'épigraphie et d'histoire religieuse*. Pessac.

BIBLIOGRAPHY   235

Develin, R. (1989), *Athenian Officials: 684–321 BCE*. Cambridge.

Dimas, P., Lane, M., and Sauvé Meier, S. (eds) (2021), *Plato's Stateman: A Philosophical Discussion*. Oxford.

Dimopoulou, A. (2014), 'Ἄκυρον ἔστω: Legal Invalidity in Greek Inscriptions', in M. Gagarin and A. Lanni (eds), *Symposion 2013: Papers in Greek and Hellenistic Legal History*. Vienna, 249–79.

Dimopoulou-Piliouni, A. (2015), *Lesbion Politeiai: Politeuma kai dikaio ton poleon tes Lesbou (archaikoi, klassikoi, ellenistikoi, romaïkoi chronoi)*. Athens.

Dixon, M. D. (2001), 'IG V² 1.75 and the Date of Arbitration between Epidauros and Hermione', *ZPE* 137, 169–73.

Dmitriev, S. (2005), *City Government in Hellenistic and Roman Asia Minor*. Oxford.

Domingo Gygax, M. (2016), *Benefaction and Rewards in the Ancient Greek City: The Origins of Euergetism*. Cambridge.

Domínguez, A. J. (2004), 'Spain and France (Including Corsica)', in M. H. Hansen and T. H. Nielsen (eds), *Inventory of the Archaic and Classical Poleis*. Oxford, 162–7.

Dover, K. J. (1955), '*Anapsephisis* in Fifth-Century Athens', *JHS* 75, 17–20.

Dreher, M. (2022), 'Das Ungültigwerden von Gesetzen in den griechischen *Poleis*', *Dike* 25, 7–76.

Dryzek, J. S. (2011), *Foundations and Frontiers of Deliberative Democracy*. Oxford.

Dössel, A. (2003), *Die Beilegung innerstaatlicher Konflikte in den griechischen Poleis vom 5.–3. Jahrhundert v. Chr.* Frankfurt.

Ehrenberg, V. (1969), *The Greek State*. London (2nd edition).

Eidinow, E. (2007), *Oracles, Curses, and Risk among the Ancient Greeks*. Oxford.

Ellis-Evans, A. (2012), 'The Tyrants Dossier from Eresos', *Chiron* 42, 183–212.

Ellis-Evans, A. (2019), *The Kingdom of Priam. Lesbos and the Troad between Anatolia and the Aegean*. Oxford.

Elmer, D. F. (2020), 'Assembly and Councils', in C. Ondine Pache (ed.) (in association with C. Dué, S. Lupack, and R. Lamberton), *The Cambridge Guide to Homer*. Cambridge, 293–5.

Elstub, S., Ercan, S., and Mendonça, R. F. (2016), 'Editorial Introduction: The Fourth Generation of Deliberative Democracy', *Critical Policy Studies* 10.2, 139–51.

Engen, D. T. (2010), *Honor and Profit: Athenian Trade Policy and the Economy and Society of Greece 415–307 BCE*. Ann Arbor.

Epstein, S. (2009), 'Quorum in People's Assembly in Classical Athens', *C&M* 60, 69–98.

Epstein, S. (2013), 'Attic Building Accounts from *Euthynae* to *Stelae*', in M. Faraguna (ed.), *Archives* and *Archival Documents in Ancient Societies*. Trieste, 127–42.

Esu, A. (2017), 'Divided Power and *EYNOMIA*: Deliberative Procedures in Ancient Sparta', *CQ* 67.2, 353–73.

Esu, A. (2020), 'After the Empire: Judicial Review and Athenian Interstate Relations in the Age of Demosthenes, 354–22 BCE', in E. Cavanagh (ed.), *Empire and Legal Thought*. Leiden, 69–104.

Esu, A. (2021a), '*Adeia* in Fifth-Century Athens', *JHS* 141, 153–78.

Esu, A. (2021b), 'Hegemony, Coercion and Consensus: A Gramscian Approach to Greek Cultural and Political History', in E. Zucchetti and A. Cimino (eds), *Gramsci and the Ancient World*. London, 341–51.

Esu, A. (2021c), Review of 'E. Carawan (2020), *Control of the Laws in the Ancient Democracy at Athens*, Baltimore', *Bryn Mawr Classical Review* 2021.12.33.

Esu, A. (forthcoming), 'Law, Office and Honour: Legal Relevance and Forensic Arguments in Demosthenes's *Against Androtion*', in E. M. Harris and A. Esu (eds) *Keeping to the Point in Athenian Forensic Oratory: Law, Character and Rhetoric*, Edinburgh.

236 BIBLIOGRAPHY

Fabiani, R. (2012), 'Dedochthai tei boulei kai toi demoi: protagonisti e prassi della procedura deliberativa a Iasos', in C. Mann and P. Scholz (eds), 'Demokratie' im Hellenismus: von der Herrschaft des Volkes zur Herrschaft der Honoratioren? Mainz, 109–68.

Fabiani, R. (2015), I decreti onorari di Iasos: cronologia e storia. Munich.

Fabiani, R. (2021), Review of 'H. Börm (2019), Mordende Mitbürger. Stasis und Bürgerkrieg in griechischen Poleis des Hellenismus, Stuttgart', Klio 103.1, 320–6.

Fabiani, R. (forthcoming), 'Deliberative Institutions, Political Culture and Society from Classical to Hellenistic Iasos', in M. Barbato, M. Canevaro, and A. Esu (eds), Rediscovering Greek Institutions: New Institutionalist Approaches to Greek History. Edinburgh.

Fantasia, U. (1987), 'Il grano di Leucone e le finanze di Atene: nota a Demostene 20,33'. ASNP 17.1, 89–117.

Faraguna, M. (1992), Atene nell'età di Alessandro: problemi economici, politici, finanziari. Rome.

Faraguna, M. (2005), 'La figura dell'aisymnetes tra realtà storica e teoria politica', in R. W. Wallace and M. Gagarin (eds), Symposion 2001, Papers on Greek and Hellenistic Legal History. Vienna, 321–38.

Faraguna, M. (2007), 'Tra oralità e scrittura: diritto e forme della comunicazione dai poemi omerici a Teofrasto', Etica & Politica 9, 75–111.

Faraguna, M. (2011), 'Lykourgan Athens?', in V. Azoulay and P. Ismard (eds), Clisthène et Lycurgue d'Athènes: autour du politique dans la cité classique. Paris.

Faraguna, M. (2012), 'Pistis and Apistia: Aspects of the Development of Social and Economic Relations in Classical Greece', MediterrAnt 15.1–2, 355–74.

Faraguna, M. (2015a), 'I nomophylakes tra utopia e realtà istituzionale delle città greche'. Politica Antica 5, 141–59.

Faraguna, M. (2015b), 'Citizen Registers in Archaic Greece: The Evidence Reconsidered', in A. Matthaiou and N. Papazarkadas (eds), Axon. Studies in Honour of R. S. Stroud. Athens, 649–67.

Faraguna, M. (2015c), 'Archives, Documents and Legal Practices in the Greek polis', in E. M. Harris and M. Canevaro (eds),The Oxford Handbook of Ancient Greek Law. Oxford, https://doi.org/10.1093/oxfordhb/9780199599257.013.14

Faraguna, M. (forthcoming), 'Citizenship in the Greek Polis: An Institutional Approach', in M. Barbato, M. Canevaro, and A. Esu (eds), Rediscovering Greek Institutions: New Institutionalist Approaches to Greek History. Edinburgh.

Ferejohn, J. and Pasquino, P. (2002), 'Constitutional Court as Deliberative Institutions: Towards an Institutional Theory of Constitutional Justice', in W. Sadurski (ed.), Constitutional Justice, East and West Democratic Legitimacy and Constitutional Courts in Post-Communist Europe in a Comparative Perspective. The Hague, London, and New York, 21–36.

Ferejohn, J. and Pasquino, P. (2010), 'The Countermajoritarian Opportunity', Journal of Constitutional Law 13.2, 353–95.

Ferguson, W. S. (1944), Attic Orgeones and the Cult of Heroes. Cambridge, MA.

Ferrary, J. L. (1987-9), 'Les Romains de la République et les démocracies grecques', Opus: rivista internazionale per la storia economica e sociale dell'antichità 6–7, 203–16.

Ferrucci, S. (2013), La democrazia diseguale. Riflessioni sull'Athenaion Politeia dello pseudo-Senofonte I, 1–9. Pisa.

Feyel, C. (2009), Dokimasia: la place et le rôle de l'examen préliminaire dans les institutions des cités grecques. Paris.

Filias, D. (2020), 'Grammateis (Secretaries) in Legal Procedure in Ancient Athens', JAH 8.2, 187–207.

BIBLIOGRAPHY 237

Filonik, J. (2019), '"Living as Anyone Wishes" in Athens: The (Anti-)Democratic Polemics', *CPh* 114.1, 1–24.

Filonik, J. (forthcoming), *The Concept of Freedom in Classical Athens*. Cambridge.

Finley, M. I. (1983), *Politics in the Ancient World*. Cambridge.

Fioretos, O., Falleti, T., and Sheingate, A. (2016), 'Historical Institutionalism in Political Science', in O. Fioretos, T. Falleti, and A. Sheingate (eds), *The Oxford Handbook of Historical Institutionalism*. Oxford, 4–22.

Fisher, N. (2001), *Aeschines. Against Timarchos. Introduction, Translation and Commentary*. Oxford.

Flaig, E. (1994), 'Das Konsensprinzip im homerischen Olymp: Überlegungen zum göttlichen Entscheidungsprozeß Ilias 4. 1–72', *Hermes* 122, 13–31.

Flaig, E. (2011), 'La révolution athénienne de 507. Un mythe fondateur «oublié»', in V. Azoulay and P. Ismard (eds), *Clisthène et Lycurgue d'Athenes: autour de la politique dans la cité classique*. Paris, 59–66.

Flaig, E. (2013), *Die Mehrheitsentscheidung: Entstehung und kulturelle Dynamik*. Padeborn.

Flower, M. (2002), 'The Invention of Tradition in Classical and Hellenistic Sparta', in A. Powell and S. Hodkinson (eds), *Sparta beyond the Mirage*. London, 191–217.

Flower, M. (2018), 'Spartan Religion', in A. Powell (ed.), *A Companion to Sparta*, vol. 2, Chichester, 425–51.

Fornara, C. W. and Samons, Jr, L. J. (1991), *Athens from Cleisthenes to Pericles*. Berkeley and Los Angeles.

Forrest, W. G. (1960), 'The Tribal Organisation of Chios', *ABSA* 55, 172–89.

Forrest, W. G. (1967), 'Legislation in Sparta', *Phoenix* 21, 11–19.

Forsdyke, S. (2005), *Exile, Ostracism and Democracy: The Politics of Exile in Ancient Greece*. Princeton.

Forsdyke, S. (2006), 'Herodotus, Political History and Political Thought', in C. Dewald and J. Marincola (eds), *The Cambridge Companion to Herodotus*. Cambridge, 224–41.

Forsdyke, S. (2018), 'Ancient and Modern Conceptions of Rule of Law', in M. Canevaro, A. Erskine, B. Gray, and J. Ober (eds), *Ancient Greek History and the Contemporary Social Sciences*. Edinburgh, 184–212.

Forsdyke, S. (2019), 'Slave Agency and Citizenship in Classical Athens', in G. Thür, U. Yiftach, and R. Zelnick-Abramovitz (eds), *Symposion 2017: Vorträge zur griechischen und hellenistischen Rechtsgeschichte*. Vienna, 345–66.

Forster, F. R. (2018), *Die Polis im Wandel: Ehrendekreten für eigene Bürger im Kontext der hellenistischen Polisgesellschaft*. Göttingen.

Foucart, P. (1889), 'Décret athénien de l'année 352 trouvé à Eleusis', *BCEH* 13, 433–67.

Freitag, K. (2007), 'Überlegungen zur Konstruktion von Grenzen im antiken Griechenland', in R. Albertz, A. Blöbaum, and P. Funke (eds), *Räume und Grenzen: Topologische Konzepte in den antiken Kulturen des östlichen Mittelmeerraums*. Munich, 49–70.

Fröhlich, P. (2004), *Les Cités grecques et le contrôle des magistrats (IVe-Ier siècle avant J.-C.)*. Geneva and Paris.

Fröhlich, P. (2013), 'Governmental Checks and Balances', in H. Beck (eds), *A Companion to Ancient Greek Government*. Chichester, 252–66.

Fröhlich, P. (2016), 'La citoyenneté grecque entre Aristote et le modernes', *CCG* 27, 91–136.

Fuller, L. L. (1969), *The Morality of Law*. New Haven.

Funke, P. (2015), 'Aitolia and the Aitolian League', in H. Beck and P. Funke (eds), *Federalism in Greek Antiquity*. Cambridge, 86–117.

Gabba, E. (1957), 'Studi su Filarco', *Athenaeum* 35, 3–55.

238   BIBLIOGRAPHY

Gabrielsen, V. (1994), *Financing the Athenian Fleet: Public Taxation and Social Relations.* Baltimore.

Gabrielsen, V. (2000), 'The Synoikized Polis of Rhodes', in T. H. Nielsen, L. Rubinstein, and P. Flensted-Jensen (eds), *Studies in Ancient Greek History presented to Mogens Herman Hansen on His Sixtieth Birthday, August 20, 2000.* Copenhagen, 177–205.

Gabrielsen, V. (2009), 'Brotherhoods of Faith and Provident Planning: The Non-Public Associations of the Greek World', I. Malkin, C. Constantakopoulou, and K. Panagopoulou (eds), *Greek and Roman Networks in the Mediterranean.* Oxford, 176–203.

Gabrielsen, V. and Paganini, M. (2021), 'Associations' Regulations from the Ancient Greek World and Beyond: An Introduction', in V. Gabrielsen and M. Paganini (eds), *Private Associations in the Ancient Greek World: Regulations and Creation of Group Identity.* Cambridge, 1–38.

Gabrielsen, V. and Thomsen, C. A. (2015), 'Introduction: Private Groups, Public Functions?', in V. Gabrielsen and C. A. Thomsen (eds), *Private Associations and the Public Sphere.* Copenhagen, 7–24.

Gagarin, M. (2005), 'The Unity of Greek Law', in M. Gagarin and D. Cohen (eds), *The Cambridge Companion of Ancient Greek Law.* Cambridge, 29–40.

Gagarin, M. (2008), *Writing Greek Law.* Cambridge.

Gagarin, M. (2012), 'Observations on the Great *Rhetra*: A Response to Francoise Ruzé', in B. Legras and G. Thür (eds), *Symposion 2011: Études d'histoire du droit grec et hellénistique.* Vienna, 17–20.

Gagarin, M. and MacDowell, D. (1998), *Antiphon and Andocides.* Austin.

Gagarin, M. and Perlman, P. (2016), *The Laws of Ancient Crete: 650–400 BCE.* Oxford.

Gamauf, R. (2013), 'Zu den Rechtsfolgen der *abolitio* im klassischen römischen Recht', in K. Harter-Uibopuu and F. Mitthof (eds), *Vergeben und Vergessen? Amnistie in der Antike.* Vienna, 299–318.

Garland, R. (1992), *Introducing New Gods: The Politics of Athenian Religion.* New York.

Gauthier, P. (1972), *Symbola: les étrangers et la justice dans les cités grecques.* Nancy.

Gauthier, P. (1985), *Les cités grecques et leurs bienfaiteurs (IVe-Ier siècle avant J.-C.). Contribution à l'histoire des institutions.* Paris.

Gauthier, P. (1987), 'Bulletin épigraphique: Institutions', *REG* 100, 308–37.

Gauthier, P. (1990), 'Quorum et participation civique dans lés démocraties grecques', in C. Nicolet (ed.), *Du pouvoir dans l'Antiquité: mots et réalités.* Geneva, 73–99.

Gauthier, P. (1993), *Études d'histoire et d'institutions grecques: choix d'écrits* (édité et indexé par Denis Rousset). Paris.

Gauthier, P. (1997), 'Compte Rendu, Guy Labarre, Les Cité de Lesbos aux époques hellénistique et impériale'. *Topoi* 7, 349–61.

Gauthier, P. (1999), 'Bulletin Epigraphique: Îles de l'Égée', *REG* 112.2, 397–437.

Gawlinski, L. (2012), *The Sacred Law of Andania: A New Text with Commentary.* Berlin and Boston.

Gehrke, H. J. (1985), *Stasis: Untersuchungen zu den inneren Kriegen in den griechischen Staaten des 5. Und 4. Jahrhunderts v.Chr.* Munich.

Gehrke, H. J. (2001), 'Myth, History, and Collective Identity: Uses of the Past in Ancient Greece and Beyond', in N. Luraghi (ed.), *The Historian's Craft in the Age of Herodotus.* Oxford, 286–313.

Gehrke, H. J. (2010), 'Representation of the Past in Greek Culture', in L. Foxhall, H. J. Gehrke, and N. Luraghi (eds), *Intentional History. Spinning the Time in Ancient History.* Stuttgart, 15–34.

BIBLIOGRAPHY 239

Georgiadou, A. (1997), *Plutarch's Pelopidas: A Historical and Philological Commentary*. Berlin.

Giangiulio, M. (2015), *Democrazie greche: Atene, Sicilia, Magna Grecia*. Rome.

Giangiulio, M. (2018), 'Oligarchies of "Fixed Number" or Citizen Bodies in the Making', in A. Duplouy and R. Brock (eds), *Defining Citizenship in Archaic Greece*. Oxford, 275–94.

Giangiulio, M. (2019), 'Do Societies Remember? The Notion of "Collective Memory": Paradigms and Problems (from Maurice Halbwachs On)', in M. Giangiulio, E. Franchi, and G. Proietti (eds), *Commemorating War and War Dead: Ancient and Modern*. Stuttgart, 17–33.

Giannadaki, I. (2014), 'The Time Limit (*Prothesmia*) in the *Graphe Paranomon*', *Dike* 17, 15–33.

Giannadaki, I. (2020), *A Commentary on Demosthenes* Against Androtion: *Introduction, Text and Translation*. Oxford.

Giannakopoulos, N. (2008), Ὁ θεσμὸς τῆς γερουσίας τῶν ἑλληνικῶν πόλεων κατὰ τοὺς Ῥωμαϊκοὺς χρόνους. Ὀργάνωση καὶ λειτουργίες. Thessaloniki.

Giovannini, A. (2007), *Les relations entre États dans la Grèce antique du temps d'Homère à l'intervention romaine (ca. 700–200 a. J.-C.)*. Stuttgart.

Girdvainyte, L. (2020), 'Law and Citizenship in Roman Achaia: Continuity and Change', in K. Czajkowski, B. Eckhardt, and M. Strothmann (eds), *Law in the Roman Provinces*. Oxford, 210–42.

Goffman, E. (1967), *Interaction Ritual: Essays on Face-to-Face Behavior*. New York.

Goldstaub, M. (1889), *De ΑΔΕΙΑΣ notione et usu in iure publico Attico*. Breslau.

Gomme, A. W. (1962), *An Historical Commentary on Thucydides*, Vol. 2: *Books II–III*. Oxford.

Gotter, U. (2008), 'Cultural Differences and Cross-Cultural Contacts: Greek and Roman Concepts of Power', *HSPh* 104, 179–230.

Gottesman, A. (2014), *The Politics of the Street in Democratic Athens*. Cambridge.

Gouschin, V. (2009), 'Athenian Ostracism and *Ostraka*: Some Historical and Statistical Observations', in L. Mitchell and L. Rubinstein (eds), *Greek History and Epigraphy: Essays in Honour of P. J. Rhodes*. Swansea, 233–45.

Gray, B. D. (2013), 'Justice or Harmony? Reconciliation after *Stasis* at Dikaia and the Fourth-Century Polis'. *REA* 115.2, 369–401.

Gray, B. D. (2015), *Stasis and Stability: Exile, the Polis, and Political Thought, c.404–146 BCE*. Oxford.

Gray, B. D. (2018a), 'Approaching the Hellenistic *Polis* through Modern Political Theory: The Public Sphere, Pluralism and Prosperity', in M. Canevaro, A. Erskine, B. Gray, and J. Ober (eds), *Ancient Greek History and the Contemporary Social Sciences*. Edinburgh, 68–97.

Gray, B. D. (2018b), 'Civic Alternative to Stoicism: The Ethics of Hellenistic Honorary Decrees', *ClAnt* 37.2, 187–225.

Gray, B. D. (2020), 'Historical Consciousness and Political Agency among Ancient Greek Refugees', in L. Loddo (ed.), *Political Refugees in the Ancient Greek World. Literary, Philosophical and Historical Essays* (= *Pallas* 112). Toulouse, 231–45.

Gray, V. (2007), *Xenophon: On Government*. Cambridge.

Green, P. (2006), *Diodorus Siculus. Books 11–12.37.1. Greek History, 489–431. The Alternative Version*. Austin.

Grieb, V. (2008), *Hellenistische Demokratie: politische Organisation und Struktur in freien griechischen Poleis nach Alexander dem Grossen*. Stuttgart.

240 BIBLIOGRAPHY

Griffith, G. T. (1966), 'Isegoria in the Assembly at Athens', in E. Badian (ed.), Ancient Society and Institutions: Studies Presented to Victor Ehrenberg on His 75th Birthday. Oxford, 115–38.

Griffiths, P. E. (1997), What Emotions Really Are: The Problem of Psychological Categories. Chicago.

Grimm, D. (2015), Sovereignty: The Origin and Future of a Political and Legal Concept. New York.

Grote, G. (reprinted 1906), History of Greece from the Earleast Period to the Close of the Generation Contemporary to Alexander the Great (12 vols). London.

Guarducci, M. (1967), Epigrafia greca I. Caratteri e storia della disciplina. La scrittura greca dale origini all'età imperiale. Rome.

Haake, M. (2009), '"Doing Philosophy"—soziales Kapital versus politischer Mißkredit? Zur Funktionalität und Dysfunktionalität von Philosophie im sozialen und politischen Raum des klassischen Athen', in C. Mann, M. Haake, and R. von den Hoff (eds), Rollenbilder in der athenischen Demokratie: Medien, Gruppen, Räume im politischen und sozialen System. Wiesbaden, 114–45.

Haake, M. (2020), 'The Academy in Athenian Politics and Society. Between Integration and Disintegration. The First Eighty Years (387/6–306/5)', in P. Kalligas, C. Balla, E. Baziotopoulou-Valavani and V. Karasmanis (eds), Plato's Academy: Its Working and Its History. Cambridge, 65–88.

Habicht, C. (2008), 'Judicial Control of the Legislature in Greek States', Studi Ellenistici 20, 17–23.

Hacker, J. S. and Pierson, P. (2010), Winner-Take-All Politics. New York.

Hacker, J. S., Pierson, P., and Thelen, K. (2015), 'Drift and Conversion: Hidden Faces of Institutional Change', in J. Mahoney and K. Thelen (eds), Advances in Comparative-Historical Analysis. Cambridge, 180–208.

Hagerdon, A. (2005), Between Moses and Plato: Individual and Society in Deuteronomy and Ancient Greek Law. Göttingen.

Hahm, D. E. (1995), 'Polybius' Applied Political Theory', in M. Schofield and A. Laks (eds), Justice and Generosity: Studies in Hellenistic Political Theory. Cambridge, 7–47.

Hahm, D. E. (2009), 'The Mixed Constitution in Greek Thought', in R. K. Balot (ed.), A Companion to Greek and Roman Political Thought. Chichester, 178–98.

Halbwachs, M. (1950), La mémoire collective. Paris.

Hall, P. A. and Taylor, R. C. (1996), 'Political Science and the Three New Institutionalisms'. Political Studies 49, 936–57.

Hallof, L., Hallof, K., and Habicht, C. (1998), 'Aus der Arbeit der «Inscriptiones Graecae» II. Ehrendekrete aus dem Asklepieion von Kos', Chiron 28, 101–42.

Hamel, D. (1998), Athenian Generals: Military Authority in the Classical Period. Leiden.

Hammer, D. (2002), The Iliad as Politics: The Performance of Political Thought. Norman.

Hamon, P. (2005), 'Le Conseil et la partécipation des citoyens: les mutations de la basse époque hellénistique', in P. Fröhlich and C. Müller (eds), Citoyenneté et participation à la basse époque hellénistique. Geneva, 121–44.

Hamon, P. (2007), 'Kymè d'Éolide, cité libre et démocratique, et le pouvoir des stratèges', Chiron 38, 63–106.

Hamon, P. (2009), 'Démocraties grecques après d'Alexandre: à propos de trois ouvrages recents', Topoi 16, 347–82.

Hamon, P. (2012), 'Mander des juges dans la cité: notes sur l'organisation des missions judiciaries à l'époque hellénistique', CCG 23, 195–22.

BIBLIOGRAPHY 241

Hanink, J. (2014), *Lycurgan Athens and the Making of Classical Tragedy*. Cambridge.

Hannick, J. M. (1981), 'Note sur la graphe paranomon', *AC* 50, 393-7.

Hansen, M. H. (1974), *The Sovereignty of the People's Court in Athens in the Fourth Century B.C. and the Public Actions against Uncostitutional Proposals*. Odense.

Hansen, M. H. (1975), Eisangelia: *The Sovereignty of the People's Court in the Fourth Century BCE and the Impeachment for Generals and Politicians*. Odense.

Hansen, M. H. (1976), Apagoge, Endeixis, *and* Ephegesis *against* Kakourgoi, Atimoi *and* Pheugontes. Odense.

Hansen, M. H. (1977), 'How Often Did the Athenian Ecclesia Meet?', *GRBS* 18, 43-70. Republished in *The Athenian Ecclesia* I (1983). Copenhagen.

Hansen, M. H. (1978), 'Nomos and psephisma in Fourth-Century Athens', *GRBS* 19, 315-30.

Hansen, M. H. (1979), 'Did the Athenian Ecclesia Legislate after 403/2?', *GRBS* 20, 23-49. Republished in *The Athenian Ecclesia I* (1983a). Copenhagen.

Hansen, M. H. (1980), 'Eisangelia at Athens. A Reply', *JHS* 100, 81-88.

Hansen, M. H. (1981), 'Initiative and Decision: The Separation of Powers in Fourth-Century Athens', *GRBS* 22.4, 345-70.

Hansen, M. H. (1983), *The Athenian Ecclesia: A Collection of Articles*. Odense.

Hansen, M. H. (1985a), 'Athenian nomothesia', *GRBS* 26, 345-71.

Hansen, M. H. (1985b), *Demography and Democracy: The Number of Athenian Citizens in the Fourth Century BCE*. Herning.

Hansen, M. H. (1987a), 'How Often Did the Athenian Assembly Meet? A Reply'. *GRBS* 28, 35-50.

Hansen, M. H. (1987b), *The Athenian Assembly in the Age of Demosthenes*. Oxford.

Hansen, M. H. (1989a), *The Athenian Ecclesia*, Vol. II: *A Collection of Articles, 1983-1989*. Odense.

Hansen, M. H. (1989b), 'Solonian Democracy in Fourth-Century Athens', *C&M* 40, 71-99.

Hansen, M. H. (1991), *The Athenian Democracy in the Age of Demosthenes: Structure, Principles and Ideology*. London.

Hansen, M. H. (1994), 'Polis, Politeuma and Politeia: A Note on Arist. Pol. 1278b6-14', in D. Whitehead (ed.), *From Political Architecture to Stephanus Byzantius*. Stuttgart, 91-8.

Hansen, M. H. (1996), 'Reflections on the Number of Citizens Accommodated in the Assembly Place on the Pnyx', in B. Fórsen and G. R. Stanton (eds), *The Pnyx in the History of Athens: Proceedings of an International Colloquium Organized by the Finnish Institute at Athens, 7-9 October, 1994*. Helsinki, 23-34.

Hansen, M. H. (1998), *Polis and City-State: An Ancient Concept and Its Modern Equivalent*. Acts of the Copenhangen Polis Centre, vol. 5. Copenhagen.

Hansen, M. H. (2000), 'Conclusion: The Impact of City-State Cultures on the World', in M. H. Hansen (ed.), *A Comparative Study of Thirty City-State Cultures*. Copenhagen, 597-623.

Hansen, M. H. (2002), 'Was the Polis a State or a Stateless Society?', in T. H. Nielsen (ed.), *Even More Studies in the Ancient Greek Polis: Papers from the Copenhagen Polis Centre 6*. Stuttgart, 17-47.

Hansen, M. H. (2004), 'How did the Athenian ecclesia vote?', in P.J. Rhodes (ed.) *The Athenian Democracy*, Edinburgh, 40-61.

Hansen, M. H. (ed.) (2010), *Démocratie athénienne—démocratie moderne: tradition et influences. Neuf exposés suivis de discussions. Entretiens sur l'Antiquité classique 56*. Geneva.

Hansen, M. H. (2015), 'Is Teisamenos' Decree (Andoc. 1.83-84) a Genuine Document?', *GRBS* 56, 34-48.

242 BIBLIOGRAPHY

Hansen, M. H. (2019), Review of 'Ismard (2017) *Democracy's Slaves* (*La démocratie contre les experts*)', *Polis* 36, 337–45.

Hansen, M. H. and Hodkinson, S. (2009), 'Spartan Exceptionalism? Continuing the Debate', in S. Hodkinson (ed.), *Sparta: Comparative Approaches*. Swansea, 473–98.

Hansen, M. H. and Nielsen, T. H. (2004), *The Inventory of Archaic and Classical Poleis*. Oxford.

Harding, P. (1994), *Androtion and the Atthis: The Fragments Translated with Introduction and Commentary*. Oxford.

Harris, E. M. (1986), 'How Often Did the Athenian Assembly Meet?', *CQ* 36, 363–77.

Harris, E. M. (1990), 'The Constitution of the Five Thousand', *HSPh* 93, 243–80.

Harris, E. M. (1991), 'Response to Trevor Saunders', in M. Gagarin (ed.), *Symposion 1990: Vorträge zur griechischen und hellenistischen Rechtsgeschichte*. Vienna, 133–8.

Harris, E. M. (1995), *Aeschines and Athenian Politics*. Oxford.

Harris, E. M. (2000), 'The Authenticity of Andokides' *De Pace*: A Subversive Essay', in P. Flensted-Jensen, T. H. Nielsen, and L. Rubinstein (eds), *Polis and Politics: Studies in Ancient Greek History Presented to Mogens Herman Hansen on His Sixtieth Birthday, August 20, 2000*. Copenhagen, 479–506.

Harris, E. M. (2006), *Democracy and Rule of Law in Classical Athens: Essays in Law, Society and Politics*. Cambridge.

Harris, E. M. (2008), *Demosthenes, Speeches 20–22*. Austin.

Harris, E. M. (2013a), 'How to Address the Athenian Assembly: Rhetoric and Political Tactics in the Debate about Mytilene (Thuc. 3.37–50)', *CQ* 63.1, 94–109.

Harris, E. M. (2013b), 'The Plaint in Athenian Law and Legal Procedure', in M. Faraguna (ed.), *Archives and Archival Documents in Ancient Societies*. Trieste, 143–62.

Harris, E. M. (2013c), *The Rule of Law in Action in Democratic Athens*. Oxford.

Harris, E. M. (2014), 'Nicias' Illegal Proposal in the Debate about the Sicilian Expedition (Thuc. 6.14)', *CPh* 109, 66–72.

Harris, E. M. (2015a), 'Military Organization and One-Man Rule in the Greek *Polis*'. *Ktema* 40, 83–91.

Harris, E. M. (2015b), 'Toward a Typology of Greek Sacred Regulations: A Legal Approach', *Kernos* 28, 55–84.

Harris, E. M. (2015c), 'The Meaning of *Symbolaion* and Maritime Cases in Athenian Law', *Dike* 18, 7–36.

Harris, E. M. (2015d), 'The Family, the Community and Murder: The Role of Pollution in Athenian Homicide Cases', in C. Ando and J. Rüpke (eds), *Public and Private in Ancient Mediterrean Law and Religion*. Berlin, 11–34.

Harris, E. M. (2016a), 'From Democracy to the Rule of Law: Constitutional Changes in Athens during the Fifth and Fourth Centuries BCE', in C. Tiersch (ed.), *Die Athenische Demokratie im 4. Jahrhundert. Zwischen Modernisierung und Tradition*. Stuttgart, 73–87.

Harris, E. M. (2016b), 'The Flawed Origins of Ancient Greek Democracy', in A. Havílček, C. Horn, and J. Jinek (eds), *Nous, Polis, Nomos. Festschrift Francesco L. Lisi*. St. Augustine, 43–55.

Harris, E. M. (2017a), 'How to Act in an Athenian Court: Emotions and Forensic Performance', in S. Papaioannou, A. Serafim, and B. da Vela (eds), *The Theatre of Justice: Aspects of Performance in Greco-Roman Oratory and Rhetoric*. Leiden, 223–42.

Harris, E. M. (2017b), 'Applying the Law about the Award of Crowns to Magistrates (Aeschin. 3.9–31; Dem. 18.113–117): Epigraphic Evidence for the Legal Arguments at the Trial of Ctesiphon', *ZPE* 202, 105–18.

BIBLIOGRAPHY 243

Harris, E. M. (2017c), *Demosthenes, Speeches 23–26*. Austin.

Harris, E. M. (2018a), 'Trials, Private Arbitration, and Public Arbitration in Classical Athens or the Background to [Arist.] *Ath. Pol.* 53.1–7', in C. Bearzot, M. Canevaro, T. Gargiulo, and E. Poddighe (eds), *Athenaion Politeiai tra storia, sociologia e politica: Aristotele e Ps. Senofonte*. Milan, 213–30.

Harris, E. M. (2018b), 'The Athenian View of an Athenian Trial', in C. Carey, I. Giannadaki, and B. Griffith-Williams (eds), *Use and Abuse of Law in the Athenian Courts*. Leiden, 42–74.

Harris, E. M. (2019a), 'Aeschylus' Eumenides: The Role of Areopagus, the Rule of Law and Political Discourse in Attic Tragedy', in A. Markantonatos and E. Volonaki (eds), *Poet and Orator: A Symbiotic Relationship in Democratic Athens*. Berlin and Boston, 389–418.

Harris, E. M. (2019b), 'The Crown Trial and Athenian Legal Procedures in Cases Against Illegal Decrees', *Dike* 22, 81–111.

Harris, E. M. (2020), 'Legal Expertise and Legal Experts in Athenian Democracy', *Journal of Juristic Papyrology* 50, 149–68.

Harris, E. M. with Esu, A. (2021), 'Policing Major Crimes in Classical Athens: *Eisangelia* and Other Public Procedures', *Rivista di Diritto Ellenico* 11, 39–119.

Harris, E. M. and Lewis, D. M. (2022), 'What Are Early Greek Laws About? Substance and Procedure in Archaic Statutes, c. 650–450 BC', in J. Berhardt and M. Canevaro (eds), *From Homer to Solon: Continuity and Change in Archaic Greece*. Leiden, 229–64.

Harrison, A. R. W. (1968), *The Law of Athens*, vol. 1. Oxford.

Hart, H. L. A. (1961), *The Concept of Law*. Oxford.

Harte, V. and Lane, M. (2013), Politeia *in Greek and Roman Philosophy*. Cambridge.

Harter-Uibopuu, K. (1998), *Das zwischenstaatliche Schiedsverfahren im Achäischen Koinon: Zur friedlichen Streitbeilegung nach den epigraphischen Quellen*. Vienna.

Hau, L. I. (2016), *Moral History from Herodotus to Diodorus Siculus*. Edinburgh.

Hau, L. I. (2021), 'The Fragments of Polybius Compared with Those of the "Tragic" Historians Duris and Phylarchus', *Histos* 15, 238–82.

Hay, C. (2006), 'Constructivist Institutionalism', in R. A. W. Rhodes, S. A. Binder, and B. A. Rockman (eds), *The Oxford Handbook of Political Institutions*. Oxford, 56–74.

Heisserer, A. J. (1980), *Alexander the Great and the Greeks: The Epigraphical Evidence*. Norman, OK.

Heisserer, A. J. and Hodot, R. (1986), 'The Mytilenian Decree on Concord', *ZPE* 63, 109–28.

Heller, A. (2009), 'La cité grecque d'époque imperial: vers une société d'ordres?', *Annales HSS* 64.2, 341–73.

Helly, B. (1971), 'Décrets de Démetrias pour des juges étrangers', *BCH* 95, 543–59.

Helly, B. (1973), *Gonnoi I: la cité et son histoire*. Amsterdam.

Henry, A. S. (1977), *The Prescripts of Athenian Decrees*. Leiden.

Henry, A. S. (1983), *Honours and Privileges in Athenian Decrees: The Principal Formulae of Athenian Honorary Decrees*. Hildesheim, Zürich, and New York.

Henry, A. S. (1989), 'The Provisions for the Payment in Athenian Decrees: A Study in Formulaic Language', *ZPE* 78, 247–95.

Henry, A. S. (1996), 'The Hortatory Intention in Athenian State Decrees', *ZPE* 112, 105–19.

Herman, G. (2006), *Morality and Behaviour in Democratic Athens: A Social History*. Cambridge.

Hobbes, T. (1651), *Leviathan* (R. Tuck ed., 1991). Cambridge.

Hodkinson, S. (1994), '"Blind Ploutos"? Contemporary Images of the Role of Wealth in Classical Sparta', in S. Hodkinson and A. Powell (eds), *The Shadow of Sparta*. London, 183–222.

244 BIBLIOGRAPHY

Hodkinson, S. (1999), 'An Agonistic Culture? Athletic Competition in Archaic and Classical Spartan Society', in S. Hodkinson and A. Powell (eds), *Sparta: New Perspectives*. London, 147–88.

Hodkinson, S. (2000), *Property and Wealth in Classical Sparta*. Swansea.

Hodkinson, S. (2002), 'Social Order and Conflict of Values in Classical Sparta', in M. Whitby (ed.), *Sparta*. New York, 104–30.

Hodkinson, S. (2004), 'Female Property Ownership and Empowerment in Classical and Hellenistic Sparta', in T. Figueira (ed.), *Spartan Society*. Swansea, 103–36.

Hodkinson, S. (2005), 'The Imaginary Spartan *Politeia*', in M. H. Hansen (ed.), *The Imaginary Polis. Acts of the Copenhagen Polis Centre 7*. Copenhagen, 222–81.

Hodkinson, S. (ed.) (2009a), *Sparta: Comparative Approaches*. Swansea.

Hodkinson, S. (2009b), 'Was Sparta an Exceptional *polis?*', in S. Hodkinson (ed.), *Sparta: Comparative Approaches*. Swansea, 417–22.

Hodkinson, S. and Powell, A. (1994), *The Shadow of Sparta*. London.

Hoekstra, K. (2016), 'Athenian Democracy and Popular Tyranny', in R. Bourke and Q. Skinner (eds), *Popular Sovereignty in Historical Perspective*. Cambridge, 15–51.

Hölkeskamp, K. J. (1999), *Schiedsrichter, Geseztgeber und Geseztgebung im archaischen Griechenland*. Stuttgart.

Hölkeskamp, K. J. (2002), '*Nomos, Thesmos*, und Verwandtes. Vergleichende Überlegungen zur Konzeptualisierung geschriebenen Rechts im klassischen Griechenland', in D. Cohen (ed.), *Demokratie, Recht und soziale Kontrolle im klassischen Athen*, Munich, 115–46.

Honneth, A. (1995), *Struggle for Recognition: The Moral Grammar of Social Conflict*. Cambridge.

Horky, P. S. and Johnson R. M. (2020), 'On Law and Justice Attributed to Archytas of Tarentum' in D. Wolfsdorf (ed.), *Early Greek Ethics*. Cambridge, 455–90.

Hornblower, S. (1996), *A Commentary on Thucydides*, vols I–II. Oxford.

Hornblower, S. (2006), 'Thucydides and the Argives', in A. Rengakos and A. Tsakmakis (eds), *Brill's Companion to Thucydides*. Leiden, 615–28.

Hornblower, S. (2009), 'Thucydides and the Athenian *Boule* (Council of Five Hundred)', in L. Mitchell and L. Rubinstein (eds), *Greek History and Epigraphy: Essays in Honour of P. J. Rhodes*. Swansea, 251–64.

Humble, N. (2021), *Xenophon of Athens. A Socratic on Sparta*. Cambridge.

Hunter, V. (1994), *Policing Athens: Social Control in the Attic Lawsuits 420–320 BCE*. Princeton.

Ismard, P. (2010), *La cité des réseaux: Athènes et ses associations, vie-ier siècle av. J.-C*. Paris.

Ismard, P. (2012), 'Le périmètre de la légalité dans l'Athènes classique: réponse à Robert Wallace', in B. Legras and G. Thür (eds), *Symposion 2011 Études d'histoire du droit grec et hellénistique*. Vienna, 127–34.

Ismard, P. (2013), 'Les génè athéniens de la basse époque hellénistique: naissance d'une aristocratie?', in P. Fröhlich and P. Hamon (eds), *Groupes et associations dans les cités grecques (IIIe s.av. J.-C./IIe s. ap. J.-C.)*. Geneva, 179–200.

Ismard, P. (2015), *La démocratie contre les experts: les escalves publics en Grèce ancienne*. Paris.

Jeffery, L. H. (1976), *Archaic Greece: The City-States 700–500 BCE*. London.

Jensen, C., Wenzelburger, G., and Zohlnhöfer, R. (2019), 'Dismantling the Welfare State? After Twenty-Five Years: What Have We Learned and What Should We Learn?', *Journal of European Policy* 29.5, 681–91.

BIBLIOGRAPHY 245

Jestaedt, M., Lepsius, O., Möllers, C., and Schönberger, C. (2011), *Das entgrenzte Gericht—Eine kritische Bilanz nach sechzig Jahren Bundesverfassungsgericht.* Berlin.

Johnstone, S. (2011), *A History of Trust in Ancient Greece.* Chicago.

Jones, N. F. (1999), *The Associations of Classical Athens: The Response to Democracy.* Oxford.

Jordan, B. (1990), 'The Ceremony of the Helots in Thucydides IV 80', *AC* 59, 37–69.

Jordan, D. R. (1995), 'A Curse Tablet against Opponents at Law', in A. L. Boegehold (ed.), *The Lawcourts at Athens: Sites, Building, Equipments, Procedure and Testimonia.* Princeton, 55–7.

Joyce, C. J. (2008), 'The Athenian Amnesty and the Scrutiny of 403', *CQ* 58.2, 507–18.

Joyce, C. J. (2014), 'Μὴ μνησικακεῖν and "All the Laws" (Andocides *On the Mysteries 81–2*): A Reply to E. Carawan', *Antichthon* 48, 37–54.

Joyce, C. J. (2015), 'Oaths (ὅρκοι), Covenants (συνθῆκαι) and Laws (νόμοι) in the Athenian Reconciliation Agreement of 403 BCE', *Antichthon* 49, 24–49.

Joyce, C. J. (2016), 'A Political and Legal Paradigm: The Athenian Reconciliation Agreement of 403 BCE and Its Legacy for Greek City States in the Classical and Hellenistic Ages', in E. M. Harris and M. Canevaro (eds), *The Oxford Handbook of Ancient Greek Law.* Oxford, https://doi.org/10.1093/oxfordhb/9780199599257.013.26

Joyce, C. J. (2022), *Amnesty and Reconciliation in Late Fifth Century Athens: Rule of Law under the Restored Democracy.* Edinburgh.

Kahrstedt, U. (1922), *Griechisches Staatsrecht,* Vol. 1: *Sparta und seine Symmachie.* Göttingen.

Kahrstedt, U. (1934), *Studien zum öffentlichen Recht Athens,* Vol. 1: *Staatsgebiet und Staatsangehörige in Athen.* Stuttgart.

Kahrstedt, U. (1938a), *Untersuchungen zur Magistratur in Athen.* Stuttgart and Berlin.

Kahrstedt, U. (1938b), 'Die Nomotheten und die Legislative in Athen'. *Klio* 3, 1–25.

Kallet-Marx, L. (1994), 'Money Talks: *Rhetor, Demos* and the Resources of the Athenian Empire', in R. Osborne and S. Hornblower (eds), *Ritual, Finance and Politics: Athenian Democracy Accounts Presented to David Lewis.* Oxford, 227–51.

Kallet, L. (2022), 'A Counting People: Valuing Numeracy in Democratic Athens', in R. Sing, A. T. van Berkel, and R. Osborne (eds), *Numbers and Numeracy in the Greek Polis.* Leiden, 27–57.

Kantor, G. (2012), 'Ideas of Law in Hellenistic and Roman Legal Practice', in P. Dresch and H. Skoda (eds), *Legalism: Anthropology and History.* Oxford, 55–83.

Kantor, G. (2013), 'Local Courts of Chersonesus Taurica in the Roman Age', in P. Martzavou and N. Papazarkadas (eds), *Epigraphical Approaches to the Post-Classical Polis.* Oxford, 69–86.

Kantor, G. (2015), 'Greek Law under the Romans', in E. M. Harris and M. Canevaro (eds), *The Oxford Handbook of Ancient Greek Law.* Oxford, https://doi.org/10.1093/oxfordhb/9780199599257.013.25

Keaney, J. J. (1974), 'Theophrastus on Greek Judicial Procedure', *TAPhA* 104, 179–94.

Keim, B. (2018), 'Communities of Honor in Herodotus' Histories', *AHB* 32.3–4, 129–47.

Kelly, G. H. (1981), 'Policy-Making in the Spartan Assembly', *Antichthon* 15, 47–61.

Kelsen, H. (1961), *General Theory of Law and State.* New York.

Kennell, N. M. (2010), *Spartans: A New History.* New York, Oxford, and Chichester.

Kloppenborg, J. S. and Ascough, R. S. (2011), *Greco-Roman Associations. Texts, Translation, Commentary,* Vol. 1: *Attica, Central Greece, Macedonia, Thrace.* Berlin and New York.

Knoepfler, D. (1990), 'Contributions à l'épigraphie de Chalcis', *BCH* 114, 473–98.

Knoepfler, D. (2001), *Décrets érétriens de proxénie et de citoyenneté, Eretria IX.* Lausanne.

246 BIBLIOGRAPHY

Koch, C. (1995–6), 'Der Bouleuten-Eid. Ein Beitrag zur Verfassungsentwicklung in Athen'. *Bulletino dell' Istituto di Diritto Romano 'Vittorio Scajola'*, n. 37–38, 277–301.

Koch, C. (2001), 'Prozesse gegen Tyrannis: Die Vorgänge in Eresos in der 2. Hälfte des 4. Jh. v. Chr.', *Dike* 4, 169–217.

Kockel, V. (1995), '*Bouleuteria*. Arkitektonische Form und urbanischer Kontext', in M. Wörrle and P. Zanker (eds), *Stadtbild und Bürgerbild im Hellenismus*. Munich, 241–50.

Konstan, D. (2006), *The Emotions of the Ancient Greeks*. Toronto.

Konstantinidou, K. (2014), 'Oath and Curse', in A. H. Sommerstein and I. C. Torrance (eds), *Oaths and Swearing in Ancient Greece*. Berlin, 6–47.

Körner, R. (Hallof, K. ed.) (1993), *Inschriftliche Gesetzestexte der frühen griechischen Polis*. Cologne.

Kourinou-Pikoula, E. (1992–8), '$M\nu\hat{\alpha}\mu\alpha$ $\gamma\epsilon\rho\sigma\nu\tau\epsilon\iota\alpha s$', *Horos* 10–12, 259–76.

Kralli, I. (1999), 'Athens and Her Leading Citizens in the Early Hellenistic Period (338–261 BCE): The Evidence of the Decrees Awarding the Highest Honours', *Archaiognosia* 10, 133–61.

Kremmydas, C. (2012), *Commentary on Demosthenes' Against Leptines with Introduction, Text and Translation*. Oxford.

Kremmydas, C. (2018), '*Anakrisis* and the Framing of Strategies of Argumentation in Athenian Public Trials', in C. Carey, I. Giannadaki, and B. Griffith-Williams (eds), *Use and Abuse of Law in the Athenian Courts*. Leiden, 110–31.

Kritzas, C. (2006), 'Nouvelles inscriptions d'Argos : les archives des comptes du trésor sacré (IV s. av. J.-C.)', *CRAI* 150.1, 397–434.

Kritzas, C. (2009), '$OBOAOI$ $AP\Gamma O\Lambda IKOI$', in S. Drougou, D. Evgenidou, C. Kritzas, N. Kaltsas, V. Penna, H., Tsourti, M. Galani-Krikou, and E. Palli (eds), *KEPMATIA $\Phi I\Lambda IA\Sigma$. $T\iota\mu\eta\tau\iota\kappa\acute{o}s$ $\tau\acute{o}\mu os$ $\gamma\iota\alpha$ $\tau o\nu$ $I\omega\acute{\alpha}\nu\nu\eta$ $To\upsilon\rho\acute{\alpha}\tau\sigma o\gamma\lambda o\upsilon$*. Athens, 9–23.

Labarre, G. (1996), *Les cités de Lesbos aux époques hellénistique et impériale*. Lyon.

Laks, A. (2000), 'The *Laws*', in C. J. Rowe and M. Schofield (eds), *The Cambridge History of Greek and Roman Political Thought*. Cambridge, 258–92.

Lalonde, G. V. (1991), '*Horoi*', in *The Athenian Agora: The Results of the Excavations Conducted by the American School of Classical Studies at Athens. Inscriptions*, vol. XIX. Princeton, 1–51.

Lambert, S. D. (1993), *The Phratries of Attica*. Ann Arbor.

Lambert, S. D. (2010), 'A Polis and Its Priests: Athenian Priesthoods before and after Pericles' Citizenship Law', *Historia* 59.2, 143–75.

Lambert, S. D. (2011a), 'Some Political Shifts in Lykourgan Athens', in V. Azoulay and P. Ismard (eds), *Clisthène et Lycurgue d'Athènes: autour du politique dans la cité classique*. Paris, 175–90.

Lambert, S. D. (2011b), 'What Was the Point of Inscribing Honorific Decrees in Classical Athens', in S. Lambert (ed.), *A Sociable Man: Essays on Ancient Greek Social Behavious in Honour of Nick Fisher*. Swansea, 193–214.

Lambert, S. D. (2012), *Inscribed Athenian Laws and Decrees 352–322 BCE: Epigraphical Essays*. Leiden and Boston.

Lambert, S. D. (2017), *Inscribed Athenian Laws and Decrees 352–322 BCE: Historical Essays*. Leiden and Boston.

Landauer, M. (2023), 'Demos (a)kurios? Agenda Power and Democratic Control in Ancient Greece', *European Journal of Political Theory* 22.3, 375–98.

Lane, M. (1998), *Method and Politics in Plato's* Stateman. Cambridge.

Lanérès, N. (2012), 'La dédicace du «trône» d'Aléa "SEG" 46, 400, nouvelle lecture'. *RDE* 125.2, 715–25.

BIBLIOGRAPHY 247

Langdon, M. K. (2015), 'Herders' Graffiti', in A. P. Matthaiou and N. Papazarkadas (eds), *ΑΞΩΝ: Studies in Honor of Ronald S. Stroud*. Athens, 49–58.

Lanni, A. (2006), *Law and Justice in the Courts of Classical Athens*. Cambridge.

Lanni, A. (2010), 'Judicial Review and the Athenian Constitution', in M. H. Hansen (ed.), *Démocratie athénienne—Démocratie moderne: tradition et influences, Entretienes sur l'Antiquité Classique 56*. Geneva, 235–63.

Lanni, A. (2016), *Law and Order in Ancient Athens*. Cambridge.

Lanza, D. (1977), *Il tiranno e il suo pubblico*. Turin.

Larsen, J. A. O. (1955), *Greek Federal States: Their Institutions and History*. Oxford.

Leão, D. F. and Rhodes, P. J. (2015), *The Laws of Solon: A New Edition with Introduction, Translation and Commentary*. London.

Leijssenaar, B. and Walker, N. (eds) (2019), *Sovereignty in Action*. Cambridge.

Lévêque, P. and Vidal-Naquet, P. (1964), *Clisthène l'Athénien*. Paris.

Levitsky, S. and Murillo, M. (2009), 'Variation in Institutional Strength', *Annual Review of Political Science* 12, 115–33.

Lévy, E. (1993), '*Politeia* et *Politeuma* chez Aristote', in M. Piérart (éd.), *Aristote et Athènes*. Paris, 65–90.

Lewis, D. (2016), Review of P. Ismard 'La démocratie contre les experts. Les eclaves publics en Grèce ancienne', *CR* 66.2, 476–8.

Lewis, D. (2018), *Greek Slave Systems in their Eastern Mediterranean Context, c. 800-146 BC*, Oxford.

Lewis, D. M. (1954), 'Note on Attic Inscriptions', *ABSA* 49, 17–50.

Lewis, D. M. (Rhodes, P.J. ed.) (1997), *Selected Papers in Greek and Near Eastern History*. Cambridge.

Liddel, P. (2003), 'The Places of Publication of Athenian State Decrees from the 5th Century BCE to the 3rd Century AD', *ZPE* 143, 79–93.

Liddel, P. (2007), *Civic Obligation and Individual Liberty in Ancient Athens*. Oxford.

Liddel, P. (2009), 'The Decree Cultures of Ancient Megarid', *CQ* 59.2, 411–36.

Liddel, P. (2010), 'Epigraphy, Legislation and Power within the Athenian Empire', *BICS* 53.1, 99–128.

Liddel, P. (2016), 'The Honorific Decree of Fourth-Century Athens: Trends, Perceptions, Controversies', in C. Tiersch (ed.), *Die Athenische Demokratie im 4. Jahrhundert zwischen Modernisierung und Tradition*. Stuttgart, 335–58.

Liddel, P. (2020a), *The Decrees of Fourth-Century Athens (403/2–322/1 BC): The Literary Evidence*, vol. 1. Cambridge.

Liddel, P. (2020b), *The Decrees of Fourth-Century Athens (403/2–322/1 BC): Political and Cultural Perspectives*, vol. 2. Cambridge.

Liddel, P. and Low, P. (eds) (2013), *Inscriptions and Their Uses in Greek and Roman Literature*. Oxford.

Linders, T. (1975), *The Treasurers of the Other Gods in Athens and Their Functions*. Meisenheim am Glan.

Link, S. (2000), *Das frühe Sparta: Untersuchungen zu seiner staatlichen und gesellschaftlichen Entwicklung im 7. und 6. Jh. v.Chr*. St. Katharinen.

Lipka, M. (2002), *Xenophon's Spartan Constitution. Introduction. Text. Commentary*. Berlin.

Loddo, L. (2018), *Solone demotikotatos: il legislatore e il politico nella cultura democratica ateniese*. Milan.

Loddo, L. (ed.) (2020a), *Political Refugees in the Ancient Greek World: Literary, Historical and Philosophical Essays* (= Pallas 112). Toulouse.

248 BIBLIOGRAPHY

Loddo, L. (2020b), *"Ἕως ἂν κατέλθωσιν εἰς τὴν αὐτῶν*: Did the Athenians Reduce Their Reception of Refugees in the Fourth Century BC?', in L. Loddo (ed.), *Political Refugees in the Ancient Greek World: Literary, Historical and Philosophical Essays* (= Pallas 112). Toulouse, 199-230.

Loddo, L. (2022), *I rifugiati politici nella Grecia antica*. Bologna.

Lonis, R. (1991), 'La reintegration des exiles politiques en Grèce: le problème des biens', in P. Gouwkowsky and C. Brixhe (eds), *Hellènika Symmikta: Histoire, Archéologie, Epigraphie*. Nancy, 91-109.

Loraux, N. (1981), *L'invention d'Athènes: histoire de l'oraison funèbre dans la cité classique*. Paris.

Loraux, N. (2002), *The Divided City: On Memory and Forgetting in Ancient Athens*. Princeton.

Low, P. A. (2007), *Interstate Relations in Classical Greece: Morality and Power*. Cambridge.

Low, P. A. (2018), 'Hegemonic Legitimacy (and Its Absence) in Classical Greece', in M. Canevaro, A. Erskine, B. Gray, and J. Ober (eds), *Ancient Greek History and Contemporary Social Science*. Edinburgh, 433-54.

Lowdnes, V. (2005), 'Something Old, Something New, Something Borrowed: How Institutions Change (and Stay the Same) in Local Governance'. *Policy Studies* 26.3-4, 293-309.

Lowdnes, V. and Roberts, M. (2013), *Why Institutions Matter: New Institutionalism in Political Sciences*. London.

Luhmann, N. (1979), *Trust and Power*. Chichester.

Lundgreen, C. (2022), 'On the Usability of the Concept of Sovereignty for the Ancient World', in C. Smith (ed.), *Sovereignty. A Global Perspective*. Oxford, 15-37.

Lupi, M. (2014a), 'Il voto dei re spartani', *QS* 79, 33-58.

Lupi, M. (2014b), 'Testo e contesti: la Grande *Rhetra* e le procedure spartane di ammissione alla cittadinanza', *IncidAntico* 12, 9-41.

Luraghi, N. (2013), 'Ruling Alone: Monarchy in Greek Political Thought', in N. Luraghi (ed.), *The Splendors and Misery of Ruling Alone: Encounters with Monarchy from Archaic Greece to the Hellenistic Mediterrenean*. Stuttgart, 11-24.

Luraghi, N. (2015), 'Anatomy of the Monster: Discourse of Tyranny in Ancient Greece', in H. Börm (ed.), *Antimonarchic Discourse in Antiquity*. Stuttgart, 67-84.

Luraghi, N. (2018), 'Discourse of Tyranny and the Greek Roots of the Bad King', in N. Panou and H. Schadee (eds), *Evil Lords: Theories of Representations of Tyranny from Antiquity to the Reinassance*. Oxford, 11-26.

Luraghi, N. and Magnetto, A. (2012), 'The Controversy between Megalopolis and Messene in a New Inscription from Messene' (with an Appendix by C. Habicht), *Chiron* 42, 509-50.

Luther, A. (2004), *Könige und Ephoren: Untersuchungen zur spartanischen Verfassungsgeschichte*. Frankfurt am Main.

Ma, J. (1999), *Antiochus III and the Cities of Western Asia Minor*. Oxford.

Ma, J. (2005), 'Kings', in A. Erskine (ed.), *A Companion to the Hellenistic World*. Malden-Oxford, 177-95.

Ma, J. (2018), 'Whatever Happened to Athens? Thoughts on the Great Convergence and Beyond', in M. Canevaro and B. Gray (eds), *The Hellenistic and Imperial Reception of Athenian Democracy and Political Thought*. Oxford, 277-97.

MacCormick, N. (2005), *Rhetoric and the Rule of Law: A Theory of Legal Reasoning*. Oxford.

MacCormick, N. (2007), *Institutions of Law: An Essay in Legal Theory (Law, State, and Practical Reason)*. Oxford.

BIBLIOGRAPHY 249

MacDowell, D. M. (1962), *Andokides, On the Mysteries. Text Edited with Introduction and Commentary*. Oxford.

MacDowell, D. M. (1975), 'Law-Making at Athens in the Fourth Century BCE', *JHS* 95, 62–74.

MacDowell, D. M. (1978), *The Law in Classical Athens*. London.

MacDowell, D. M. (1986), *Spartan Law*. Edinburgh.

MacDowell, D. M. (1991), 'The Athenian Procedure of *Phasis*', in M. Gagarin (ed.), *Symposion 1990: Vorträge zur griechischen und hellenistischen Rechtgeschichte*. Cologne, 187–98.

MacDowell, D. M. (2000), *Demosthenes: On the False Embassy (Oration 19)*. Oxford.

MacDowell, D. M. (2005), 'The Athenian Procedure of *Dokimasia* of Orators', in R. W. Wallace, and M. Gagarin (eds), *Symposion 2001: Akten der Gesellschaft für Griechische und Hellenistische Rechtsgeschichte 16*. Vienna, 79–87.

MacDowell, D. M. (2009), *Demosthenes the Orator*. Oxford.

Mack, W. (2015), *Proxeny and Polis: Institutional Networks in the Ancient Greek World*. Oxford.

Mackil, E. (2013), *Creating a Common Polity: Religion, Economy, and Politics in the Making of Greek Koinon*. Berkeley.

Mackil, E. (2021), 'Confiscation, Exile, and Return: The Property Problem and Its Legal Solutions', in K. Harter-Uibopuu and W. Riess (eds), *Symposion 2019. Vörträge zur griechischen und hellenistischen Rechtsgeschichte*. Vienna, 185–211.

Maddoli, G. (2007), 'Epigrafi di Iaso, Nuovo Supplemento 1', *PP* 62, 354–6.

Mæhle, I. (2018), 'Patronage in Ancient Sparta', in M. Canevaro, A. Erskine, B. Gray, and J. Ober (eds), *Ancient Greek History and the Contemporary Social Sciences*. Edinburgh, 241–68.

Maffi, A. (2002), 'Studi recenti sulla Grande *Rhetra*'. *Dike* 5, 195–235.

Maffi, A. (2015), 'Il consiglio degli anziani e le istituzioni politiche delle città cretesi: risposta a Maria Youni', in M. Gagarin and A. Lanni (eds), *Symposion 2013: Vorträge zur griechischen und hellenistischen Rechtsgeschichte*. Vienna, 127–30.

Magnetto, A. (2013), 'Ambasciatori plenipotenziari delle città greche in età classica ed ellenistica: terminologia e prerogative', in M. Mari and J. Thornton (eds), *Parole in movimento: linguaggio politico e lessico storiografico nel mondo ellenistico, Atti del Convegno Internazionale, Roma 21–23 febbraio 2011* (= *Studi Ellenistici* 27). Pisa, 223–41.

Magnetto, A. (2016), 'Interstate Arbitration and Foreign Judges', in E. M. Harris and M. Canevaro (eds), *The Oxford Handbook of Ancient Greek Law*. Oxford, https://doi.org/10.1093/oxfordhb/9780199599257.013.20

Mahoney, J. (2006), 'Analyzing Path Dependence: Lessons from the Social Sciences', in A. Wimmer and R. Kössler (eds),*Understanding Change. Models, Methodologies, and Metaphors*. New York.

Manfredini, M. and Piccirilli, L. (1980), *Plutarco: la Vita di Solone*. Milan.

Mann, C. (2001), *Athlet und Polis im archaischen und frühklassischen Griechenland*. Göttingen.

Mann, C. (2007), *Die Demagogen und das Volk: zur politischen Kommunikation im Athen des 5. Jahrhunderts v. Chr*. Berlin.

Mann, C. (2012), 'Gleichheiten und Ungleichheiten in der hellenistischen Polis: Überlegungen zum Stand der Forschung', in Mann, C. and Scholz, P. (2012), *'Demokratie' im Hellenismus: von der Herrschaft des Volkes zur Herrschaft der Honoratioren? Die hellenistische Polis als Lebensform*. Berlin, 11–27.

250 BIBLIOGRAPHY

Mann, C. and Scholz, P. (2012), *'Demokratie' im Hellenismus: von der Herrschaft des Volkes zur Herrschaft der Honoratioren? Die hellenistische Polis als Lebensform.* Berlin.

Mansbridge, J., Bohman, J., Chambers, S., Christiano, T., Fung, A., Parkinson, J., Thompson, D. and Warren, M. E. (2012), 'A Systemic Approach to Deliberative Democracy', in J. Parkinson and J. Mansbridge (eds), *Deliberative Systems—Deliberative Democracy at the Large Scale.* Cambridge, 2–26.

March, J. G. and Olsen, P. J. (1984), 'The New Institutionalism: Organizational Factors in Political Life', *APSR* 78.3, 734–49.

March, J. G. and Olsen, P. J. (1989), *Rediscovering Institutions: Organizational Basis of Politics.* New York.

Mari, M. (2018), 'Powers in Dialogue: The Letters and *Diagrammata* of Macedonians Kings to Local Communities', in P. Ceccarelli, L. Doering, T. Fögen, and I. Gildenhard (eds), *Letters and Communities: Studies in Socio-Political Dimension of Ancient Epistolography.* Oxford, 122–46.

Marr, J. L. and Rhodes, P. J. (eds) (2008), *The 'Old Oligarch' Constitution of the Athenian Attributed to Xenophon.* Liverpool.

Martin, G. (2006), 'Forms of Address in Athenian Courts', *Museum Helveticum* 63.2, 75–88.

Mason, H. J. (1974), *Greek Terms for Roman Institutions: A Lexicon and Analysis.* Toronto.

Mattingly, H. B. (1961), 'Athens and Euboea', *JHS* 81, 124–32.

Mattingly, H. B. (1996), *The Athenian Empire Restored: Epigraphical and Historical Studies.* Ann Arbor.

McElwee, L. A. (1975), ΑΔΕΙΑ: *Amnesty and Immunity at Athens from Solon to Demosthenes.* PhD Diss. Albany, NY.

McLean I., and McMillan, A. (eds) (2009), *Concise Oxford Dictionary of Politics.* Oxford (4th edition).

Migeotte, P. (2014), *Les finances des cités grecques aux périodes classique et hellénistique.* Paris.

Millender, E. G. (1999), 'Athenian Ideology and the Empowered Spartan Woman', in S. Hodkinson and A. Powell (eds), *Sparta: New Perspectives.* Swansea, 355–91.

Millender, E. G. (2001), 'Spartan Literacy Revisited', *ClAnt* 20.1, 127–41.

Millender, E. G. (2009), 'The Spartan Dyarchy: A Comparative Perspective', in S. Hodkinson (ed.), *Sparta: Comparative Approaches.* London, 31–40.

Millender, E. G. (2017a), 'Kingship: The History, Power, and Prerogatives of the Spartans' "Divine" Dyarchy', in A. Powell (ed.), *A Companion to Sparta*, vol. 2. Chichester, 452–79.

Millender, E. G. (2017b), 'Spartan Women', in A. Powell (ed.), *A Companion to Sparta*, vol. 2. Chichester, 500–24.

Miller, F. D. (1997), *Nature, Justice and Rights in Aristotle's* Politics. Oxford.

Miller, F. D. (ed.), (in association with) Biondi, C. A. (2007), *A History of the Philosophy of Law from the Ancient Greeks to the Scholiastics*, in E. Pattaro (gen. ed.), *A Treatise of Legal Philosophy and General Jurisprudence* 6. Dordrecht.

Mirhady, D. (2007), 'The Dikast's Oath and the Question of Fact', in A. Sommerstein and J. Fletcher (eds), *Horkos: The Oath in Greek Society.* Exeter, 48–59, 228–33.

Missiou-Ladi, A. (1987), 'Coercive Diplomacy in Greek Interstate Relations'. *CQ* 37, 336–45.

Missou, A. (2011), *Literacy and Democracy in Fifth-Century Athens.* Cambridge.

Mitchell, L. (1997), *Greeks Bearing Gifts: The Public Use of Private Relationships 435–323 BC.* Cambridge.

Moatti, C. and Müller, C. (eds) (2018), *Statuts personnels et espaces sociaux: questions grecques et romaines.* Nanterre.

BIBLIOGRAPHY 251

Møller, J. and Skaaning, S. E. (2014), *The Rule of Law: Definitions, Measures, Patterns, and Causes.* London.

Moreno, A. (2007), *Feeding the Democracy: The Athenian Grain Supply in the Fifth and Fourth Centuries B.C.* Oxford.

Moreno, A. (2009), '"The Attic Neighbour": The Cleruchy in the Athenian Empire', in J. Ma, N. Papazarkadas, and R. Parker (eds), *Interpreting the Athenian Empire.* London, 211–21.

Morrow, G. R. (1960), *Plato's Cretan City: A Historical Interpretation of the Laws.* Princeton.

Mosconi, G. (2021), *Democrazia e buon governo: cinque tesi democratiche nella Grecia del V secolo a.C.* Milan.

Mosley, D. J. (1973), *Envoys and Diplomacy in Ancient Greece.* Wiesbaden.

Mouritsen, H. (2015), 'Incongruence of Power: The Roman Constitution in Theory and Practice', in D. Hammer (ed.), *A Companion to Greek Democracy and the Roman Republic.* London, 146–63.

Mouritsen, H. (2017), *Politics in the Roman Republic.* Cambridge.

Murray, O. (1990), 'Cities of Reason', in O. Murray and S. Price (eds), *The Greek City from Homer to Alexander.* Oxford, 1–27.

Müller, C. (2005), 'La procédure d'adoption des décrets en Béotie de la fin du IIIe s. av. J-C. au Ier s. apr. J.-C.', in P. Fröhlich and C. Müller (eds), *Citoyenneté et partecipation a la basse époque hellenistique.* Geneva, 95–120.

Müller, C. (2014), 'A *koinon* after 146? Reflections about the Political and Institutional Situation of Boeotia in the Late Hellenistic Period', in N. Papazarkadas (ed.), *The Epigraphy and History of Boeotia: New Finds, New Prospects.* Leiden, 119–46.

Nafissi, M. (1991), *La nascita del* kosmos: *studi sulla storia e la società di Sparta.* Perugia.

Nafissi, M. (2007), 'Forme di controllo a Sparta', *Il Pensiero Politico* 2, 329–44.

Nafissi, M. (2009), 'Sparta', in K. Raaflaub and H. van Wees (eds), *A Companion to Archaic Greece,* Chichester, 117–37.

Nafissi, M. (2008), 'Asteropos e Epitadeus: storie di due efori spartani e di altri personaggi dai nomi parlanti', *L'Incidenza dell'Antico* 6, 46–90.

Nafissi, M. (2010), 'The Great *Rhetra* (Plut. Lyc. 6): A Retrospective and Intentional Construct?', in L. Foxhall, H. J. Gehrke, and N. Luraghi (eds), *Intentional History: Spinning the Time in Ancient History.* Stuttgart, 89–120.

Nafissi, M. (2017), 'Lykourgos the Spartan "Lawgiver": Ancient Beliefs and Modern Scholarship', in A. Powell (ed.), *A Companion to Sparta,* vol. 1. Chichester, 93–123.

Nagy, G. and Noussia Fantuzzi, M. (2015), *Solon in the Making: The Early Reception in the Fifth and Fourth Centuries.* Berlin.

Naiden, F. S. (2006), *Ancient Supplication.* Oxford.

Netz, R. (2002), 'Counter Culture: Towards a History of Greek Numeracy'. *History of Science* 40.3, 321–52.

Nielsen, T. H. (2002), *Arkadia and Its Poleis in the Archaic and Classical Periods.* Göttingen.

Nielsen, T. H. (2015), 'The Arkadian Confederacy', in H. Beck and P. Funke (eds), *Federalism in Antiquity.* Cambridge, 250–68.

ní Mheallaigh, K. (2014), *Reading Fiction with Lucian: Fakes, Freaks and Hyperreality.* Cambridge.

Nippel, W. (1980), *Mischverfassungstheorie und Verfassungsrealität in Antike und früher Neuzeit.* Stuttgart.

Nippel, W. (1994), 'Ancient and Modern Republicanism: "Mixed Constitution" and "Ephors"', in B. Fontana (ed.), *The Invention of the Modern Republic.* Cambridge, 6–26.

BIBLIOGRAPHY

North, D. (1990), *Institutions, Institutional Change, and Economic Performance.* Cambridge.

Ober, J. (1985), *Fortress Attica: Defense of the Athenian Land Frontier 404–322 BCE.* Leiden.

Ober, J. (1989a), *Mass and Elite in Democratic Athens: Rhetoric, Ideology and the Power of the People.* Princeton.

Ober, J. (1989b), 'Review Article: The Nature of Athenian Democracy', *CPh* 84.4, 322–34.

Ober, J. (1996), *The Athenian Revolution: Essays on Ancient Greek Democracy and Political Theory.* Princeton.

Ober, J. (2006), 'Thucydides and the Invention of Political Science', in A. Tsakmakis and A. Rengakos (eds), *Brill's Companion to Thucydides.* Leiden, 131–59.

Ober, J. (2007), '"I Besiege That Man": Democracy Revolutionary Start', in K. A. Raaflaub, J. Ober, and R. W. Wallace (eds), *Origins of Democracy in Ancient Greece.* Berkeley, 83–104.

Ober, J. (2008), *Democracy and Knowledge: Innovation and Learning in Classical Athens.* Princeton.

Ober, J. (2015), *Rise and Fall of Classical Greece.* Princeton.

Oliver, G. J. (2003), 'Oligarchy at Athens after the War: Epigraphic Evidence for the *Boule* and the *Ekklesia*', in O. Palagia and S. Tracy (eds), *The Macedonians in Athens 322–229 BCE: Proceedings of the International Conference Held at the University of Athens, May 24–26, 2001.* Oxford, 38–51.

Oliver, G. J. (2007), *War, Food and Politics in Early Hellenistic Athens.* Oxford.

Ollier, F. (1933), *Le Mirage Spartiate. Étude sur l'idéalisation de Sparta dans l'antiquité grecque de l'origine jusqu'aux Cyniques.* Paris.

O'Neil, J. L. (2000), 'Royal Authority and City Law under Alexander and His Hellenistic Successors', *CQ* 50.2, 424–31.

Oranges, A. (2021), Euthyna: *Il rendiconto dei magistrati nella democrazia ateniese (V-IV secolo a.C.).* Milan.

Osborne, M. J. (1981–3), *Naturalization in Athens.* 4 vols. Brussels.

Osborne, R. (1985a), Demos: *The Discovery of Classical Attika.* Cambridge.

Osborne, R. (1985b), 'Law in Action in Classical Athens', *JHS* 105, 40–58.

Ostwald, M. (1969), *Nomos and the Beginnings of Athenian Democracy.* Oxford.

Ostwald, M. (1986), *From Popular Sovereignty to the Sovereignty of Law: Law, Society, and Politics in Fifth-Century Athens.* Berkley and Los Angeles.

O'Sullivan, L. (2009), *The Regime of Demetrius of Phalerum in Athens, 317–307 BCE.* Leiden.

Paga, J. (2020), *Building Democracy in Late Archaic Athens.* Oxford.

Palier, U. (2010), 'Ordering Change: Understanding the "Bismarckian" Welfare Reform Trajectory', in B. Palier (ed.), *A Long Goodbye to Bismarck? The Politics of Welfare Reforms in Continental Europe.* Amsterdam, 19–35.

Paoli, U. E. (1933), *Studi sul processo attico.* Padua.

Paoli, U. E. (1953), 'La sauvegarde de la légalité dans la démocratie athénienne', *Festschrift Hans Lewald.* Basel, 133–41.

Paoli, U. E. (1960), 'Diadicasia', *Novissimo Digesto Italiano* 5, 572–78.

Papakonstantinou, Z. (2008), *Lawmaking and Adjudication in Archaic Greece.* London.

Papazarkadas, N. (2009), 'Epigraphy and the Athenian Empire: Reshuffling the Chronological Cards', in J. Ma, N. Papazarkadas, and R. Parker (eds), *Interpreting the Athenian Empire.* London, 67–88.

Papazarkadas, N. (2011), *Sacred and Public Land in Ancient Athens.* Oxford.

Parker, R. (1983), *Miasma: Pollution and Purification in Early Greek Religion.* Oxford.

BIBLIOGRAPHY 253

Parker, R. (1989), 'Spartan Religion', in A. Powell (ed.), *Classical Sparta: Techniques behind Her Success*. London, 142–72.

Parker, R. (1997), *Athenian Religion: A History*. Oxford.

Parker, R. (2005), *Polytheism and Society at Athens*. Oxford.

Parker, R. and Obbink, D. (2001). 'Aus der Arbeit der «Inscriptiones Graecae» VIII: Three Further Inscriptions Concerning Coan Cults', *Chiron* 31, 256–76.

Pasquino, P. (1998), *Emmanuel Sieyes et l'invention de la constitution en France*. Paris.

Pasquino, P. (2003), 'Prolegomena to a Theory of Judicial Power: The Concept of Judicial Independence in Theory and History', *LPICT* 2, 11–25.

Pasquino, P. (2005), 'Il potere diviso. Dalla *graphé paranomon* nella democrazia ateniese, a John Locke e James Madison', in A. Arienzo and D. Caruso (eds), *Conflitti*. Naples, 89–99.

Pasquino, P. (2010), 'Democracy Ancient and Modern: Divided Power', in M. H. Hansen (ed.), *Démocratie athénienne—Démocratie moderne: tradition et influences: Neuf exposés suivis de discussions. Entretiens sur l'Antiquité classique* 56. Geneva, 1–49.

Pasquino, P. (2012), 'Introduction to the Articles on Rule of Law and Divided Power', *Justice System Journal* 33.2, 131–5.

Pasquino, P. (2015), 'The New Separation of Powers: Horizontal Accountability', *Italian Journal of Public Law* 1, 157–69.

Pasquino, P. (2019), 'Popular Sovereignty: The People's Two Bodies', in B. Leijssnaar and N. Walker (eds), *Sovereignty in Action*. Cambridge, 144–58.

Patera, M. (2013), 'Reflections on the Discourse of Fear in Greek Sources', in A. Chaniotis and P. Ducrey (eds), *Unveiling Emotions*, Vol. II: *Emotions in Greece and Rome: Texts, Images, Material Culture*. Heidelberg, 109–34.

Pébarthe, C. (2006), *Cité, démocratie et écriture: histoire de l'alphabétisation d'Athènes à l'époque classique*. Paris.

Pébarthe, C. (2013), 'Les archives de la cité de raison: démocratie athénienne et pratiques documentaires à l'époque classique', in M. Faraguna (ed.), *Archives and Archival Documents in Ancient Societies*. Trieste, 107–25.

Pečírka, J. (1966), *The Formula for the Grant of Enktesis in Attic Inscriptions*. Prague.

Pecorella Longo, C. (2004), 'Il condono della pena in Atene in età classica', *Dike* 7, 85–111.

Pédech, P. (1989), *Trois historiens méconnus: Théopompe, Duris, Phylarque*. Paris.

Pelling, C. (2002), 'Herodotus' Debates on Constitutions', *Proceedings of the Cambridge Philological Society* 48, 123–58.

Pelling, C. (2009), *Plutarch and History: Eighteen Studies*. London.

Pelling, C. (2023), 'A Doubles Match: Agis-Cleomenes and the Gracchi', in Ph. Davies and J. Mossman (eds), *Plutarch and Sparta*. Swansea, 113–38.

Pelloso, C. (2016), '*Ephesis eis to dikasterion*: Remarks and Speculations on the Legal Nature of the Solonian Reform', in D. Leão and G. Thür (eds), *Symposion 2015: Vorträge zur griechischen und hellenistischen Rechtgeschichte*. Vienna, 33–54.

Pelloso, C. (2017), 'L'ἔφεσις al tribunale popolare in diritto processuale ateniese. "Impugnazione", "rimessione" o tertium datur?', *Index* 45: 517–56.

Peters, G. B. (2014), 'Implementation Structures as Institutions'. *PPA* 29.2, 131–44.

Petersen, W. (1922), 'Studies in Greek Noun-Formation: Dental Terminations III'. *CPh* 17.1, 44–85.

Petrovic, A. and Petrovic, I. (2016), *Inner Purity and Pollution in Greek Religion*, Vol. I: *Early Greek Religion*. Oxford.

Piérart, M. (1971), 'Les *euthunoi* atheniens', *AC* 40, 526–73.

Piérart, M. (2000), 'Qui étaient les nomothètes à Athènes à l'époque de Démosthène?', in E. Lèvy (ed.), *La codification des lois dans l'antiquité*. Paris, 229–56.

254   BIBLIOGRAPHY

Piérart, M. (2016), 'Plato and the Reform of Athenian Law', in E. M. Harris and M. Canevaro (eds), *Oxford Handbook of Ancient Greek Law*. Oxford, https://doi.org/10.1093/oxfordhb/9780199599257.013.23

Pierson, P. (1995), *Dismantling the Welfare State? Reagan, Thatcher and the Politics of Retrenchment*. Cambridge.

Pierson, P. (2000a), 'Increasing Returns, Path Dependence, and the Study of Politics', *APSR* 94.2, 251–67.

Pierson, P. (2000b), 'Not Just What, but *When*: Issues of Timing and Sequence in Political Processes', *Studies in American Political Development* 14, 72–92.

Pierson, P. (2016), 'Power in Historical Institutionalism', in O. Fioretos, T. G. Falleti, and A. Sheingate (eds), *The Oxford Handbook of Historical Institutionalism*. Oxford, 125–38.

Pierson, P. and Skocpol, T. (2002), 'Historical Institutionalism in Contemporary Political Science', in I. Katznelson and H. V. Miller (eds), *Political Science: State of the Discipline*. New York, 693–721.

Pietragnoli, L. (2010), 'I *probouloi* nel pensiero politico e nella pratica istituzionale: un tentativo di sintesi', in C. Antonetti (ed.), *Lo spazio ionico e le comunità della Grecia nord-occidentale: territorio, società, istituzioni*. Pisa, 245–56.

Planeaux, C. (2000), 'The Date of Bendis' Entry into Attica', *CJ* 96.2, 165–92.

Poddighe, E. (2002), *Nel segno di Antipatro: l'eclissi della democrazia ateniese dal 323/2 al 319/8 a.C.* Rome.

Poddighe, E. (2006), 'Ateniesi infami (*atimoi*) ed ex Ateniesi senza i requisiti (*apepsephis-menoi*). Nuove osservazioni in margine al Fr. 29 Jensen di Iperide sulle diverse forme di esclusione dal corpo civico di Atene', *AFCL* 61, 5–24.

Poddighe, E. (2010), 'Riflessioni sul fondamento etico-legale e sul carattere finanziario dell'*eisphora* ateniese tra V e IV sec. a.C.', in M. R. Cataudella, A. Greco, and G. Mariotta (eds), *Strumenti e tecniche della riscossione dei tributi nel mondo antico*. Padua, 97–117.

Pospisil, L. J. (1974), *The Anthropology of Laws: A Comparative Theory*. New Haven.

Powell, A. (1999), 'Spartan Women Assertive in Politics? Plutarch's *Lives of Agis and Kleomenes*', in S. Hodkinson and A. Powell (eds), *Sparta New Perspectives*. London, 401–15.

Powell, A. and Richer, N. (2020), *Xenophon and Sparta*. Swansea.

Pressman, J. L. and Wildavsky, A. (1973), *Implementation*. Berkeley.

Price, J. J. (2001), *Thucydides and Internal War*. Cambridge.

Pritchard, D. (2015), *Public Spending and Democracy in Classical Athens*. Austin.

Proietti, G. (2021), *Prima di Erodoto: aspetti della memoria delle Guerre persiane*. Stuttgart.

Psoma, S. (2009), 'Thucydide I, 61,4: Béroia et la nouvelle localisation de Bréa', *REG* 122.2, 263–80.

Psoma, S. (2016), 'From Corcyra to Potidaea: The Decree of Brea (IG I3 46)', *ZPE* 199, 55–7.

Quass, F. (1971), *Nomos und Psephisma: Untersuchung zum griechiscen Staatsrecht*. Munich.

Raaflaub, K. A. (2000), 'Poets, Lawgivers, and the Beginning of Political Reflection in Ancient Greece', in C. J. Rowe and M. Schofield (eds), *The Cambridge History of Greek and Roman Political Thought*. Cambridge, 23–57.

Raaflaub, K. A. (2002), 'Philosophy, Science, Politics: Herodotus and the Intellectual Trends of His Time', in E. J. Bekker, I. J. F. de Jong, and H. van Wees (eds), *Brill's Companion to Herodotus*. Leiden, 149–86.

Raaflaub, K. A. (2006), 'Athenian and Spartan *Eunomia*, Or: What to Do with Solon's Timocracy?', in J. H. Blok and A. P. H. M. Lardinois (eds), *Solon of Athens: New Historical and Philological Approaches*. Leiden, 390–428.

BIBLIOGRAPHY 255

Raaflaub, K. A. (2007), 'The Breakthrough of *demokratia* in Mid-Fifth-Century Athens', in K. A. Raaflaub, J. Ober, and R. W. Wallace (eds), *Origins of Democracy in Ancient Greece*. Berkeley, 105–54.

Raaflaub, K. A. (2013), 'Archaic and Classical Greek Reflections on Politics and Government', in H. Beck (ed.), *A Companion to Ancient Greek Government*. Chichester, 73–92.

Raaflaub, K. A. and Wallace, R. W. (2007), '"People's Power" and Egalitarian Trends in Archaic Greece', in K. A. Raaflaub, J. Ober, and R. W. Wallace (eds), *Origins of Democracy in Ancient Greece*. Berkeley, 22–48.

Rebenich, S. (1997), 'Historical Prose', in S. E. Porter (ed.), *Handbook of Classical Rhetoric in the Hellenistic Period, 330 B.C.–A.D. 400*. Leiden, 265–337.

Rebenich, S. (1998), *Xenophon, Lakedaimonion Politeia. Griechisch und Deutsch, mit Einführung und Kommentar*. Darmstadt.

Rhodes, P. J. (1972), *The Athenian Boule*. Oxford.

Rhodes, P. J. (1979), 'εἰσαγγελία in Athens', *JHS* 109, 103–14.

Rhodes, P. J. (1980), 'Athenian Democracy after 403 BCE', *CJ* 75.4, 305–23.

Rhodes, P. J. (1981), *A Commentary on the Aristotelian Athenaion Politeia*. Oxford.

Rhodes, P. J. (1984), 'Members Serving in the Athenian *Boule* and the Population of Athens Again', *ZPE* 57, 200–2.

Rhodes, P. J. (1987), '*Nomothesia* in Classical Athens', *L' educazione giuridica* 5.2, 5–26.

Rhodes, P. J. (1994), *Thucydides, History III*. Warminster.

Rhodes, P. J. (1998), *Thucydides: History Books IV,1–V,24*. Warminster.

Rhodes, P. J. (2003a), *Athenian Democracy and Modern Ideology*. London.

Rhodes, P. J. (2003b), 'After the Three-Bar Sigma Controversy: The History of Athenian Imperialism Reassessed', *CQ* 58.2, 500–6.

Rhodes, P. J. (2004), 'Keeping to the Point', in E. M. Harris and L. Rubinstein (eds), *The Law and Courts in Ancient Greece*. London, 137–58.

Rhodes, P. J. (2007), 'Documents and the Greek Historians', in J. Marincola (ed.), *A Companion to Greek and Roman Historiography*. Chichester, 56–66.

Rhodes, P. J. (2008), 'Making and Breaking Treaties in the Greek World', in P. De Souza and J. France (eds), *War and Peace in Ancient and Medieval History*. Cambridge, 6–27.

Rhodes, P. J. (2009), 'State and Religion in Athenian Inscriptions', *G&R* 56, 1–13.

Rhodes, P. J. (2013), 'The Organization of Athenian Public Finance', *G&R* 60, 203–31.

Rhodes, P. J. (2015), 'Constitutional Law in the Greek World', in E. M. Harris and M. Canevaro (eds), *The Oxford Handbook of Ancient Greek Law*. Oxford, https://doi.org/10.1093/oxfordhb/9780199599257.013.12

Rhodes, P. J. (2016a), 'Boiotian Democracy?', in S. D. Gartland (ed.), *Boiotia in the Fourth Century BCE*. Philadelphia, 59–64.

Rhodes, P. J. (2016b), 'Demagogues and *demos* in Athens', *Polis* 33, 243–64.

Rhodes, P. J. with Lewis D. M. (1997), *The Decrees of the Greek States*. Oxford.

Rhodes, P. J. and Osborne R. (2003), *Greek Historical Inscriptions, 404–323 BCE*. Oxford.

Rhodes, R. A. W. (2006), 'Old Institutionalism', in R. A. W. Rhodes, S. A. Binder, and B. A. Rockman (eds), *The Oxford Handbook of Political Institutions*. Oxford, 90–108.

Richer, N. (1998), *Les éphores: études sur l'histoire et sur l'image de Sparte (VIIIe-IIIe siècle av. J. C.)*. Paris.

Richer, N. (1999), '*Aidōs* at Sparta', in S. Hodkinson and A. Powell (eds), *Sparta. New Perspectives*. Swansea, 91–115.

Richer, N. (2007), 'The Religious System at Sparta', in D. Ogden (ed.), *A Companion to Greek Religion*. Chichester, 236–52.

256 BIBLIOGRAPHY

Rizakis, A. (1998), *Achaie II. La cité de Patras. Epigraphie et histoire, Meletemata 25.* Athens.

Rizakis, A. (2008), *Achaie III. Les cités achéennes. Epigraphie et histoire.* Paris.

Rizakis, A. (2015), 'The Achaian League', in H. Beck and P. Funke (eds), *Federalism in Greek Antiquity.* Cambridge, 118–31.

Robert J., and Robert J. L. (1960), 'Bulletin épigraphique', in *RDA* 73, 134–213.

Robert, J. L. (1973), 'Les juges étrangers dans la cite grecque', in E. von Caemmemer (ed.), *Xenion: Festschrift für Pan. J. Zepos anlässlich seines 65. Geburtstages am 1. Dezember 1973.* Athens, 765–82.

Robinson, E. W. (1997), *The First Democracies: Early Popular Government outside Athens.* Stuttgart.

Robinson, E. W. (2011), *Democracy beyond Athens: Popular Government in the Greek Classical Age.* Cambridge.

Rocchi, L. (2023a), *Atimia: Dishonour, Disenfranchisment, and Civic Disability in Archaic and Classical Athens.* PhD Diss. Edinburgh.

Rocchi, L. (2023b), 'Identity, Status, and Dishonour: Was *Atimia* Relevant Only to Citizens?', in J. Filonik, C. Plastow, and R. Zelnick-Abramovitz (eds), *Citizenship in Antiquity. Civic Communities in the Mediterranean.* London, 313–26.

Rocchi, L. (2023c), 'From (Apt) Contempt to (Legal) Dishonor: Two Kinds of Contempt and the Penalty of Atimia', *Emotion Review* 15.3, 200–6.

Rohde, D. (2019), *Von der Deliberationsdemokratie zur Zustimmungsdemokratie. Die öffentlichen Finanzen Athens und die Ausbildung einer Kompetenzelite im 4. Jahrhundert v. Chr.* Stuttgart.

Rosivach, V. J. (1994), *The System of Public Sacrifice in Fourth-Century Athens.* Atlanta.

Roubineau, J.-M. (2015), *Les cités grecques (VIe-IIe siècle av. J.-C.). Essai d'histoire sociale.* Paris.

Rousset, D. (1994), 'Les frontières des cités grecques: premières réflexions à partir du recueil des documents épigraphiques', *CCG* 5, 97–126.

Rowe, C. J. (2007), 'The Place of the Republic in Plato's Political Thought', in G. R. F. Ferrari (ed.), *The Cambridge Companion to Plato's Republic.* Cambridge, 27–54.

Roy, J. (2003), 'The Achaean League', in K. Buraselis and K. Zoumboulakis (eds), *The Idea of European Community in History. Conference proceedings*, Vol. II: *Aspects of Connecting poleis and ethne in Ancient Greece.* Athens, 81–95.

Roy, J. (2008), '*Homonoia* in *Inscriften von Olympia* 260: The Problem of Dating Concord at Elis', *ZPE* 167, 67–72.

Rubinelli, L. (2020), *Constituent Power: A History.* Cambridge.

Rubinstein, L. (1998), 'Political Perception of the *Idiotes*', in P. Cartledge, P. Millett, and S. Von Reden (eds), *Kosmos: Essays in Order, Community and Conflict in Classical Athens.* Cambridge, 125–44.

Rubinstein, L. (2000), *Litigation and Cooperation: Supporting Speakers in the Courts of Classical Athens.* Stuttgart.

Rubinstein, L. (2003), 'Volunteer Prosecutors in the Greek World', *Dike* 6, 87–113.

Rubinstein, L. (2007), ' "Arai" in Greek Laws in the Classical and Hellenistic Periods: Deterrence or Concessions to Traditions?', in E. Cantarella (ed.), *Symposion 2005, Vorträge zur griechischen und hellenistischen Rechtgeschichte.* Vienna, 269–86.

Rubinstein, L. (2008), 'Response to James P. Sickinger', in E. M. Harris and G. Thür (eds) *Symposion 2007, Vorträge zur griechischen und hellenistischen Rechtgeschichte. Vienna,* 113–124.

BIBLIOGRAPHY 257

Rubinstein, L. (2010), '*Praxis*: Enforcement of Penalties in the Late Classical and Early Hellenistic Periods', in G. Thür (ed.), *Symposion 2009, Vorträge zur griechischen und hellenistischen Rechtsgeschichte*. Vienna, 193–216.

Rubinstein, L. (2013), 'Forget or Forgive? Amnesty in the Hellenistic Period', in K. Harter-Uibopuu and F. Mitthof (eds), *Vergeben und Vergessen? Amnistie in der Antike*. Vienna, 127–62.

Rubinstein, L. (2016), 'Reward and Deterrence in Classical and Hellenistic Enactments', in D. F. Leão and G. Thür (eds), *Symposion 2015: Vorträge zur griechischen und hellenistischen Rechtgeschicht*. Vienna, 419–50.

Rubinstein, L. (2018), 'Immigration and Refugee Crises in Fourth-Century Greece: An Athenian Perspective', in J. Filonik, B. Griffith-Williams, and J. Kucharski (eds), *The Greeks in a Changing World: Ancient Answers to Modern Questions* (= *The European Legacy. Towards New Paradigms* 23.1–2), 5–24.

Russell, A. (2020), 'The Economic World of the *Populus Romanus*', *Journal of the History of International Law* 22.4, 536–64.

Ruzé, F. (1997), *Dèliberation et pouvoir dans la cité grecque de Nestor à Socrate*. Paris.

Ruzé, F. (2012), 'Dire le droit: retour sur la grande rhètra', in B. Legras and G. Thür (eds), *Symposion 2011: Études d'histoire du droit grec et hellénistique (Paris, 7–10 September 2011)*. Vienna, 5–15.

Sakurai, M. (2014), 'The Date of *IG* I³ 136 and the Cults of Bendis in Fifth-Century Athens', in A. P. Matthaiou and R. K. Pitt (eds), *ΑΘΗΝΑΙΩΝ ΕΠΙΣΚΟΠΟΣ: Studies in Honour of Harold B. Mattingly*. Athens, 203–14.

Saldutti, V. (2014), *Cleone: un politico ateniese*. Bari.

Saldutti, V. (2022), 'The Mixed Constitution of Demetrius Phalereus', *Klio* 104.1, 159–90.

Samons, Jr, L. J. (2000), *Empire of the Owl: Athenian Imperial Finance*. Stuttgart.

Sanders, E. (2006), 'Historical Institutionalism', in R. A. W. Rhodes, S. A. Binder, and B. A. Rockman (eds), *The Oxford Handbook of Political Institutions*. Oxford, 39–55.

Scafuro, A. (2003), '*IG* II² 204: Boundary Setting and Legal Process in Classical Athens', in G. Thür and F. J. Fernández Neito (eds), *Symposion 1999. Vorträge zur griechischen und hellenistischen Rechtsgeschichte*. Cologne, 123–43.

Scafuro, A. (2011), *Demosthenes, Speeches 39–49*. Austin.

Scafuro, A. (2014a), 'Patterns of Penalty in Fifth-Century Attic Decrees', in A. P. Matthaiou and R.-K. Pitt (eds), *ΑΘΗΝΑΙΩΝ ΕΠΙΣΚΟΠΟΣ. Studies in Honour of Harold B. Mattingly*. Athens, 299–326.

Scafuro, A. (2014b), 'Decrees for Foreign Judges: Judging Conventions—or Epigraphic Habits?', in M. Gagarin and A. Lanni (eds), *Symposion 2013: Vorträge zur griechischen und hellenistischen Rechtsgeschichte* 24. Vienna, 365–96.

Scheibelreiter, P. (2018), '*Nomos, enklema* and *factum*', in G. Thür and U. Yiftach-Firanko (eds), *Symposion 2017: Vorträge zur griechischen und hellenistischen Rechtsgeschichte*. Vienna, 211–49.

Schepens, G. (1980), *L'autopsie dans la méthode des historiens grecs du Ve siècle avant J.-C.* Brussels.

Schepens, G. (2005), 'Polybius on Phylarchus' "Tragic" Historiography', in G. Schepens and J. Bollansée (eds), *The Shadow of Polybius: Intertextuality as a Research Tool in Greek Historiography. Proceedings of the International Colloquium, Leuven, 21–22 September 2001*. Leuven, Paris, and Dudley, 141–64.

Schmidt, V. (2008), 'Discursive Institutionalism: The Explanatory Power of Ideas and Discourse', *Annual Review of Political Science* 11, 303–26.

258 BIBLIOGRAPHY

Schmidt, V. (2010), 'Reconciling Ideas and Institutions through Discursive Institutionalism', in D. Béland and R. Henry Cox (eds), *Ideas and Politics in Social Science Research*. Oxford, 47–64.

Schoemann, G. F. (1819), *De comitiis Atheniensium libri tres*. Greifswald.

Schofield, M. (1999), *Saving the City: Philosopher-Kings and Other Classical Paradigms*. London.

Schofield, M. (2000a), 'Approaching the Republic', in C. J. Rowe and M. Schofield (eds), *The Cambridge History of Greek and Roman Political Thought*. Cambridge, 190–228.

Schofield, M. (2000b), 'Plato and Practical Politics', in C. J. Rowe and M. Schofield (eds), *The Cambridge History of Greek and Roman Political Thought*. Cambridge, 293–302.

Schuler, C. and Zimmermann, K. (2012), 'Neue Inschriften aus Patara I: zur Elite der Stadt in Hellenismus und früher Kaiserzeit', *Chiron* 42, 567–626.

Schulz, F. (2011), *Die homerische Räte und die spartanische Gerusie*. Düsseldorf.

Schütrumpf, E. (1994), 'Aristotle on Sparta', in S. Hodkinson and A. Powell (eds), *The Shadow of Sparta*. London, 323–45.

Schütrumpf, E. and Gehrke, H. J. (1996), *Aristoteles Politik Buch IV–VI*. Berlin and Darmstadt.

Schwartzberg, M. (2004), 'Athenian Democracy and Legal Change', *APSR* 98.2, 311–25.

Schwartzberg, M. (2013), 'Was the *Graphe Paranomon* a Form of Judicial Review?', *Cardozo Law Review* 34, 1049–59.

Schwartzberg, M. (2014), *Counting the Many: The Origins and Limits of Supermajority Rule*. Cambridge.

Scodel, R. (2008), *Epic Facework: Self-Presentation and Social Interaction in Homer*. Swansea.

Sealey, R. (1987), *The Athenian Republic: Democracy or Rule of Law?* London.

Sears, M. A. (2013), *Athens, Thrace and the Shaping of Athenian Leadership*. Cambridge.

Sebillotte Cuchet, V. (2017), 'Gender Studies et domination masculine: les citoyennes de l'Athènes classique, un défi pour l'historien des institutions', *CCG* 28, 7–30.

Seelentag, G. (2015), *Das archaische Kreta. Institutionalisierung im frühen Griechenland*. Berlin.

Sellers, M. N. S. (ed.) (2017), *Law, Reason and Emotions*. Cambridge.

Shepsle, K. A. (1986), 'Institutional Equilibrium and Equilibrium Institutions', in H. Weisberg (ed.), *Political Science: The Science of Politics*. New York, 51–82.

Shepsle, K. A. (2006), 'Rational Choice Institutionalism', in R. A. W. Rhodes, S. A. Binder, and B. A. Rockman (eds), *The Oxford Handbook of Political Institutions*. Oxford, 23–38.

Sickinger, J. P. (1999), *Public Records and Archives in Classical Athens*, Chapel Hill and London.

Sickinger, J. P. (2008), 'Indeterminacy in Greek Law: Statutory Gaps and Conflicts', in E. M. Harris and G. Thür (eds), *Symposion 2007. Vorträge zur griechischen und hellenistischen Rechtsgeschichte*. Vienna, 99–112.

Siewert, P. (ed.) (2002), *Ostrakismos—Testimonien I. Die Zeugnisse antiker Autoren, der Inschriften und Ostraka über das athenische Scherbengericht aus vorhellenisticher Zeit (487–322 V. Chr.)*. Stuttgart.

Simms, R. (1988), 'The Cult of the Goddess Bendis in Athens and Attica'. *AncW* 18, 59–76.

Simonton, M. (2017), *Classical Greek Oligarchy: A Political History*. Princeton.

Simonton, M. (2019), 'The Telos Reconciliation Dossier (*IG* XII.4.132): Democracy, Demagogues and *Stasis* in an Early Hellenistic Polis', *JHS* 139, 187–209.

Simonton, M. (2021), 'Representing the *Demos*: Adapting Insights from the Constructivist Turn in Political Representation', in J. Hanink and D. Kasimis (eds), *In Terms of Athens* (= *Ramus* 50, Special Issue 1–2). Cambridge, 129–44.

BIBLIOGRAPHY 259

Simonton, M. (2022), 'Demagogues and Demagogery in Hellenistic Greece', *Polis* 39.1, 35–76.

Simonton, M. (forthcoming), 'Non-democratic Assemblies: The Procedure and Function of Mass Meetings in Oligarchies', in T. Oppeneer and A. Zuiderhoeck (eds), *Popular Political Participation from Archaic Greece to the Late Hellenistic Period: The Assemblies of the Greek Cities beyond Athens*. London.

Sing, R., van Berkel, A. T., and Osborne, R. (eds) (2022), *Numbers and Numeracy in the Greek Polis*. Leiden.

Siron, N. (2020), 'Quel est votre verdict? Le résultat des discours contenus dans le canon des dieux orateurs attiques'. *Dike* 23, 83–110.

Sizov, S. (2017), 'On the Composition of the Achaian *Synodos* in Polybios' Time'. *AAntHung* 57, 381–414.

Skoczylas Pownall, F. (1995), '"*Presbeis autokratores*": Andokides' *De Pace*'. *Phoenix* 49.2, 140–9.

Smarczyk, B. (2006), 'Thucydides and Epigraphy', in A. Rengakos and A. Tsamakis (eds), *Brill's Companion to Thucydides*. Leiden and Boston, 495–522.

Smith, C. (ed.) (2022), *Sovereignty: A Global Perspective*. Oxford.

Sommerstein, A. H. (2008), *Aeschylus II: Oresteia: Agamemnon, Libation Bearers, Eumenides*. Cambridge.

Sommerstein, A. H. (2014), 'The Authenticity of the Demophantus Decree', *CQ* 64, 49–57.

Sommerstein, A. H. and Bayliss, A. J. (with contributions by L. A. Kozak and I. C. Torrance) (2013), *Oath and State in Ancient Greece*. Göttingen.

Spencer, N. (1995), *A Gazeteer of Ancient Sites in Lesbos*. Oxford.

Spencer, N. (2000), 'Exchange and *Stasis* in Archaic Mytilene', in R. Brock and S. Hodkinson (eds), *Alternatives to Athens: Varieties of Political Organization in Ancient Greece*. Oxford, 68–81.

Stalley, R. F. (2007), 'Platonic Philosophy of Law', in F. D. Miller, Jr (ed.) (in association with) C. A. Biondi (2007), *A History of the Philosophy of Law from the Ancient Greeks to the Scholiastics*, in E. Pattaro (gen. ed.), *A Treatise of Legal Philosophy and General Jurisprudence* 6. Dordrecht, 57–77.

Stanton, G. R. (1996), 'The Shape and Size of the Athenian Assembly Place in Its Second Phase', in B. Fórsen and G.R. Stanton (eds), *The Pnyx in the History of Athens: Proceedings of an International Colloquium Organized by the Finnish Institute at Athens, 7–9 October 1994*. Helsinki, 7–21.

Staveley, E. S. (1972), *Greek and Roman Voting and Elections*. New York.

Steinbock, B. (2013), *Social Memory in Athenian Public Discourse: Uses and Meanings of the Past*. Ann Arbor.

Steinmo, S., Thelen, K., and Longstreth, F. (1992), *Structuring Politics: Historical Institutionalism in Comparative Analysis*. Cambridge.

Stoneman, R. (1987), *The Land of Lost Gods: In Search of Classical Greece*. London.

Straumann, B. (2016), *Crisis and Constitutionalism. Roman Political Thought from the Fall of the Republic to the Age of Revolution*. Oxford.

Streeck, W. and Thelen, K. (2005), *Beyond Continuity: Institutional Change in Advanced Political Economies*. Oxford.

Stroud, R. S. (1998), *The Athenian Grain Tax Law of 374/3 BCE* (= *Hesperia* Supplement 29). Princeton.

Sundahl, M. (2000), *The Use of Statutes in the Seven Extant* Graphe Paranomon *and* Graphe Nomon Me Epitedeion Theinai *Speeches*. PhD Diss. Brown University.

Svara, J. H. (2001), 'The Myth of the Dichotomy: Complementarity of Politics and Administration in the Past and Future of Public Administration', *PAR* 61.2, 173–86.

260 BIBLIOGRAPHY

Szegedy-Maszak, A. (1978), 'Legends of the Greek Lawgivers', *GRBS* 19, 199–209.

Tamanaha, B. (2004), *On the Rule of Law: History, Politics, Theory*. Cambridge.

Taylor, C. (2007), 'From the Whole Citizen Body? The Sociology of Election and Lot in Athenian Democracy', *Hesperia* 76.2, 323–45.

Taylor, C. and Vlassopoulos, K. (eds) (2015), *Communities and Networks in the Ancient Greek World*. Oxford.

Taylor, J. (2022), '*Turannoi* in Archaic Greece: A New Phenomenon or a New Name for an Old Phenomenon?', in J. Bernhardt and M. Canevaro (eds), *From Homer to Solon: Continuity and Change in Archaic Greece*. Leiden, 301–29.

Thériault, G. (1996), *Le culte d'Homonoia dans les cités grecques*. Lyon and Québec.

Thomas, R. (1994), 'Law and Lawgiver in the Athenian Democracy', in R. Osborne and S. Hornblower (eds), *Ritual, Finance, Politics: Athenian Democratic Accounts Presented to David Lewis*. Oxford, 119–34.

Thomas, R. (2016), 'Performance, Audience, Participation and the Dynamics of Fourth-Century Assembly and Jury-Courts of Athens', in C. Tiersch (ed.), *Die athenische Demokratie im 4. Jahrhundert. Zwischen Modernisierung und Tradition*. Stuttgart, 85–103.

Thomsen, C. A. (2020), *The Politics of Associations in Hellenistic Rhodes*. Edinburgh.

Thomsen, R. (1964), *Eisphora: A Study in Direct Taxation in Ancient Athens*. Copenhagen.

Thür, G. (1977), *Beweisführung vor den Schwurgerichtshöfen Athens: die Proklesis zur Basanos*. Vienna.

Thür, G. (2007), 'Das Prinzip der Fairness im attischen Prozess', in E. Cantarella (ed.), *Symposion 2005: Vorträge zur griechischen und hellenistischen Rechtsgeschichte*. Vienna, 131–50.

Thür, G. (2008), 'The Principle of Fairness in Athenian Legal Procedure: Thoughts on the *echinos* and *enklema*', *Dike* 11, 51–74.

Thür, G. (2011), 'Amnestie in Telos (*IG* XII 4/1, 132)', *ZRG* 128, 339–51.

Thür, G. (2012), 'Dispute over Ownership in Greek Law: Preliminary Thoughts about a New Inscriptions from Messene (*SEG* LVIII 370)', in B. Legras and G. Thür (eds), *Symposion 2011: études d'histoire du droit grec et hellénistique*. Vienna, 293–31.

Tigerstedt, E. N. (1965–78), *The Legend of Sparta in Classical Antiquity*, vols I–III. Stockholm.

Todd, S. C. (1993), *The Shape of the Athenian Law*. Oxford.

Todd, S. C. (1996), 'Lysias against Nicomachus: The Fate of the Expert in Athenian Law', in L. Foxhall and D. E. Lewis (eds), *Greek Law in Its Political Setting: Justification Not Justice*. Oxford, 101–32.

Todd, S. C. (2000), *Lysias*. Austin.

Todd, S. C. (2012), 'The Publication of Voting-Figures in the Ancient Greek World: A Response to Alberto Maffi', in B. Legras and G. Thür (eds), *Symposion 2011: études d'histoire du droit grec et hellénistique*. Vienna, 33–48.

Todd, S. C. (2020), *A Commentary on Lysias' Speeches 12–16*. Oxford.

Torfing, J., Peters, B. G., Pierre, J., and Sørensen, E. (2012), *Interactive Governance: Advancing the Paradigm*. Oxford.

Tracy, V. S. (1995), *The Athenian Democracy in Transition: Attic Letter-Cutters of 390 to 230 BCE*. Berkley.

Traill, J. S. (1975), *The Political Organization of Attica: A Study of the Demes, Trittyes, and Phylai, and Their Representation in the Athenian Council* (= *Hesperia* Supplement 14). Athens.

Trampedach, K. (1994), *Platon, die Akademie und die zeitgenössische Politik*. Stuttgart.

BIBLIOGRAPHY 261

Tréheux, J. (1989), 'Sur les probouloi en Grèce'. *BCH* 113, 241–7.

Triantaphyllopoulos, J. (1985), 'ΤΡΑΦΗ ΠΑΡΑΝΟΜΟΝ fuori di Atene', in F. Broilo (ed.), *Xenia: Scritti in onore di Piero Treves*. Rome, 219–21.

Tribe, L. H. (1980), 'The Puzzling Persistence of Process-Based Constitutional Theories', *Yale Law Journal*, 1063–89.

Troper, M. (2012), 'Sovereignty', in M. Rosenfeld and A. Sajó (eds), *The Oxford Handbook of Comparative Constitutional Law*. Oxford, 351–68.

Tuplin, C. (1994), 'Xenophon, Sparta and the *Cyropaedia*', in S. Hodkinson and A. Powell (eds), *The Shadow of Sparta*. London, 127–82.

Urbinati, N. (2002), *Mill on Democracy: From the Athenian Polis to Representative Governement*. Chicago.

van Dyke Robinson, E. (1904), 'The Division of Governmental Power in Ancient Greece', *Political Science Quarterly* 18.4, 614–30.

van Effenterre, H. and Ruzé, F. (1994), *Nomima: recueil d'inscriptions politiques et juridiques de l'archaïsme grecque* I. Rome.

van Wees, H. (1999), 'Tyrtaeus' *Eunomia*: Nothing to Do with the Great Rhetra', in S. Hodkinson and A. Powell (eds), *Sparta: New Perspectives*. Swansea, 1–41.

van Wees, H. (2002), 'Gute Ordnung ohne grosse *Rhetra*: noch einmal zu Tyrtaios' *Eunomia*', *GFA* 5, 89–103.

van Wees, H. (2008), '*Stasis*, Destroyer of Men: Mass, Elite, Political Violence and Security in Archaic Greece', in C. Brélaz and P. Ducrey (eds), *Sécurité Collective et Ordre Public dans le Sociétés Anciennes*. Geneva, 1–39.

van Wees, H. (2013), *Ships and Silver, Taxes and Tributes*. New York.

Vattuone, R. (2008), 'Hetoimaridas: note di politica interna a Sparta in età classica', in C. Bearzot and F. Landucci (eds), *Partiti e fazioni nell'esperienza politica greca*. Milan, 131–51.

Versnel, H. S. (1990), *Inconsistencies in Greek and Roman Religion*. New York.

Veligianni-Terzi, C. (1997), *Wertbegriffe in den attischen Ehrendekreten der klassischen Zeit*. Stuttgart.

Vélissaropoulos-Karakostas, J. (2011), *Droit grec d'Alexandre à Auguste (323 av. J.-C.–14 ap. J.-C.): personnes, biens, justice*, vol. 2. Athens.

Vial, C. (1984), *Délos indépendante (314–167 avant J.-C.). Étude d'une communauté civique et de ses institutions*. Paris.

Villacèque, N. (2013), '*Θόρυβος τῶν πολλῶν*: le spectre du spectacle démocratique', in A. Macé (ed.), *Le savoir publique: la vocation politique du savoir en Grèce ancienne*. Besançon, 283–312.

Vlassopoulos, K. (2007), 'Free Spaces: Identity, Experience and Democracy in Classical Athens', *CQ* 57.1, 33–52.

Vlassopoulos, K. (2022), *Historicizing Ancient Slavery*. Edinburgh.

Von Fritz, K. (1968), *Platon in Sizilien und das Problem der Philosophenherrschaft*. Berlin.

Walbank, F. W. (1972), *Polybius*. Berkeley and Los Angeles.

Walbank, F. W. (1979), *A Historical Commentary on Polybius*, Vol. III: *Commentary on Books XIX–XL*. Oxford.

Walbank, M. B. (1978), *Athenian Proxenies of the Fifth Century BCE*. Toronto and Sarasota.

Wallace, R. W. (1989), *The Areopagus Council to 307 BCE*. Baltimore and London.

Wallace, R. W. (2013), 'Councils in Greek Oligarchies and Democracies', in H. Beck (ed.), *A Companion to Ancient Greek Government*. Chichester 191–204.

Walser, A. V. (2008), *Bauern und Zinsnehmer: Politik, Recht und Wirtschaft im frühhellenistischen Ephesos*. Munich.

262 BIBLIOGRAPHY

Walser, A. V. (2012), 'ΔΙΚΑΣΤΗΡΙΑ: Rechtsprechung und Demokratie in den hellenistischen Poleis', in C. Mann and P. Scholz (eds), *Demokratie' im Hellenismus: von der Herrschaft des Volkes zur Herrschaft der Honoratioren?* Mainz, 75–108.

Walthall, D. A. (2013), 'Becoming Kings: Spartan *Basileia* in the Hellenistic Period', in N. Luraghi (ed.), *The Splendors and Misery of Ruling Alone. Encounters with Monarchy from Archaic Greece to the Hellenistic Mediterrenean.* Stuttgart, 123–59.

Wankel, H. (1961), *Kalos kai Agathos.* Frankfurt am Main.

Welles, C. B. (1933), *Royal Correspondence in the Hellenistic Period: A Study in Greek Epigraphy.* New Haven.

Westwood, G. (2020), *The Rhetoric of the Past in Demosthenes and Aeschine: Oratory, History, and Politics in Classical Athens.* Oxford.

Westwood, G. (forthcoming), 'The Rhetoric of *Graphē Paranomōn* in the Trial on the Crown', in E. M. Harris and A. Esu (eds), *Keeping to the Point in Athenian Forensic Oratory: Law, Character and Rhetoric.* Edinburgh.

Whitehead, D. (1986), *The Demes of Attica 508/7 BCE–250 BCE: A Political and Social History.* Princeton.

Whitehead, D. (1993), 'Cardinal Virtues: The Language of Public Approbation in Democratic Athens', *C&M* 44, 37–75.

Whitehead, D. (2000), *Hyperides. The Forensic Speeches. Introduction, Translation and Commentary.* Oxford.

Whitehead, D. (2019), *Xenophon. Poroi: Revenue-Sources.* Oxford and New York.

Wiemer, H.-U. (2002), *Krieg, Handel und Piraterie. Untersuchungen zur Geschichte des hellenistischen Rhodos.* Berlin.

Wiemer, H.-U. (2013), 'Hellenistic Cities: The End of Greek Democracy?', in H. Beck (ed.), *A Companion to Ancient Greek Government.* Chichester, 54–69.

Wilks, M. (1963), *The Problem of Sovereignty in the Later Middle Ages.* Cambridge.

Willi, A. (2003), *The Languages of Aristophanes: Aspects of Linguistic Variation in Classical Attic Greek.* Oxford.

Wilson, J. B. (1987), *Athens and Corcyra. Strategy and Tactics in the Peloponnesian War.* Bristol.

Wolff, H. J. (1970), *'Normenkontrolle' und Gesetzesbegriff in der attischen Demokratie.* Heidelberg.

Wolff, H. J. (1975), 'Juristische Gräzistik—Aufgaben, Probleme, Möglichkeiten', in H. J. Wolff (ed.), *Symposion 1971. Vorträge zur griechischen und hellenistischen Rechtsgeschichte.* Cologne, 1–22.

Worthington, I. (1990), 'Alexander the Great and the Date of the Mytilene Decree', *ZPE* 83, 194–214.

Worthington, I. (2004), 'Oral Performance in the Athenian Assembly and the Demosthenic *Prooemia*', in C. M. Mackie (ed.), *Oral Performance and Its Context.* Leiden, 129–43.

Youni, M. (2011), 'L'imprécation et la loi: châtiment divin et sanctions pénales dans la polis grecque', in A. Helmis, N. Kálnoky, and S. Kerneis (eds), *Vertiges du Droit. Mélanges Franco-Helléniques à la mémoire de Jacques Phytilis.* Nanterre, 399–410.

Youni, M. (2015), 'Councils of Elders and Aristocratic Government in the Cretan *Poleis*', in M. Gagarin, A. Lanni, and G. Thür (eds), *Symposion 2013: Vorträge zur griechischen und hellenistischen Rechtsgeschichte.* Vienna, 103–26.

Yunis, H. (1988), 'Law, Politics, and the *Graphe paranomon* in Fourth-Century Athens'. *GRBS* 29, 361–82.

Yunis, H. (1996), *Taming Democracy: Models of Political Rhetoric in Classical Athens.* Ithaca.

BIBLIOGRAPHY 263

Zaborowski, R. (2002), *La crainte et le courage dans l'*Iliade *et l'*Odyssée. Warsaw.

Zaccarini, M. (2011), 'The Case of Cimon: The Evolution of the Meaning of Philolaconism in Athens', *Hormos* 3, 287–304.

Zaccarini, M. (2017), *The Lame Hegemony: Cimon of Athens and the Failure of Panhellenism, ca. 478–450 BC*. Bologna.

Zaccarini, M. (2018), 'The Fate of the Lawgiver: The Invention of the Reforms of Ephialtes and the *Patrios Politeia*', *Historia* 67.4, 495–512.

Zajonz, S. (2022), *Demosthenes, Gegen Aristokrates: Einleitung, Text, Übersetzung und Kommentar*. Berlin and Boston.

Zelnick-Abramovitz, R. (2004), 'Settlers and Dispossessed in the Athenian Empire', *Mnemosyne* 57, 325–45.

Zucchetti, E. (2021), 'Introduction: The Reception of Gramsci's Thought in Historical and Classical Studies', in E. Zucchetti and A. Cimino (eds), *Gramsci and the Ancient World*. London, 1–43.

Zurn, F. (2007), *Deliberative Democracy and the Institutions of Judicial Review*. Cambridge.

Index Locorum

For the benefit of digital users, indexed terms that span two pages (e.g., 52–53) may, on occasion, appear on only one of those pages.

Literary Sources

Aeschines
1.79 170 n. 97
1.108 157 n. 32
1.180 131–2
1.180–1 145–7
2.1 81 n. 156
2.11–14 185–6
2.13 185–6
2.14 187 n. 47
2.84 168 n. 84
2.109–10 54 n. 40
2.183 157 n. 32
3.6 12
3.8 196–7
3.9–31 192
3.32–48 192
3.37 74–5
3.49 192
3.103 83–4
3.125–8 57–8
3.162 157 n. 32
3.191 12, 177 n. 2
3.192 188 n. 53
3.195 219–20
3.197–8 193 n. 67
3.200 187
3.213 196–7
3.230 196–7

Aeschylus
Eumenides
  408–90 188 n. 50
  698 159–60

Alcaeus
fr. 70 Voigt 96
fr. 130b Voigt 105

Anonymus Iamblichi
7.2 DK 15 n. 60

Andocides and Pseudo-Andocides
1.11 157 n. 32, 173–4
1.12 65 n. 95, 157 n. 32
1.15 37–9, 64–5, 157 n. 32
1.17 153, 168–9
1.17–22 179 n. 9
1.20 157 n. 32
1.22 153
1.34 157 n. 32
1.43 53
1.60 173–4
1.74 13 n. 55
1.77 157 n. 32
1.86 83 n. 167
1.87 24–5, 70 n. 117, 74 n. 145
1.89 155 n. 22
1.91 46
2.22 157 n. 32
2.23 157 n. 32, 166 n. 72
2.27 157 n. 32
3.33–4 64 n. 87
3.40–1 63–4
4.3 46
4.31 72–3

Antiphon
1.12 145–7
5.77 156–7
5.77.3 157 n. 32
5.96 145–7
6.49 187 n. 49
fr. 13.47 153 n. 9

Archytas of Tarentum
On Law and Justice
  fr. 4 16 n. 62

Aristophanes
Acharnians
  19–20 143 n. 84
Birds
  1024–5 54 n. 40
  1040–5 164 n. 68
  1595 63–4
Clouds
  1178–1200 56 n. 53
Ecclesiazousae
  379 168 n. 84
Lysistrata
  1009–12 63–4
Peace
  359 63 n. 83

266 INDEX LOCORUM

Aristophanes (*cont.*)
  Thesmophoriazousae
    331–51 162 n. 59
    352–71 154
  Wasps
    662 168–9
[Aristotle]
  Constitution of the Athenians
    7.2 25 n. 101
    8.4 11–12
    9.1 35 n. 156
    21.3 5
    22.2–3 51–2
    22.8 13 n. 55
    24.3 168–9
    29.2–31.3 6–7, 136 n. 62
    29.4 177–8
    39.1 74
    41.2 83–4
    43.2 5
    43.2–49.5 43
    43.3 55 n. 46, 69 n. 114
    43.4 20 n. 87, 62 n. 78
    43.5 57–8, 167–8, 182 n. 22
    43.6 164 n. 63
    44.2–3 53
    44.3 167 n. 79
    45.2 43 n. 3
    45.4 5, 135 n. 61, 169
    45.8 171–2
    46.1 89
    47.2 59–60
    47.4–5 75 n. 149, 82 n. 160
    47–8 43 n. 2
    48.1–2 82 n. 161
    48.3 20 n. 87, 59–60
    48.3–5 166 n. 73
    49.2 46–7
    49.3 68 n. 111
    53.5–6 13 n. 55
    54.1 59 n. 69
    54.2 166 n. 73
    54.3 58–9
    55.5.3 48 n. 21
    59 48–9
    59.2 53 n. 35, 184
    59.4 43 n. 3
    61.1 82 n. 163
    61.2 62 n. 78
    63–5 182–3
    63.3 13 n. 55
    67.5 13 n. 55
    68–9 170 n. 97, 193
    68.5–15 189–90

  On Virtues and Vices
    1250b9 157 n. 32
Aristotle
  Nicomachean Ethics
    1130b31–3 22
    1130b–1131b 90 n. 190
    1132b15 157 n. 32
    1132b15–16 156
    1137b13–14 70 n. 117, 178 n. 6
    1181b15–23 194 n. 72
  Politics
    1265b378 6 n. 17
    1268b10 189 n. 56
    1269a29–1271b19 18
    1269a69 126 n. 6
    1270b24–5 133–4
    1270b39 131–2
    1271a4–6 149–50
    1271a6–7 135 n. 60
    1272a10–12 145–7
    1272a36 131–2
    1273b20 126 n. 6
    1274b18–23 96 n. 7
    1274b38 18 n. 78
    1275a38 18 n. 78
    1276b1 31–5 18 n. 78
    1278a15 18 n. 78
    1278a35–6 13 n. 55
    1278b6–11 18–19
    1279a22–8 18–19
    1285a7 130
    1285a30 96
    1289b23–6 21–2
    1291a31–2 194 n. 72
    1292a4 195 n. 73
    1292a32–7 70 n. 117, 178 n. 6
    1292a4–38 178 n. 6
    1294b29 134–5
    1297a21–4 156
    1297a22 157 n. 32
    1297b35–1298a7 20 n. 87
    1297b35–40 20
    1298a3–7 20
    1298a12–19 20–1
    1298b 145–7
    1298b26–35 136
    1299b30–1300a 4–5
    1299b–1300a 137–8
    1299b30–2 45 n. 10
    1300b19–20 20 n. 87
    1305b4 201 n. 98
    1311b19 96
    1313a25–33 135
    1317b30–1 45 n. 10

INDEX LOCORUM 267

1320b18 201 n. 98
1321a30 201 n. 98
1322b12–17 45 n. 10
1323a 6–7, 136 n. 62
1331a41 158–9
Rhetoric
1354b4–8 20 n. 84
1359b19 24
1359b 170 n. 96
Arrian
Anabasis
1.18.1 97
2.1.1 97
2.1.4 104 n. 29
Aulus Gellius
Attic Nights
2.12.1 160–2
Cicero
Philippics
1.1 155 n. 19
De Republica
1.26. 42 3 n. 6
1.27.43 3 n. 6
1.31.47 3 n. 6
3.33.45 3 n. 6
Cratinus
fr. 85 [KA] 65–6
Demosthenes and Pseudo-Demosthenes
1.1 52–3
3.5.20 55
4.24 177 n. 2
5.6 157 n. 32
5.8 157 n. 32
7.15 157 n. 32
8.64 157 n. 32
9.44 13 n. 55
10.66 157 n. 32
13.8 96–7
13.17 157 n. 32
15.19 96–7
16.5 157 n. 32
18 89, 192
18.6–7 81 n. 155
18.117 192
18.155.11 63 n. 83
18.222 157 n. 32
18.235 63 n. 83
18.249–50 219–20
18.282 162 n. 59
18.286 157 n. 32
19.32 87–8
19.70 160–2
19.149 157 n. 32

19.154 59, 70–1
19.179 91
19.190 157 n. 31
19.191 157 n. 32
19.227 177 n. 2
19.272 157 n. 32
19.289 157 n. 32
20.29–40 72–3
20.34 109 n. 50
20.52 177 n. 2
20.92 24–5
20.107 131–2, 162 n. 59, 220
21.33 157 n. 32
21.103 187
21.182 184 n. 35
21.210 157 n. 32
21.218 220 n. 8
22 49, 71 n. 121, 185
22.1–46 189
22.5 57–8, 168 n. 84, 184–6
22.5–6 5, 185
22.5–7 135 n. 61, 171–2
22.5–8 187–8
22.8 89, 185
22.9 168 n. 84
22.9–10 184
22.10 187–8
22.17 187–8
22.21 187–8
22.21–4 185
22.23 187–8
22.25 157 n. 32
22.33 187–8
22.33–4 185
22.35 187–8
22.36 57 n. 56
22.37–8 49
22.38 187–8
22.40 187–8
22.42 157 n. 32, 187–8
22.43 24–5
22.47–8 189
22.56–7 50
22.70 187–8
23 89, 91 n. 195, 189–90
23.1 13 n. 55
23.4 182–3
23.12 157 n. 32
23.22–7 191
23.28–36 191
23.37–43 191
23.42 160–2
23.44–50 191
23.51–2 191

268 INDEX LOCORUM

Demosthenes and Pseudo-Demosthenes (*cont.*)
23. 53–8 191
23.86 70 n. 117
23.87 24–5, 91
23.92–3 196–7
23.94 157 n. 32
23.97 162 n. 59
23.125 157 n. 32
23.128 157 n. 32
23.133 157 n. 32
23.159 157 n. 32
23.192 157 n. 32
23.218 70 n. 117
24 177 n. 2
24.9 157 n. 32
24.9–14 196–7
24.11 197
24.18 70 n. 117
24.25 171
24.30 24–5, 74 n. 145
24.31 157 n. 32
24.35 169–70
24.36 170 n. 96, 190
24.45 39, 152–3, 166–7, 171–2
24.45–7 157 n. 32
24.59 70 n. 117, 155 n. 22, 167 n. 82
24.63 43 n. 3
24.88 157 n. 32
24.102–3 157 n. 32
24.106 157 n. 32
24.107 162 n. 59
24.116 70 n. 117
24.139–41 25 n. 101
24.144 46
24.154 177–8
24.188 70 n. 117
24.205 157 n. 32
25.20 20 n. 84
28.4 164 n. 64
36.34 74–5
39.10 45 n. 10
39.15 187 n. 49
40.36–7 96–7
43 81 n. 155
43.4 62
44.63 157 n. 32
45.7 74–5
45.4 182–3
45.46 187
47 53–4, 85 n. 175
47.33 53–4
47.34 91, 184 n. 32
47.42–3 43 n. 3
47.67–8 55

50.52 63 n. 83
51 88 n. 184, 90
51.1 47 n. 17, 88–9
51.3 47 n. 17
51.4 89
51.8 47–8
51.15 157 n. 32
51.22 47 n. 17
53.22 187
54.21 157 n. 32
57 56
57.7 56
57.9 56
58.6 156–7
58.34 177 n. 1
58.43 187 n. 47
58.65 157 n. 32
59.4 45
59.6–8 219–20
59.15 55 n. 48
59.16 182–3
59.66 182–3
59.89 167–8
59.89–90 169
59.90 170 n. 92
59.111 157 n. 32
59.113 157 n. 32
61.2 62

Dinarchus
1.100–1 182–3
2.17 49
3.2 48 n. 22

Dio Cassius
60.3.5 155 n. 19

Dio Chrysostom
Orationes
45.3–7 116 n. 86
80.6 160–2

Diodorus Siculus
7.12.6 130 n. 27
11.37–8 96–7
11.50.2–7 129
11.50.1–7 138
11.55 167–8
12.7 25 n. 101
15.72.4 111
16.22.3 71 n. 123
17.29.1 97

Diogenes Laertius
1.81 96

Etymologicum Magnum
s.v. ὀργάδα γῆν 75 n. 148

INDEX LOCORUM   269

Euripides
  The Phoenician Women
    503–24 22 n. 93
    536 22 n. 93
    542 22 n. 93
  Suppliants
    403–8 20 n. 84
    426–55 20 n. 84

Harpocration
  s.v. νομοφύλακες 147 n. 107
  s.v. ὀργάς 75 n. 148

Hellanicus
  FGrH 31 157 n. 32

Herodotus
  1.1 223
  1.65 128–9
  1.151.2 96
  2.80 133 n. 43
  2.121 157 n. 30, 32
  3.52 50
  3.80–2 15
  3.80.1–4 15
  3.80.6 15
  3.81 20 n. 84
  4.145.4 13 n. 55
  4.161 202 n. 102
  5.39–40 135 n. 56
  5.63 133 n. 44
  5.92 109 n. 50
  6.5 96–7
  6.14 96–7
  6.26–2 96–7
  6.31 96–7
  6.57 127 n. 15, 131 n. 36
  7.104 128–9
  7.104.4 159–60
  8.120 157 n. 32
  9.28.1–3 13 n. 55
  9.28.1 133–4
  9.42 157 n. 30 n. 32

Hesiod
  Works and Days
    225–60 15

Homer
  Iliad
    4.1–72 4
    8.117 156–7
    8.120 156–7
    8.423 156–7
    21.481 156–7
  Odyssey
    1.22–95 4
    6.53–5 130–1

    7.189 130–1
    8.41 130–1
    13.10–12 130–1

Hyperides
  2.4 192–3
  2.10 192–3
  2.13 192–3
  4.15–18 220 n. 8
  5.8 157 n. 32

Isaeus
  4.28 83 n. 165
  5.47 72 n. 131
  6.12 187
  7.39–40 164 n. 64
  10.2 187
  11 81 n. 155

Isocrates
  3.56 157 n. 32
  14.24 157 n. 32

Lexicon Rhetoricum Cantabrigense
  s.v. νομοφυλάκες 147

Lycurgus
  1.3–4 190
  1.4 170 n. 96
  1.9–10 87–8
  1.104 157 n. 32
  1.107 160 n. 45
  1.149 145–7

Lysias
  1.36 157 n. 31, 32
  1.48 157 n. 32
  2.15 157 n. 32
  6.13 63 n. 83
  6.23 157 n. 32
  6.36 157 n. 32
  6.43 157 n. 32
  6.451 62–3
  10.10 187–8
  10.31 145–7
  12.85 157 n. 32
  12.90 145–7
  13.55 157 n. 32
  13.55–6 173–4
  13.85–7 187
  13.86 187–8
  13.9 64 n. 87
  15.3 48–9
  16.1 47 n. 17
  16.3 47 n. 17
  16.8 47 n. 17
  16.9 47 n. 17
  16.12 47 n. 17
  16.13 157 n. 32

270 INDEX LOCORUM

Lysias (*cont.*)
  16.15 47 n. 17
  16.16 47 n. 17
  16.19 47 n. 17
  16.20 47 n. 17
  19.43 164 n. 64
  20.23 164 n. 64
  21.3 164 n. 64
  22.19 157 n. 32
  24.1 47 n. 17
  24.3 47 n. 17
  24.7 47 n. 17
  24.8 47 n. 17
  24.10 47 n. 17
  24.11 47 n. 17
  24.12 47 n. 17
  24.13 47 n. 17
  24.15 47 n. 17
  24.22 47 n. 17
  24.23 47 n. 17
  24.26 47 n. 17
  25.28 157 n. 32
  26 47–8
  26.2–4 47–8
  26.6–8 47–8
  29.13 157 n. 32
  30.5 59–60
  30.24 157 n. 32
  31 49
  31.1 45, 47 n. 17
  31.1–2 50
  31.2 46
  31.8 47 n. 17
  31.33 47 n. 17
  33.7 126 n. 7
Lucian
  Toxaris or Friendship
    24 200–1
Pausanias
  3.5.2 131–2
  7.16.9 112–13
  8.52.4 96–7
Philochorus
  FGrH 328 F 140 46
  FGrH 328 F 30 167–8
Photius
  s.v. ὀργάς 75 n. 148
Plato
  Apology
    32b 48 n. 20
    37a 134–5
    35e1–38 193 n. 67

Cratylus
    413c F 63 n. 83
Epistles
    309b2 63 n. 83
    324d1 63 n. 83
    337a 16 n. 64
    337d 16 n. 64
Euthyphron
    4c8 55
Laches
    198b 158–9
Laws
    647a 159–60
    691d–692a 16 n. 68
    692a2 131 n. 36
    701 157 n. 32
    713c7 63 n. 83
    739d–e 16 n. 64
    751a–768c 17 n. 70
    875b3 63 n. 83
Statesman
    274a5 63 n. 83
    299c2 63 n. 83
Republic
    327a 65–6
    435d–436a 16–17
    555c–e 140 n. 73
[Plato]
  Definitions
    415b 70 n. 117, 178 n. 6
Plutarch
  Agesilaus
    4.2 131–2
  Agis
    5, 3–5 140 n. 73
    11.1 138–9
    8–11 138–9
    8.11 138–9
    9.11 138–9
    11.1 129, 137–8
    19 134 n. 52
    19.3 135 n. 56
  Alcibiades
    20.2–3 149 n. 110
  Apophthegmata Laconica
    217a13 134–5
  Aristides
    7.6 167–8
  Cleomenes
    9.1–4 159–60
    9.2 150 n. 114
  Dion
    48.3 200–1

INDEX LOCORUM

Lycurgus
6 131–2
6.1–10 126–7
6.3 130 n. 28, 137
26 133–5
26.1 131–2
26.3–6 134–5
Lysander
14.4 143 n. 86
16–17 140 n. 73
Nicias
14.3 149 n. 110
Pelopidas
25.7 200–1
Solon
11.2 127 n. 15
25 25 n. 101

Pollux
8.94 147 n. 107

Polybius
2.37.10–11 111
2.39.1–4 223 n. 20
2.44.5 111
2.56 138 n. 67
4.34–5 144 n. 92
6.3.5–4.5 23 n. 96
6.10 23
21.32.1 146 n. 101
21.41.2 107 n. 43
28.7.1–15 210
28.7.15 211 n. 122
31.2.12 112–13
38.12.1–6 112 n. 66
39.5.2–3 112–13
39.5.2 112 n. 69

Solon
fr. 3 G.-P.² = 4 West 35 n. 156
fr. 5 West 11–12, 15
fr. 32 West 2 n. 3
fr. 30 G.-P.² = 36 West 35 n. 156

Sophocles
Ajax
1074–6 160 n. 44
Oedipus at Colonus
447 157 n. 32

Suda
s.v. ὀργάς 75 n. 148
s.v. πρυτανεία 168–9

Strabo
4.1.5 201 n. 98

Theophrastus
Fragments
Vat. Gr. 2306 fr. A 1–30 134 n. 53

Thucydides
1.18.1 125–6, 128–9
1.19 50 n. 27
1.20.3 131 n. 36
1.79–87 143–4
1.87 133–4
1.87.1 6 n. 16
1.126.8 62–3
1.137.1 158–9
1.139 75 n. 148
2.20 50
2.24 164–5
2.37.1 35 n. 156
2.37.3 159–60
3.10.2–4 96–7
3.27–51 96–7
3.37.3–4 148–9, 154
3.37–50 221 n. 10
3.49.1 222 n. 15
3.50 96–7
3.58.3 157 n. 32
3.70–81 221–2
3.70.3 221–2
3.70.6 221–2, 222 n. 14
3.82.1 221 n. 11
4.64.1 62–3
4.76 61 n. 74
4.89–102 61 n. 74
4.92.6 157 n. 32
4.108.4 63 n. 82, 157 n. 32
4.113.3 50 n. 27
4.126.5 63 n. 82
5.27 63–4
5.27.2 62–3
5.32 81 n. 157
5.45 63–4
5.45.1 62–3
5.46 211 n. 122
5.46.1 62–3
5.77.1 6 n. 16, 143–4
5.79.1 143–4
6.8 63–4
6.8.2 62–3
6.14 135–6, 201 n. 97
6.26 64 n. 89
6.26.1 62–3
6.27.2 173–4
6.39 15–16
6.46.5–50.1 149 n. 110
6.60.3 157 n. 32
6.60.4 157 n. 32
6.67.1–3 62–3
6.72 64 n. 89
6.72.1 62–3
6.8 64 n. 89

272 INDEX LOCORUM

Thucydides (*cont.*)
6.88.10 6 n. 16
7.29.3 157 n. 32
8.1.3 6–7, 136 n. 62
8.60.1 61 n. 75
8.64.5 157 n. 32
8.65.2 50 n. 27
8.67 64 n. 89
8.67.2 152
8.73 158 n. 35
8.76.7 157 n. 32
8.77 158
8.81.1 157 n. 32
8.91 158
8.91.3 156–7
8.92.1 157 n. 32
8.97.2 15–16

Tyrtaeus
fr. 9.40 G–P 133 n. 43

Valerius Maximus
2.6.7 201 n. 98

Xenophon
Agesilaus
11.2 133 n. 44
Hellenica
1.1.18 47–8
1.5.18 62 n. 78
1.7.12–14 184
1.7.15 47–8
1.7.20 153
1.7.23 153
1.7.34 221 n. 10
2.2.19 63–4
2.4.10 65–6
2.2.5 96–7
2.3.24 47 n. 17
2.3.34 143 n. 85
3.2.23 6 n. 16, 143–4
3.3.8–11 134 n. 52
4.6.3 6 n. 16, 143–4
6.5.27 132 n. 42
7.4.2 111 n. 59
7.33–9 111 n. 59
Constitution of the Lacedaemonians
1.1 125–6
8.3 135
8.4 149–50
9.6 13 n. 55
10.1 131 n. 35, 134–5
10.1–3 131–2
15.5 126–7
15.6 132–3
15.7 130, 149–50

Memorabilia
1.1.18 45–6
1.2.35 46
1.7.14 46
2.1.5 157 n. 32
2.1.21 62–3
4.4.2 62 n. 78
4.4.16 224
Ways and Means
3.1–7 75
4.19 75 n. 149
6.1–2 75 n. 149

[Xenophon]
Constitution of the Athenians
3.2 24

Inscriptions

Agora
XV 37 105 n. 34
XVI 56 87 n. 181

Annuario n.s. 1–2 [1938–9]
158 n. 18 115 n. 84

BCH 95 (1971)
554 202 n. 105

Blumel (2007)
2 II, 40–1 186 n. 45

CIG
1.9 C 19 154 n. 15

FD III
1.362.26–35 207–8

Gonnoi II
91.20–5 208 n. 118

HGK
8.17 154 n. 15

I.Eleusis
142 84
144 75 n. 148

I.Erythrai
1 12 n. 51
116 211 n. 125

IG I³
1 143–4
7.7–9 67 n. 104
21.85 64 n. 92
40.6–7 13 n. 55
40.33–4 13
46.12–3 64 n. 92
52 163
52A 163
52B 39, 163

INDEX LOCORUM 273

52B.16–17 157 n. 32
52 59 n. 69
52B 171–2
52.9 64 n. 92
52.59 59–60
58 82 n. 161
68.43–4 74 n. 144
73 60–2
73. 5–7 62
73.12–16 62
73.21 62
73.39–40 62
76.15 158 n. 35
76.21 158
78 82 n. 161
84 82 n. 161
84.23–5 82 n. 160
85 72 n. 129
97.1–7 61
97.5–8 61
105 45
108.56 65 n. 97
127 72 n. 129
136 60, 65–7, 81 n. 157
136.24 64 n. 92
138 82 n. 161
153.19 85 n. 175
369 59 n. 69
370 39, 166–7, 171–2
370.15 157 n. 32
370.28 157 n. 32
370.30 157 n. 32
370.33 157 n. 32
370.64 157 n. 32
383 66 n. 100
1453 46, 164 n. 68

IG II²
1 72 n. 129
17 73 n. 137
19 72 n. 129
28.15–17 64 n. 92
40 72 n. 129, 97 n. 11
44.22–3 64 n. 92
103.34–5 169 n. 91
107 96–7
107. 25–6 59
111.58 158 n. 35
124 72 n. 129
127 60, 70–1
127. 27–34 72–3
127.35–6 72–3
140 84
140.7–8 153
157 62

204 68 n. 112, 75, 106
216/17 70–1
226 72 n. 129
281.3 158 n. 35
1062 190
1237.31 146 n. 102
1237.38 146 n. 102
1237.90 146 n. 102
1237.95 146 n. 102
1237.98 146 n. 102
1237.101–3 146 n. 102
1255 66 n. 102
1275 75 n. 146
1283 66–7
1328.13–14 54 n. 39
1361 67 n. 108
1437 97 n. 11
1496. 86 67 n. 109
1604–32 85 n. 175
1623 85 n. 175
1628 85 n. 175
1631 82 n. 161, 85 n. 175, 87 n. 179
1631.350–403 87
1666 76 n. 150
2490 75

IG II³ 1
292 60, 74 n. 140, 75 n. 148
303 73 n. 133
304 73 n. 133
309 73 n. 133
313 73 n. 133
337 66–7
370 60
370 74 n. 140, 85
404 73 n. 135, 74 n. 140, 84 n. 171
452.43–6 82 n. 161

IG IV 2
1.75 210 n. 121
506 159–60
679 217 n. 1

IG IV² 2
749 107 n. 43

IG V 1
1390 87 n. 180

IG V 2
1 111 n. 60
433 38, 113
433.8 114
434 114–15
456.1–2, 6 117 n. 88

IG IX 1
109.10 6
119.7 157 n. 32

274 INDEX LOCORUM

IG IX 1 (*cont.*)
682 7 n. 26
686 7 n. 26
694 217 n. 1

IG IX 1²
583.75–6 115 n. 80, 217 n. 1
609 6, 137 n. 64, 160–2

IG XI 4
541 6
1063 64 n. 91

IG XII 2
4 96–7, 105
4.1 105
4.3 105

IG XII 3
249.39 185–6

IG XII 4, 1
59 206–7
132, face A, fr. b, 40–3 223

IG XII 5
444 64 n. 91

IG XII 7
515 217 n. 1
515.131–2 199–200

IG XII 8
51.5–6 199–200

IG XII 9
211.23 157 n. 32
212.16 157 n. 32
231.10 157 n. 32

*IG*Bulg. I²
388 64 n. 91

I.Kyme
1 202 n. 101
12 178 n. 7, 199–200

I.Labraunda
56 203–4

I.Magnesia
35 217 n. 1
38 217 n. 1
38.45–50 115 n. 81
56 217 n. 1
90 210–11
92 a.13–14 200–1
92 b.18–19, 94 200–1

I.Mylasa
134, 4–5 208 n. 118

IPArk
5 104 n. 29
5.59 158 n. 35

24.5 158 n. 35
30 113

I.Priene²
119 204

IscM
1 64 64 n. 91

IvO
260 224

IvP I
5 64
246.59–61 199–200

Körner (1993)
7 12
90 110

Maddoli (2007)
306–20 B 186 n. 45

ML
8.10–2 6 n. 19

Milet
148.62 157 n. 32, 158
150.36 158

Miletos
61 64 n. 91

Nomima I
48 161 n. 51
62 12 n. 51
81 109–10
102 154 n. 15

OR
73.5 81 n. 157
102 160–2
131.64–7 81 n. 157
142 170 n. 92
142.24–9 160–2

RC
1 64

RO
2.74–5 59
19.18–22 25
20.36–8 59
22 97 n. 11
22.41–6 116 n. 85
31 96–7
50 70–1
53 70–1
58 81 n. 153, 157, 82 n. 159, 163
84 102 n. 18
85 (A+B) 98–100
83 108–9
88 48 n. 21

INDEX LOCORUM 275

100 85
278 82 n. 163

SdA
429.6 157 n. 32
429.12 157 n. 32
429.14 157 n. 32

SEG
3.416 6 n. 20
9.1, 7–8 107 n. 43
9.1, 32–4 7 n. 25
22.506 102 n. 18
24.51 75
24.52 75
26.677 23–4 207
26.909 105 n. 36
28.2 46
32.329 188 n. 52
33.275 5–6
33.637 64 n. 91
36.750 98
36.752 98
36.752 38
36.982 B1 6

39.1244 col. III, 48–51 185–6
41.932, 10–12 186 n. 45
46.400 132–3
55.838 199–200

SGDI
3621 6

Syll.[3]
283 107 n. 43
344 107 n. 43

Teos
51 105 n. 34

Hypotheses

hyp. Andr.
1.2 5
1.9 5

Scholia

Scholia on Aeschines
3.4 (Dilts 14) 43

General Index

For the benefit of digital users, indexed terms that span two pages (e.g., 52–53) may, on occasion, appear on only one of those pages.

Abdera 156–7
Academy 15 n. 56
Accattino, P. 19–20
accountability 1–2, 15, 29, 59–60, 191–2, 195
  horizontal 2, 11, 69
  vertical 11 n. 48
Achaean League 111–12, 119–20, 181–2, 210–11, 213
Acharnae 49–50
adeia 39, 64–5, 68–9, 152–76, 178–9, 216–17
Agis IV, (Spartan king) 134–5, 137–43, 145, 147–9
agōgimos 191
agora 48–9, 105, 187
agoranomoi 16–17
Agoratus 173–4
agronomoi 16–17
Aegina 107 n. 43
Aeschines 12, 43, 74–5, 80–1, 83–4, 145–7, 177–8, 185–6, 192, 194–7, 219–20
aidōs 158–60
aischunē 159–60
aisumnētēs 96 n. 7, 160–2
Alcaeus 96, 105–6
Alcibiades 63–4, 72–3, 156–8, 173–4
Alexander 94–5, 97, 102, 107 n. 43, 108–9, 211–12
Alexandria Troas 37, 204–5, 211–12
allotment machine 182 n. 23
amnesty 74, 103 n. 27, 107 n. 44, 154–5, 158, 224 n. 22
Amorgus 217 n. 1
Amphipolis 70–1
anakrisis 134–5, 184 n. 33, 187–9, 207–8
anapsēphisis 201 n. 97
Anaxandrias 135 n. 56
Andania, law of 87 n. 180, 114, 119
Andocides 53, 64–5, 72–3, 166, 173–5, 177–8
Andronicus 173–4
Androtion 49–50, 57 n. 56, 71 n. 121, 185–9, 197
anepitēdeios 50–2
Antigone 156–7
Antigonus 64 n. 91, 107 n. 43, 108–9, 202 n. 101
Antipater 3 n. 6
Antiphon 177–8
apepsēphismenoi 145–7
apocheirotonia 10 n. 44

apodektai 81–2, 86–7
apoklēsia 137–8, 165
Apollodorus 169, 219–20
Apollonia 64 n. 91
aprepēs 210–11
arbitration 81–2, 111, 187–8, 193–4, 207–8, 210 n. 121
Arcadian Confederacy 111
archē 20 n. 86, 37–8, 43–4, 45 n. 10, 52, 76, 83–4, 112–13
Archebius 197
archive 58–9, 114–15, 199–200
  of Argos 59 n. 66
  and the Athenian Council 58–9, 166
  of Sparta 142–3
Archidamus, (king of Sparta) 50, 143–4
Archinus 219–20
archons 11–12, 46–9, 49 n. 25, 82 n. 160, 167 n. 81, 207–8
Areopagus 8–9, 28 n. 113, 55, 71–2, 75, 82, 159–60, 191
Argos 5–6, 59 n. 66, 143–4, 158–62
aristocracy 23
Aristophon 194–5, 197
Aristotle
  constitutional methodology of 18–22
  on *probouleusis* 5
  on Spartan society 18
  on *stasis* 22–3
Arnaoutoglou, I. 67
Asia Minor 6, 29, 102, 117, 202
Assembly
  agenda of 43
  advisory 127–8, 139–40, 145
  Athenian 8–9, 10 n. 44, 12–14, 25–9, 39–40, 43–5, 47–9, 51 n. 28, 52–3, 56–65, 69–72, 74–6, 80–1, 83–9, 91–2, 125, 135–6, 152–76, 178–90, 192–9, 218–19
  federal 111–13
  of the gods 4
  Mytilenian 95–8, 102–5, 107–10
  and quorum 64–5, 152–5, 166–72, 175–6
  Spartan 125, 127, 129, 145
associations 66–7, 115 n. 84
astunomoi 16–17

GENERAL INDEX 277

ateleia 72–3
Athena (goddess) 132–3, 159–60, 163, 188 n. 50
  treasury of 164–5
  treasurers of 166, 173 n. 101
Athenagoras 97–8
atimia 10 n. 44, 13 n. 55, 22 n. 92, 74, 134–5,
  160–2, 162 n. 60, 184, 200–1
Atrometus 105 n. 36
Attalus 210
autokratōr
  ambassador 62–4
  Athenians at Eleusis 74
  clause 38, 62–4
  council 64–9
  general 63–4
axones 154 n. 13

Barbato, M. 35–6
basileus (archon) 81–2
Beck, H. 29
behaviouralism 30–1
Bendis 60, 64 n. 92, 65–9, 83, 92–3
bicameralism 11, 179–83
Bodin, J. 9–10
Boeotia 34–5, 117, 200–1, 207–8
Boffo, L. 107–8
bouleutērion 52, 166
boulomenos, ho 8, 148, 150 n. 113, 182–3
Boumelita 207–8
Busolt, G. 26–7

Callixenus 47–8, 177–8
Cammack, D. 52, 54 n. 41, 74 n. 142, 179–81
Canevaro, M. 13–14, 25, 34–5, 53, 84–5, 154,
  164–5, 171, 181–2
Carawan, E. 179–81
Cassander 147
Cephallenia 217 n. 1
Cephisophon of Cholargus 86–7
Cetriporis (king of the Thracians) 71–3
Chalcis 64 n. 92, 117
change
  bounded 33–4
  endogenous 34, 94–5, 117
  exogenous 94–5, 117
  institutional 34–5, 94–5, 105, 117, 120–1
Chaniotis, A. 199–200
Charidemus 91 n. 195, 191
charis (reciprocity) 90
Charon 200–1
Charondas 24–5, 156
Cheronaea 72–3, 192–3
Chersonesus in Tauris 199–200
China 105 n. 37
Chios 6, 96–7, 102, 107 n. 43
Cinadon 134–5

Cleisthenes 43, 51–2
Cleitor 111
Cleon 10 n. 44, 221, 222 n. 15
Cnidus 217 n. 1
collective memory 29–30, 126
common mess 134–5
constitution, mixed 14–20, 23–4, 131–2
conversion 34, 117–21
Corcyra 7, 217 n. 1, 221–3
Corinth 6–7, 112 n. 66, 221–2
council
  federal 111–13
  Homeric 4
  of Mytilene (*bolla*) 95–8, 102–3, 105–10
  of Megalopolis, (see *sunedrion*)
Council of Five Hundred (Athenian *boulē*)
  addressing the 47–8
  and administration 57–60
  bouleutic oratory 45–54, 88–92
  and decree-making, (*see* decree of the council)
  demography of 56–7
  and diplomacy 59, 70–4
  etiquette of 49
  sessions of 57
courts
  arguments in 179–82, 187–93, 219–20
  constitutional 182–3, 193 n. 65, 198–9,
    218 n. 4
  lawmaking (*nomothetikon*
    dikastērion) 178 n. 7, 199–200
  of law (*dikastēria*) 1, 3–4, 8–9, 12–13, 21,
    26–30, 34–7, 39–40, 43–4, 46–9, 56, 69,
    84–5, 87, 89, 103–4, 109–10, 127–8,
    148–9, 169–71, 174–5, 177–213, 217–21
  U.S. supreme 11 n. 47, 183
Crete 2 n. 3, 145–7
Critias 47 n. 17
Crowther, C. 206–7
Ctesiphon 185–6, 192, 196–7
curse 160–3
Cyrene 7 n. 25, 107 n. 43

dadouchos 81–2
decision-making
  consensual 53, 181–3
  deliberative 39, 57–8, 183–6
  informal 128, 139–40, 145, 147
  and magistrates 17–18, 37–8, 48–9, 61, 75–6,
    82–4, 92, 107–8, 136, 145–50
  majoritarian 40, 52 n. 32, 181–4, 194–6,
    205–6, 209–10, 217–18
  unanimous 57–8, 138–40, 142–4, 144 n. 92,
    147–51, 185–6
decree
  Adriatic 85–8
  of Androtion 5, 185–9, 192–3

278 GENERAL INDEX

decree (*cont.*)
  for Arconidas of Anaphe 185–6
  of Callias 64 n. 92, 162–7, 169–70, 172, 174–6
  on Concord 98–102
  of the council 48–9, 53–4, 57–8, 62, 68, 70,
    72–3, 85, 87–91, 181–2, 184 n. 32, 218–19
  of Ctesiphon 12
  filling the gaps in 38, 65, 106, 109–10, 114,
    120–1, 218–19
  for Hekatomnus 185–6
  honorary 49, 57 n. 56, 70, 89–91, 96–7, 177–8,
    185–6, 192–3, 199–200, 203–4, 206–7
  naturalization 166–7
  non-probouleumatic 7 n. 28, 102, 145 n. 97
  of Patrocleides 154–5
  probouleumatic 6, 57–8, 102
  for the property of Codros, Neleus and
    Basile 81–2
  on Reconciliation 102–8
  of Scamander 53
  of Speusippus 177–8
  of Teisamenus 155 n. 24
delegation
  clause (see *autokratōr*-clause; *kurios*-
    clause) 61–121
  and divided power 37–8, 215–17
Delos 6
deliberative
  democracy 60, 183–4, 187, 194–5
  expectations 183–4
  non-deliberative moments 189–90, 195–7
  system 92, 183–4, 214
Delian League 59 n. 68, 96–7
Demaratus 159–60
Demeter 75
Demetrias 37, 202–7, 212–13
Demetrius of Phalerum 6–7, 147
democratic *koine* 107–8
dēmokratia 128–9
Demosthenes 5, 49–50, 52–3, 57–8, 71–5, 83–4,
  88–91, 96–7, 131–2, 152–5, 160–2, 166–7, 171,
  177–8, 185, 189–92, 196–8, 219–20
Demosthenes of Aphidna 177–8
Deuteronomy 161 n. 53
diacheirotonia 53, 171, 185–6
diadikasia 80–1, 88–9
diagramma
  as civic decree 1, 38, 102, 120–1
  royal 102, 107 n. 43, 108–10, 114–15
diagraphē (*see* royal *diagramma*) 102–9, 120
diamarturia 188 n. 52
diapheromenoi 223
diaphora 223
diapsēphisis 56
diathesis (disposition) 22 n. 92

Dikaia 107 n. 42
dikaskopoi 103–4
dikastagōgos 206–10
dike 204–5
Diodorus (supporting speaker) 177–8, 185–9
Diodorus Siculus 71–2, 129, 135–6,
  138–41, 145
Diopeithes 210
diorthōma 210–11
dogma 1, 5–6, 199–200
dokimasia 27–8, 37–8, 43, 43 n. 3, 52, 56, 88
  of *adunatoi* 46–7
  of archons 46–9
  of councillors 45, 49
  rhēthōron 10 n. 44, 51 n. 28
dokimastai 54–5
Draco 24–5, 154, 165
Dreros, law of 2 n. 3, 110 n. 56, 161 n. 51
drift 34, 117 n. 94

echinos 188
eisangelia
  to the Council 10 n. 44
  to court 43, 190
eisphora 75, 164–7, 179
Elaea 199–200
Eleusinian Mysteries
  profanation of 173–4
Eleusis 74–6, 80–1
Elis 143–4
elite-capture 94–5, 116
Ellis-Evans, A. 108
empire
  Athenian 164 n. 68
  Persian 96–7
enklēma 82–3, 184, 187 n. 46, 202, 210–11
entrenchment clause 87 n. 180, 137 n. 64, 154–5,
  160–6, 169–76, 178–9
Epakreis 75
Ephialtes 51 n. 29
ephors 16, 18, 23, 39, 125, 127, 130–3, 135–6,
  138–41, 143–4, 216, 220
  control of kings 149–50
  election of 133–4
  eponymous 143–4
  interacting with the *gerontes* 127–9, 150–1
  introducing motions to the Spartan
    assembly 131, 138, 142–3
  judicial power of 134–5
  nomophylakia of 20 n. 87, 125, 129, 149–50,
    159–60
  probouleutic power of 5–6, 125, 140, 143–7
  summoning the Spartan assembly 63–4, 143–4
epigraphic habit 64 n. 91, 129
epitēdeios 25, 50–1, 210–11

GENERAL INDEX   279

epitimos 74
Eponymus Heroes 187
equality by worth 22
Eresus 108–9
Eretria 117, 157 n. 32
Erythrai 12 n. 51
Eteocles 22 n. 93
Euctemon 185, 187, 197
Eumenes II 210, 211 n. 122
Eumolpidai 81–2, 87 n. 181
Euryptolemus of Alopeke 177–8
euthunai 27–8, 49, 56 n. 51, 135 n. 60, 149–50, 166, 192
euthunoi (magistrates) 16–18
Euthycles 191
Euxitheus 56
Evander 47–8
exēgētai 16–17, 55
exō tou pragmatos 187–8
expertise
   deliberative 54–61
   financial 60
   horizontal 56, 221
   legal 36–7, 39–40, 55 n. 48, 179–81, 195–6, 198, 211–12
   and literacy 59–60, 59 n. 66
   and numeracy 59–60, 60 n. 70
   vertical 56

Fabiani, R. 94–5, 116
Faraguna, M. 56, 208
fear of the law 156–63, 175
Filias, D. 188
first-fruits, (*aparchē*) 84–5
Five Thousand, the 15–16
Flower, M. 126
Four Hundred, the 6–7, 64 n. 89, 158
Fuller, L. 195–6

Gauthier, P. 167–9
genē 67, 81–2, 117
gerousia 5–6, 8–9, 23, 38–9, 125–51, 216, 220
   election to the 132–4
   honours for 134–5
   prerogatives of 134–5, 137–8
   symbolic capital of 131–3
   unanimity of 138–40, 144 n. 92, 147–51
   veto power 38–9, 128, 133–4, 137, 145–51
Glaucetes 197
Glotz, G. 27–8
gnōme 198
   tou dēmou 109 n. 52
Goldstaub, M. 154–5, 164 n. 63
Gotter, U. 22 n. 93

Grabus (king of the Illyrians) 70–1
grammatophulakes 114–15
grammatophulakion 114–15
graphē 82–3, 184, 187, 189, 190 n. 59
   nomon mē epitēdeion theinai 25, 50, 148–9, 152 n. 3, 153, 179–83, 181 n. 18, 190, 194–5, 197 n. 81, 210–11
   paranomōn 10 n. 44, 12, 25–7, 39–40, 57 n. 56, 70 n. 119, 89, 91, 109–10, 148, 152 n. 3, 153, 175–206, 209–13, 217–19
   proedrikē 53 n. 35
graphos 1, 153
gumnasia 158–9

Habicht, C. 202, 204–7, 210
Hacker, J. 117–18
Hagnodorus of Amphitrope 173–4
Halai 207–8
Hallof, K. 206–7
Hallof, L. 206–7
Hamon, P. 94–5, 112–13, 115–17, 119 n. 96, 206, 207 n. 117
Hannick, J. M. 196–8
Hansen, M. H. 7–9, 27–9, 39–40, 43–4, 56–8, 70, 85–6, 153, 166–8, 179–81, 185–6, 196–8
Harris, E. M. 34–5, 71–2, 187–8
Harter-Uibopuu, K. 111
Hector 156–7
hegemony (Gramscian) 51 n. 30, 170 n. 93
Heller, A. 117
Hermione 217 n. 1
Hermocrates 62–3
Hermocreon 51–2
Herms, mutilation of 53, 65, 173–4
Hetoimaridas 138–41
hidrusis 66–7
hierophant 81–2
hieropoioi 67 n. 108
Hippansidas 132–3
hipparchoi 16–17
Hobbes, T. 9–10
Hodkinson, S. 126
Hoekstra, K. 10 n. 44
homonoia 103, 211–12, 222–4
Hornblower, S. 57–8
hybris 15, 22 n. 92
hupōmosia 184, 187, 209–10

Iasos 6, 7 n. 25, 94–5, 116, 143–4, 185–6
Illyrians 60, 70–2, 84
institutionalization of advantage 51–2
institutions
   complexity of 21, 23–4, 25 n. 103, 37, 69, 85–6, 152–3, 171, 216–18

280 GENERAL INDEX

institutions (*cont.*)
design of 1–2, 7, 12–37, 89, 92, 95, 117–18,
130, 175–6, 181–4, 194–5, 206, 214–15,
217–19, 224
federal 111–13, 116
ideology of 7, 34–6, 51–2, 83–4, 90–2, 95, 110,
117–18, 125, 129, 133–4, 136, 147–50, 154,
162, 170–3, 178–9, 181, 195–6
mixing of 3, 14, 16–18, 20–1, 23–4, 37
modern scholarship on 26–30
normativity of 2, 12–13, 18, 40, 45, 48–9,
69–70, 210–11, 214, 217–21, 223–5
strength of 105–6
theory of 23–4, 218–19
welfare 33–4
Ismard, P. 54–5, 66–7, 117

judge
bribery of 48–9, 207–8, 208 n. 118
foreign 37, 186 n. 45, 202–13, 217–18

kaloi kai agathoi 131–2, 206–7
Kammys 96–7
Kantor, G. 114, 199–200
Kelly, D. 139–40
kerdos 22 n. 92
Kerukes 81–2, 87 n. 181
kōlakretai 62, 66–7
kosmos (official) 2 n. 3, 110 n. 56, 161 n. 51
kurbeis 154 n. 13
kurios-clause 37–8, 60–3, 70–5, 92–3, 105,
114–15, 218–19
Kyme 143–4, 178 n. 7, 199–200

Lambert, S. 71–3
Lamian, War 217–18
Lanni, A. 39–40, 49, 179–81
Larisa 206–7
law (*nomos*)
of Cannonus 153
of Chairemonides 84
Common 183, 194 n. 68
and emotions 156–63
ep'andri 154–5, 191
established 16, 130, 152–3, 159–60, 170–2,
174–5, 216–17
on homicide 160–2
invalidity of 74 n. 143
rule of 11, 194–6, 202
suspension of (see *adeia*) 163–76
Leagoras of Cydathanaeum 177–8
Lebedus 107 n. 43
legal
certainty 195 n. 75
change 25, 34–5, 70, 154, 162–5, 172, 175,
178–9

coherence 175, 179, 193–4, 218
consistency 13, 39–40, 152, 175–6, 179,
181–3, 191, 198–201, 211–12, 219–20
control 37, 125, 179–81, 212–13, 215–17
hierarchy 25, 34–5, 70, 91, 114, 153, 165,
177–82, 203–4
precedents 192
reforms 25, 178, 195–6
stability 13–14, 38–9, 152, 175, 216
substance 3–4, 109–10, 181, 213
terminology 50, 58–9, 156–60
legislation
Archaic 24–5, 160–2
distinction from decree-making 24–6
local and royal 107–8, 110, 202, 213
legitimacy
of institutions 22–3, 118, 148, 165, 179, 192–3,
202, 209–11, 221–3
political 11, 69–70, 107–9, 215–16, 224
Leonidas (Spartan king) 138–43
Leptines 72–3
Lesbos 6, 96–7, 108–9
Leucon 72–3
Lewis, D. M. 7, 102, 160–2, 164–5
lex posterior derogat priori 172
lex superior derogat inferiori 179
lēxiarchika grammateia 56, 145–7
Liddel, P. 29, 58–9, 72–3, 90–1
liturgy 90
Locris 24–5
Ozolian (western) Locris 6, 137 n. 64, 160–2
Loddo, L. 72–3
logic
of appropriateness 30–1, 50–1
of increasing returns 33–4
Lowdnes, V. 33–4
Luraghi, N. 130–1
Lycinus 185–6
Lycurgus (Spartan legislator) 24–5, 125–7, 131–2
Lydiadas (tyrant) 111
Lyppeus (king of the Paeonians) 71–2
Lysander (ephor) 138–9, 142–3, 145
Lysander (Spartan general) 96–7
Lysimachus 63–4
Lysitheides 197

Ma, J. 107–8, 109 n. 52
MacDowell, D. 88–9, 134–5
Mack, W. 34–5
Macedonia 112–13, 185–6
Mackil, E. 34–5
Magnesia (Platonic) 16–17
Magnesia on the Meander 105 n. 36, 200–1
Magnetto, A. 63–4, 210–12
Mainalians 111
Mantinea 111

GENERAL INDEX 281

March, J. 30–1, 118–19
Massalia 200–1
Megacles 96
Megalopolis 37–8, 94–5, 110–21, 147–8,
 152, 215–16
Megara 64–5, 75, 80–1, 173–4
Melanopos 197
Meletus 173–4
Menecleidas 200–1
Menestratus 173–4
Menippus 185–6
merismos 25, 81–2
Messene 111
metabolē 21–2
metic (resident alien) 64–5, 182 n. 22
Metroon 185
Miletus 64 n. 91, 157 n. 32
Millender, E. 126, 142–3
Miltiades 86 n. 178
moichos 191
monarchy 15, 119–20
Monounius 72–3
Mummius 112–13
Munichia 173–4
Mylasa 202–5
Myrsilus 96
Mytilene 37–8, 94–110, 114, 118–20, 147–8, 152,
 215–16

Nafissi, M. 126–7, 135, 145
Naucratis 197
Naupactus 160–2, 165
Neapolis in Thrace 72–3
New Institutionalism 3, 30–5, 54, 218–19
 Discursive Institutionalism 31 n. 133
 Historical Institutionalism 31–5
 Old Institutionalism 26, 30 n. 129
 Rational-choice Institutionalism 30–3
 Sociological Institutionalism 31–2
Nicias 63–4, 135–6
Nicides 173–4
nomographoi 111–12, 114–15, 217 n. 1
nomophulakes 6–7, 7 n. 25, 16–18, 136–8, 145–7,
 149–51
nomophulakia 125, 127–9, 137–8, 145–51,
 160–2, 216
nomothesia (law-making) 13–14, 25–6,
 34–5, 70, 82 n. 161, 115 n. 80, 153, 162–3,
 170–2, 174–5, 178, 199–200, 216–17,
 217 n. 1
nomothetai 7–8, 13–14, 25–7, 43–4, 70, 84–5,
 153, 172, 178
 first 24–5, 154, 160–2
 identity of 25 n. 103, 70 n. 118, 172 n. 100,
 197 n. 81
North, D. 218–19

oath
 of the archons 48–9
 bouleutic 37–8, 45–54, 92, 164 n. 68
 judicial 45–6, 80–1, 182–3, 192–3
Ober, J. 28–9, 35–6, 43–4, 85–6
Oedipus 156–7
oligarchia 128–9
oligarchy 12, 15–16, 18–20, 47–8,
 96–7, 128–9, 149–50, 201 n. 98,
 221–2
Olsen, J. 30–1, 118–19
Olympia 12 n. 51, 115 n. 80
O'Neil, J. 107–8
Oreos 83–4
orgas, sacred 60, 70, 75–83, 92–3, 106
orgeōnes 66–7
Oropus 52
Osborne, M. 166–7
Ostwald, M. 8–9
Otanes 15

Paeonians 60, 70–2, 84
pannuchis 65–6
Paga, J. 51–2
Pagai 119 n. 96
Paoli, E. U. 154–5
Papazarkadas, N. 75–6, 80–2
paranomia 181–3, 193–4, 203–4
parepidēmia 207 n. 117
parousia 207 n. 117
Parrhasians 111
Pasquino, P. 10–11, 182–3
path dependence 33–5, 51–2, 54–5, 95, 118–21,
 128–9, 135–6, 164 n. 63, 170–1
Peithias 221–3
Pelopidas 200–1
Peloponnesian War 10 n. 44, 50, 128–9
Penthilides 96
Peparethus 206–7
peridromoi 103–4
peripolarchoi 82
Pergamon 64 n. 91, 210
Pericles 159–60
Persephone 75
Philip II 70–2, 75, 185–6
Philip III 108–9
Philocrates, peace of 70–2
Philon 49–51
philotimia 22 n. 93, 72–3, 86–8, 208
phularchoi 16–17
Phylarchus 138–9
Pierson, P. 31–4, 117–18
Pinax 72–3
Piraeus 65–7
Pisada 64 n. 91
Pisander 53

282 GENERAL INDEX

pistis (trust) 208
  and honour 206–7, 209
Pittacus 96
Plato 3, 10 n. 44, 14–18, 15 n. 56, 23–4,
    57–8, 66
Plutarch 127, 129–30, 133–5, 137–43, 145–7,
    150–1, 159–60, 167 n. 81, 200–1
Pnyx 167–9
politeia 12, 14–16, 18–19, 22, 75, 112–13, 125–6,
    145–7, 194–5, 194 n. 72, 201 n. 98, 217–20
  division of 20–1, 20 n. 84
  ethos of 225
  mesē 19
  memigmenē (*see* constitution, mixed) 19–20
  parts of 20–1
  patrios 126
politeuma 18–19
pollution (*miasma*) 159–60
Polybius 14, 17–18, 23, 111–12, 138–9, 210–12
Polydorus (king of Sparta) 126–7
Polytion 173–4
Potamodorus of Orchomenos 60–2, 64–5, 69,
    72 n. 128
power
  definition of divided 10–14
  constituent 23 n. 95
  constituted 10
  separation of 3, 7–8, 10–11, 27–9
preiga 6, 137 n. 64, 165
Priene 202, 204–7
priest 16–17
priestess 16–17
probouleuma 1–2, 5–6, 9, 43, 57–8, 83–4,
    91 n. 195, 102–3, 108–9, 135–6, 139–40,
    143–4, 147–8, 150–1, 169, 184 n. 31, 192–3,
    195–8
  closed 43, 57–8
  open 43, 145, 145 n. 97, 171–2, 197
probouleusis 4–7, 36–8, 44–5, 57–8, 69, 83–4,
    108–9, 125, 128–9, 135–8, 143, 144 n. 92,
    145–51, 187, 214–16
probouloi 63–4, 136–8, 143–7
procheirotonia 57–8, 197
proedroi 49, 53, 53 n. 35, 82, 147, 166–7, 185–6,
    192–3
proklēsis 111 n. 62
prostagma 107 n. 43
prothesmia 184
prutaneion 59, 72–3
prutaneis 7 n. 25, 18, 47–9, 53–5, 57, 59, 62, 82,
    86–8, 116, 135–6, 143–4, 166–9, 171–2
  epistatēs of 47–8
prytany 5, 57–60, 166
Ptolemy I 107 n. 43

Pydna, battle of 117
Pythilles 61
Pythonicus 173–4

Quass, F. 178–9

refugees 72–3
  reintegration of property of 103–4
régime, ancient 10
review
  judicial 30, 37, 39–40, 109–10, 148–9,
    177–213, 217–19
  legislative 13, 137–8, 148–9, 216
Rhetra
  of Agis IV 137–9, 141–3, 147–9
  of Epitadeus 140 n. 73
  Great 5–6, 126–8, 130–1, 135–7, 145–7, 150–1
Rhodes 116, 210–11
Rhodes, P. J. 7, 27–8, 45–6, 57–8, 68, 87, 102
Richer, N. 139–40
Rohde, D. 8–9
Roman
  abolitio publica 155 n. 19
  assemblies (*comitia*) 3–4
  constitution 23
  institutional influence 112–13, 116
  praetor 83 n. 167
  Republic 3–4, 174 n. 105
  Staatsrecht 26–7
Ruzé, F. 43–4, 127–8, 139–40, 143–4

Samos 96–7, 156–7
sanides 185
Scafuro, A. 80–1
Schulz, F. 8–9, 127–8, 139–40
Schwartzberg, M. 133–4, 179–81
secretaries (*grammateis*) 5–6, 188, 206–7
  of the Council (*grammateus tēs boulēs*) 58–9
  kata prutaneian 58 n. 64
Sicily 135–6, 173–4
Simonton, M. 29
sitēsis 72–3, 73 n. 137
Six Hundred, the 200–1
Sizov, S. 111–12
Skepsis 64 n. 91
Skocpol, T. 31–3
slavery 29, 50
  and expertise 54–5
  public 55, 58–9
  and recognition 55 n. 47
  Spartan (helotage) 18
Social War 71–2, 75–6
Socrates 47–8, 66, 159–60
Solon 2 n. 3, 15, 24–5, 126, 154, 160–2, 165

GENERAL INDEX   283

Sopolis 87
sovereignty
  of the courts 8, 179–83, 217–18
  of the *gerousia* 8–9
  as *Herrschaft* 218–19
  of the law 8–9, 179–81, 194–5
  locus of 2, 8–11, 218–21
  as *Souveränität* 218
  as *Staatsgewalt* 218
  terminology of 9–11, 19 n. 80
Spartan
  constitution 6, 8–9, 16, 126–30
  double kingship 16, 23, 130–3, 149–50
  eunomia 38–9, 125–6, 128–9, 135–6, 145–7
  invention of tradition 126–7
  kosmos of 126, 138–9, 142–3
  mirage 125–6
  patronage 143
  stasis 21–2, 29, 96–7, 106, 109–10, 125–6, 194–5, 221–4
  causes of 22–3
Stephanus 219–20
Sthenelaidas 143–4
stratēgoi (generals) 17–18, 62, 73, 111–12, 143–4
  federal 111–12
  for the protection of the countryside 82
strotagoi 102–4
sumbolaion 202, 207
sunedrion 6, 38, 95, 114–17, 120–1
sunodos 113
supervisors of the dockyards 85, 87
supplication 159–60, 164 n. 63
Syracuse 16 n. 64, 201 n. 97

tamiai (*see also* treasurers) 16–17
taxiarchoi 16–17
Tegea 104 n. 29, 111
Teithras 75
Telos 223
Temnos 64 n. 91
Ten, board of 96–7
Teos 107 n. 43, 160–2
Teucrus 64–5, 173–4
Thargelion 67 n. 108
Thelen, K. 117–18
Theomnestus 219–20
Theopompus (king of Sparta) 126–7, 135
Theramenes 47 n. 17, 63–4
thesmos 154, 154 n. 15, 199–200
thesmothetai 39–40, 82–3, 86–7, 184, 187, 207–8
Thessaly 112–13, 154 n. 15, 202 n. 102
Theugenes 206–9

Thomsen, C. A. 116
thorubos 53
Thracians 60, 65–7, 70–3, 72 n. 132, 84
Thrasybulus 47–8, 158, 219–20
Thucydides 6–7, 15–16, 50, 57–8, 61–4, 126, 143–4, 156–9, 164–5, 177–8, 221–3
timē (honour) 11–12, 13 n. 55, 21, 22 n. 92, 23, 118–19, 132–3, 150–1, 159–60, 185–6, 192–3, 207
  civic 1, 35–6, 59–60, 72–3, 72 n. 129, 87–91, 117, 134–5, 208, 210–12
  as office 21–2, 76, 117, 132–5
  as right 13, 13 n. 55
  of slaves 54–5
timai, megistai 72 n. 129
timouchoi 201 n. 98
timoumenoi 206–7
timēsis 184, 187 n. 47, 193, 193 n. 67
treasurers 17–18, 59–60, 89, 190
  of Athena 166, 173 n. 101
  of the Other Gods 66–7, 82 n. 161
Triantaphyllopoulos, J. 202
trierarch 53–4, 86–90, 197
Troper, M. 218
tyranny 10 n. 44, 12, 15–16, 96–7, 108–9, 128–9, 195

Vietnam 105 n. 37
voting
  by ballots (*psēphophoria*) 154–5, 166–7, 170–2, 216–17
  and distinct political behaviour 166–7
  by ostraka (*ostrakophoria*) 167–8
  by shouts 53, 133–4
  by show of hands (*cheirotonia*) 166–71, 185–6

Wallace, R. 8–9
Wolff, H. J. 179–81
women 63–4
  citizenship of 5 n. 10, 29
  Spartan 18, 134–5, 134 n. 49, 138–9
  written documents 142–3, 187–8

Xenophon 57–8, 143–4
Xerxes 96–7, 156–7, 159–60

Yunis, H. 179–81

Zaleucus (legislator) 24–5
zēmia 22 n. 92
Zeus and Alcinous, sanctuary of 221–2